I0819477

COMIC CHARACTER METAL
SAND TOYS

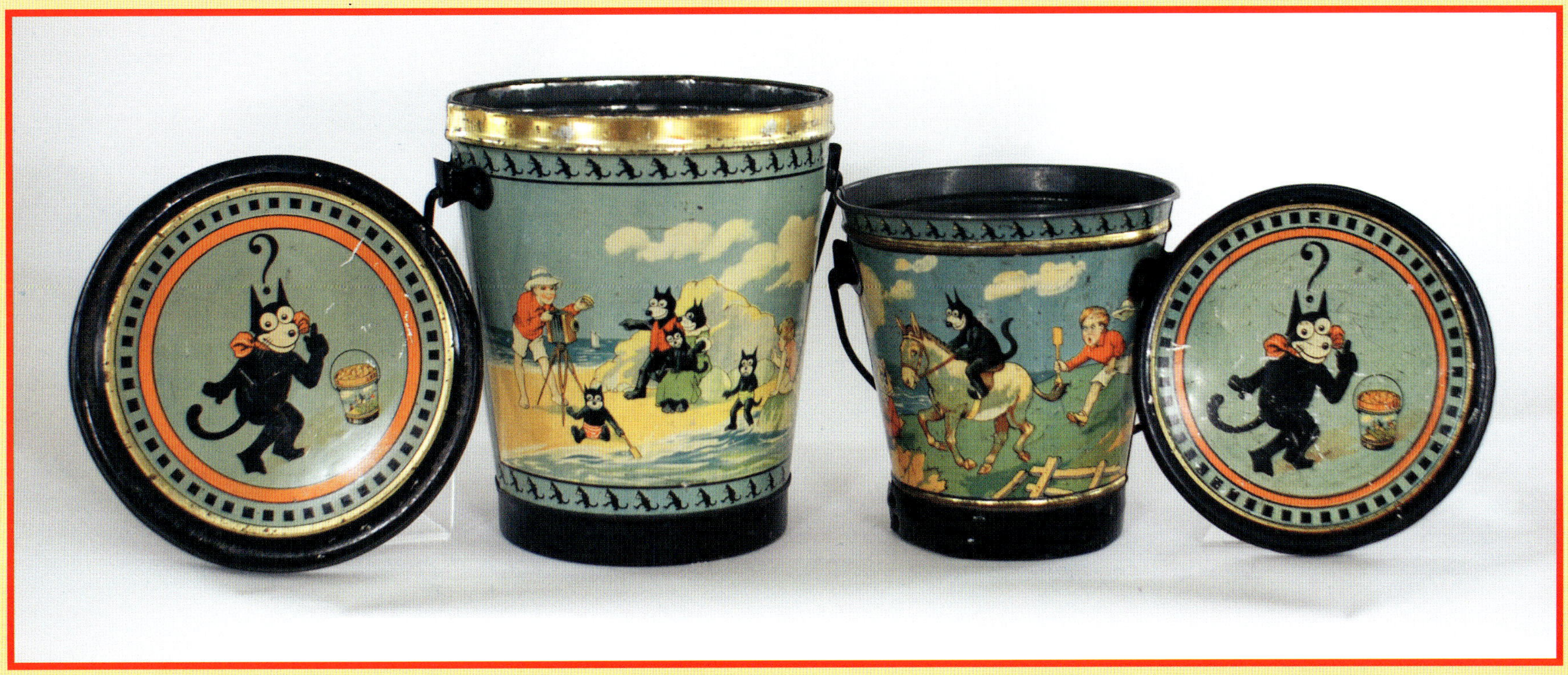

Doug & Pat Wengel

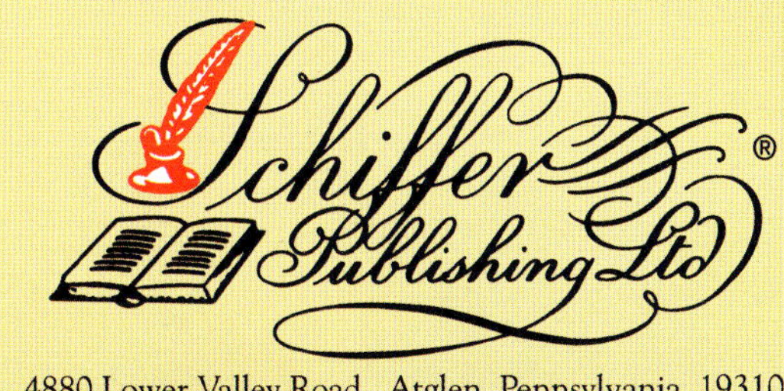

4880 Lower Valley Road Atglen, Pennsylvania 19310

DEDICATION

This book is lovingly dedicated to our children, Kathy, Deb, and Dave and to their children Riley, Ella Beth, Ruby, Malcolm, and Reese.

And to the children in all of us!

Library of Congress Control Number: 2007940912

Type set in Eros Bd / Zurich Bt

ISBN: 978-0-7643-2851-0
Printed in China

Schiffer Books are available at special discounts for bulk purchases for sales promotions or premiums. Special editions, including personalized covers, corporate imprints, and excerpts can be created in large quantities for special needs. For more information contact the publisher:

Published by Schiffer Publishing Ltd.
4880 Lower Valley Road
Atglen, PA 19310
Phone: (610) 593-1777; Fax: (610) 593-2002
E-mail: Info@schifferbooks.com

For the largest selection of fine reference books on this and related subjects, please visit our web site at **www.schifferbooks.com**
We are always looking for people to write books on new and related subjects. If you have an idea for a book please contact us at the above address.

This book may be purchased from the publisher.
Include $3.95 for shipping.
Please try your bookstore first.
You may write for a free catalog.

In Europe, Schiffer books are distributed by
Bushwood Books
6 Marksbury Ave.
Kew Gardens
Surrey TW9 4JF England
Phone: 44 (0) 20 8392-8585; Fax: 44 (0) 20 8392-9876
E-mail: info@bushwoodbooks.co.uk
Website: www.bushwoodbooks.co.uk
Free postage in the U.K., Europe; air mail at cost.

Contents

ACKNOWLEDGMENTS AND SPECIAL MENTION

With over 30 years of enjoying the toy collecting fraternity, we can not possibly recognize all those who have made such a positive impact on our enjoyment and enthusiasm for the hobby we love. Therefore we are able to acknowledge here only those who have made a specific contribution to this book. To the others, our heartfelt thanks for lifetime friendships.

In Alphabetical Order:

Bob Bernabe: For almost a quarter of a century, our associate and helper at the Atlantique City show and before that a tennis friend. Bob has one of the finest sand pail collections in the world as shown by the number of his quality pieces pictured here in this book. Bob, we couldn't have done it without you!

Mel Birnkrant: It should come as no surprise that several of the rarest sand toy examples in this book are from the legendary character collection of Mel. A friend and mentor since the late 1970s, Mel started collecting 25 years before that and has, without doubt, the finest character collection in the world. A heartfelt thank you, Mel.

Nigel Boyle: Our source and friend in New Zealand who found the wonderful Alex Harvey sand pail for us. A great New Zealand host as well.

"El Duende," Andres Diego: A source for some of the finest Spanish and European sand toys and for information on Rogelio Sanchis. We miss you, Andres.

Jim Gilcher: Jim, recently retired from the Ohio Art Co., has often been very helpful to us and has provided us with a number of catalog sheets of the company that we have used to expand the information on this outstanding company and important Disney licensee.

John and Adrian Haley: Friends from the beginning and source for some of our finest collectibles including the marvelous Felix covered toffee pail. Why were we so foolish not to buy the 8" Charlie Chaplin covered toffee pail when they offered it to us 20 years ago!

Deb Wengel Heitmann: The principal photographer for the book, she is also the mother of some of our beautiful granddaughters. While studying in Australia in 1990, she made some great dealer contacts and found some exciting items for us. She has always been a great shopper. We love you, Deb.

David Huxtable: A major collector and dealer of biscuit tins and related containers, David provided us with several important sand toys.

Larry Langer: Larry brought us his extensive collection of Happynak sand toys for the book. He also provided valuable insight about today's market, particularly eBay. Larry is a perfect example of a great friend found when sharing the same hobby.

Carl Lobel: Carl graciously provided us with images of some of his rare sand toys. He has been a collector and dealer from before we got started and has a truly magnificent collection.

Barbara Moran: Barbara was our source for a couple of rare unauthorized Disney pails from Japan. She is a well-known expert on Japanese toys and has been very helpful in providing information about them.

John Reynolds: John brought us a number of sand toys from his extensive Popeye collection. He also provided a Donald Duck watering can we needed. If it's a Popeye item, John probably has it in his collection.

The Schiffer organization, led by Peter B. Schiffer who has been encouraging us for over a decade to publish a book with them, has gone the extra mile in helping us with our first book. The next one has to be easier! Special thanks to our editor, Doug Congdon-Martin, who has been so helpful in answering some of our naïve questions.

Catherine Saunders-Watson: From mentoring our daughter, Deb, when she was studying in Australia in 1990, to being a source for intriguing information, Catherine has always been available to us and we appreciate that very much.

Wikipedia, the Free Encyclopedia: In researching for this book, particularly early characters, we found this to be the best source for information which is continuously updated.

Dave Zarodnansky: Although unknown in our hobby field, Dave possesses computer skills without boundaries. His help with getting all our photos onto DVDs, and rescuing us from other seemingly insurmountable computer issues, merits a special thanks. Dave isn't sure he ever owned a sand toy, but he has been building electronic devices since age 8.

All images, not otherwise credited, are from the Wengel collection.

Introduction

Metal sand toys, usually made of tin, have been around for a century or more. Pails (sometimes referred to as buckets), shovels, sieves, and watering cans have been popular with children for years. Recently they have become very desirable to adults to be used as collectible decorative accents.

Character metal sand toys have been produced from the 1920s through to the present day. Sometimes the pails, usually with lids, were made to contain candy or toffee. The popularity of the comic characters helped market the products. After the treats were consumed, the pails could be used at the beach or in sand boxes.

Condition and rarity are the two most important factors in placing a value on these toys. Because they were played with in sand and water, condition is often a concern. Several years ago we purchased a Mickey Mouse Atlantic City pail at an estate sale. It turns out that the couple had their honeymoon over 50 years before in Atlantic City. They purchased the pail as a souvenir and partially filled it with sand from the beach. The outside of the bucket is great; however the sand absorbed moisture over the years and there is corrosion to that level!

Generally the larger the pail or shovel, the greater its value. Almost always a shovel came with the pail, although usually it was a plain shovel with no decoration. Occasionally a shovel would include an image of the character or characters. This was particularly true with boxed sets that might include a pail, shovel, watering can and sand moulds. A box increases the value of the items and greatly increases the value if the characters are pictured on the box. The value of the bucket is also increased if the images are embossed around the pail.

This book is organized by character in alphabetical order by chapter. The long Disney chapters start with the Ohio Art Co. toys followed by items from J. Chein and other U.S. companies. The second Disney chapter includes pieces of foreign manufacture.

The values we have given are for items in as pictured condition. Examples in better or mint condition command greater values, just as poorer items have lower values. Recently produced items, although beautiful, have a nominal value.

Finally, this book is not an encyclopedia. All character items are not included, although we feel a representative selection is present. Enjoy!

Chapter 1:

Baby Snooks

Baby Snooks was the creation of Fanny Brice. The sketches first appeared on the radio in 1936 and in 1940 became the main attraction on the Maxwell House Coffee Time show. In 1944 Fanny headlined her own program, "The Baby Snooks Show," that lasted until Fanny's death at age 60 in 1951. Other characters on the program were Mom, Dad, and baby brother, Robespierre.

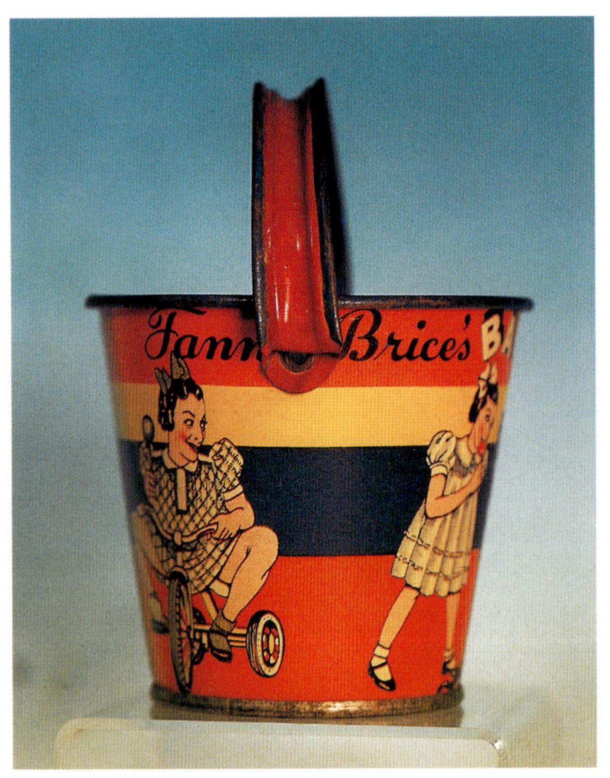

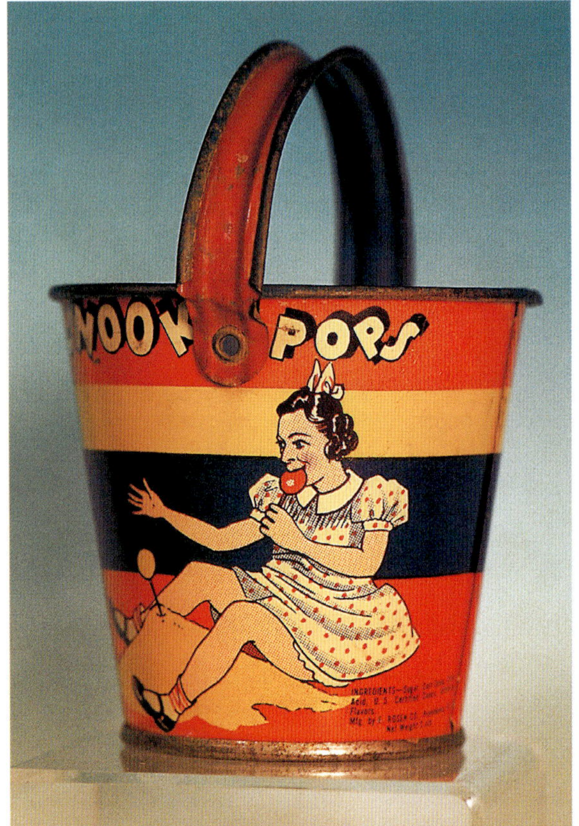

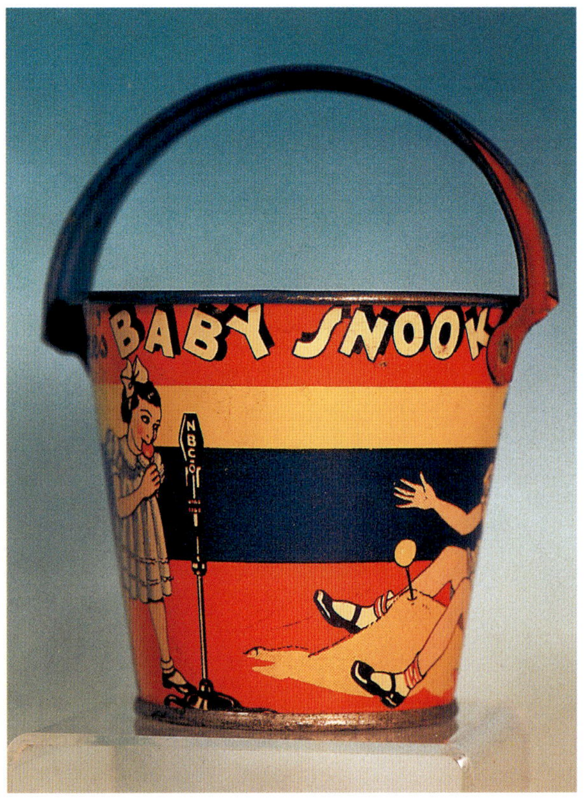

Fanny Brice's Baby Snooks Pops 3" tin lithographed candy pail. A lobster mould is on the bottom of the small pail. The pail is marked: "Ingredients-sugar, corn syrup, citric acid, U.S. certified flavors, and artificial colors. Mfg. by E. Rosen Co., Providence, R.I. Net wt.2 oz." $200-300

Chapter 2:

Barney Google

Barney Google was created by Billy DeBeck in 1919, first appearing in the sports section of the *Chicago Herald and Examiner* as "Take Barney Google, F'rinstance."

In October 1919, the comic strip was being syndicated by King Features all over the country. In 1922, the strip added greatly to its popularity when Barney's horse Spark Plug joined the strip. The strip took an even greater jump in popularity when moonshiner Snuffy Smith was added to the strip. Fred Laswell took over drawing the strip in 1942 and continued to draw it until his death on March 3, 2001. John Rose, who inked the strip for Lasswell, continues it today. "Barney Google" appears in 21 countries in 11 languages.

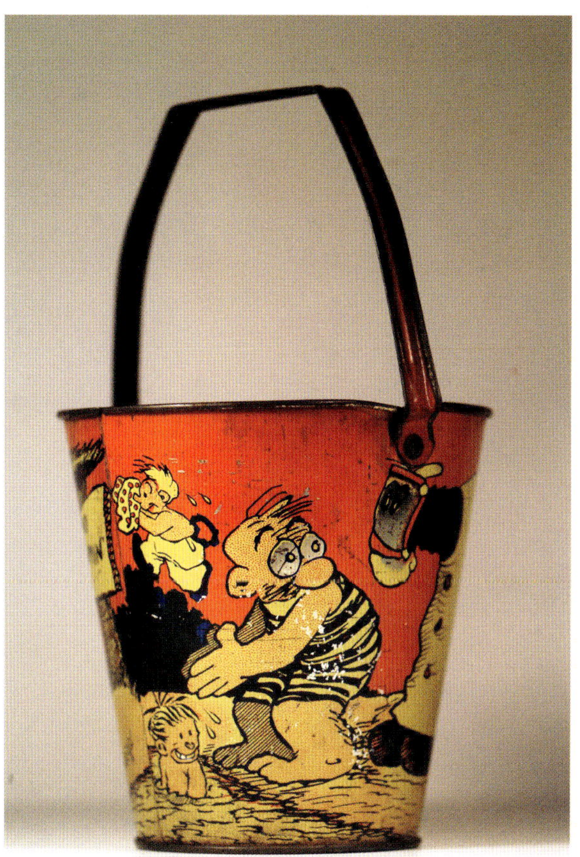

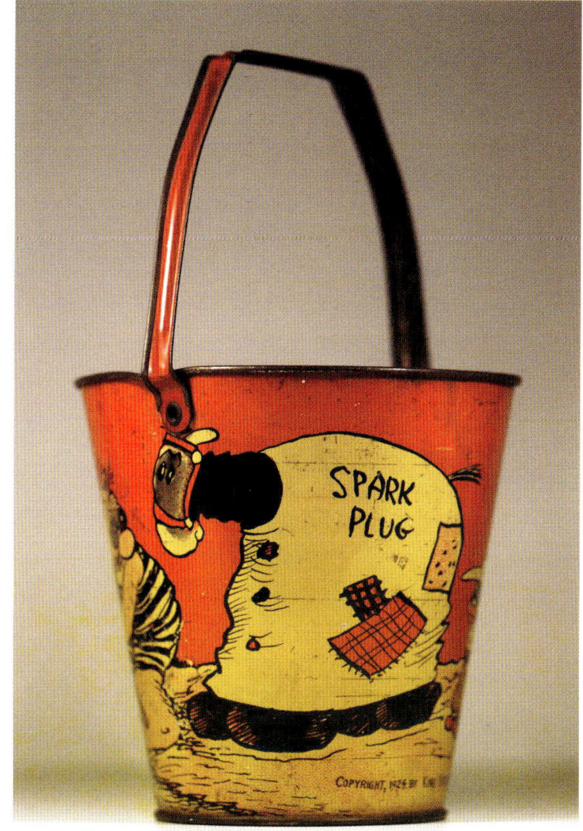

Four views of the very rare Barney Google and Spark Plug sand pail. Produced in 1924, it is one of the earliest character pails known. It is 6" tall. "Copyright 1924. By King Features Syndicate, Inc." *Collection of Mel Birnkrant*. $400-750.
Continued on following page.

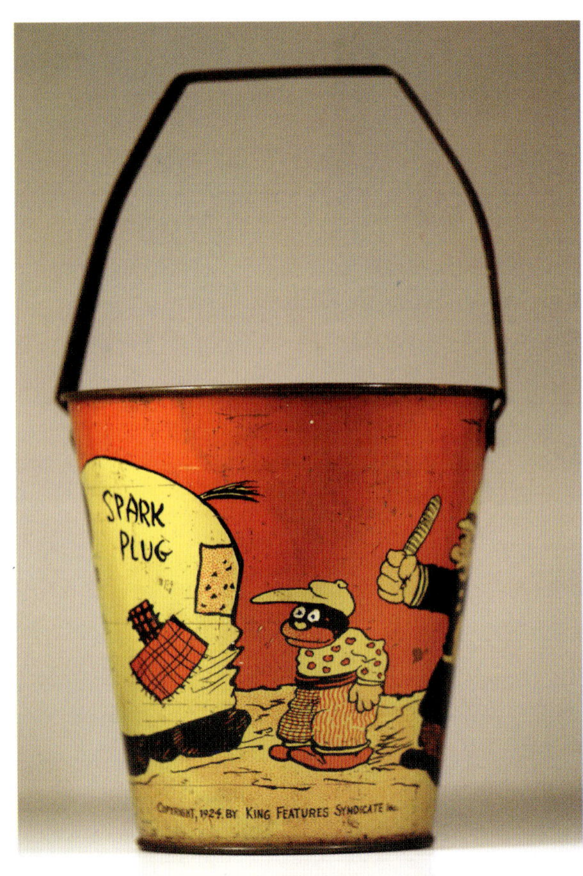

The very rare Barney Google continued from preceding page.

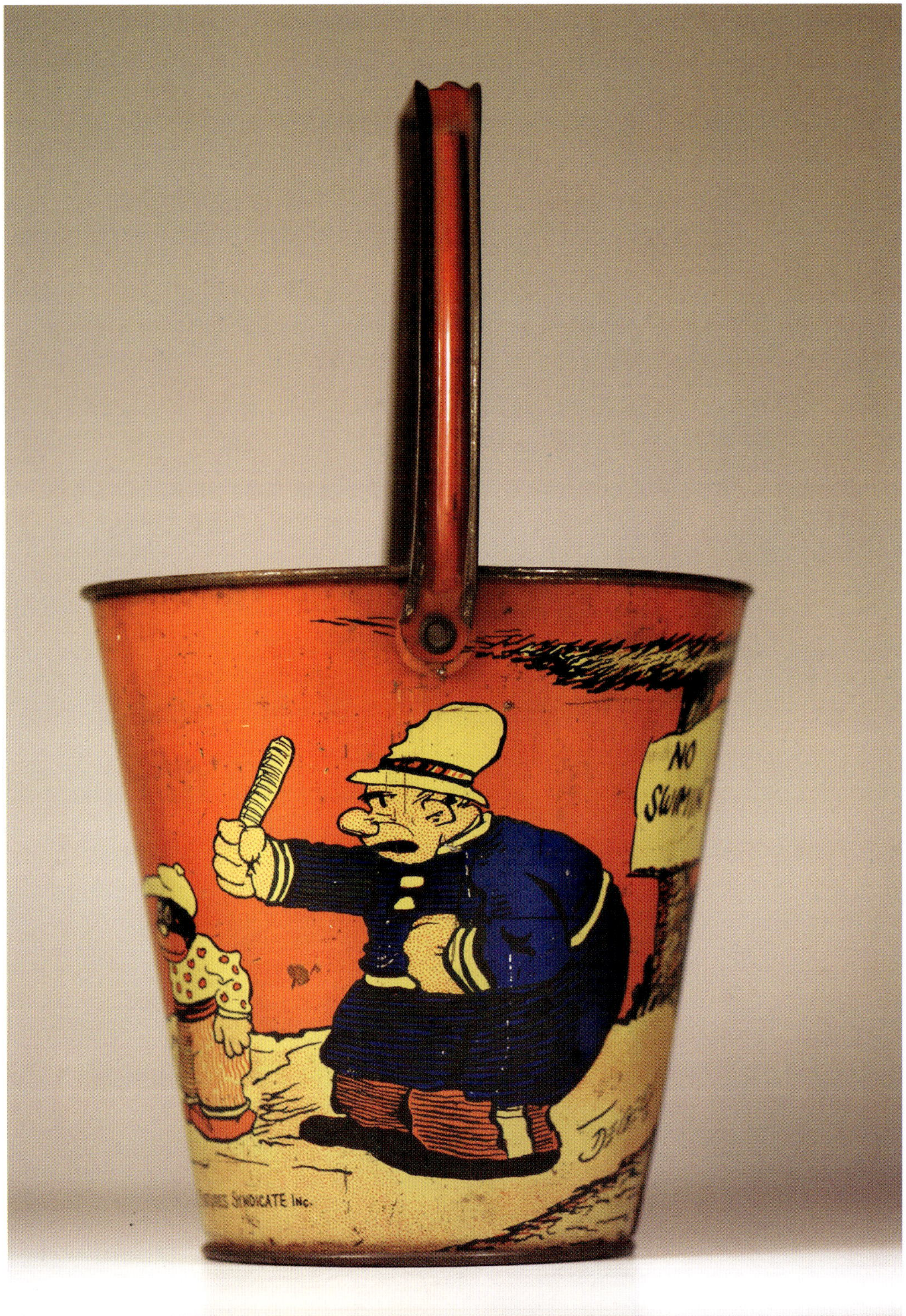

Chapter 3:

Betty Boop

Max Fleischer produced a series of *Talkertoon and Betty Boop* films featuring Boop, released by Paramount during the 1930s. She was the first cartoon to depict a sexy lady and was an immediate sensation.

Accompanied by her dog, Bimbo, and Koko, the clown, she participated in a series of adventures. Because of her world-wide popularity, it was not long before licensed and unlicensed merchandise was produced in a number of items. These included products made in ceramics, paper, and tin, plus dolls and toys. Often unlicensed merchandise included other comic characters like Mickey Mouse or Felix the Cat to help sell the items.

Betty Boop items have been continued to be produced to the present day and a couple of the pails pictured are contemporary.

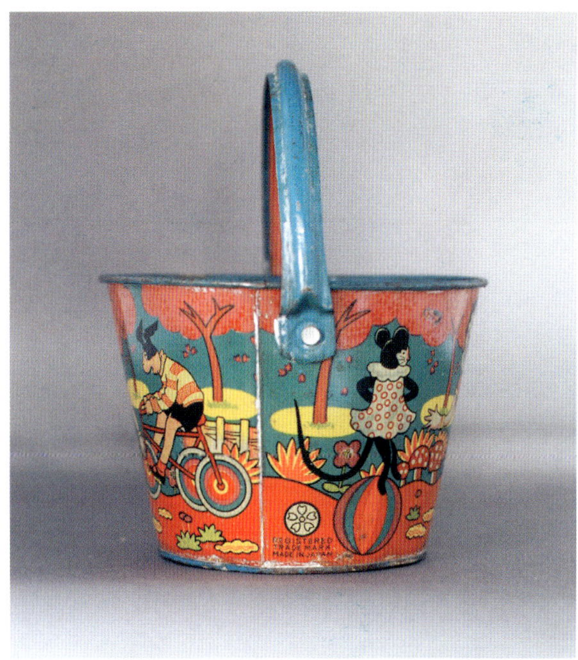

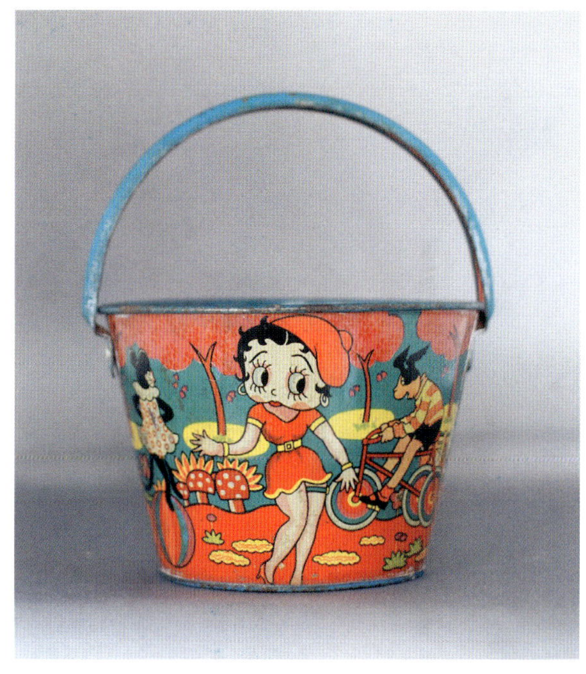

Two views of an early 3" sand pail from Japan. The first image shows the manufacturer's logo and the words "Registered Trademark, Made in Japan." The second depicts Betty wondering who or what is riding the tricycle. The reverse side has the same images. Rare. $850-1,250.

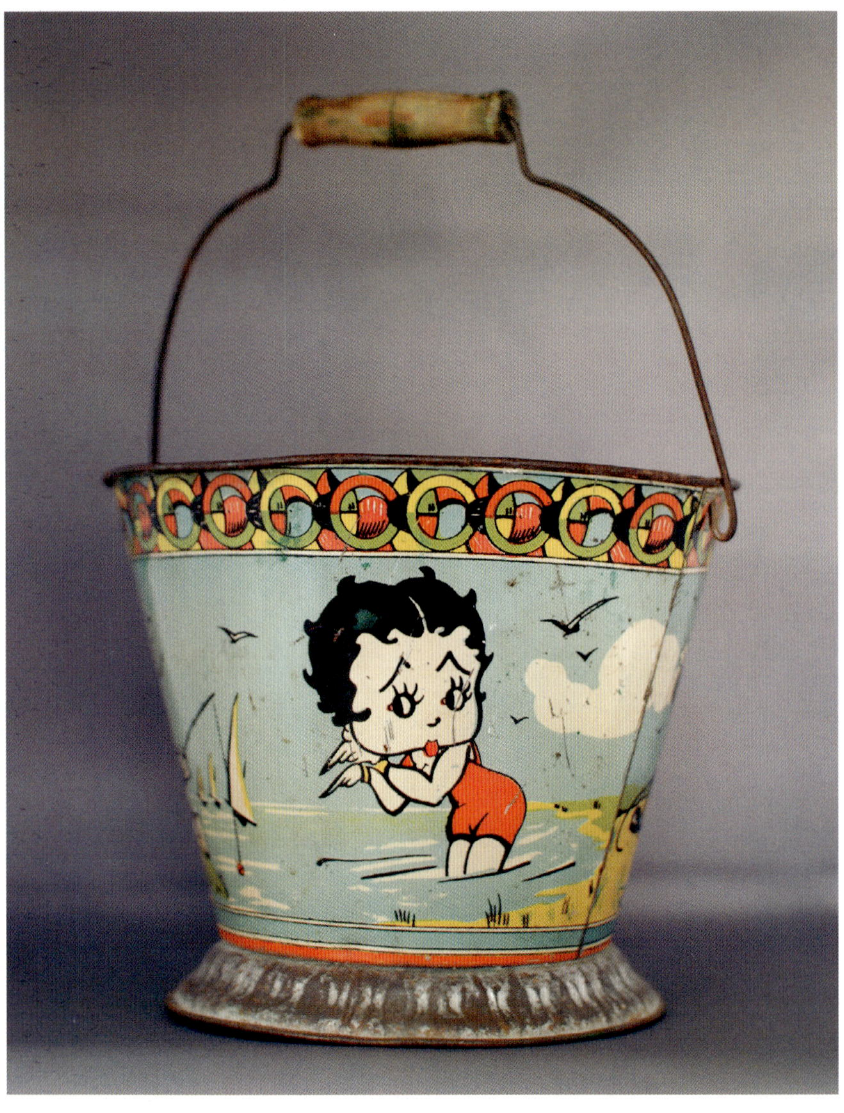

A 5.5″ pail with a raised bottom featuring Betty Boop from the 1930s. Made in Japan. The pail also features images of Oswald and Mickey Mouse. Very rare. $1,000-$1,500

Two contemporary 7″ pails featuring Betty Boop in various poses. Images are the same on both sides of the pails. Each is marked © 2000 King Features Syndicate, Inc. / Fleischer Studios Inc./ ™Hearst Holdings Inc./ Imported from China by The Tin Box Company. Each $10-15

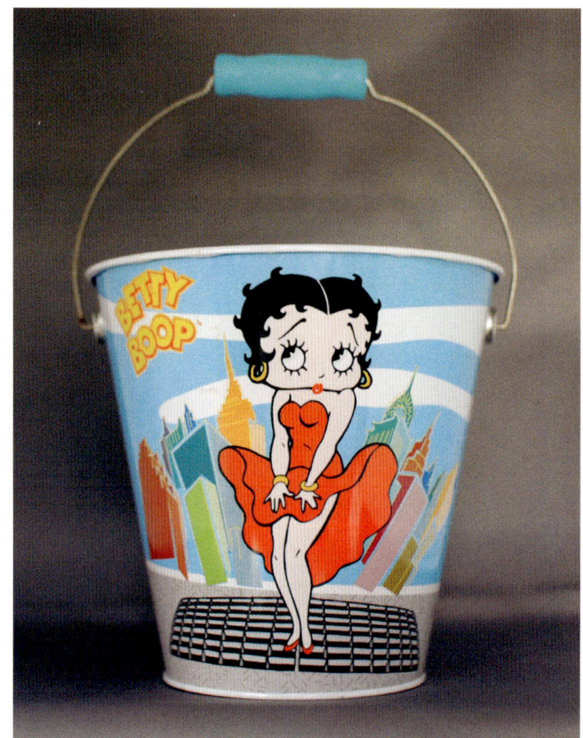

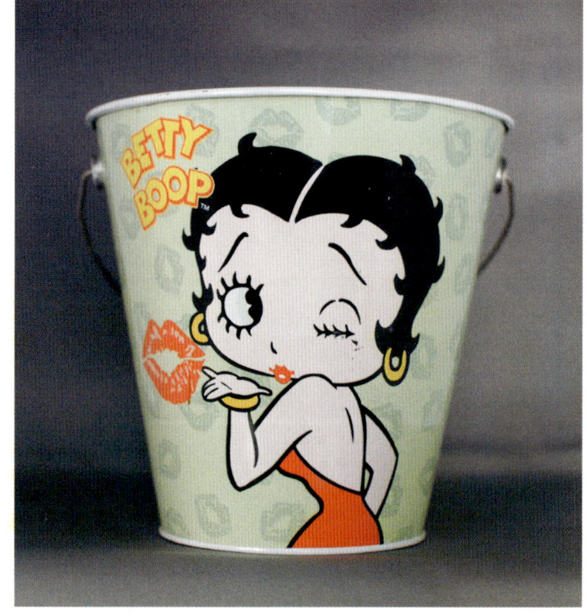

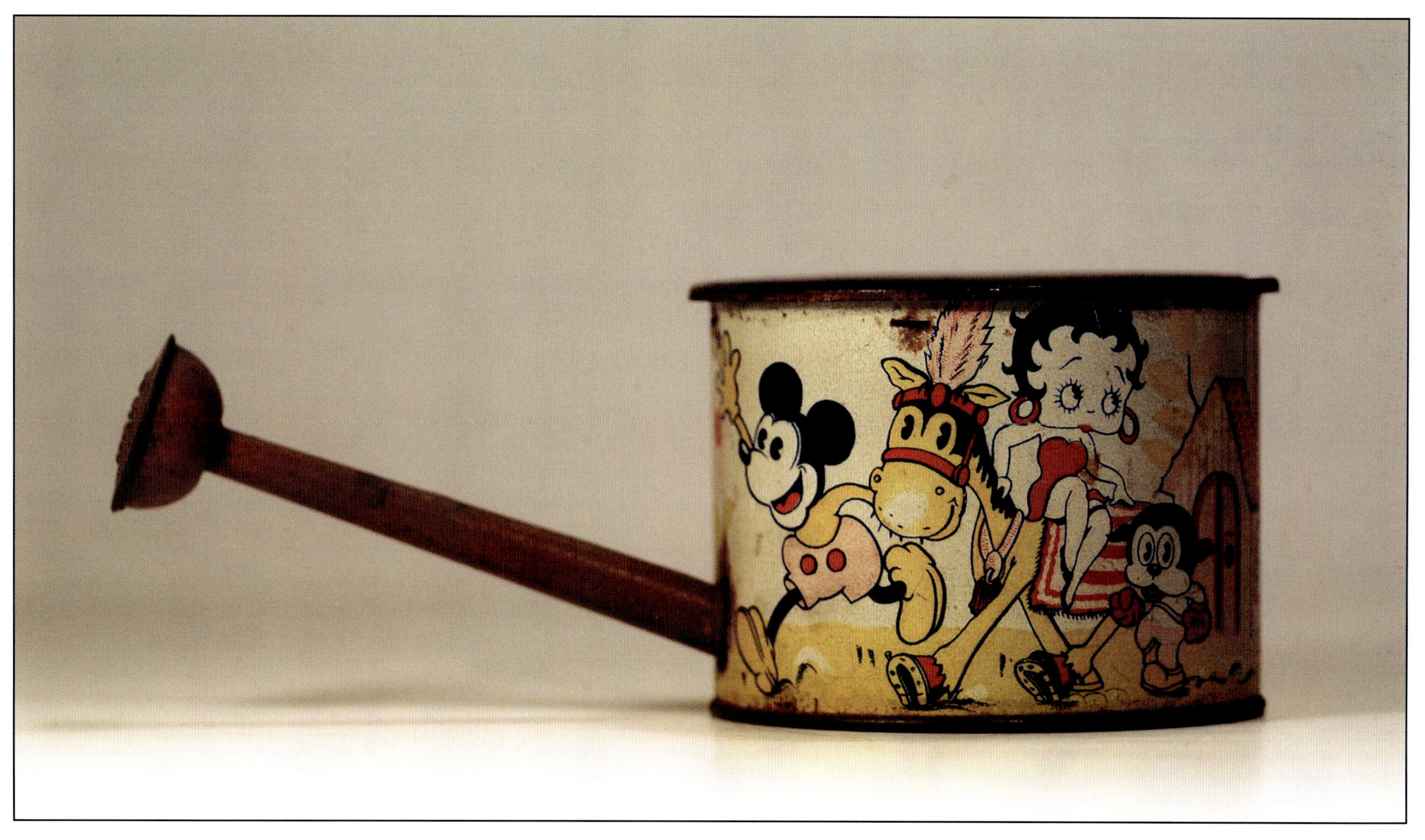

This rare Betty Boop and Mickey Mouse vintage watering can is probably from the early to mid 1930s. Missing the handle. The can measures 2.5" high by 3.5" in diameter. Including the spout it is 7" wide. Unmarked. *Birnkrant Collection*. $450-850

Chapter 4:
Bonzo

Bonzo the Dog was the creation of George E. Studdy in 1922. Bonzo is very much a British character and is still avidly collected today. Among the most collected items are post cards and figurines. The sand pail example shown is quite rare and has some outstanding images of Bonzo.

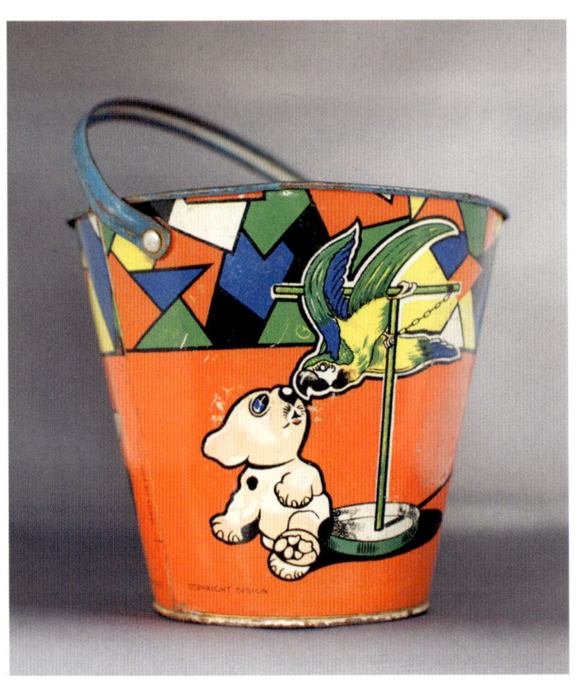

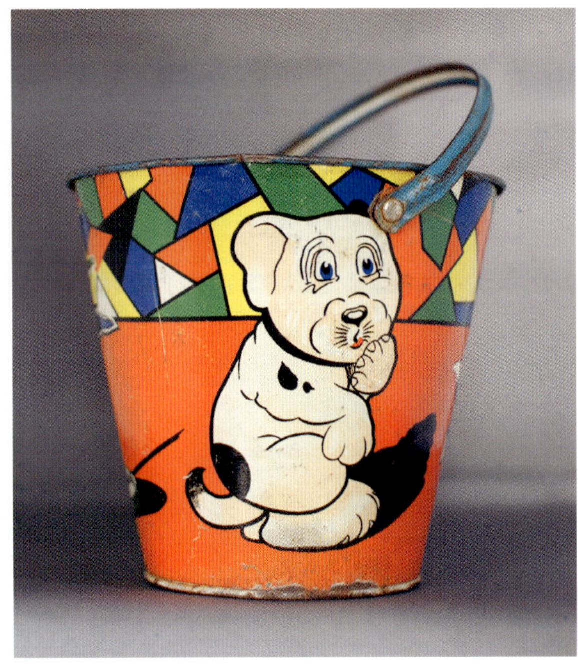

Three views of the 6" Bonzo pail. This colorful pail is extremely rare. The only markings include "Reliable Series, Made in England, IR" and "copyright design" A covered toffee pail was also produced in 1925. It was very similar to the Felix toffee pails shown in the Felix chapter. $700-900

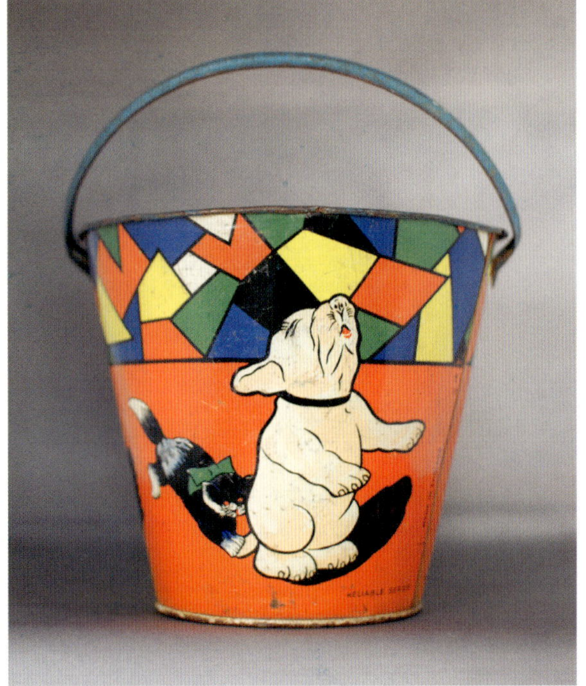

Chapter 5:

Charlie Chaplin

Born in Walworth, London, England in April, 1889, Charlie was the son of parents who were entertainers in London music halls. His first performance on stage was in 1894 at the age of five.

Charlie came to America in 1910 and stayed until early 1912, when he returned to England. After five months there, he returned to the U.S. where he remained until 1952. Film producer Mack Sennett of Keystone Studios had Charlie make his first film appearance in 1914 in a one-reel comedy, *Making a Living.*

His most famous character was "The Tramp" which he first played in 1914. It was his signature role and he continued playing it until the *Modern Times* which was released in 1936.

With Mary Pickford, Douglas Fairbanks, and D.W.Griffith, Charlie co-founded United Artists film distribution company. This was a successful attempt to get away from the ever growing power of the film distributors and financiers. Charlie continued serving on the U.A. board until the early 1950s.

With few exceptions most of Charlie's films were produced during the "silent" era. His first dialogue film was *The Great Dictator*, released in 1940. The film ridiculed Adolph Hitler and Nazism a year before the United States abandoned its policy of isolationism regarding Nazi Germany. Charlie lived in Switzerland from 1952 until his death on Christmas Day, 1977, at age 88.

Because of his great popularity and longevity, lots of merchandise was created with Charlie's image. Examples include dolls, toys, ceramics, and paper items. We know of one fabulous covered 8" toffee pail featuring Charlie on one side and, we believe, Mary Pickford on the other. An example is not pictured in this book. We have pictured several Charlie Royal Paragon ceramic pieces.

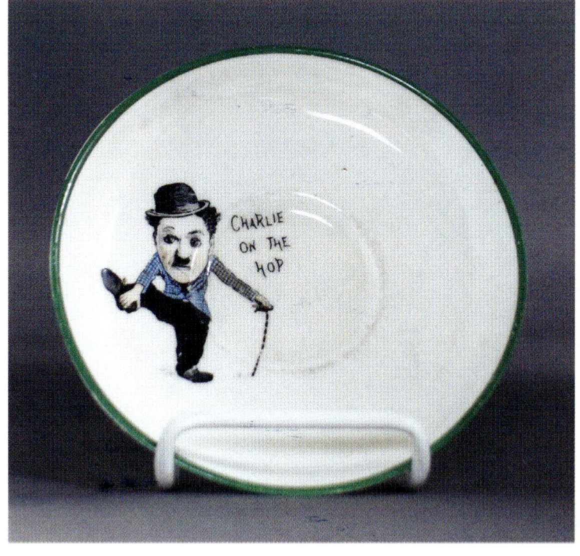

In addition to some great Mickey Mouse china pieces, Royal Paragon of Great Britain produced some unique Charlie Chaplin ceramic pieces. Shown are a cup, saucer and both sides of a rare Charlie match safe. Each $250-500

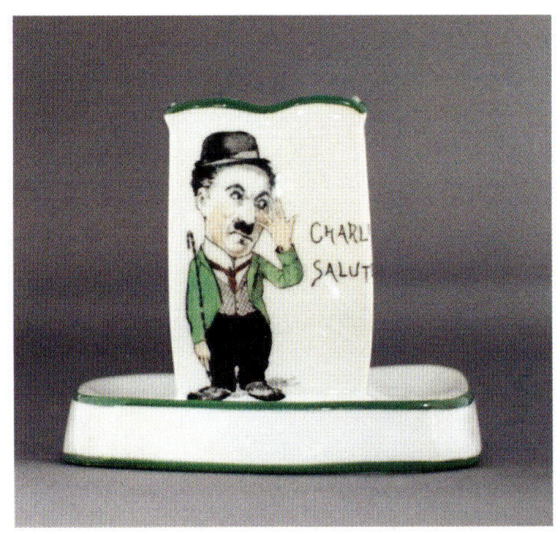

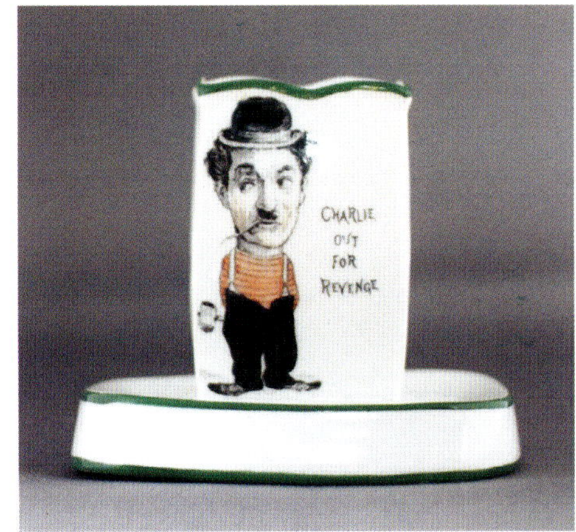

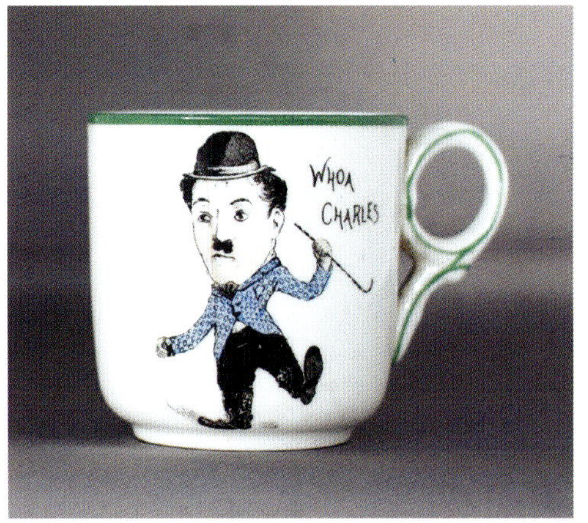

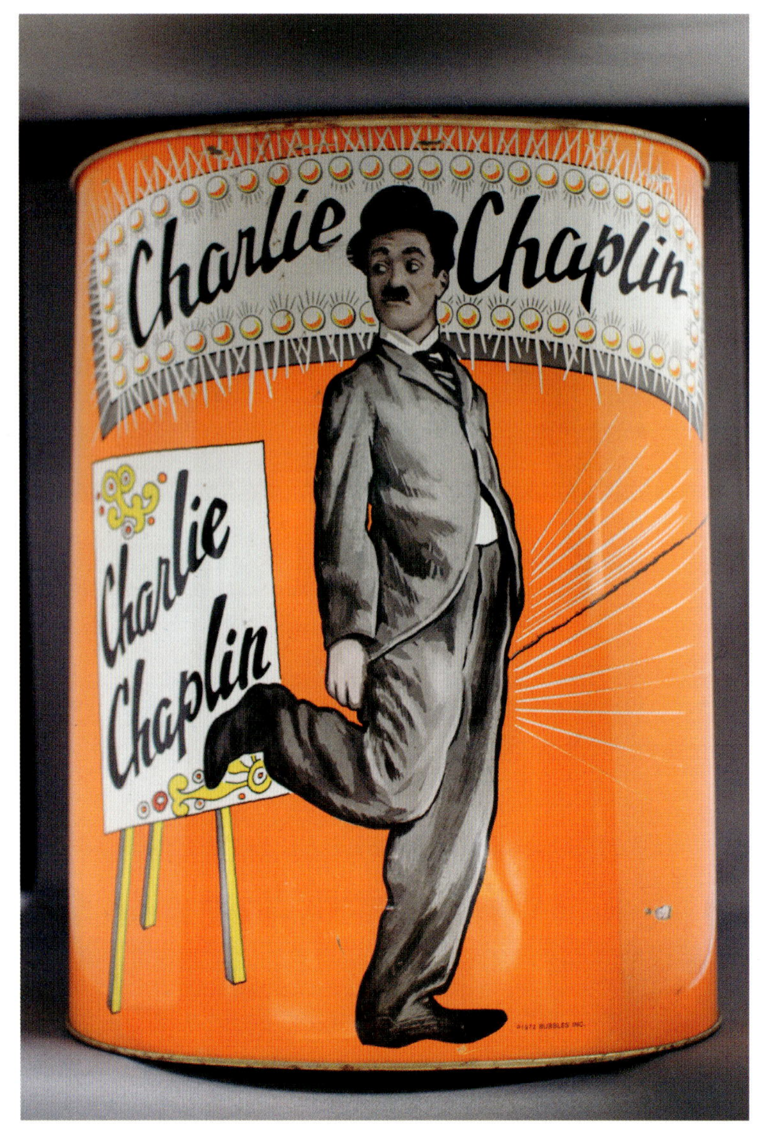

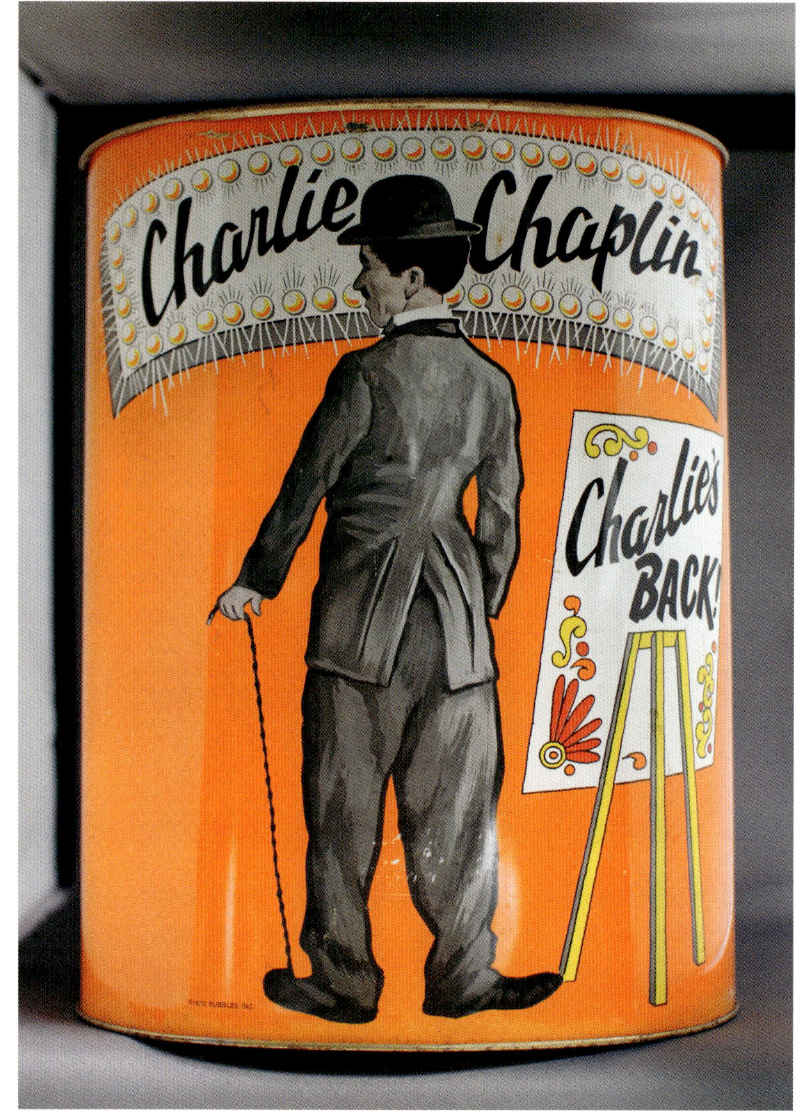

Two views of a Charlie Chaplin 13″ waste can as we were unable to secure an 8″ Chaplin and Mary Pickford toffee pail with cover in time for this printing. The waste can is ©1972 by Bubbles, Inc. Made by J. Chein. $25-50

Chapter 6:

Davy Crockett

King of the Wild Frontier

Colonel David Crockett was born August 17, 1786, and died defending the Alamo March 6, 1836. He was born in Tennessee and named after his grandfather who was killed there by Indians. Davy Crockett served several terms in the U.S. House of Representatives representing Tennessee. Before his 20th birthday he had become a skilled backwoodsman, hunter, and trapper. In 1806 he married Polly Finley and they had three children. In 1815 he fought in the Creek war and in 1818 was elected a lieutenant colonel in the Tennessee militia.

After he served three terms in Congress he was defeated for re-election in 1835 and he was reported to have said: "I told the people of my district that I would serve them as faithfully as I had done but if not…you may all go to hell and I will go to Texas." And so on October 31, 1835, he left for Texas. He died in defense of the Alamo.

Over the years, Davy Crockett became a folk hero. Stories, books, and silent films all served to support the legend. Then in late 1954 and early 1955, Walt Disney produced a series of three television specials featuring Fess Parker as Davy Crockett. The shows were a huge success and Disney was sorry he killed him off at the Alamo in the third episode. Coonskin caps and other products became all the rage. The series spawned a Davy Crockett craze around the world, particularly in Great Britain. John Wayne starred as Davy in *The Alamo* in 1960. The sand pail included is but a small part of the excitement.

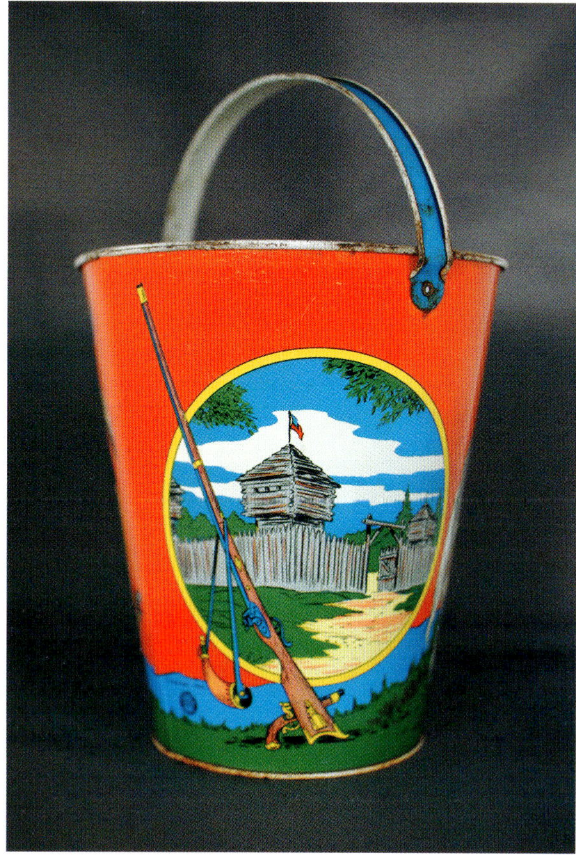

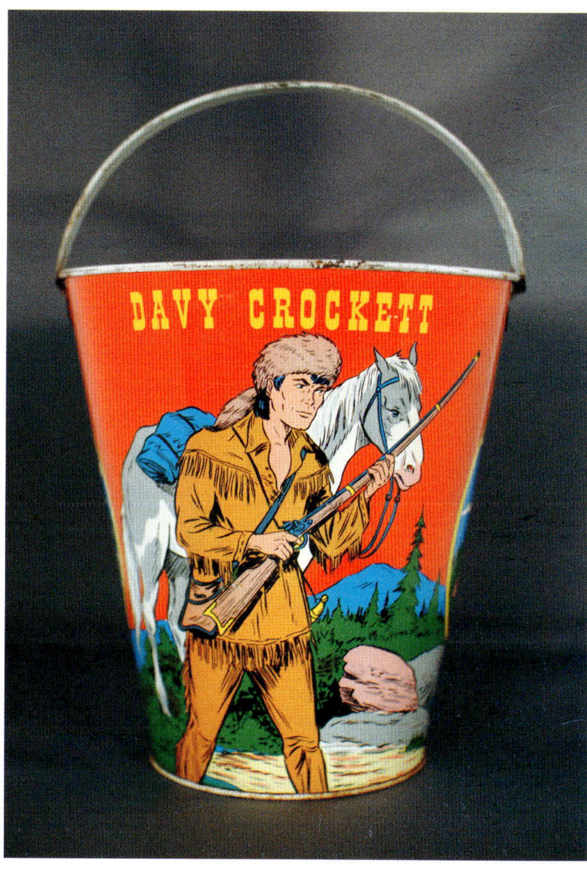

Three views of the 7.75" Davy Crockett sand pail plus a detail of the Ohio Art logo and copyright. The logo reads: Copyright 1955 the Ohio Art Co. Bryan, Ohio Made in Ohio U.S.A. $125-200

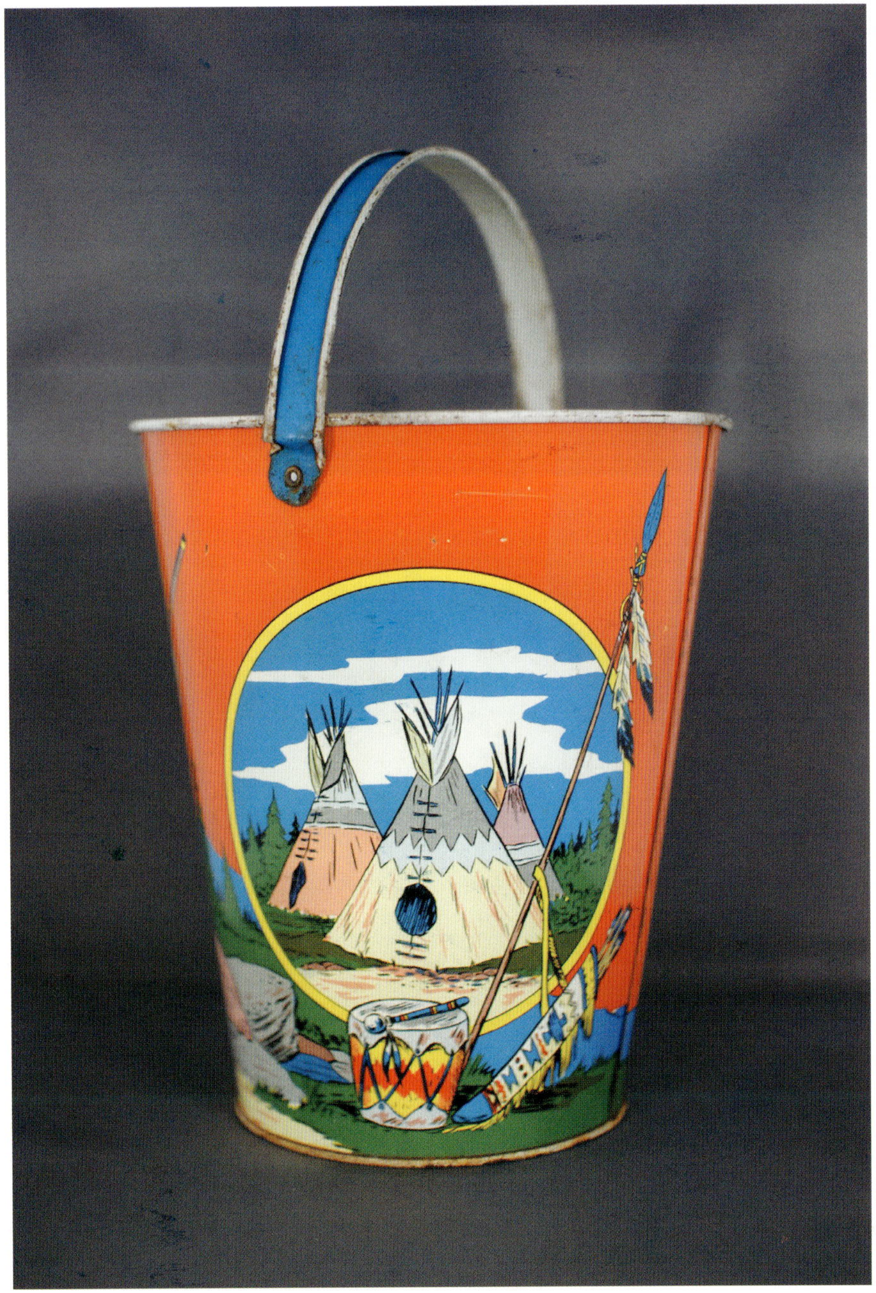

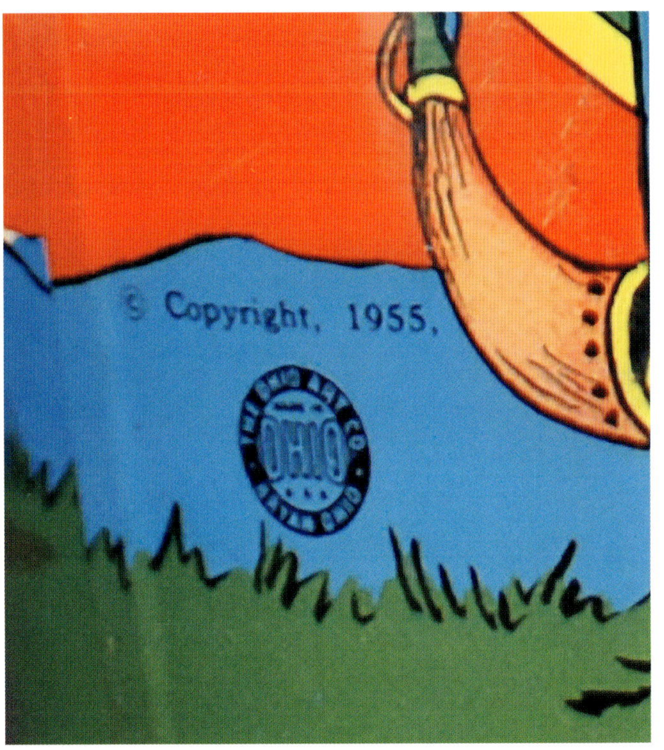
© Copyright, 1955,
OHIO

Chapter 7:

Walt Disney® Characters: U.S.A.

Ohio Art, J. Chein, and other U.S. manufacturers.

Without doubt more licensed and unlicensed merchandise was produced involving Disney characters than any other. No other character is even close. This production of merchandise started in the 1920s and continues to the present day.

In fact, more Disney metal sand toys were produced than for all other characters combined. For this reason, the Disney chapters will be organized by both licensed (authorized) and unlicensed (un-authorized) within the United States in Chapter 7. Chapter 8 will cover the more than ten foreign countries where the metal toys were produced.

Special mention must be made of the Ohio Art Company, Bryan Ohio, USA that by themselves produced more metal character sand toys than all other companies combined. Because the life and genius of Walter Elias Disney has been well documented elsewhere, that subject will not be covered here.

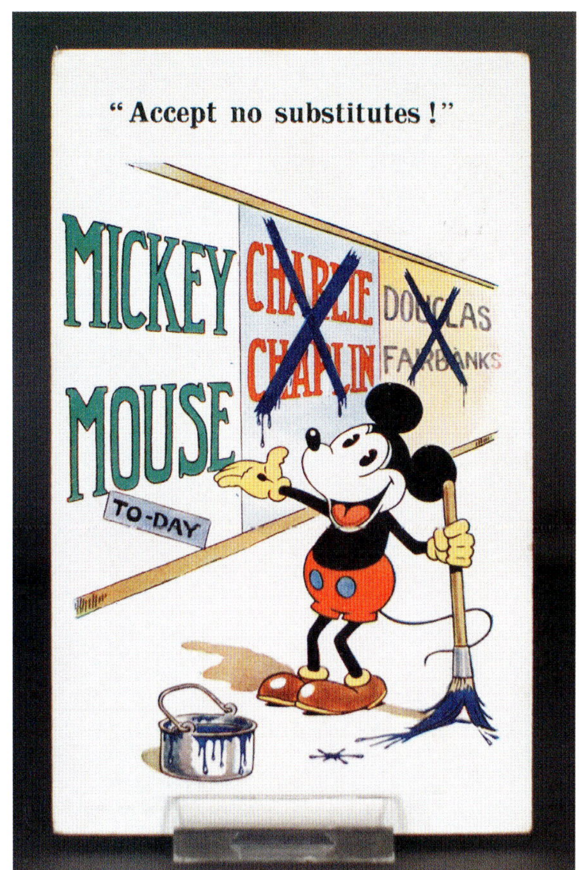

"Accept No Substitutes!" is one in the series of outstanding post cards produced by two British companies: INTER-ART CO. Florence House, Barnes, S.W. 13 and WOOLSTONE BROS., London, E.C. 1 This example is from WOOLSTONE #513. $35-85

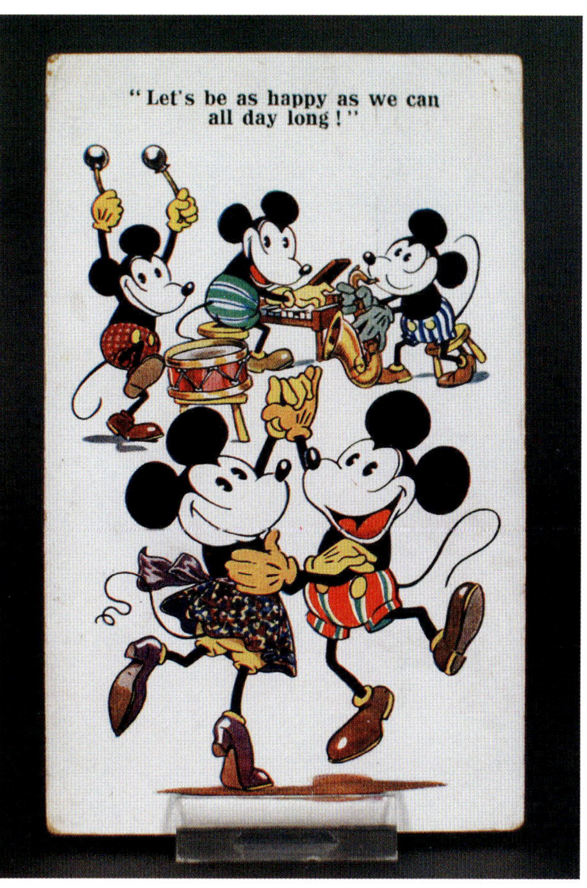

"Let's be as happy as we can all day long!" All these post cards are: Copyright reserved. Mickey Mouse Films distributed in British Isles by Ideal Films Ltd. This one is by Woolstone #506 $35-85

THE OHIO ART COMPANY (all items licensed)

In late 1933, Kay Kamen was appointed by Disney to handle all merchandise licensing for the company world wide. In 1934, Kay appointed his nephew, George Kamen, to be headquartered in London to handle the licensing of countries other than those in North America.

This section begins with three sets of Ohio Art catalog pages from 1936, 1938, and 1942. These will be followed by a Mickey sand set in a great Mickey box and a Donald Duck set in a generic box. Following will be the special images of Disney metal sand toys together with additional images.

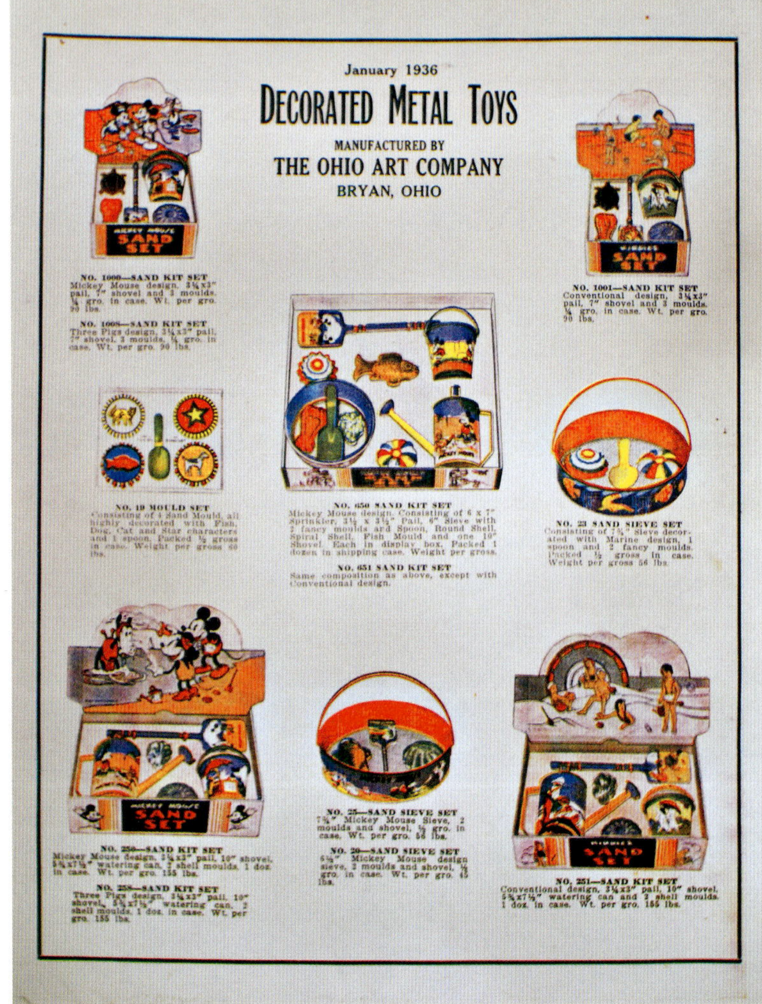

January 1936

DECORATED METAL TOYS

MANUFACTURED BY

THE OHIO ART COMPANY

BRYAN, OHIO

NO. 1000—SAND KIT SET
Mickey Mouse design. 3¼x3" pail, 7" shovel and 3 moulds. ¼ gro. in case. Wt. per gro. 90 lbs.

NO. 1008—SAND KIT SET
Three Pigs design, 3¼x3" pail, 7" shovel, 3 moulds, ¼ gro. in case. Wt. per gro. 90 lbs.

NO. 1001—SAND KIT SET
Conventional design, 3¼x3" pail, 7" shovel and 3 moulds. ¼ gro. in case. Wt. per gro. 90 lbs.

NO. 19 MOULD SET
Consisting of 4 Sand Mould, all highly decorated with Fish, Dog, Cat and Star characters and 1 spoon. Packed ½ gross in case. Weight per gross 60 lbs.

NO. 650 SAND KIT SET
Mickey Mouse design. Consisting of 6 x 7" Sprinkler, 3½ x 3½" Pail, 6" Sieve with 2 fancy moulds and Spoon, Round Shell, Spiral Shell, Fish Mould and one 10" Shovel. Each in display box. Packed 1 dozen in shipping case. Weight per gross.

NO. 651 SAND KIT SET
Same composition as above, except with Conventional design.

NO. 23 SAND SIEVE SET
Consisting of 7½" Sieve decorated with Marine design, 1 spoon and 2 fancy moulds. Packed ½ gross in case. Weight per gross 56 lbs.

NO. 250—SAND KIT SET
Mickey Mouse design, 3¼x3" pail, 10" shovel, 5⅝x7½" watering can, 2 shell moulds, 1 doz. in case. Wt. per gro. 155 lbs.

NO. 258—SAND KIT SET
Three Pigs design, 3¼x3" pail, 10" shovel, 5⅝x7½" watering can, 2 shell moulds, 1 doz. in case. Wt. per gro. 155 lbs.

NO. 25—SAND SIEVE SET
7½" Mickey Mouse Sieve, 2 moulds and shovel, ½ gro. in case. Wt. per gro. 56 lbs.

NO. 20—SAND SIEVE SET
6½" Mickey Mouse design sieve, 2 moulds and shovel, ½ gro. in case. Wt. per gro. 45 lbs.

NO. 251—SAND KIT SET
Conventional design, 3¼x3" pail, 10" shovel, 5⅝x7½" watering can and 2 shell moulds. 1 doz. in case. Wt. per gro. 155 lbs.

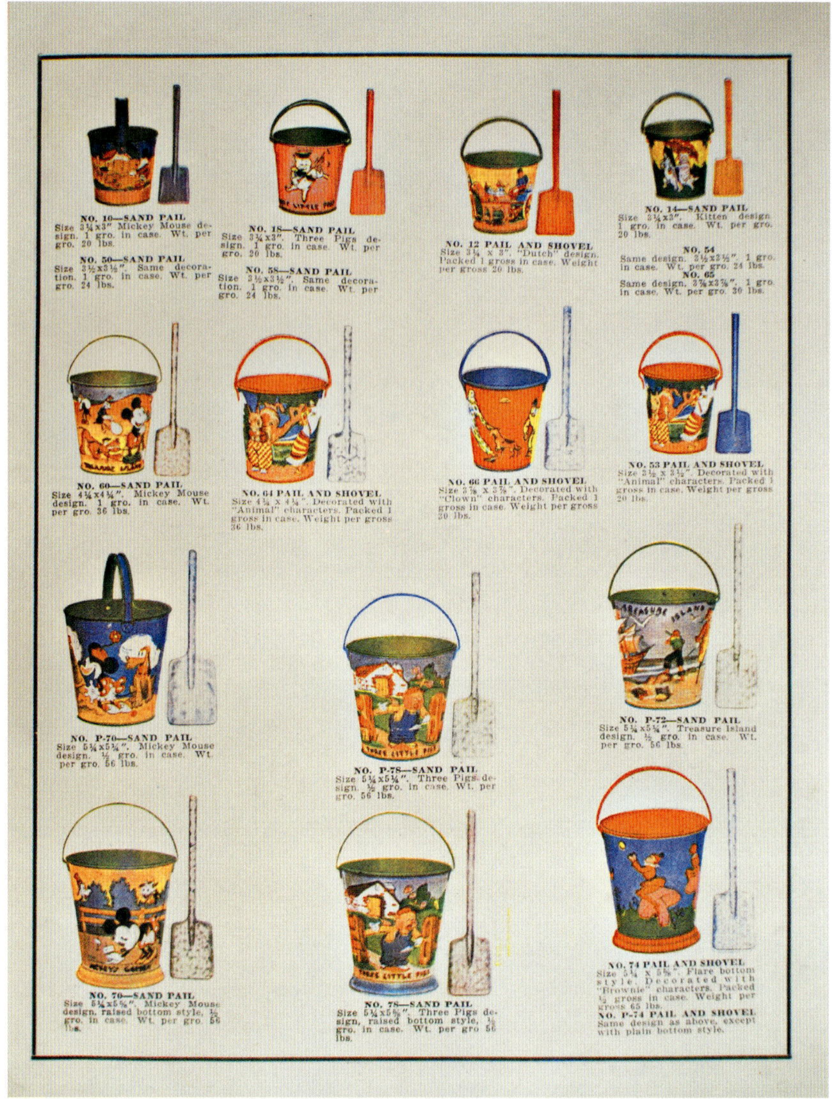

NO. 10—SAND PAIL
Size 3¼x3" Mickey Mouse design. 1 gro. in case. Wt. per gro. 20 lbs.

NO. 50—SAND PAIL
Size 3½x3½". Same decoration. 1 gro. in case. Wt. per gro. 24 lbs.

NO. 18—SAND PAIL
Size 3¼x3". Three Pigs design. 1 gro. in case. Wt. per gro. 20 lbs.

NO. 58—SAND PAIL
Size 3½x3½". Same decoration. 1 gro. in case. Wt. per gro. 24 lbs.

NO. 12 PAIL AND SHOVEL
Size 3¼ x 3". "Dutch" design. Packed 1 gross in case. Weight per gross 20 lbs.

NO. 14—SAND PAIL
Size 3¼x3". Kitten design 1 gro. in case. Wt. per gro. 20 lbs.

NO. 54
Same design. 3½x3½". 1 gro. in case. Wt. per gro. 24 lbs.

NO. 65
Same design. 3⅞x3⅞". 1 gro. in case. Wt. per gro. 30 lbs.

NO. 60—SAND PAIL
Size 4¼x4¼". Mickey Mouse design. 1 gro. in case. Wt. per gro. 36 lbs.

NO. 64 PAIL AND SHOVEL
Size 4¼ x 4¼". Decorated with "Animal" characters. Packed 1 gross in case. Weight per gross 36 lbs.

NO. 66 PAIL AND SHOVEL
Size 3⅞ x 3⅞". Decorated with "Clown" characters. Packed 1 gross in case. Weight per gross 30 lbs.

NO. 53 PAIL AND SHOVEL
Size 3½ x 3½". Decorated with "Animal" characters. Packed 1 gross in case. Weight per gross 20 lbs.

NO. P-70—SAND PAIL
Size 5¼x5¼". Mickey Mouse design. ½ gro. in case. Wt. per gro. 56 lbs.

NO. P-78—SAND PAIL
Size 5¼x5¼". Three Pigs design. ½ gro. in case. Wt. per gro. 56 lbs.

NO. P-72—SAND PAIL
Size 5¼x5¼". Treasure Island design. ½ gro. in case. Wt. per gro. 56 lbs.

NO. 70—SAND PAIL
Size 5¼x5⅝". Mickey Mouse design, raised bottom style, ½ gro. in case. Wt. per gro. 56 lbs.

NO. 78—SAND PAIL
Size 5¼x5⅝". Three Pigs design, raised bottom style, ½ gro. in case. Wt. per gro 56 lbs.

NO. 74 PAIL AND SHOVEL
Size 5¼ x 5⅝". Flare bottom style. Decorated with "Brownie" characters. Packed ½ gross in case. Weight per gross 65 lbs.

NO. P-74 PAIL AND SHOVEL
Same design as above, except with plain bottom style.

The first two pages from the January 1936 catalog and price list. Note the number of boxed sets on the first page.

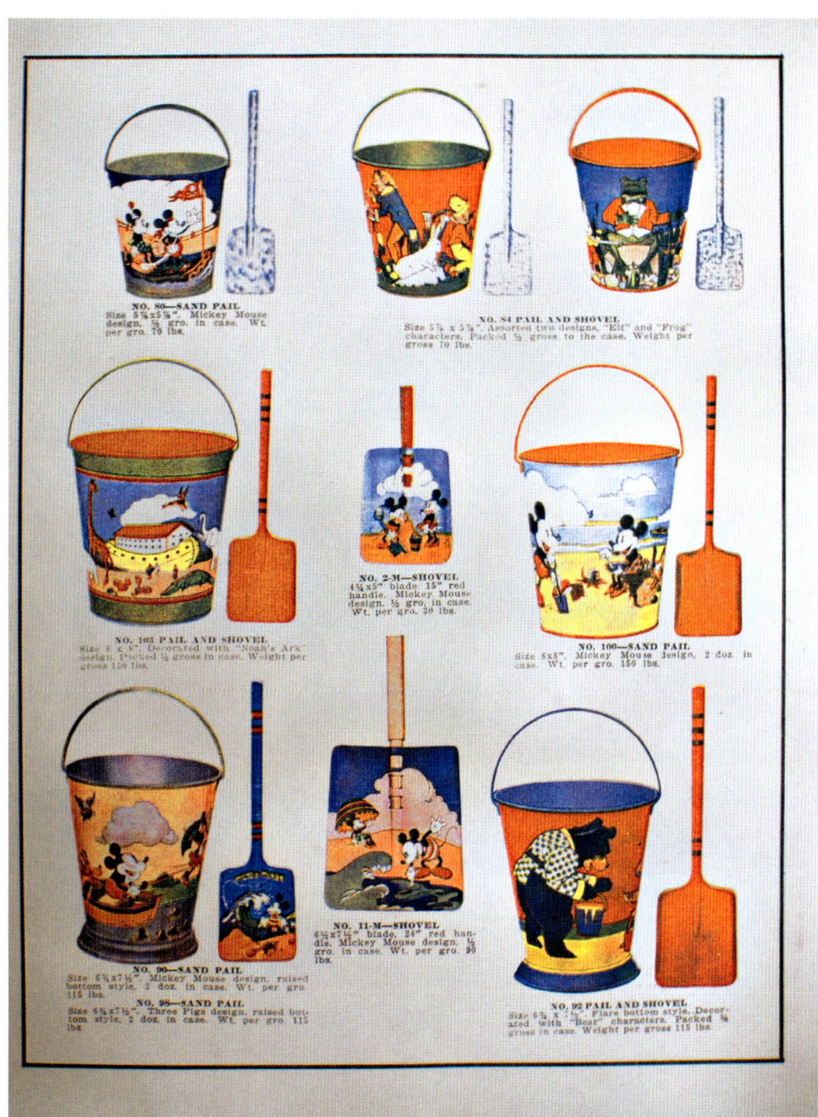

NO. 80—SAND PAIL
Size 5⅝x5⅞". Mickey Mouse design. ½ gro. in case. Wt. per gro. 70 lbs.

NO. 84 PAIL AND SHOVEL
Size 5¼ x 5⅞". Assorted two designs, "Elf" and "Frog" characters. Packed ½ gross to the case. Weight per gross 70 lbs.

NO. 103 PAIL AND SHOVEL
Size 8 x 8". Decorated with "Noah's Ark" design. Packed ⅓ gross in case. Weight per gross 150 lbs.

NO. 2-M—SHOVEL
4¾x5" blade 15" red handle. Mickey Mouse design. ½ gro. in case. Wt. per gro. 30 lbs.

NO. 100—SAND PAIL
Size 8x8". Mickey Mouse design. 2 doz. in case. Wt. per gro. 150 lbs.

NO. 90—SAND PAIL
Size 6¾x7½". Mickey Mouse design, raised bottom style. 2 doz. in case. Wt. per gro 115 lbs.

NO. 98—SAND PAIL
Size 6¾x7½". Three Pigs design, raised bottom style. 2 doz. in case. Wt. per gro 115 lbs.

NO. 11-M—SHOVEL
6½x7¼" blade, 24" red handle. Mickey Mouse design. ⅙ gro. in case. Wt. per gro. 90 lbs.

NO. 92 PAIL AND SHOVEL
Size 6¾ x 7½". Flare bottom style. Decorated with "Bear" characters. Packed ⅙ gross in case. Weight per gross 115 lbs.

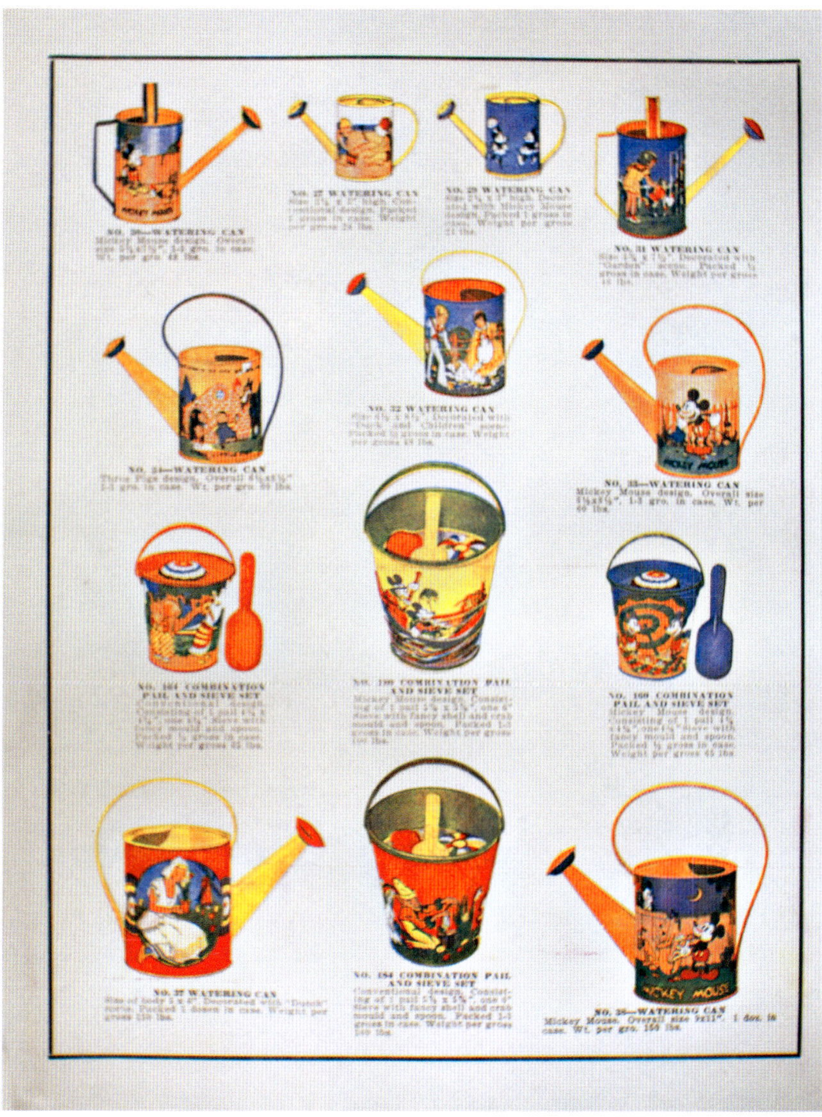

NO. [illegible]—WATERING CAN

NO. 27 WATERING CAN

NO. 29 WATERING CAN

NO. 31 WATERING CAN

NO. 24—WATERING CAN

NO. 32 WATERING CAN

NO. 33—WATERING CAN

NO. [illegible] COMBINATION PAIL AND SIEVE SET

NO. [illegible] COMBINATION PAIL AND SIEVE SET

NO. [illegible] COMBINATION PAIL AND SIEVE SET

NO. 37 WATERING CAN

NO. [illegible] COMBINATION PAIL AND SIEVE SET

NO. 38—WATERING CAN
Mickey Mouse. Overall size 9x11". 1 doz. in case. Wt. per gro. 150 lbs.

In addition to the sand pails, note the number of shovels and watering cans featured on the final two pages of the 1936 catalog.

SPRING & SUMMER TOYS

1936 PRICE LIST

		Quantity Case	Pric Gros
10	Pail and Shovel, "Mickey Mouse"	144	3.48
12	Pail and Shovel, "Dutch" design	144	3.36
14	Pail and Shovel, "Kitten" design	144	3.36
18	Pail and Shovel, "Three Pigs"	144	3.48
50	Pail and Shovel, "Mickey Mouse"	144	3.72
53	Pail and Shovel, "Animal" design	144	3.60
54	Pail and Shovel, "Kitten" design	144	3.60
58	Pail and Shovel, "Three Pigs"	144	3.72
60	Pail and Shovel, "Mickey Mouse"	144	4.50
64	Pail and Shovel, "Animal" design	144	4.26
65	Pail and Shovel, "Kitten" design	144	3.84
66	Pail and Shovel, "Clown" design	144	3.84
68	Pail and Shovel, "Three Pigs"	144	4.50
P-70	Pail and Shovel, "Mickey Mouse"	72	6.84
P-72	Pail and Shovel, "Treasure Island"	72	6.60
P-74	Pail and Shovel, "Brownie" design	72	6.60
P-78	Pail and Shovel, "Three Pigs"	72	6.84
70	Pail and Shovel, "Mickey Mouse"	72	8.28
74	Pail and Shovel, "Brownie" design	72	7.92
78	Pail and Shovel, "Three Pigs"	72	8.28
80	Pail and Shovel, "Mickey Mouse"	72	7.80
84	Pail and Shovel, "Elf" and "Frog" Asst.	72	7.50
88	Pail and Shovel, "Three Pigs"	72	7.80
90	Pail and Shovel, "Mickey Mouse"	24	17.76
92	Pail and Shovel, "Bear" design	24	16.80
98	Pail and Shovel, "Three Pigs"	24	17.76
100	Pail and Shovel, "Mickey Mouse"	24	16.80
103	Pail and Shovel, "Noah's Ark" design	24	16.56
108	Pail and Shovel, "Three Pigs"	24	16.80
160	Combination Pail Set, "Mickey Mouse"	72	8.76
164	Combination Pail Set, "Conventional"	72	8.64
180	Combination Pail Set, "Mickey Mouse"	48	16.80
184	Combination Pail Set, "Conventional"	48	15.84

		Quantity Case	Price Gross
19	Sand Mould Set, "Conventional"	72	7.92
1000	Sand Kit Set, "Mickey Mouse"	36	8.40
1001	Sand Kit Set, "Conventional"	36	7.92
1008	Sand Kit Set, "Three Pigs"	36	8.40
250	Sand Kit Set, "Mickey Mouse"	12	17.76
251	Sand Kit Set, "Conventional"	12	16.80
258	Sand Kit Set, "Three Pigs"	12	17.76
650	Sand Kit Set, "Mickey Mouse"	12	33.00
651	Sand Kit Set, "Conventional"	12	31.50
20	Sand Sieve Set, "Mickey Mouse"	72	7.00
23	Sand Sieve Set, "Marine" design	72	8.28
25	Sand Sieve Set, "Mickey Mouse"	72	8.40
2M	Sand Shovel, "Mickey Mouse"	72	3.96
11M	Sand Shovel, "Mickey Mouse"	72	7.92
27	Sprinkler, "Juvenile" design	144	4.20
29	Sprinkler, "Mickey Mouse"	144	4.38
28	Sprinkler, "Three Pigs"	48	7.00
30	Sprinkler, "Mickey Mouse"	48	7.00
31	Sprinkler, "Juvenile"	48	6.96
32	Sprinkler, "Duck and Children"	48	8.76
33	Sprinkler, "Mickey Mouse"	48	9.00
34	Sprinkler, "Three Pigs"	48	9.00
37	Sprinkler, "Dutch" scene	12	16.80
38	Sprinkler, "Mickey Mouse"	12	17.76

—

Terms Net 30 days, Less 2% 10 da. F. O. B. Factory

—

THE OHIO ART COMPANY, Bryan, Ohio

The price list for the Spring and Summer Toys for 1936. Note how inexpensive the toys were during these Depression era times.

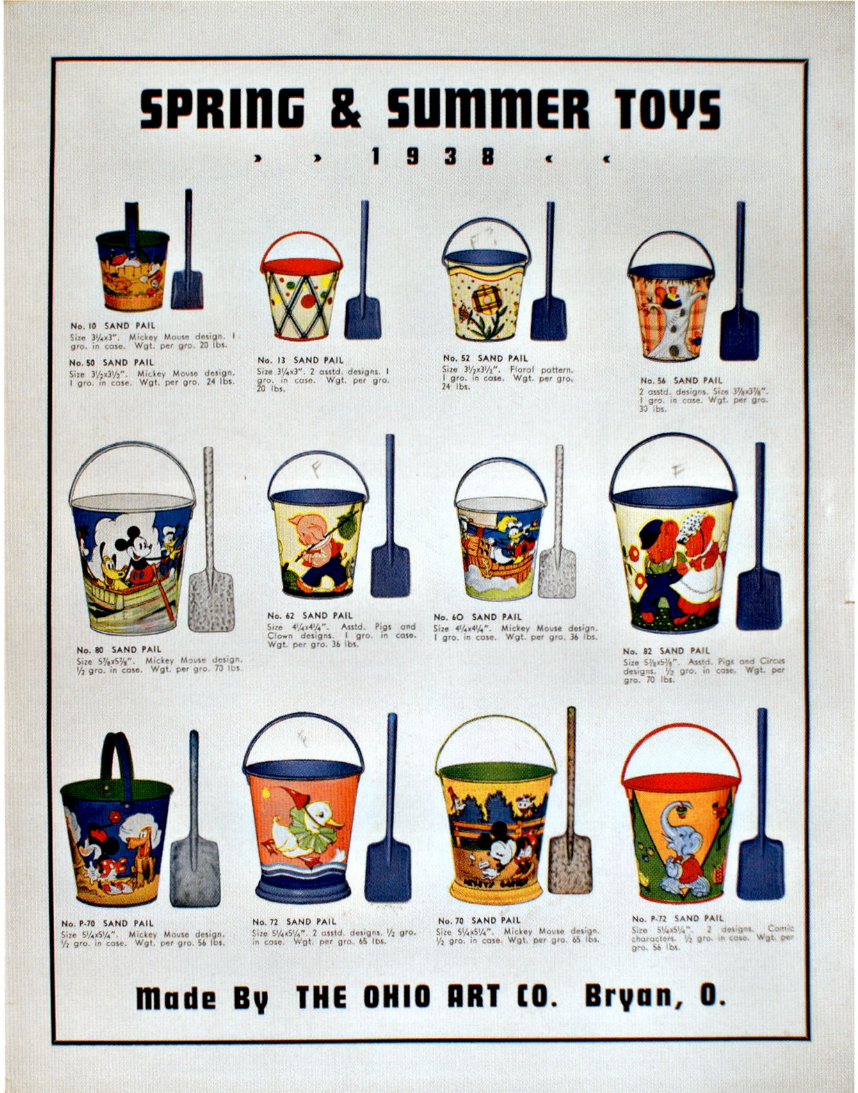

Spring and Summer Toys 1938, page one. Every sand pail on this page has a generic shovel included.

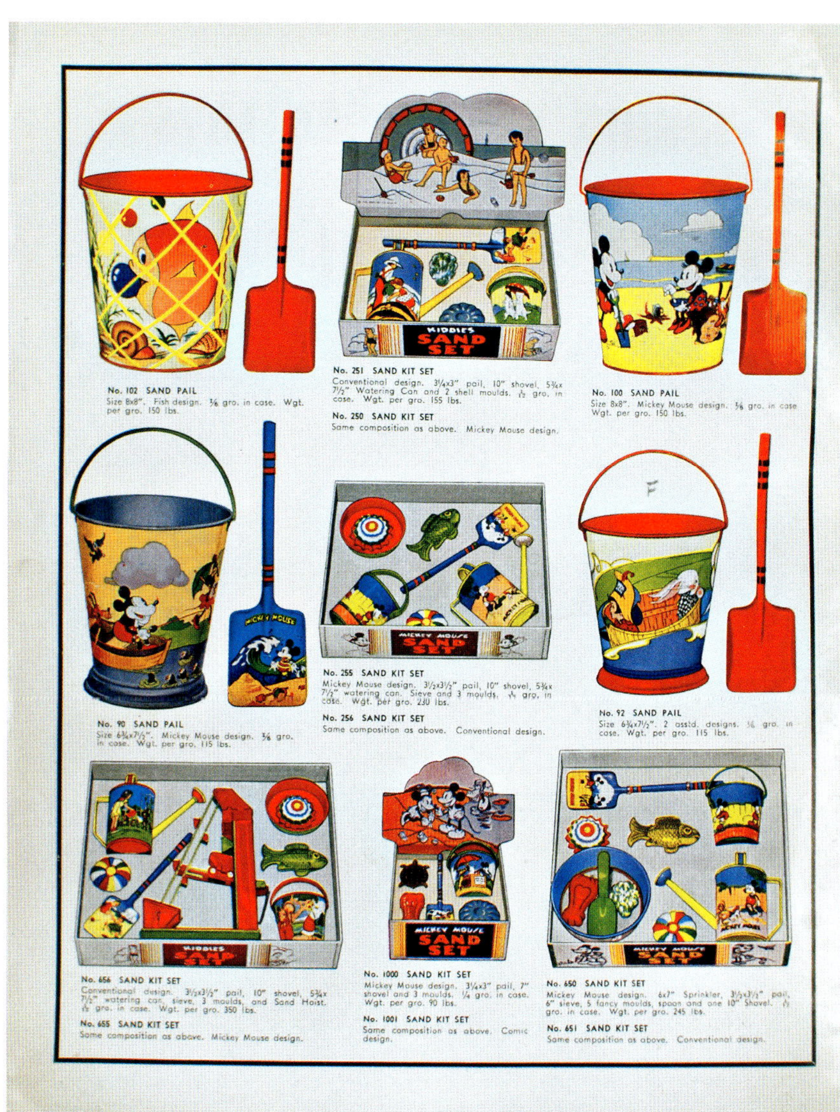

No. 102 SAND PAIL
Size 8x8". Fish design. 5/6 gro. in case. Wgt. per gro. 150 lbs.

No. 251 SAND KIT SET
Conventional design. 3¼x3" pail, 10" shovel, 5¾x7½" Watering Can and 2 shell moulds. 1/12 gro. in case. Wgt. per gro. 155 lbs.

No. 250 SAND KIT SET
Same composition as above. Mickey Mouse design.

No. 100 SAND PAIL
Size 8x8". Mickey Mouse design. 5/6 gro. in case Wgt. per gro. 150 lbs.

No. 90 SAND PAIL
Size 6¾x7½". Mickey Mouse design. 5/6 gro. in case. Wgt. per gro. 115 lbs.

No. 255 SAND KIT SET
Mickey Mouse design. 3½x3½" pail, 10" shovel, 5¾x7½" watering can. Sieve and 3 moulds. 1/4 gro. in case. Wgt. per gro. 230 lbs.

No. 256 SAND KIT SET
Same composition as above. Conventional design.

No. 92 SAND PAIL
Size 6¾x7½". 2 asstd. designs. 1/6 gro. in case. Wgt. per gro. 115 lbs.

No. 656 SAND KIT SET
Conventional design. 3½x3½" pail, 10" shovel, 5¾x7½" watering can, sieve, 3 moulds, and Sand Hoist. 1/12 gro. in case. Wgt. per gro. 350 lbs.

No. 655 SAND KIT SET
Same composition as above. Mickey Mouse design.

No. 1000 SAND KIT SET
Mickey Mouse design. 3¼x3" pail, 7" shovel and 3 moulds. ¼ gro. in case. Wgt. per gro. 90 lbs.

No. 1001 SAND KIT SET
Same composition as above. Comic design.

No. 650 SAND KIT SET
Mickey Mouse design. 6x7" Sprinkler, 3½x3½" pail, 6" sieve, 5 fancy moulds, spoon and one 10" Shovel. 1/12 gro. in case. Wgt. per gro. 245 lbs.

No. 651 SAND KIT SET
Same composition as above. Conventional design.

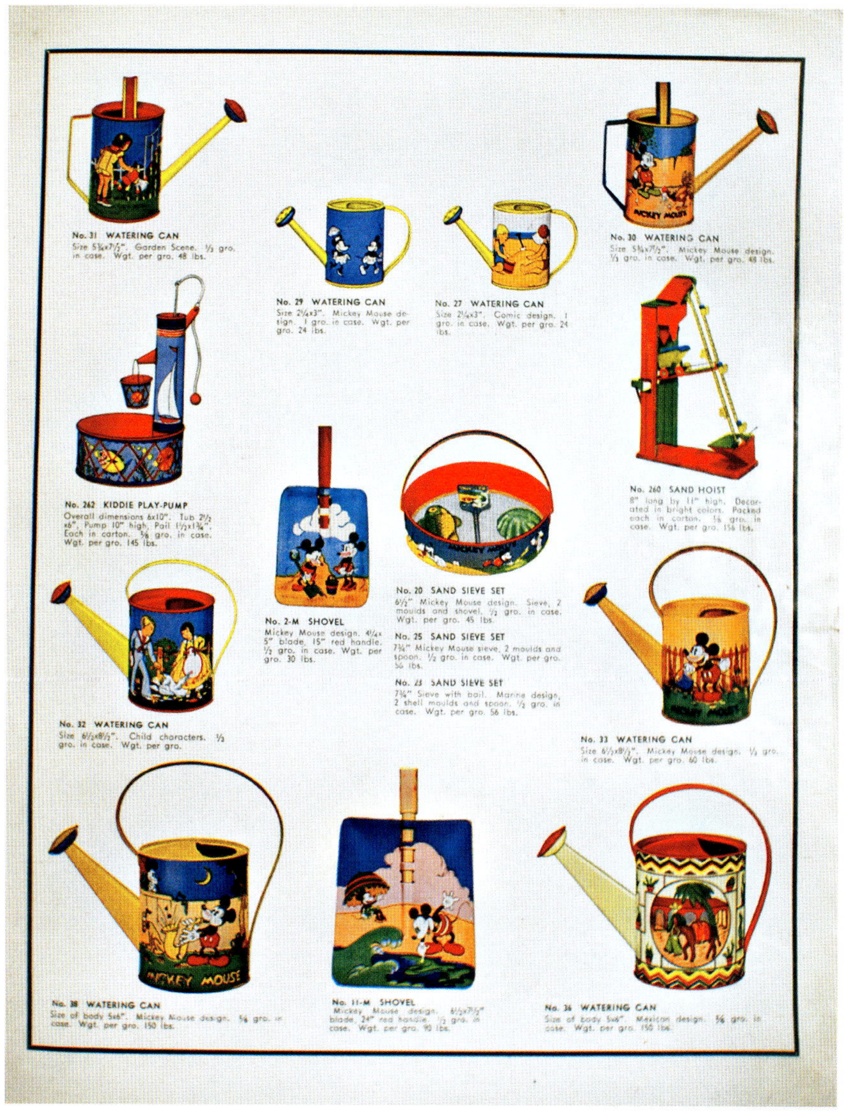

No. 31 WATERING CAN
Size 5¾x7½". Garden Scene. ⅓ gro. in case. Wgt. per gro. 48 lbs.

No. 29 WATERING CAN
Size 2¼x3". Mickey Mouse design. 1 gro. in case. Wgt. per gro. 24 lbs.

No. 27 WATERING CAN
Size 2¼x3". Comic design. 1 gro. in case. Wgt. per gro. 24 lbs.

No. 30 WATERING CAN
Size 5¾x7½". Mickey Mouse design. ⅓ gro. in case. Wgt. per gro. 48 lbs.

No. 262 KIDDIE PLAY-PUMP
Overall dimensions 6x10". Tub 2½x6", Pump 10" high, Pail 1½x1¾". Each in carton. 5/6 gro. in case. Wgt. per gro. 145 lbs.

No. 2-M SHOVEL
Mickey Mouse design. 4¼x5" blade, 15" red handle. ½ gro. in case. Wgt. per gro. 30 lbs.

No. 20 SAND SIEVE SET
6½" Mickey Mouse design. Sieve, 2 moulds and shovel, ½ gro. in case. Wgt. per gro. 45 lbs.

No. 25 SAND SIEVE SET
7¾" Mickey Mouse sieve, 2 moulds and spoon. ½ gro. in case. Wgt. per gro. 56 lbs.

No. 23 SAND SIEVE SET
7¾" Sieve with bail. Marine design, 2 shell moulds and spoon. ½ gro. in case. Wgt. per gro. 56 lbs.

No. 260 SAND HOIST
8" long by 11" high. Decorated in bright colors. Packed each in carton. 1/6 gro. in case. Wgt. per gro. 156 lbs.

No. 32 WATERING CAN
Size 6½x8½". Child characters. ⅓ gro. in case. Wgt. per gro.

No. 33 WATERING CAN
Size 6½x8½". Mickey Mouse design. ⅓ gro. in case. Wgt. per gro. 60 lbs.

No. 38 WATERING CAN
Size of body 5x6". Mickey Mouse design. 5/6 gro. in case. Wgt. per gro. 150 lbs.

No. 11-M SHOVEL
Mickey Mouse design. 6½x7½" blade, 24" red handle. ½ gro. in case. Wgt. per gro. 90 lbs.

No. 36 WATERING CAN
Size of body 5x6". Mexican design. 5/6 gro. in case. Wgt. per gro. 150 lbs.

Spring and Summer Toys 1938 catalog, pages 2 and 3. These pages feature sand kit sets, shovels, sieves, and watering cans.

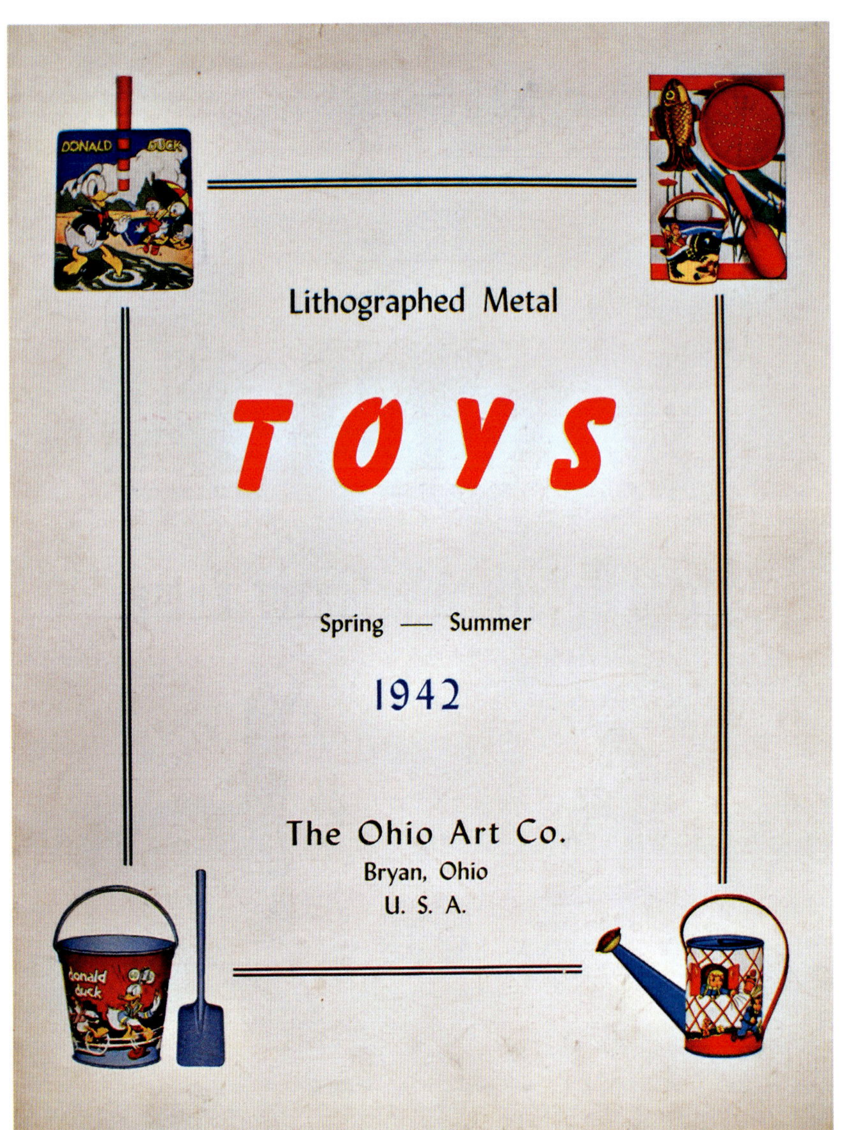

Lithographed Metal

TOYS

Spring — Summer

1942

The Ohio Art Co.
Bryan, Ohio
U. S. A.

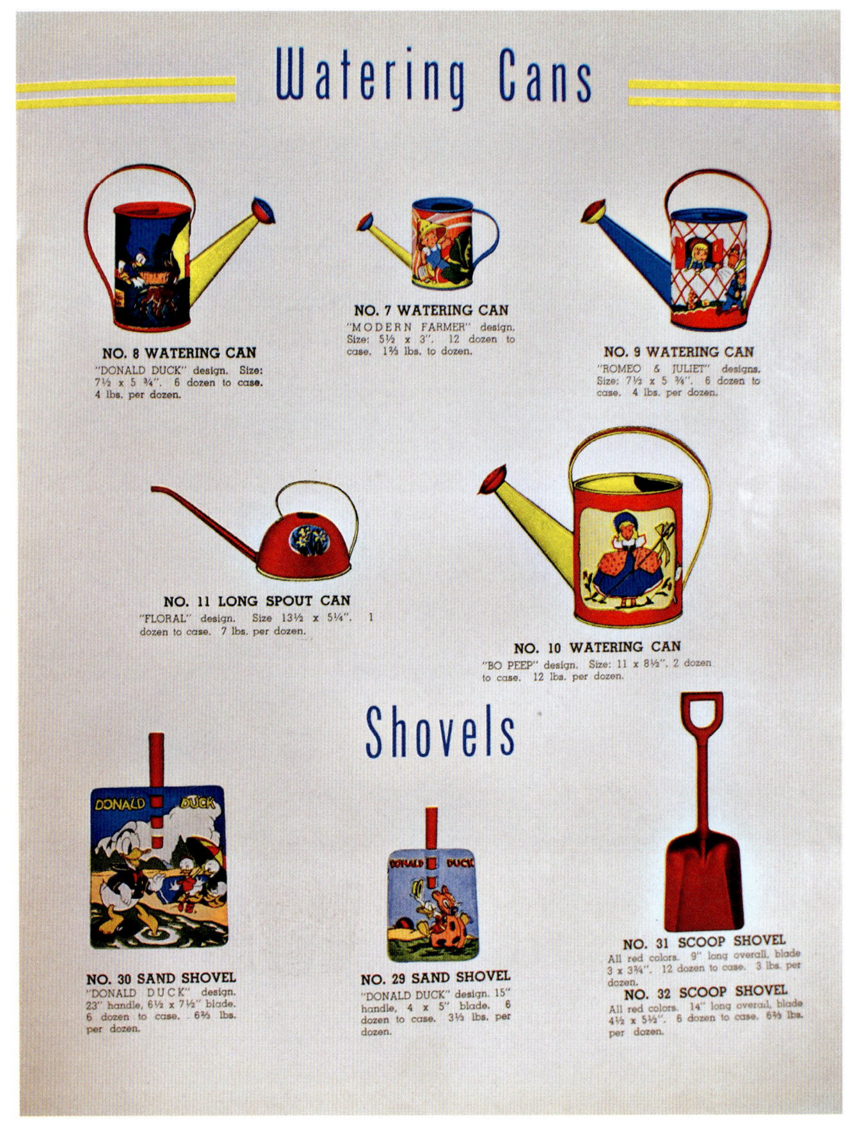

Watering Cans

NO. 8 WATERING CAN
"DONALD DUCK" design. Size: 7½ x 5 ¾". 6 dozen to case. 4 lbs. per dozen.

NO. 7 WATERING CAN
"MODERN FARMER" design. Size: 5½ x 3". 12 dozen to case. 1⅔ lbs. to dozen.

NO. 9 WATERING CAN
"ROMEO & JULIET" designs. Size: 7½ x 5 ¾". 6 dozen to case. 4 lbs. per dozen.

NO. 11 LONG SPOUT CAN
"FLORAL" design. Size 13½ x 5¼". 1 dozen to case. 7 lbs. per dozen.

NO. 10 WATERING CAN
"BO PEEP" design. Size: 11 x 8½". 2 dozen to case. 12 lbs. per dozen.

Shovels

NO. 30 SAND SHOVEL
"DONALD DUCK" design. 23" handle, 6½ x 7½" blade. 6 dozen to case. 6⅔ lbs. per dozen.

NO. 29 SAND SHOVEL
"DONALD DUCK" design. 15" handle, 4 x 5" blade. 6 dozen to case. 3⅓ lbs. per dozen.

NO. 31 SCOOP SHOVEL
All red colors. 9" long overall, blade 3 x 3¾". 12 dozen to case. 3 lbs. per dozen.

NO. 32 SCOOP SHOVEL
All red colors. 14" long overall, blade 4½ x 5½". 6 dozen to case. 6⅔ lbs. per dozen.

Lithographed Metal Toys, Spring-Summer 1942 showing title page plus page 3 that includes watering cans and shovels.

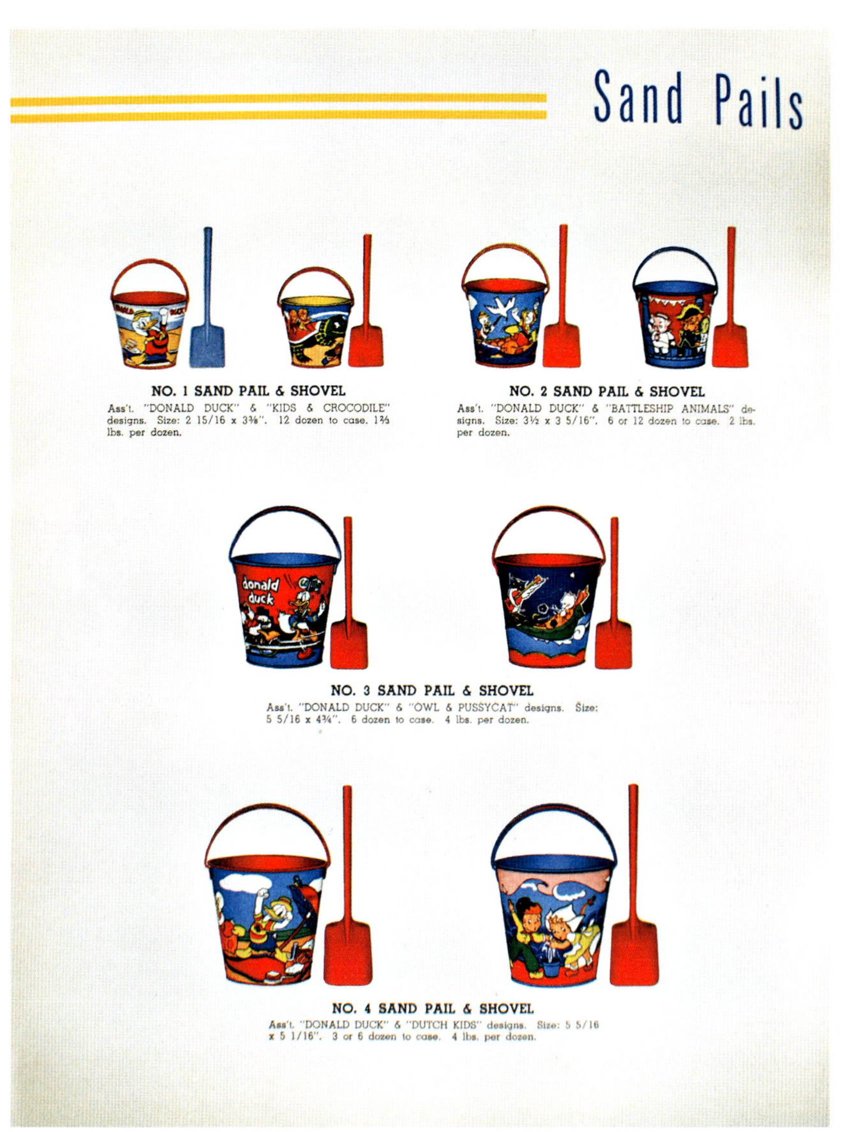
Sand Pails

NO. 1 SAND PAIL & SHOVEL

Ass't. "DONALD DUCK" & "KIDS & CROCODILE" designs. Size: 2 15/16 x 3⅜". 12 dozen to case. 1⅔ lbs. per dozen.

NO. 2 SAND PAIL & SHOVEL

Ass't. "DONALD DUCK" & "BATTLESHIP ANIMALS" designs. Size: 3½ x 3 5/16". 6 or 12 dozen to case. 2 lbs. per dozen.

NO. 3 SAND PAIL & SHOVEL

Ass't. "DONALD DUCK" & "OWL & PUSSYCAT" designs. Size: 5 5/16 x 4¾". 6 dozen to case. 4 lbs. per dozen.

NO. 4 SAND PAIL & SHOVEL

Ass't. "DONALD DUCK" & "DUTCH KIDS" designs. Size: 5 5/16 x 5 1/16". 3 or 6 dozen to case. 4 lbs. per dozen.

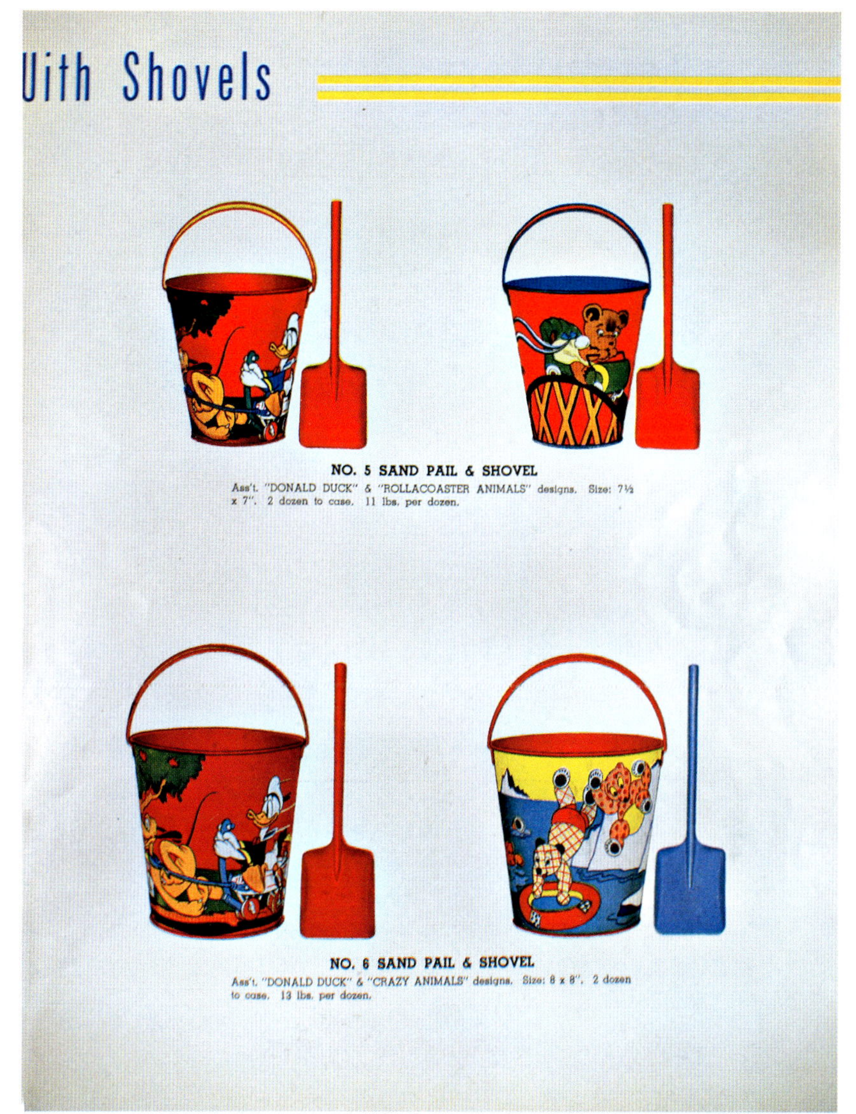
With Shovels

NO. 5 SAND PAIL & SHOVEL

Ass't. "DONALD DUCK" & "ROLLACOASTER ANIMALS" designs. Size: 7½ x 7". 2 dozen to case. 11 lbs. per dozen.

NO. 6 SAND PAIL & SHOVEL

Ass't. "DONALD DUCK" & "CRAZY ANIMALS" designs. Size: 8 x 8". 2 dozen to case. 13 lbs. per dozen.

Pages 4 and 5 of 1942 catalog featuring sand pails and shovels. Note that the Donald Duck pail on page 5 came in both 7″ and 8″ sizes.

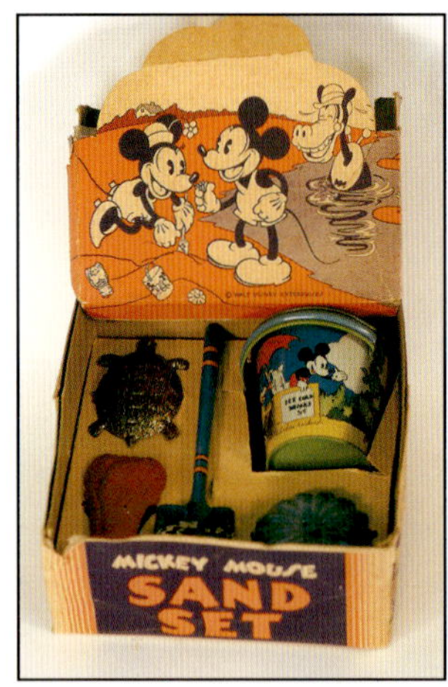

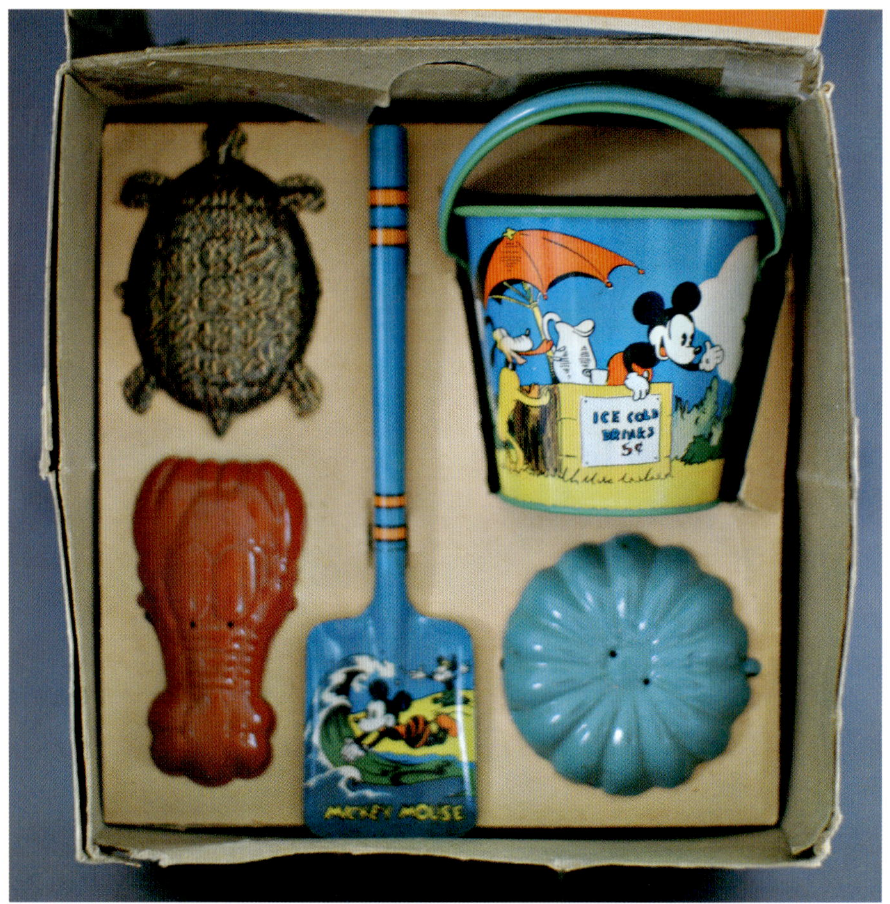

No. 1000 Mickey Mouse 3″ pail and 7″ shovel plus three generic sand molds. The box is 7″ square and is the smallest of three Mickey sand kit sets. Mint in excellent box. $1,500-2,000

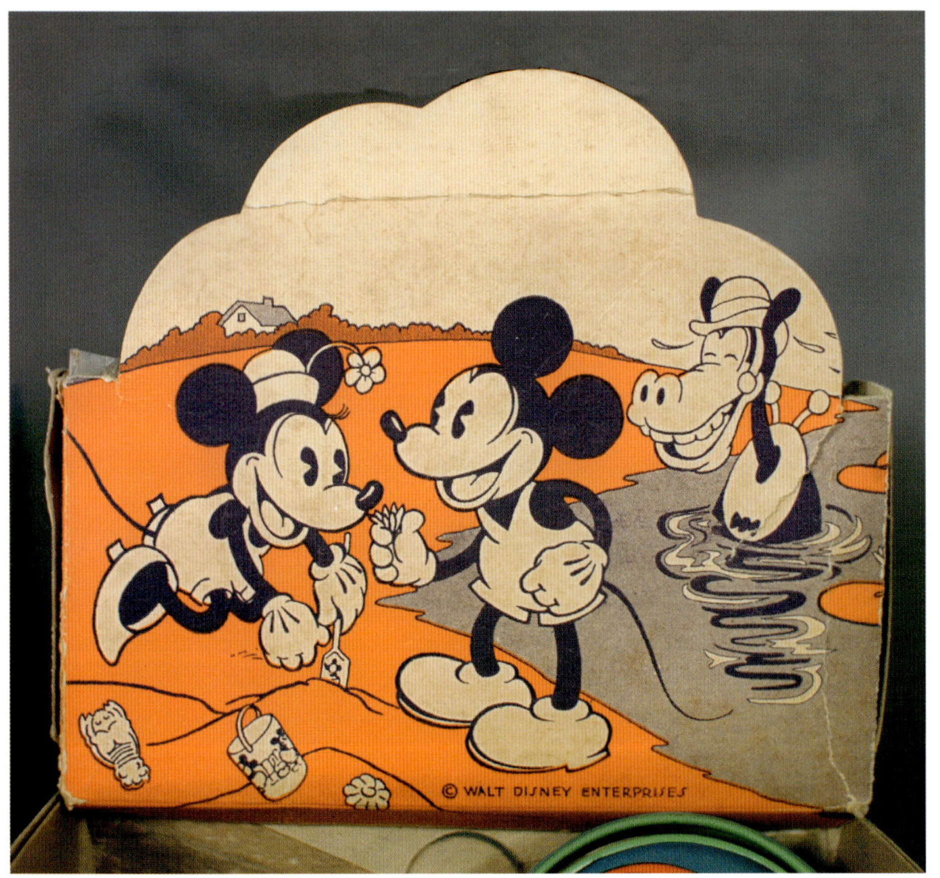

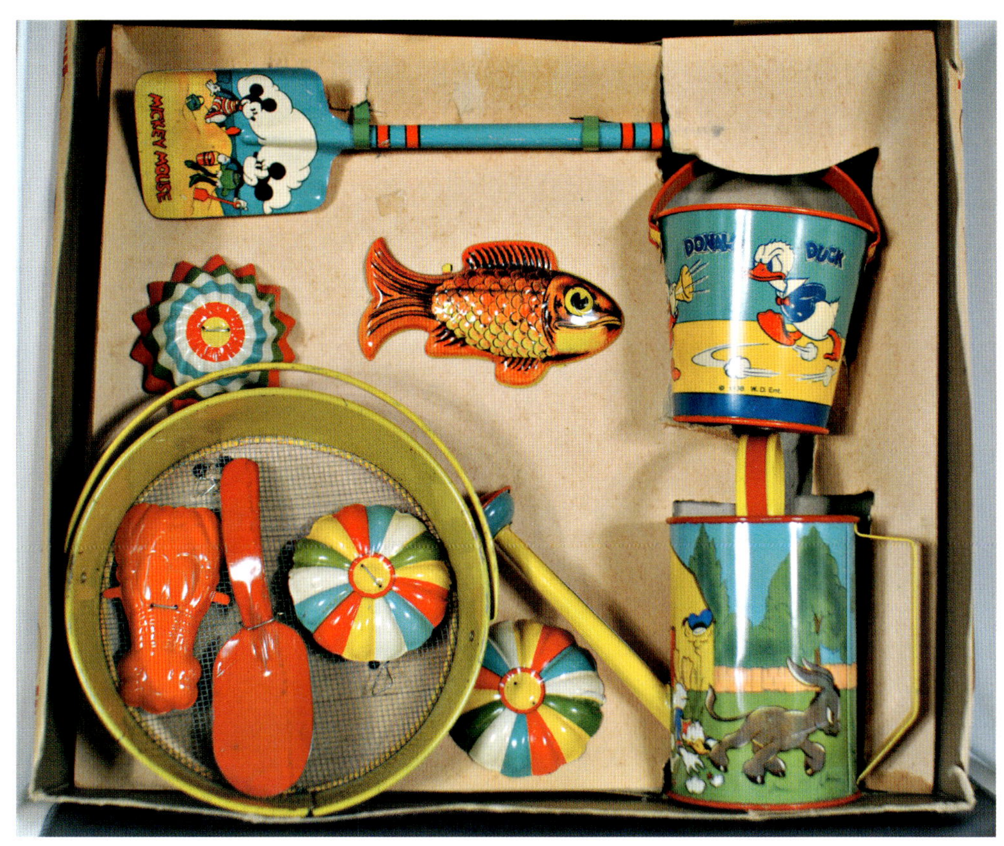

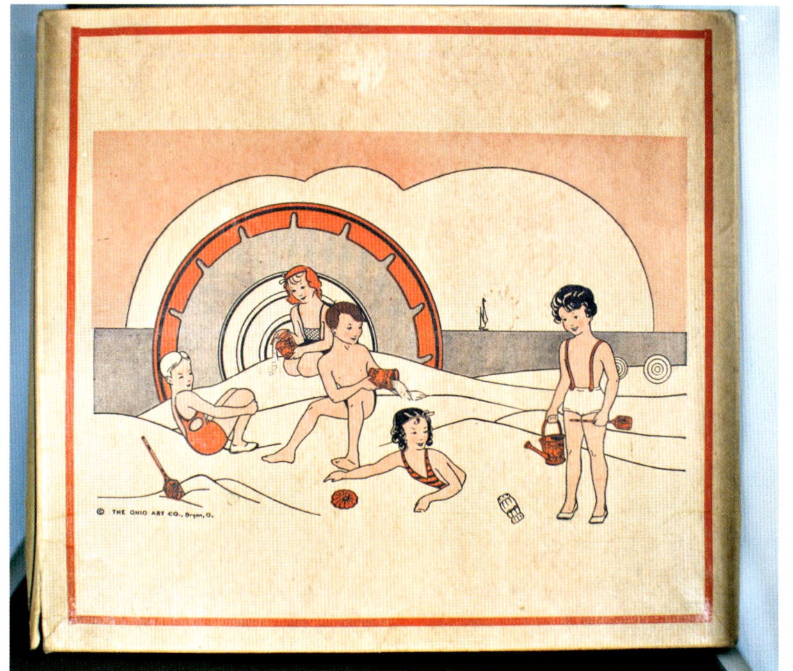

No. 650 Mickey and Donald sand kit set. Both the set and the generic box are pictured. The set includes a 3" sand pail, a 10" Mickey shovel, a sieve, a watering can, 5 sand molds and a scoop. Mint in generic excellent box $1,250-1,500

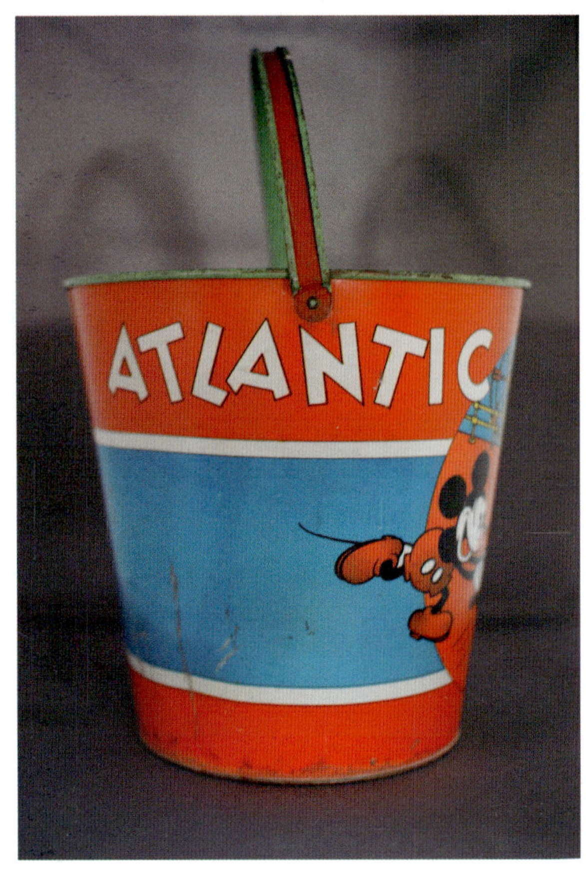

The 8" Mickey pushing Minnie in a rolling chair Atlantic City pail by Ohio Art. Probably the most desired Mickey pail. ©Walt Disney Enterprises. $1,500-2,250

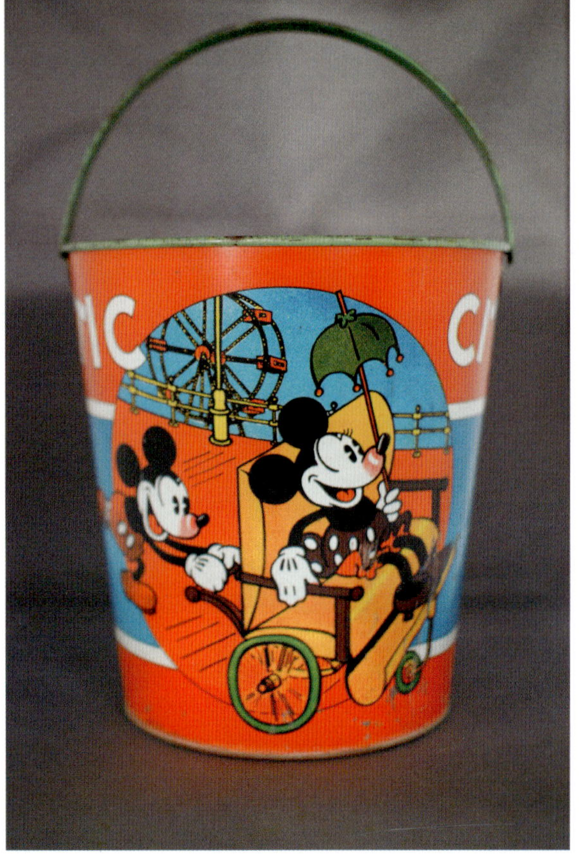

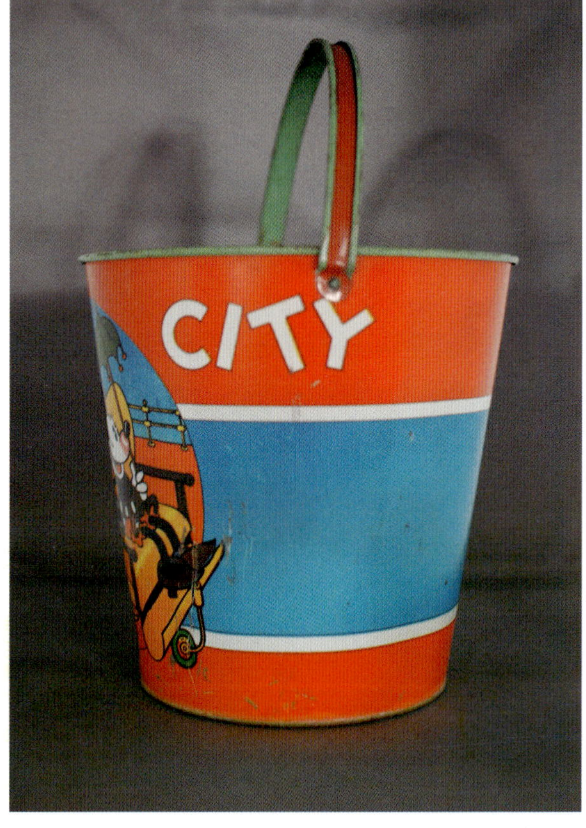

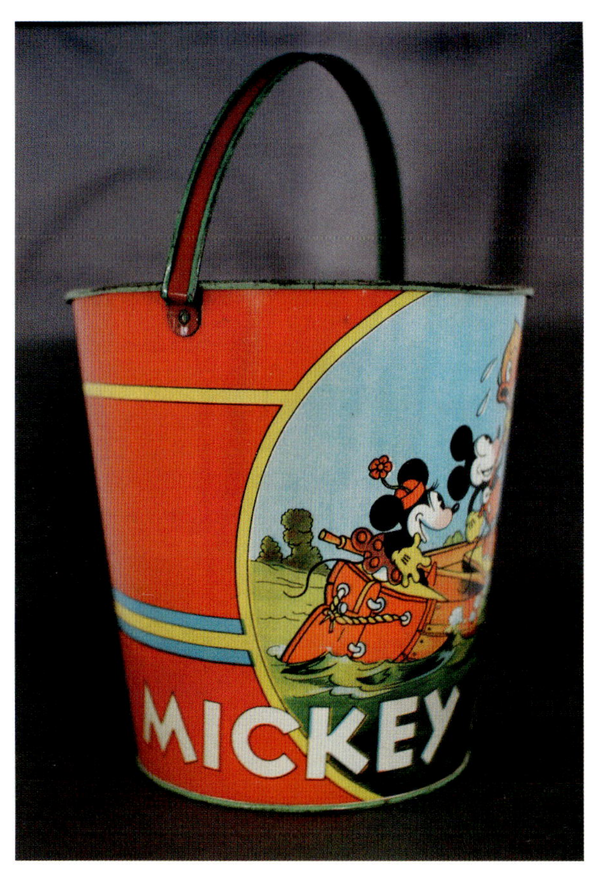

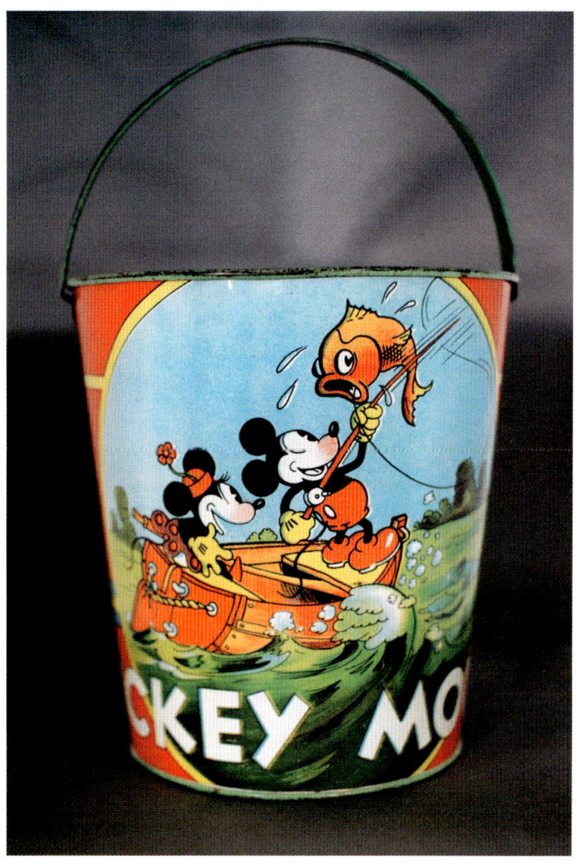

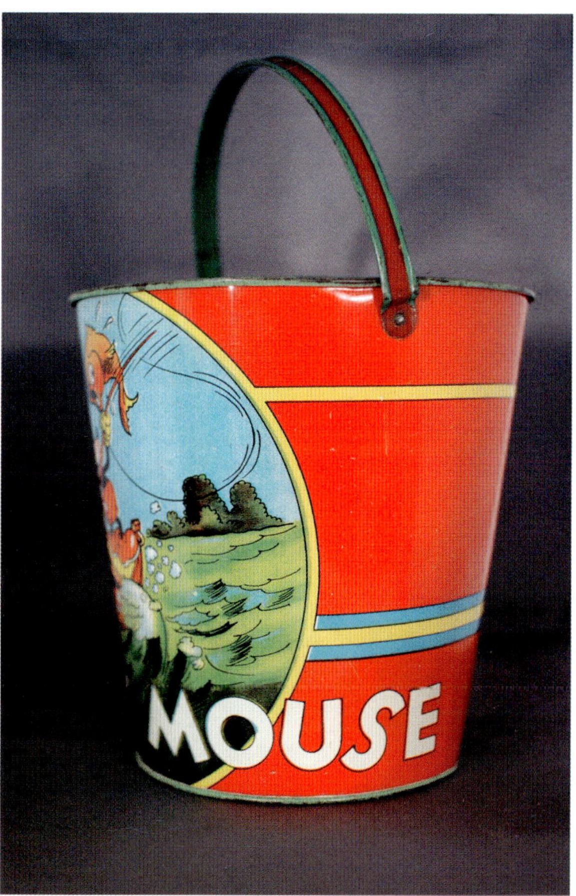

The 8" Mickey Mouse fishing pail. A mate to the previous Atlantic City pail. ©Walt Disney Enterprises. $600-1,200

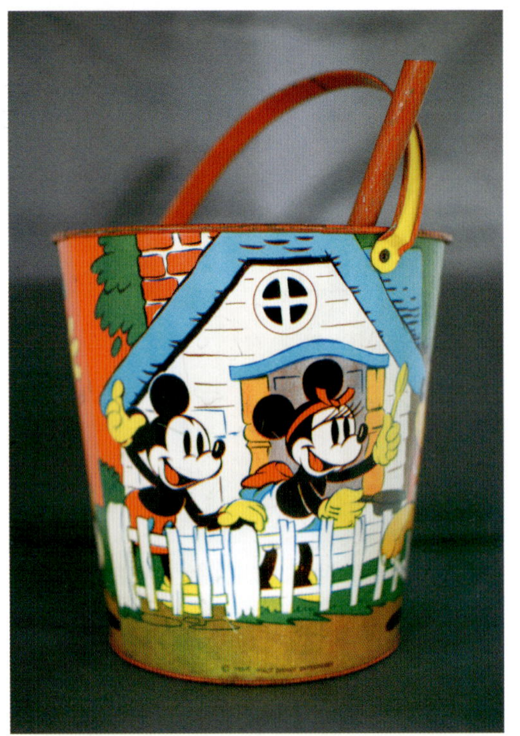

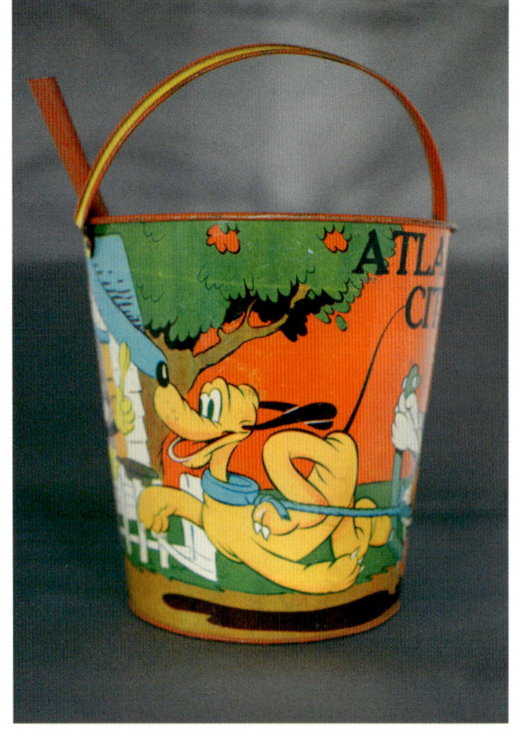

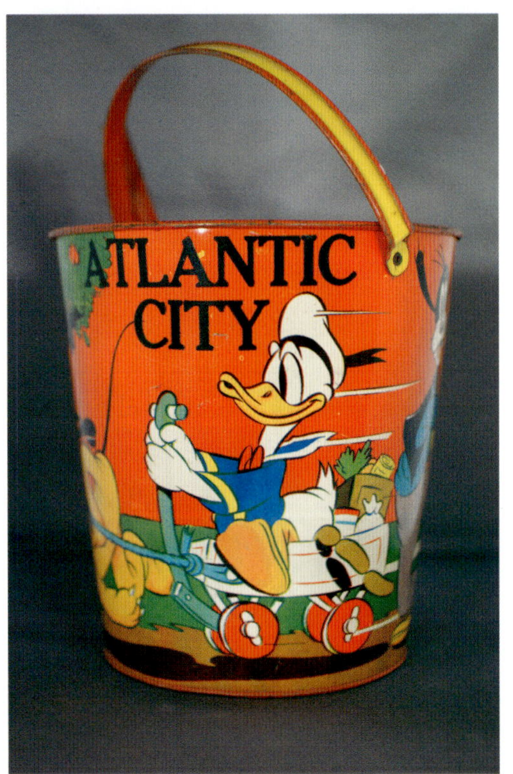

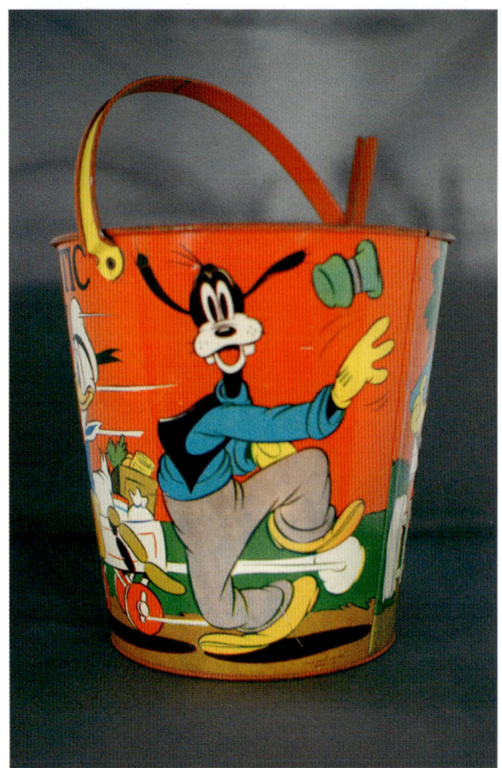

The 8″ Mickey pail with 11″ shovel featuring Mickey, Minnie, Donald, Pluto and Goofy. This example has the Atlantic City imprint. It also came without the imprint. It is marked "©1938 Walt Disney Enterprises, Ohio Art Co., Bryan, O." $500-850. A.C imprint add $100

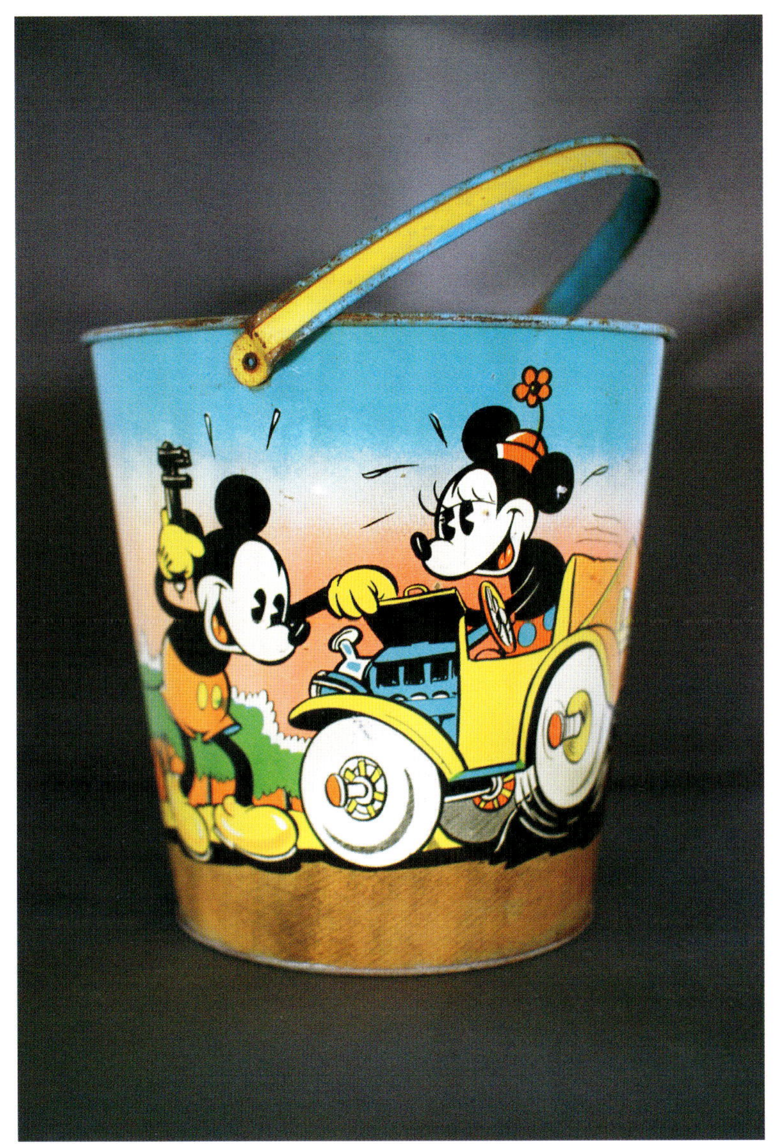

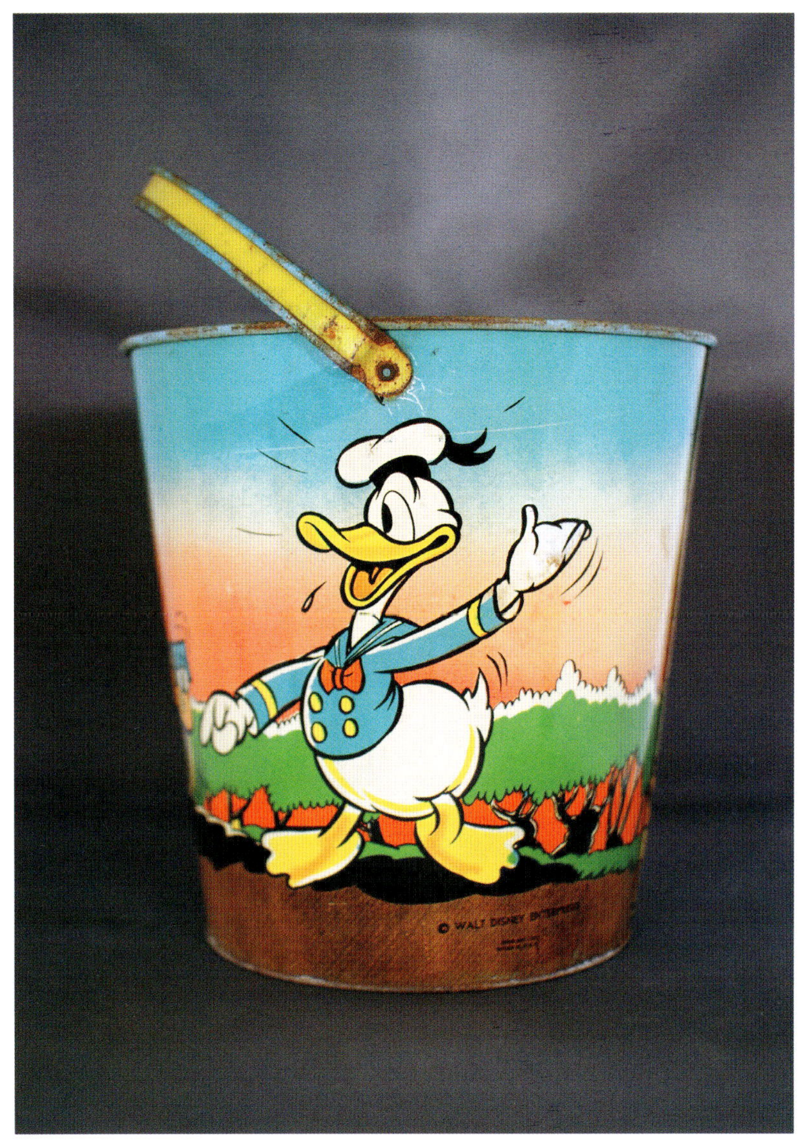

The 8" Mickey Mouse car breakdown pail. It features Mickey and Minnie with car problems, with Donald Duck looking on. This one does not have an Atlantic City imprint although it also comes with one. © Walt Disney Enterprises, Ohio Art Co., Bryan, O. U.S.A. *Collection of Bob Bernabe* $700-1,200; with A.C. imprint add $100

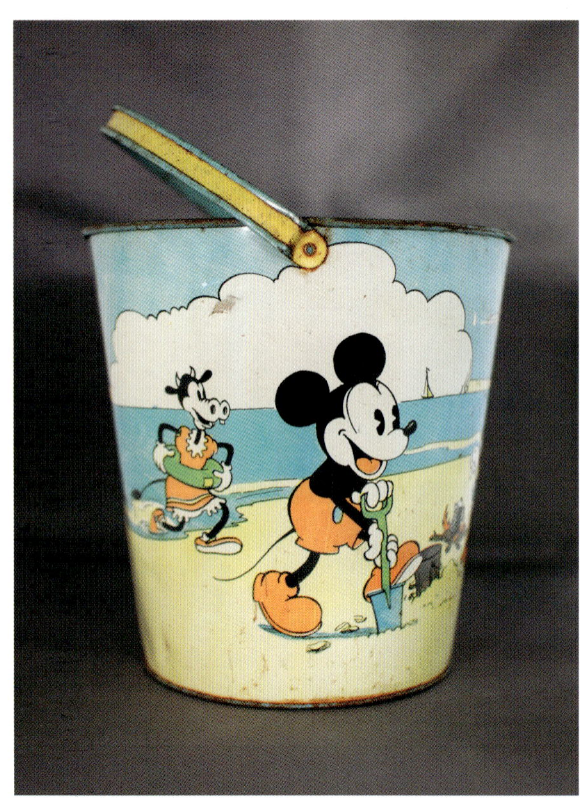

8" Mickey digging in the sand. One of the earliest Ohio Art Disney pails. ©Walt Disney, Ohio Art Co., Bryan, O. U.S.A. *Bernabe collection* $750-1,250.

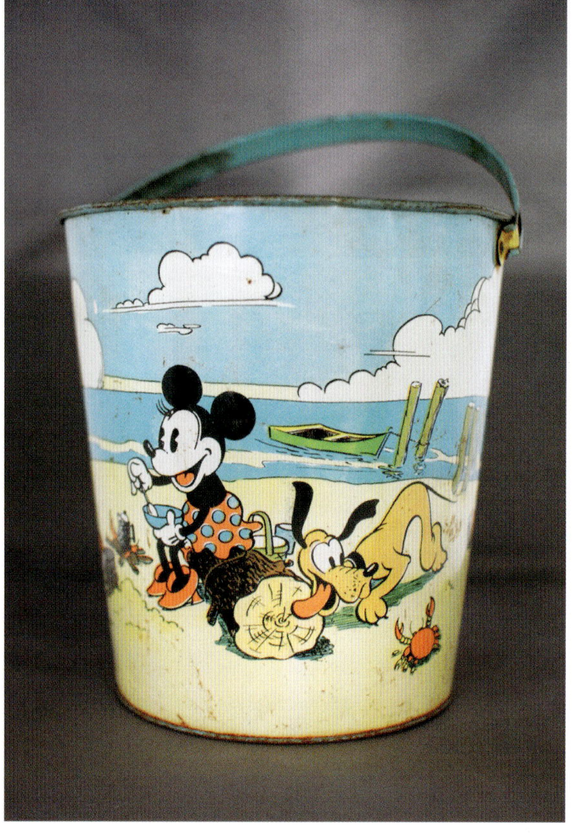

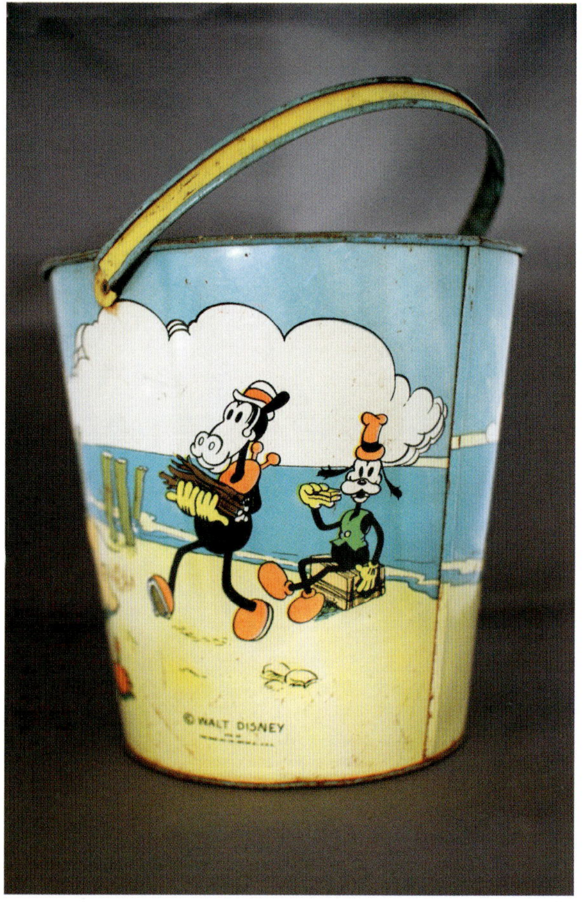

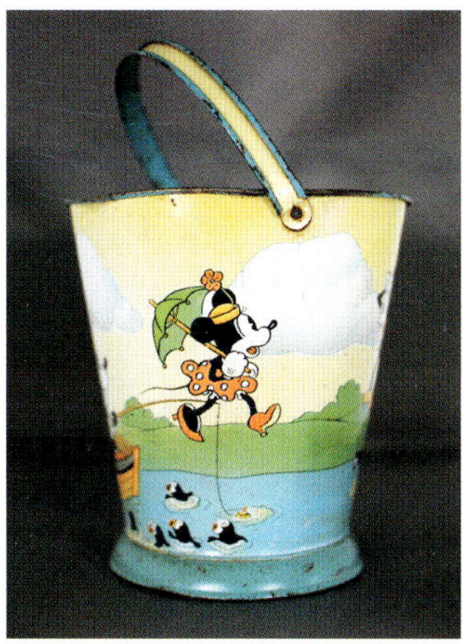

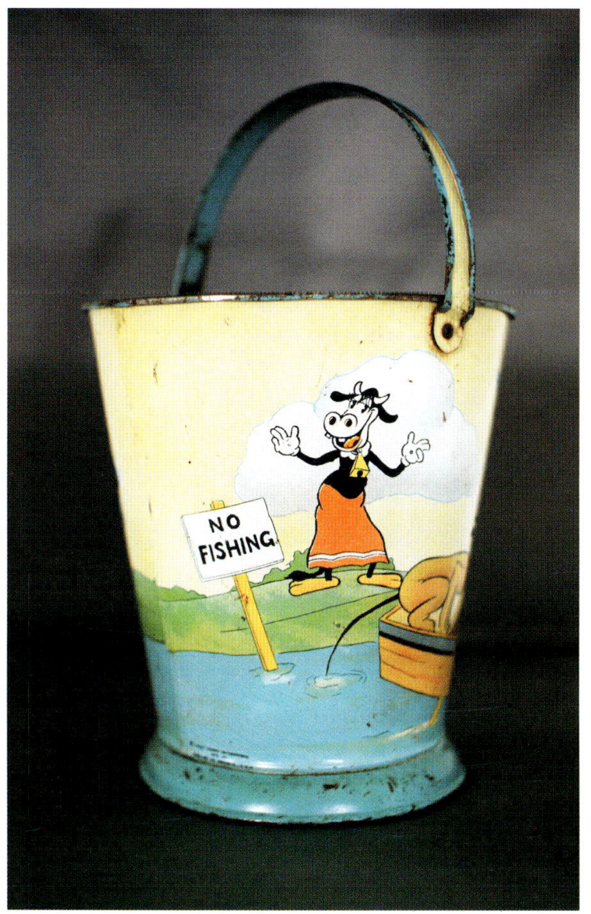

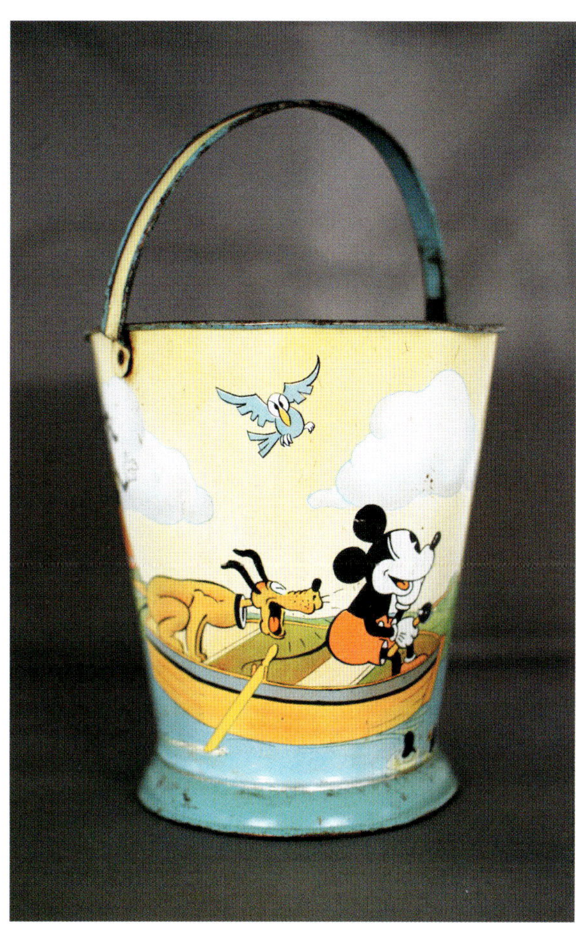

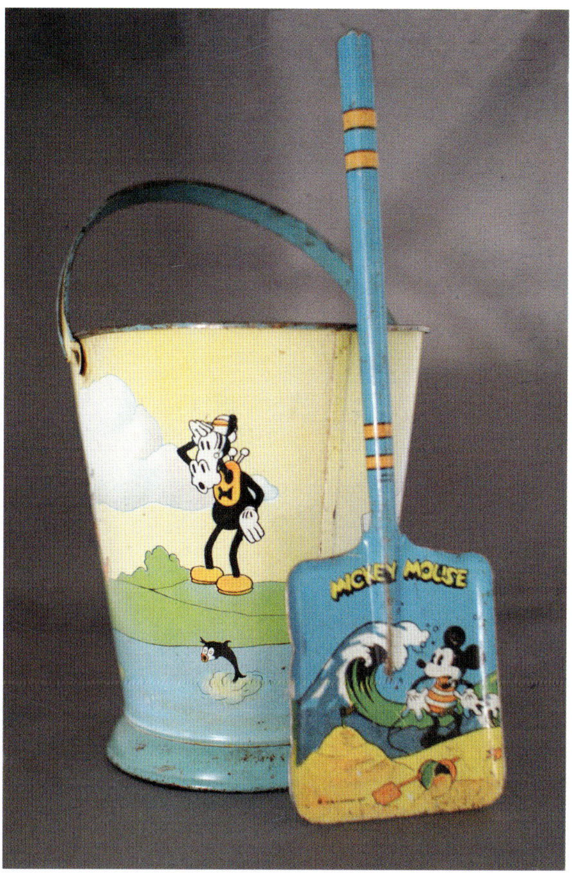

The 7" Mickey "No Fishing" pail with a raised bottom along with an 11.5" Mickey shovel. Marked "© Walt Disney Enterprises, Ohio Art Co., Bryan, O. U.S.A." $750-1,250 or with Mickey shovel $1,000-1,500

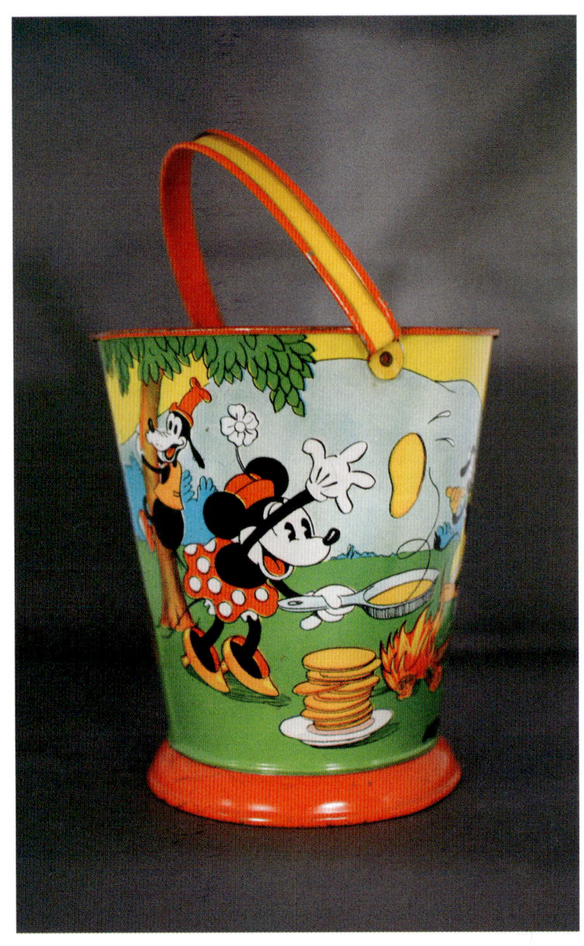

A 7" "Mickey Mouse Picnic" pail with a raised bottom and an 11" shovel. Marked "© Walt Disney, Ohio Art Co., Bryan, O. U.S.A." *Bernabe collection.* $750-1,000

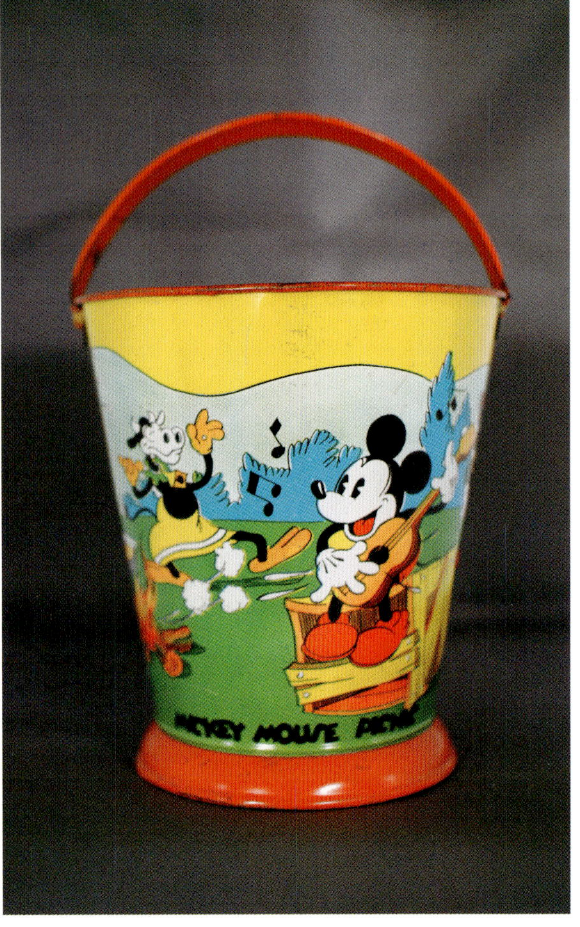

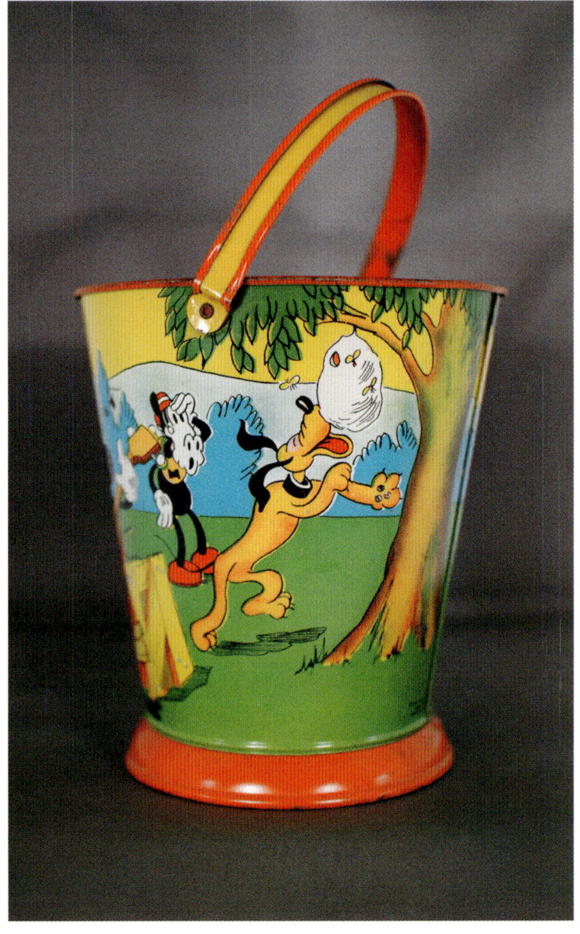

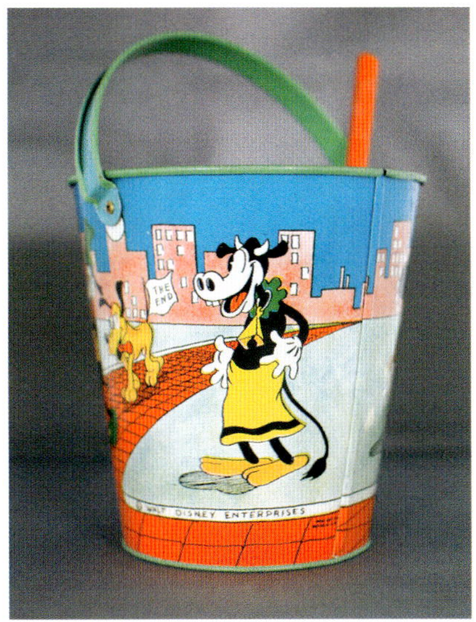

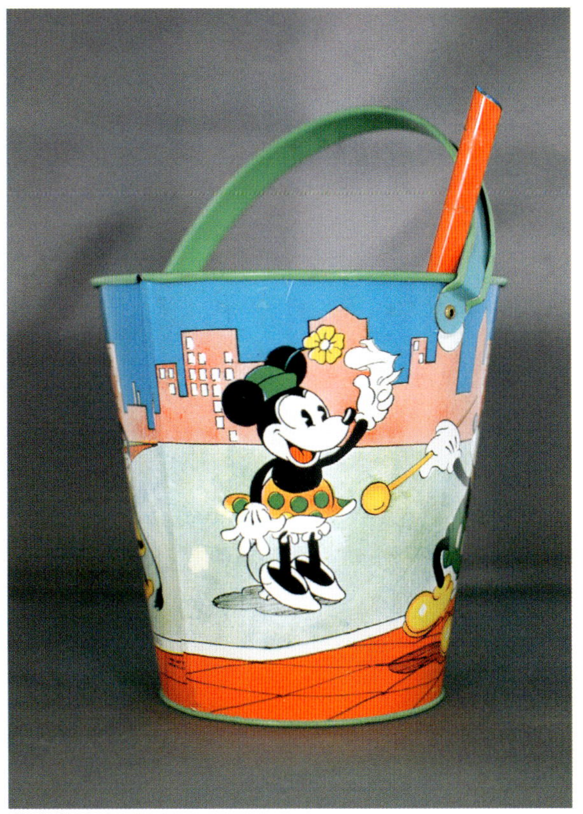

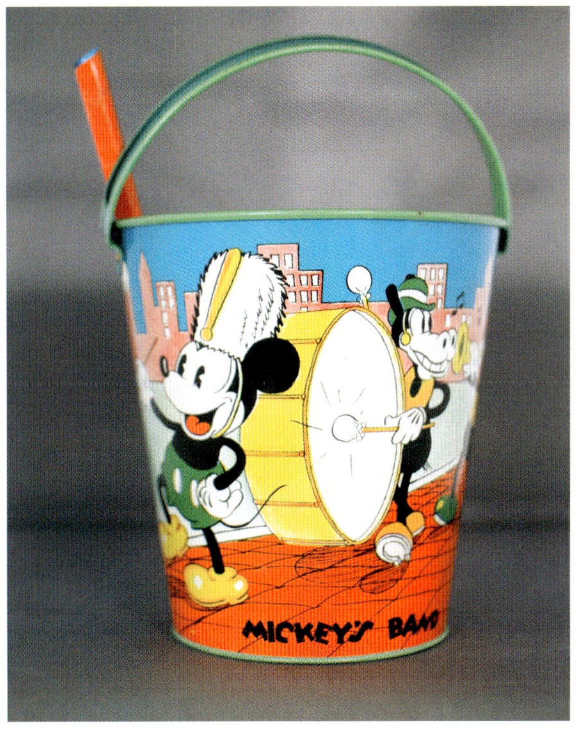

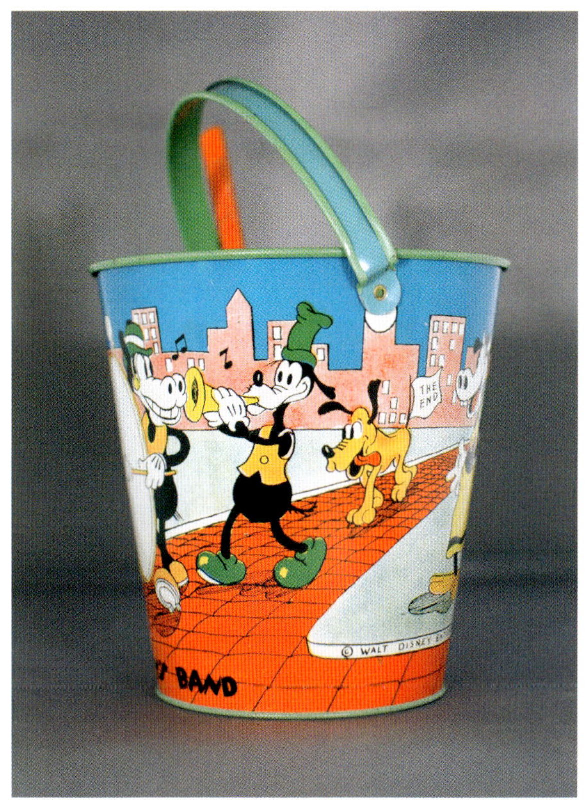

A 6″ Mickey Mouse Band″ sand pail with an 8.5″ shovel. It features all of the marvelous early Disney characters. ©Walt Disney Enterprises, Ohio Art Co., Bryan, O., U.S.A. $600-1,000

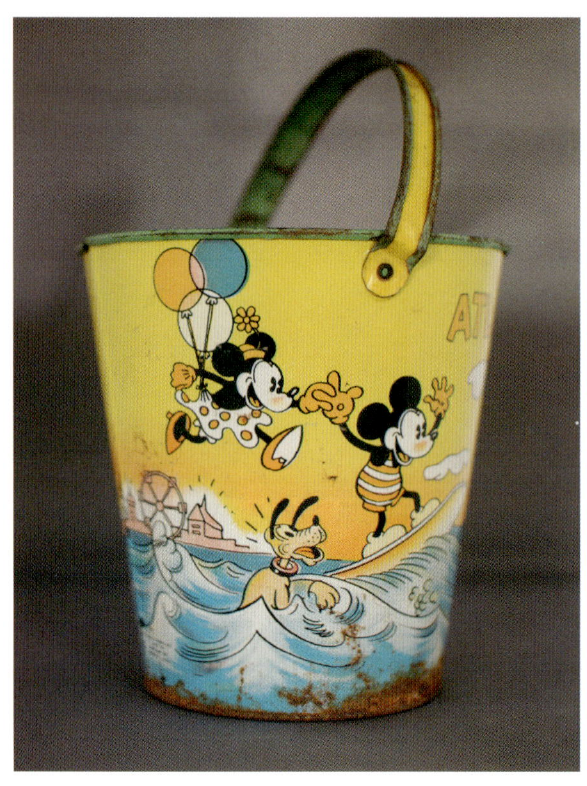

A 6" Mickey Mouse Atlantic City with sailboat sand pail. Probably the rarest Ohio Art Disney pail. Note the ferris wheel to the left has six spokes while the one on the right has eight. © Walt Disney Ent. Mfg by Ohio Art Co., Bryan O. U.S.A. $750-1250

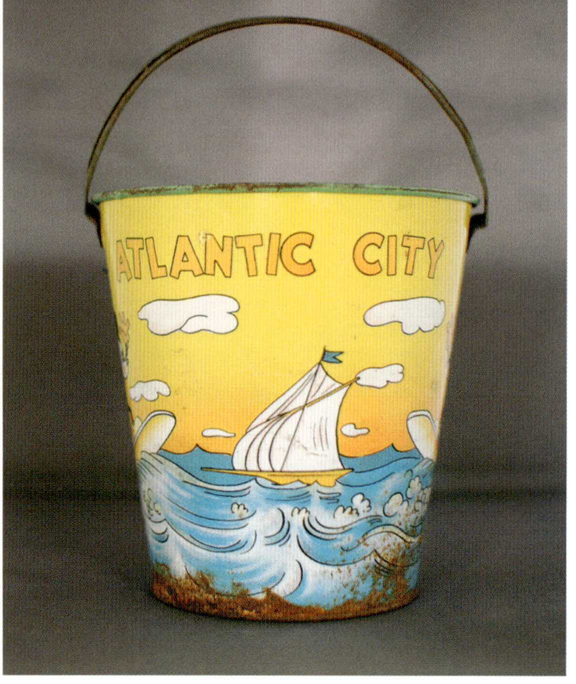

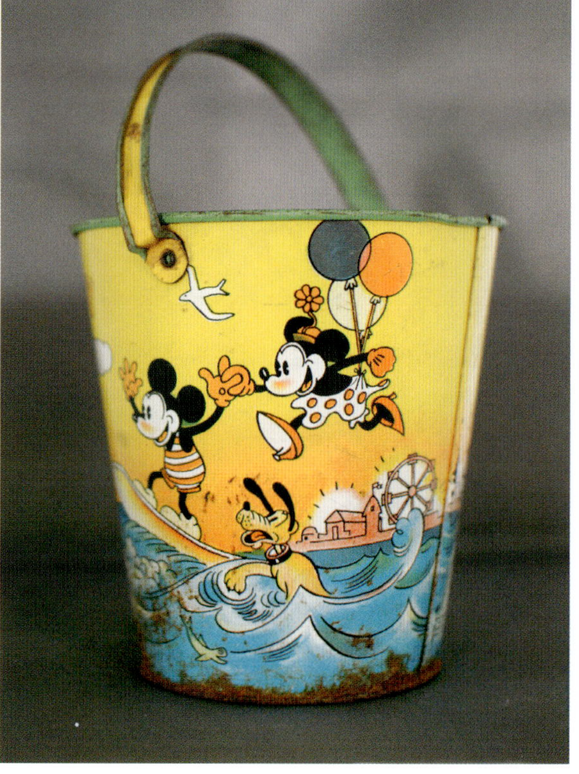

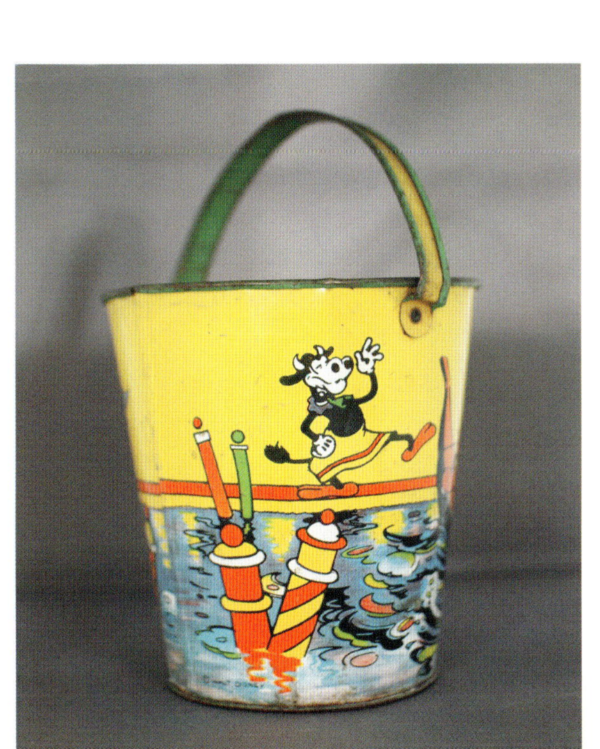

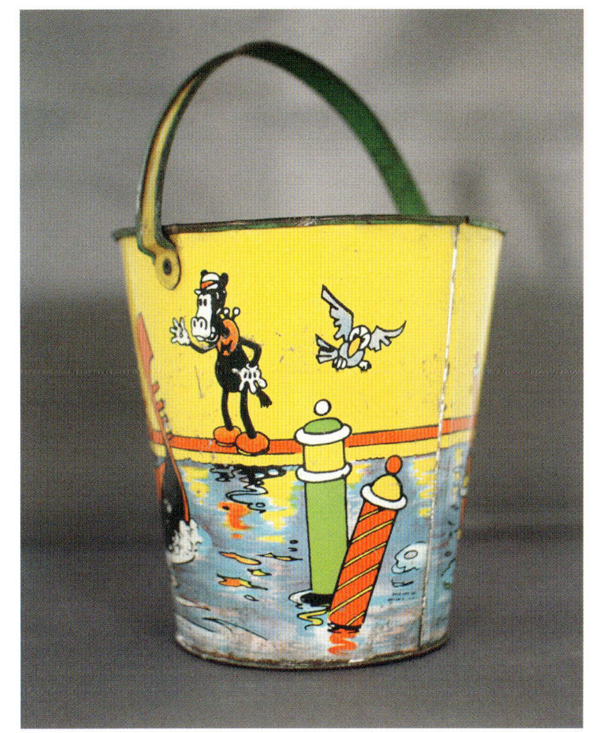

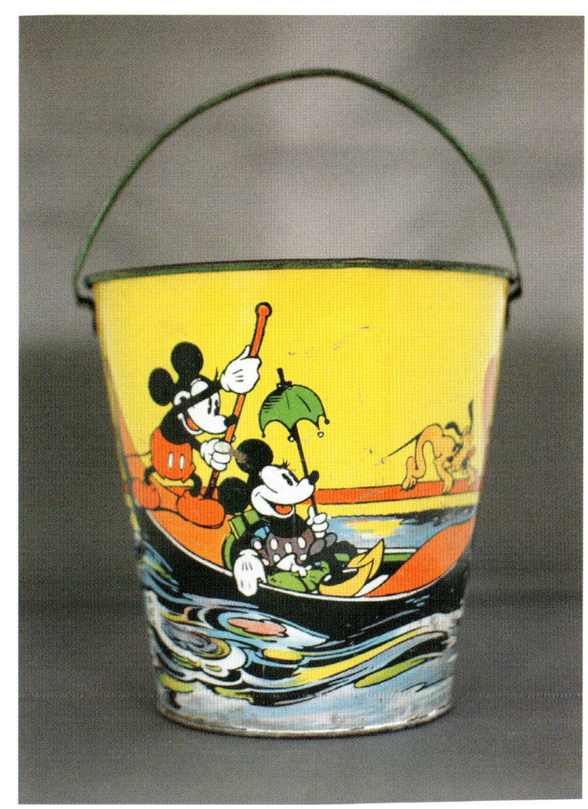

6" Mickey and Minnie in the gondola pail. One of the earliest Ohio Art Disney pails. ©Walt Disney, Ohio Art Co., Bryan, O., U.S.A. *Bernabe collection* $600-850

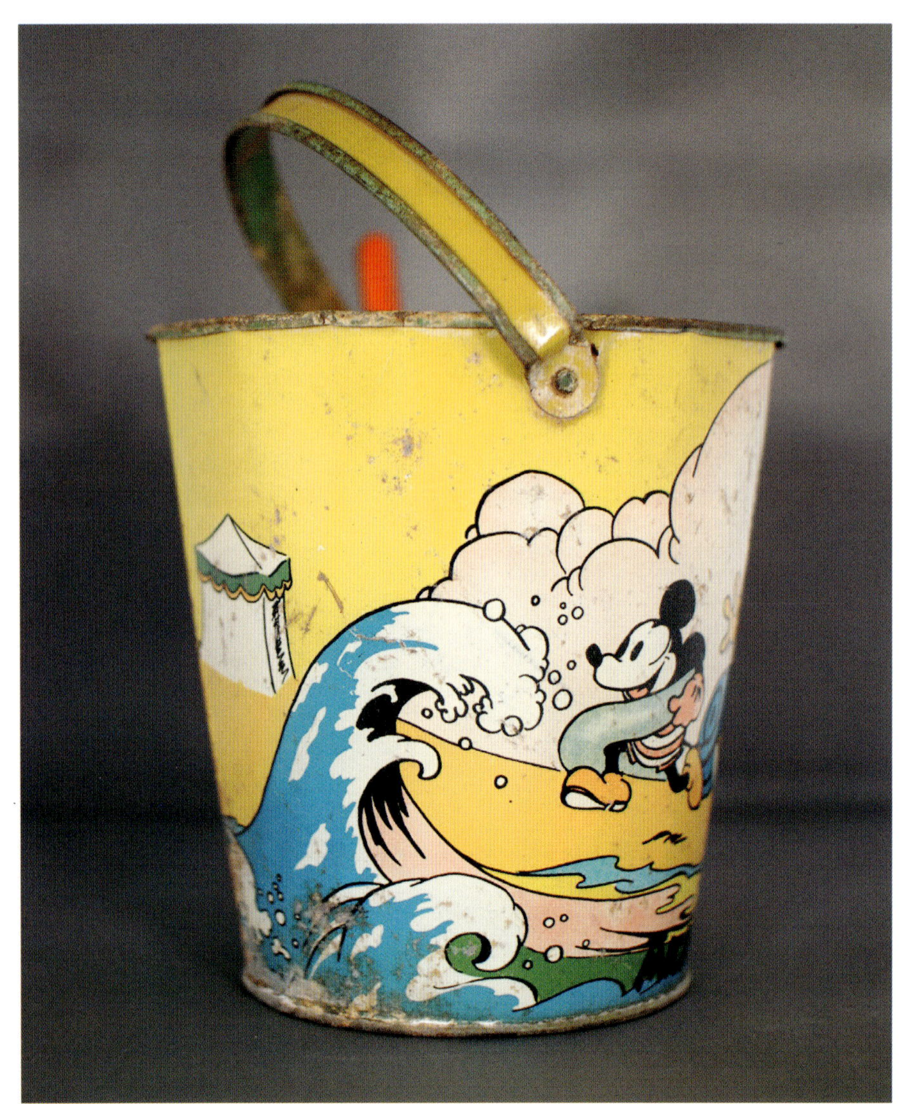

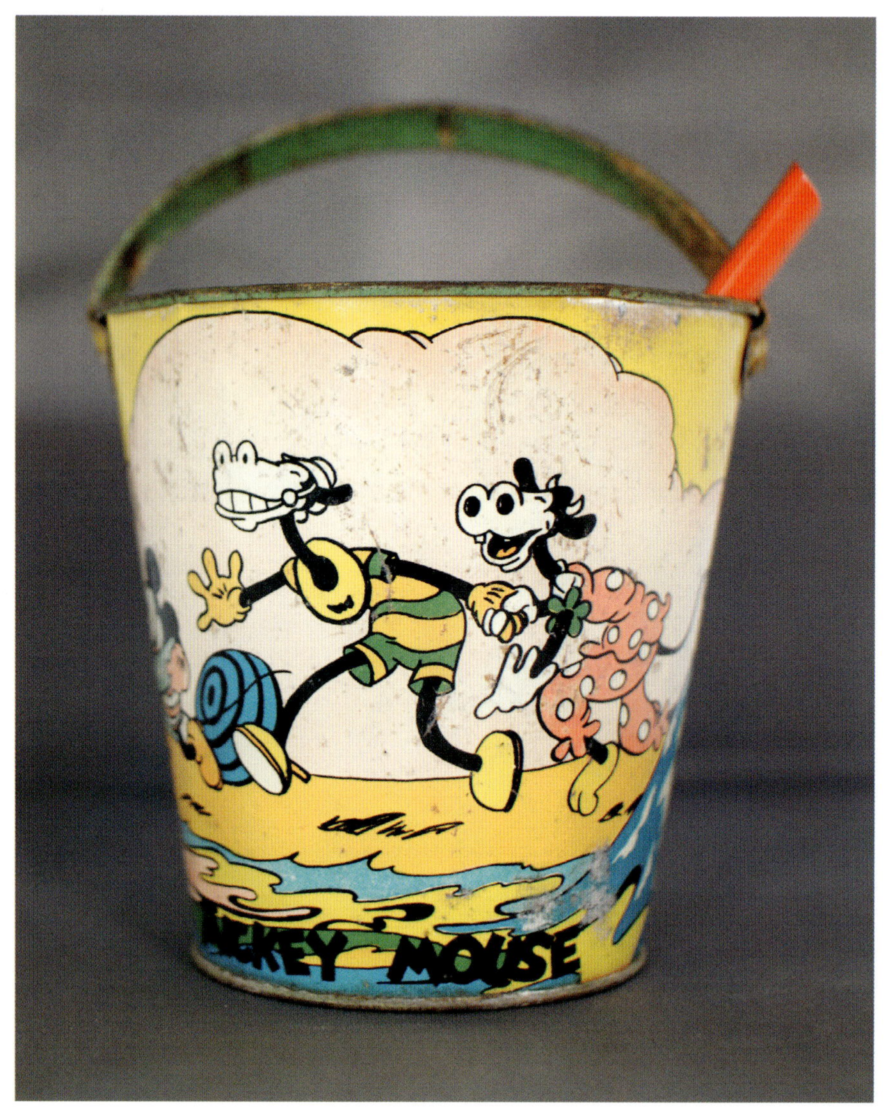

6" Mickey Mouse pail with 8.5" shovel featuring Mickey, Horace and Clarabelle at the beach. Two views. *Bernabe collection* $500-800

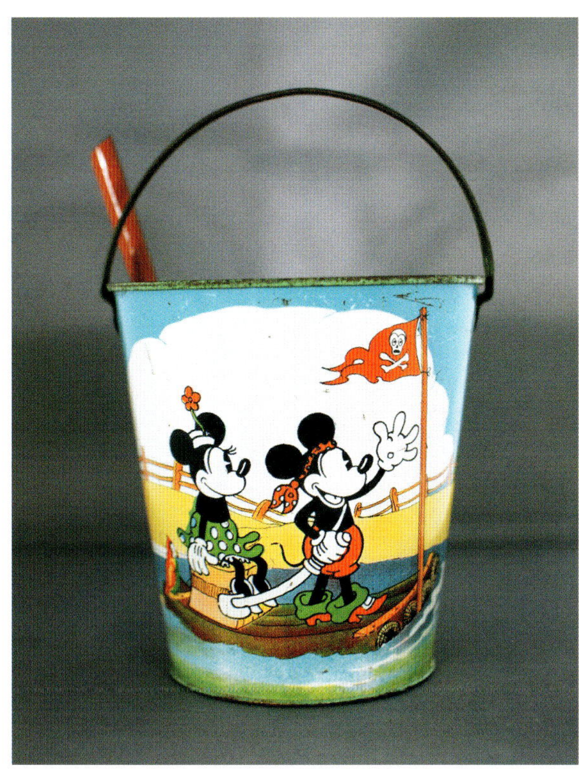

6″ Mickey Mouse pirate pail with 8.5″ shovel. ©Walt Disney Mfg by Ohio Art Co., Bryan, O. $400-700

Mickey's garden pails with and without the raised bottom. The 5″ pail came with a blue 6″ spoon that matches the color on the inside of the pail. The 5.5″ pail with the raised bottom came with an 8.5″ or 9.5″ shovel. ©Walt Disney Ent. Ohio Art Co, Bryan, O. *Bernabe collection* 5″ pail $450-750. 5.5″ pail $450-850

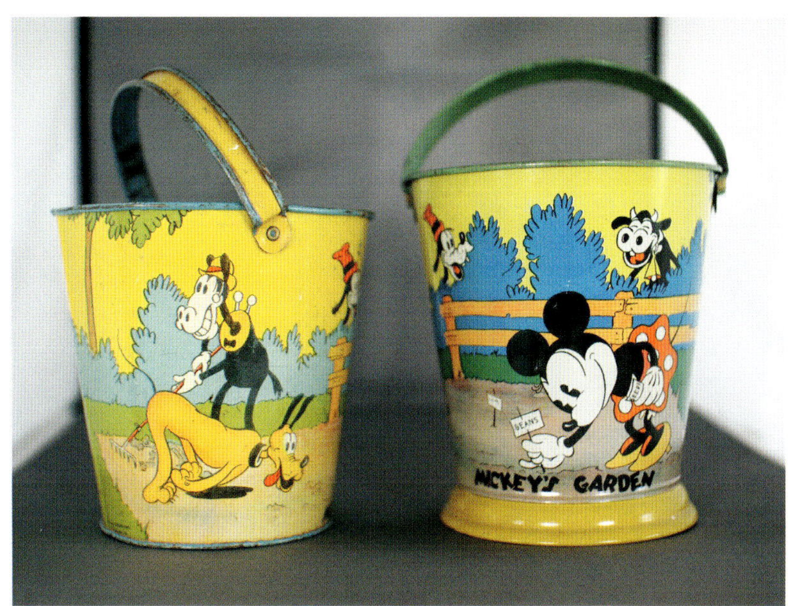

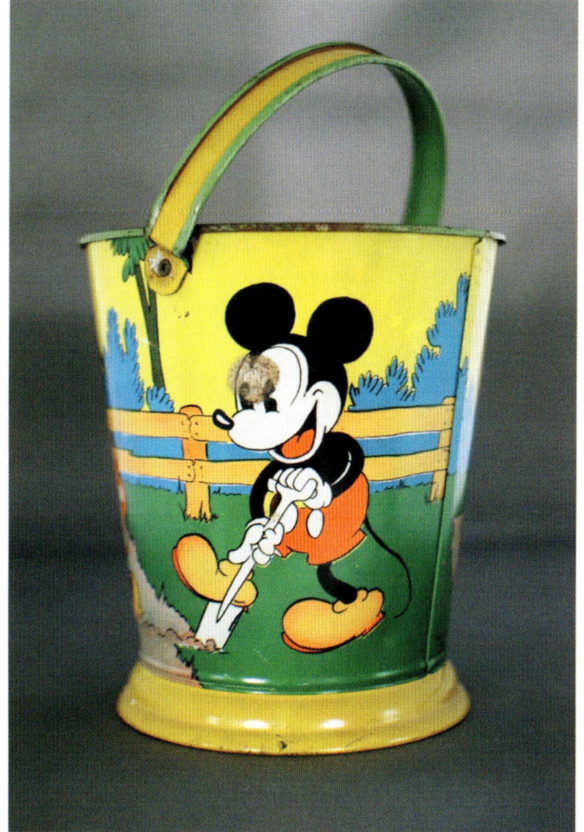

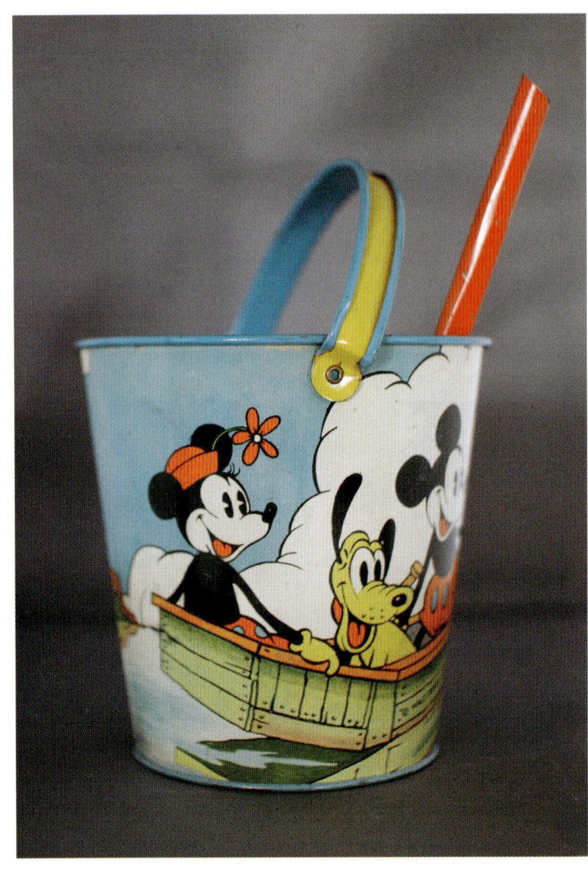

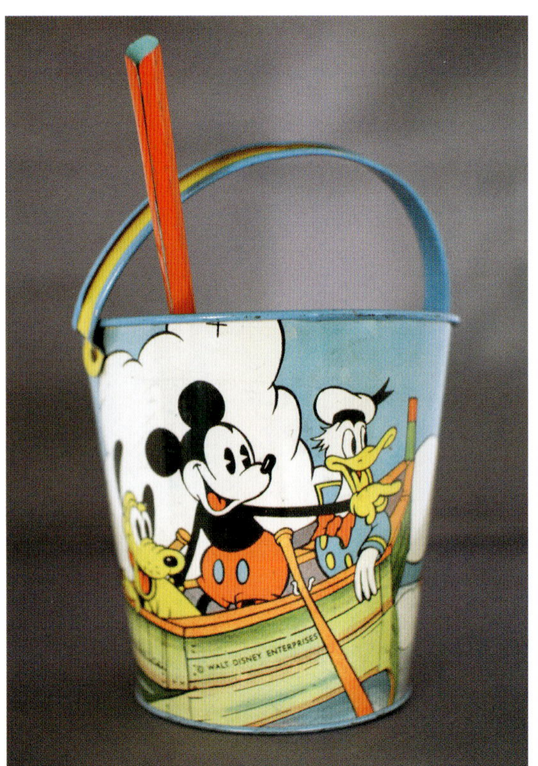

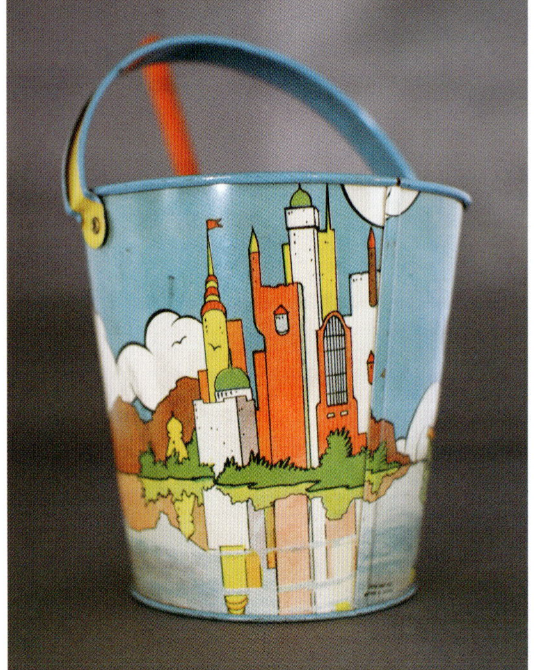

Three views of a 5″ pail with Mickey, Minnie and Donald looking at a castle. 8.5″ shovel included. ©Walt Disney Enterprises, Ohio Art Co., Bryan, O. U.S.A. $500-750

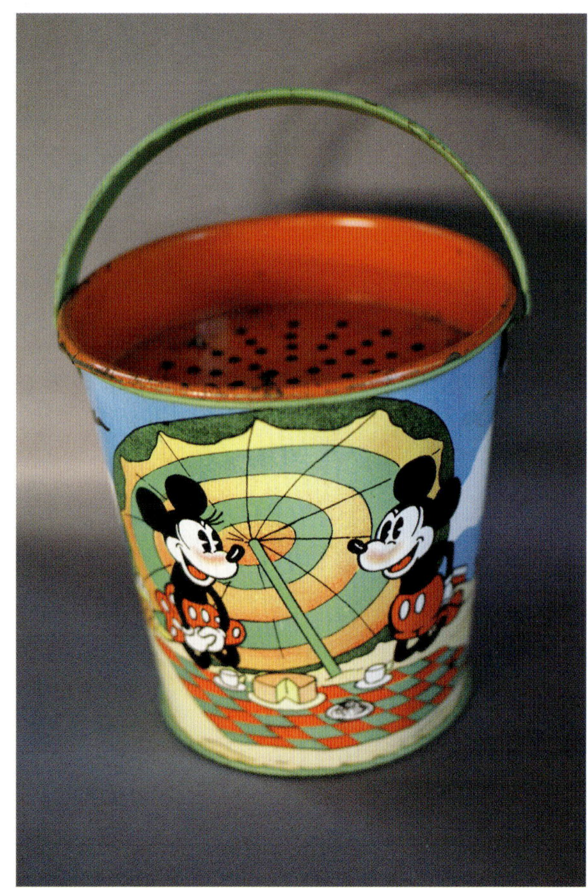

A 4.25″ pail with original sifter features Mickey, Minnie and Pluto sitting with a beach umbrella. ©Walt Disney Ent., Ohio Art Co., Bryan, O., U.S.A. $350-500. With original sifter add $25-50

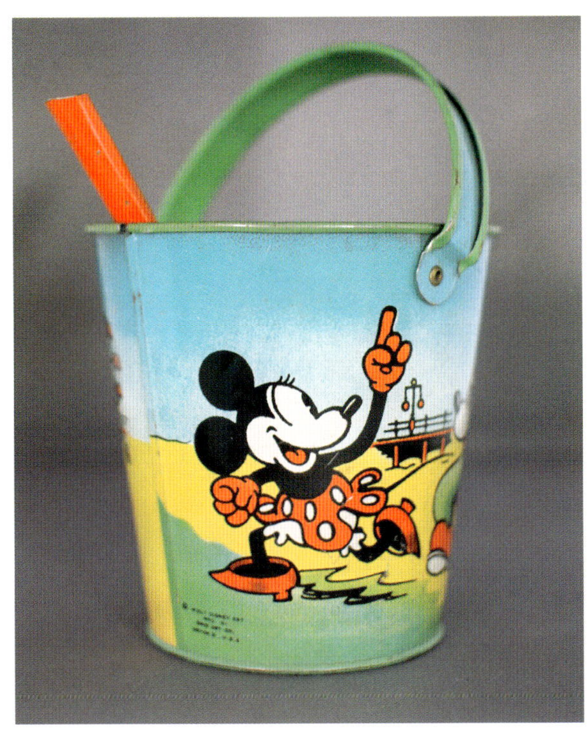

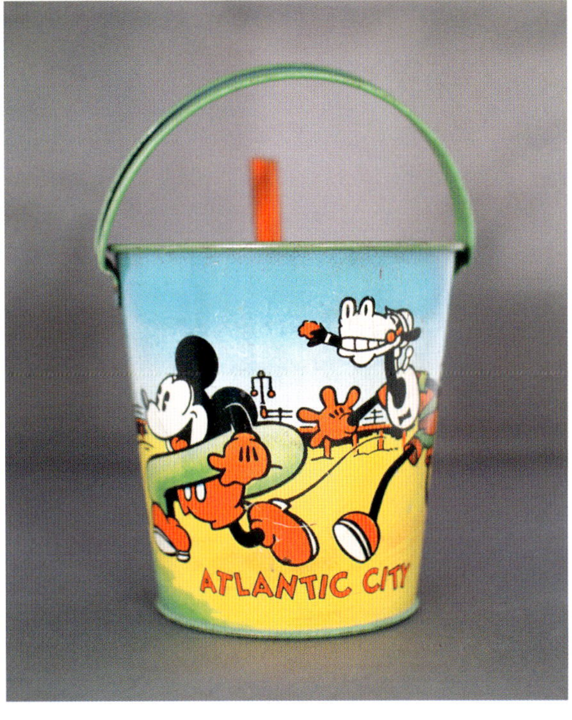

4.25″ Atlantic City sand pail with a 6.25″ shovel featuring Mickey, Minnie, Horace and Clarabelle in three different views. ©Walt Disney Ent., Mfg. by Ohio Art Co., Bryan, O., U.S.A. $500-$750

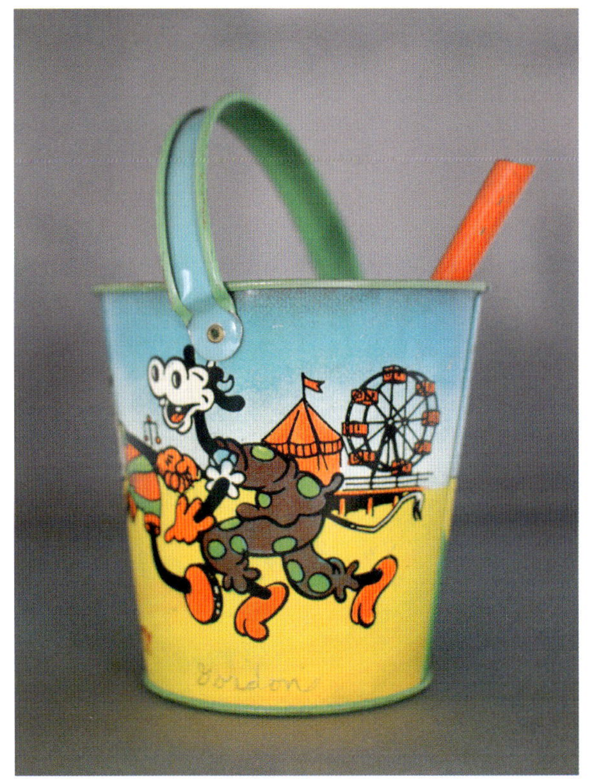

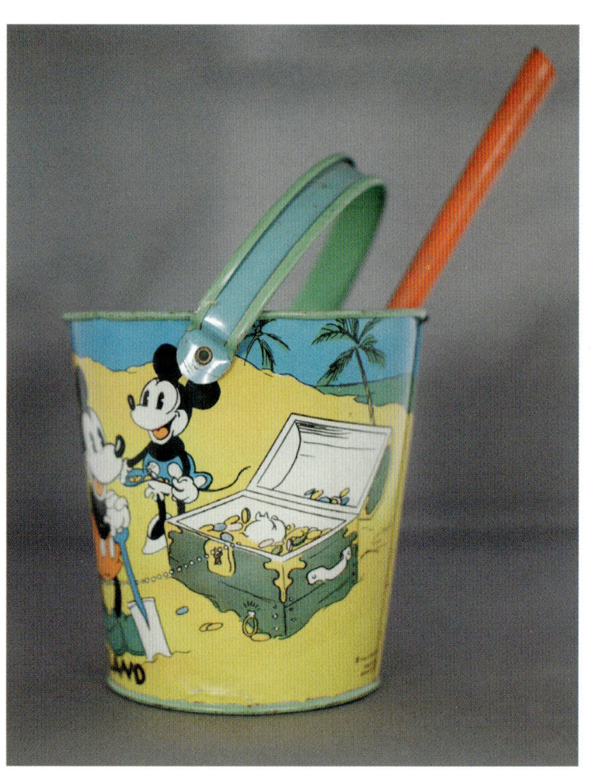

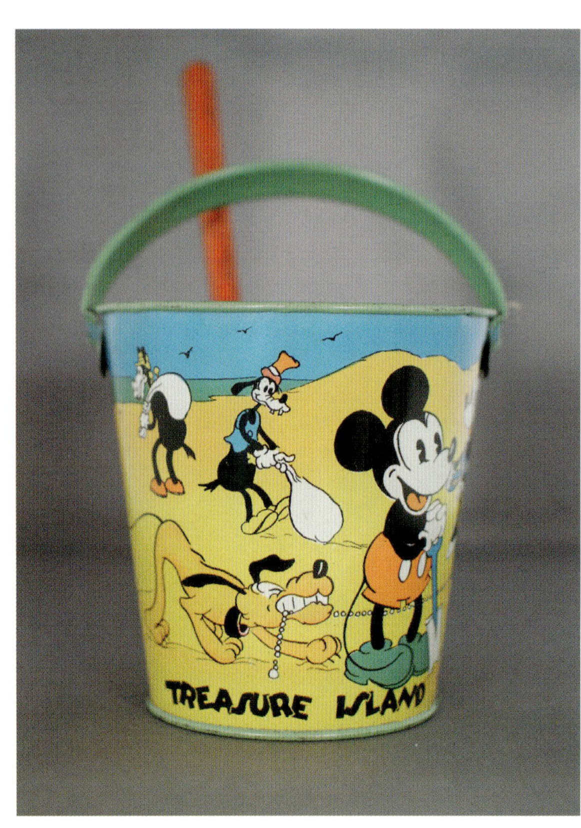

4.25" Mickey Mouse Treasure Island pail with an 8.5" shovel. Three views of this popular pail. ©Walt Disney Ent., Ohio Art Co., Bryan, O. U.S.A. $450-700

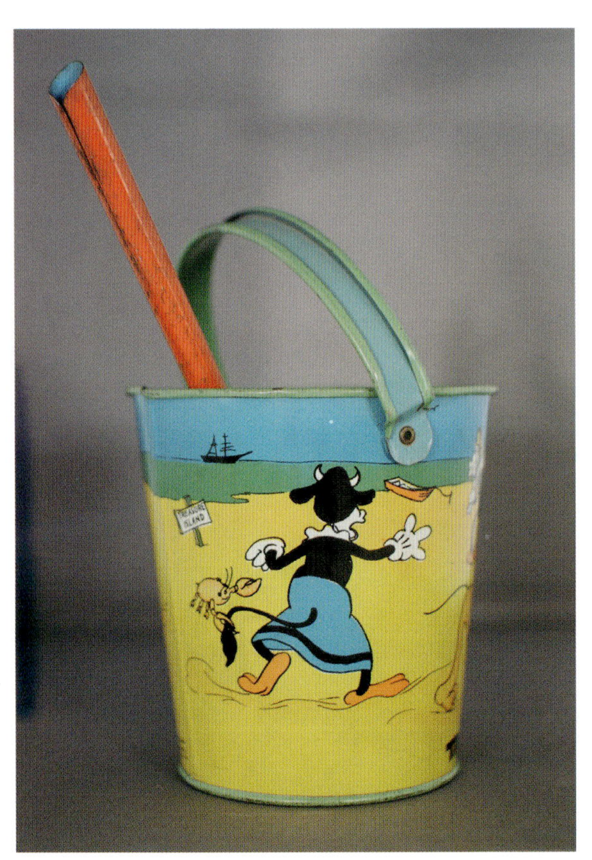

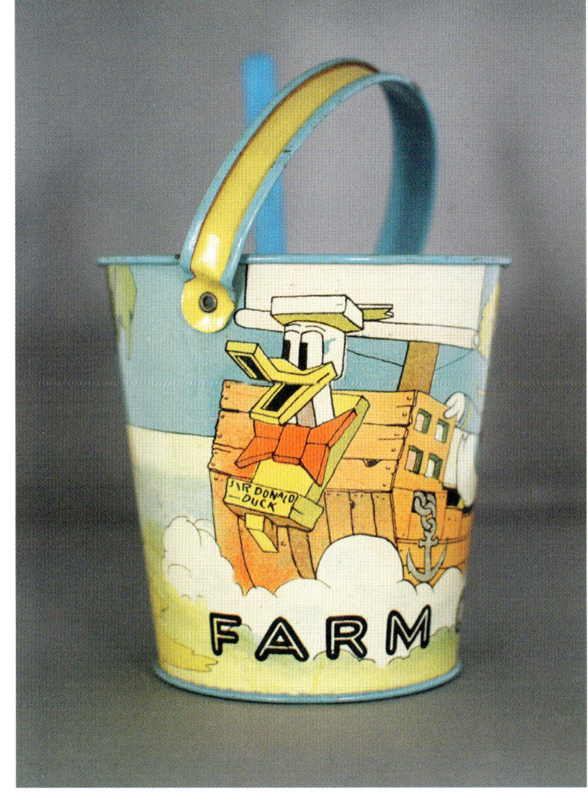

Three images of 4.25" Farm Crest pail with 7" shovel. Note stern figurehead of "Sir Donald Duck" and cannon toward bow. Also available without "Farmcrest." ©Walt Disney Enterprises, Ohio Art Co., Bryan, O., U.S.A. $300-500. With "Farmcrest" add $50-75.

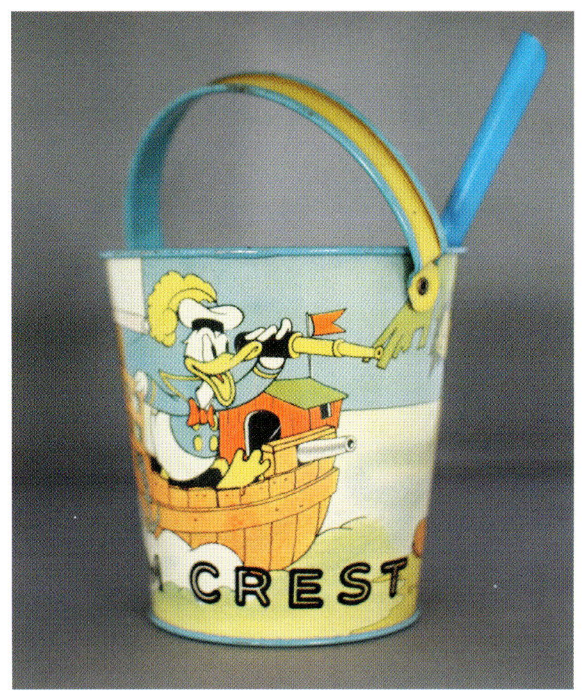

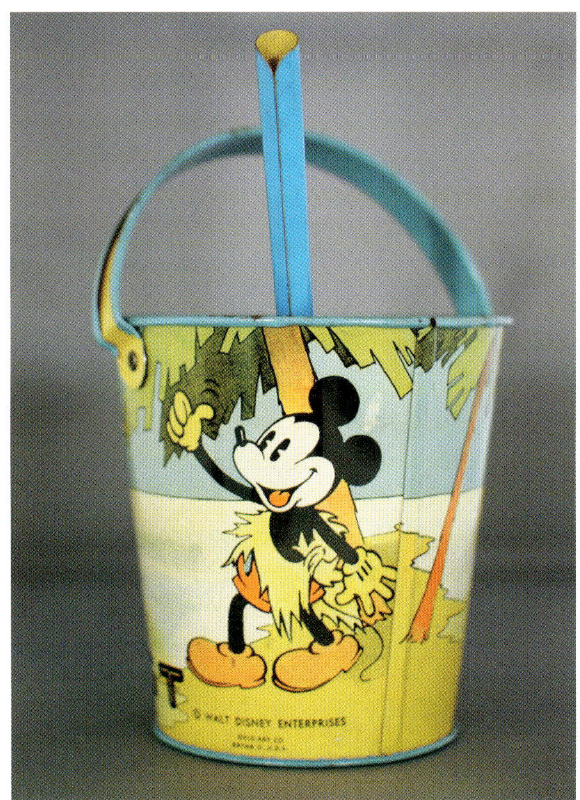

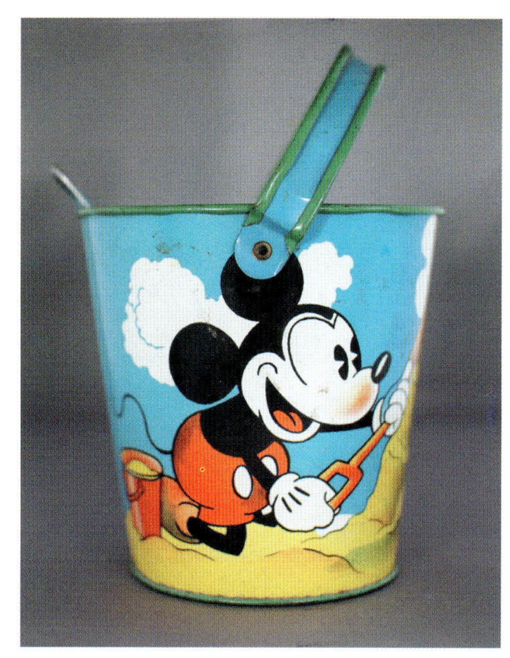

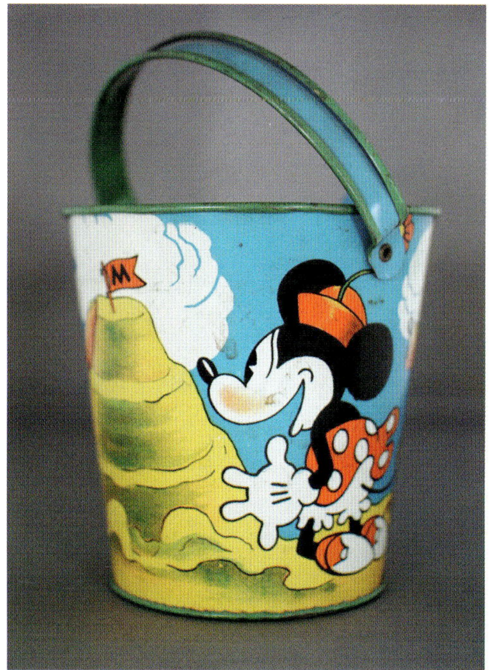

4.25" Mickey building a sand castle pail with 5.25" spoon. Be aware that a 5.5" contemporary pail of the same design exists. ©Walt Disney Ent., Mfg. by Ohio Art Co., Bryan, O., U.S.A. $300-500

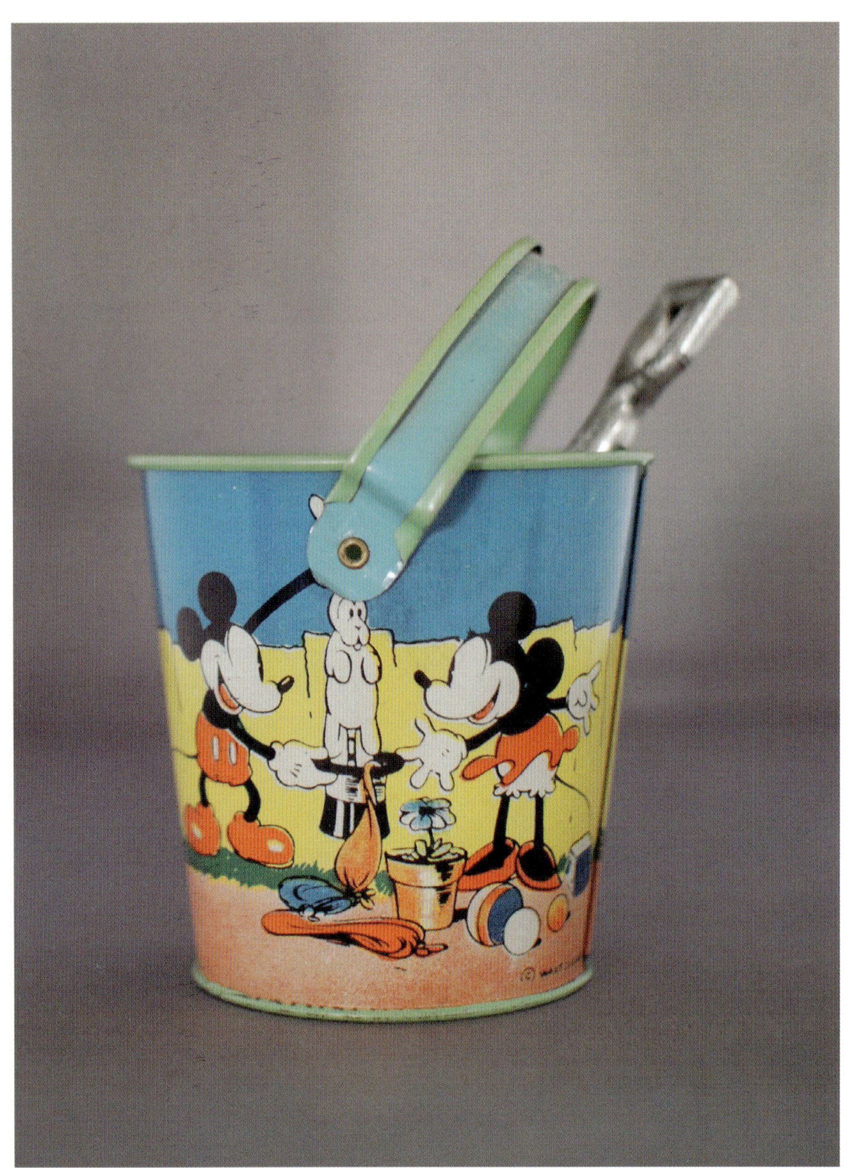

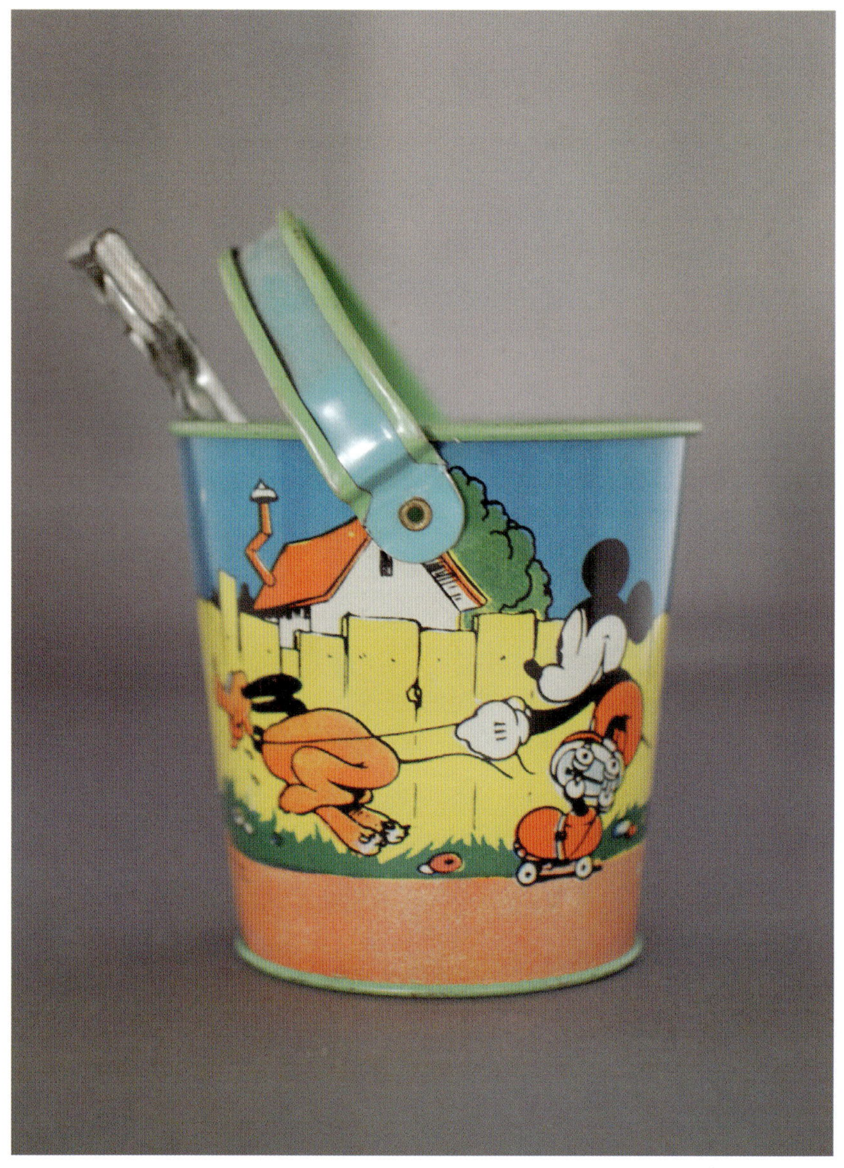

3.5" Mickey Mouse magician sand pail with 5.5" shovel. Nice images of Pluto pulling Mickey on roller skates and Mickey pulling a rabbit out of a hat for an admiring Minnie! ©Walt Disney, Ohio Art Co., U.S.A. $250-450

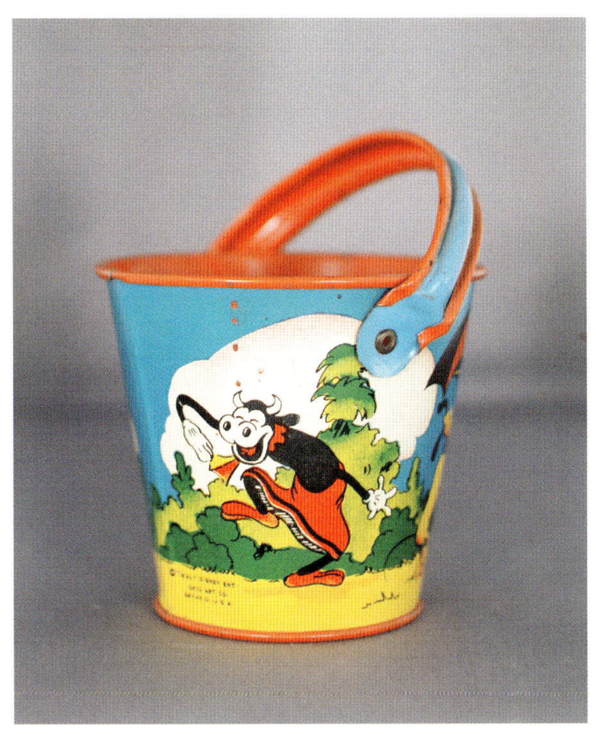

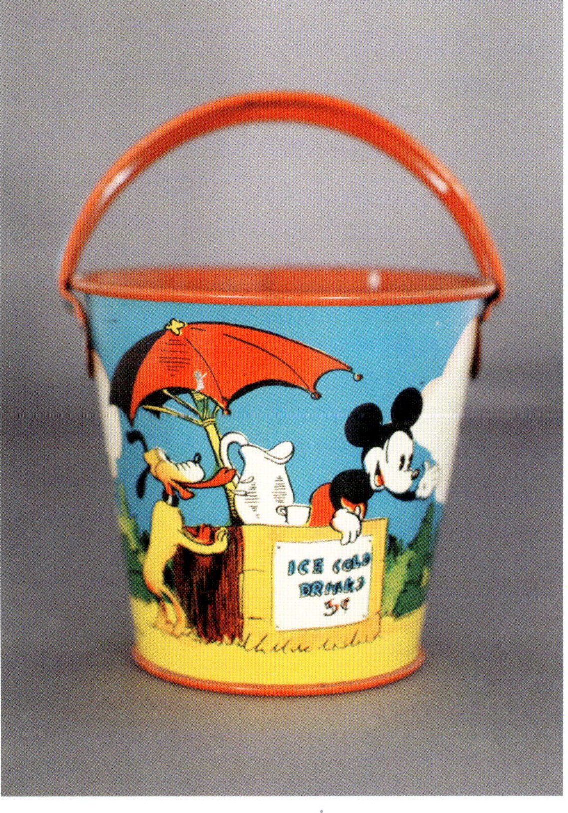

3" Mickey Mouse with a 5 cent drink stand sand pail. The images show a dancing Clarabelle, Mickey and Pluto at the "5c" stand along with a gorgeous Minnie. ©Walt Disney Ent., Ohio Art Co., Bryan, O., U.S.A. $300-500

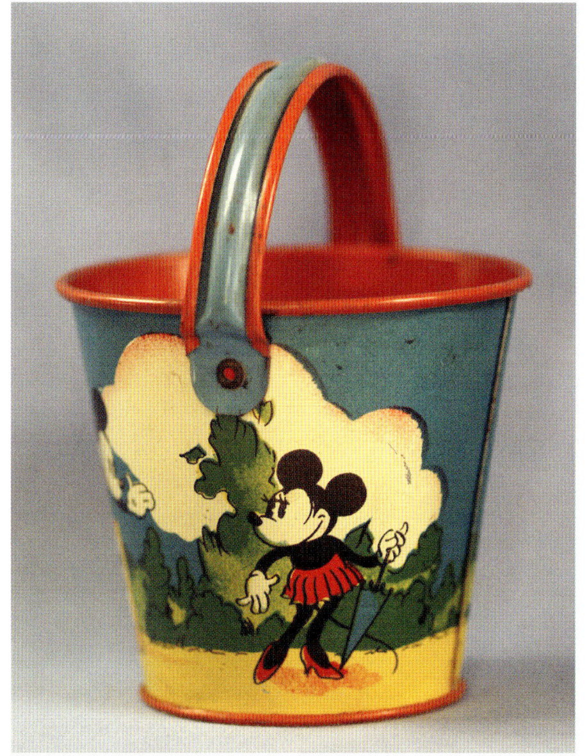

Donald Duck

Donald Duck first appeared in the Disney cartoon short *The Wise Little Hen* in 1934. Donald actually gained more popularity than Mickey Mouse, the Disney icon. He appeared in more cartoon shorts, more comics, and more stories than Mickey. Donald first appeared with a very long bill, which lasted only a short time. Therefore any long-billed Donald items are most desirable and are more valuable.

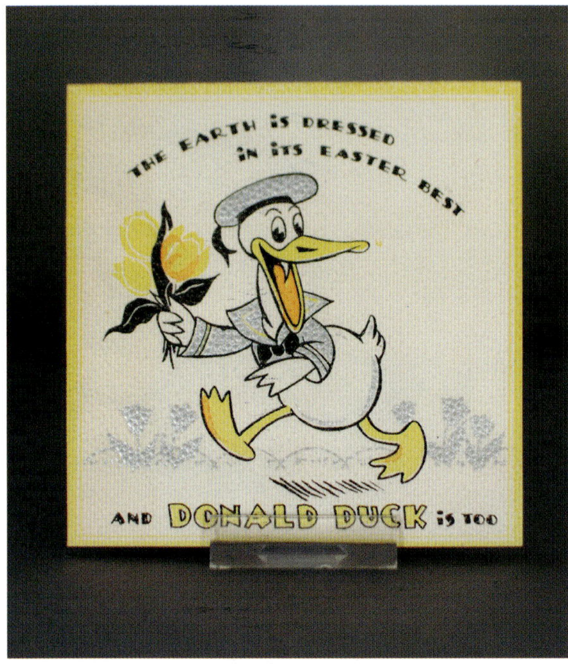

A Hallmark long-billed Donald Easter greeting card. Both cards are marked: "Copyright 1936 A Hallmark card published under exclusive license granted by Walt Disney Enterprises. Copyright owners" $50-75

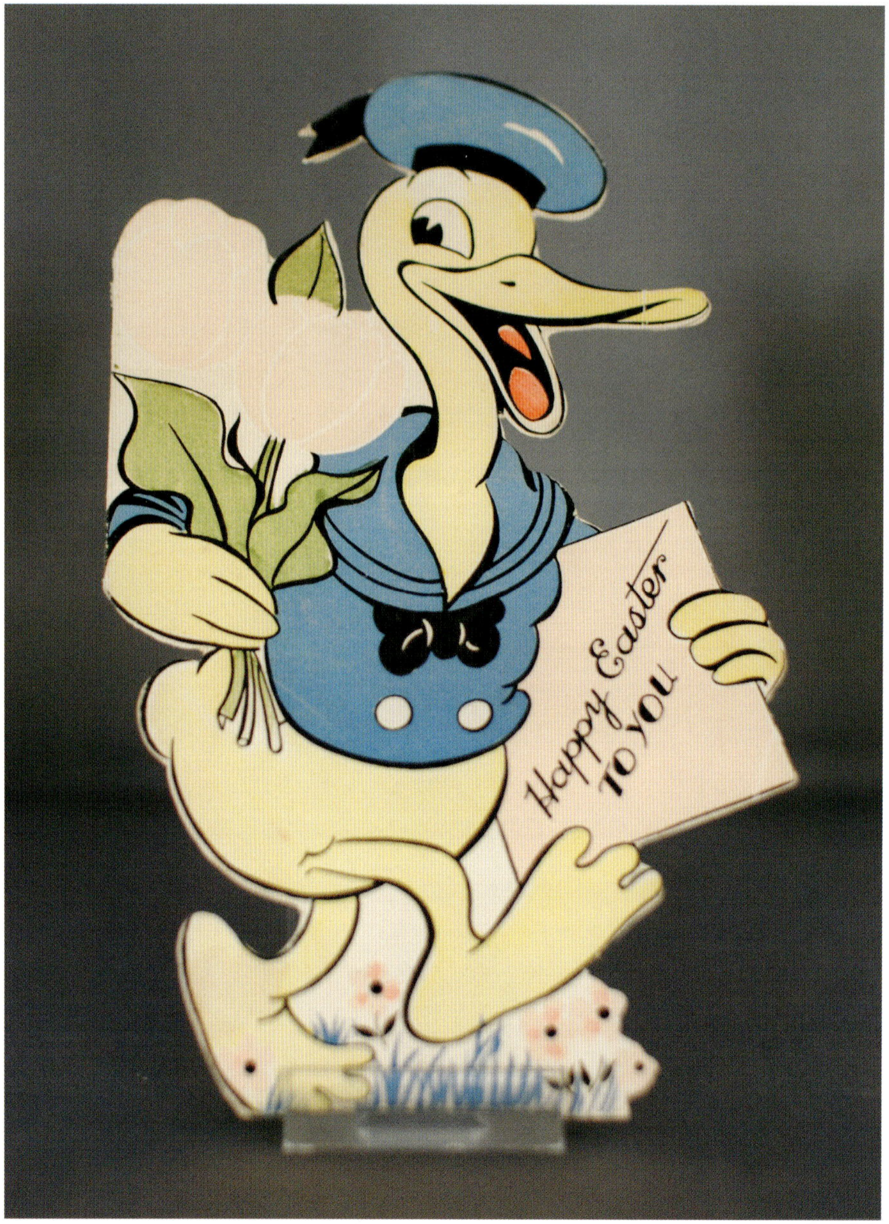

Hallmark had the Disney license to produce greeting cards during the 1930s. Long billed Donald cards are exceedingly rare. This example is an Easter greeting card and is 6.5" tall. $50-75

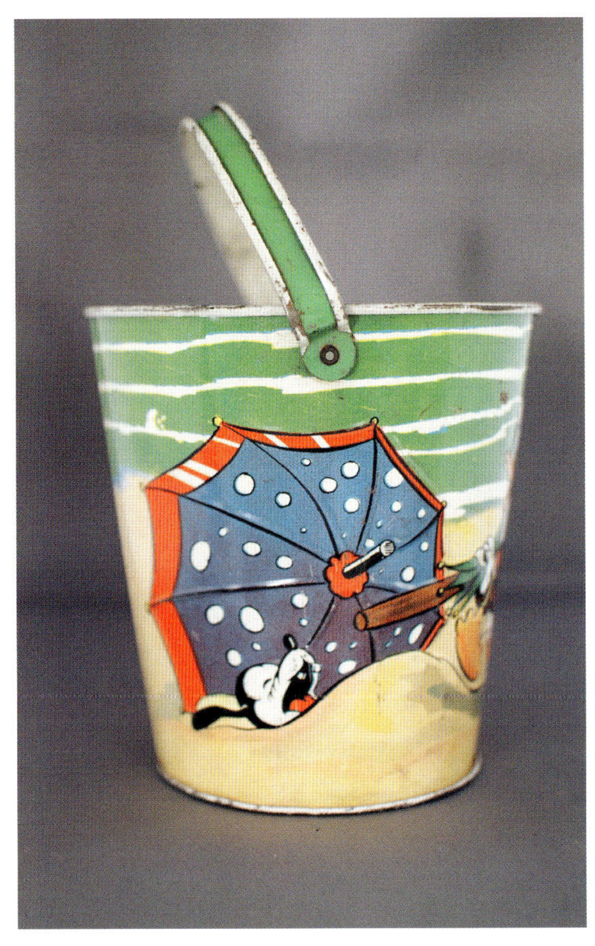

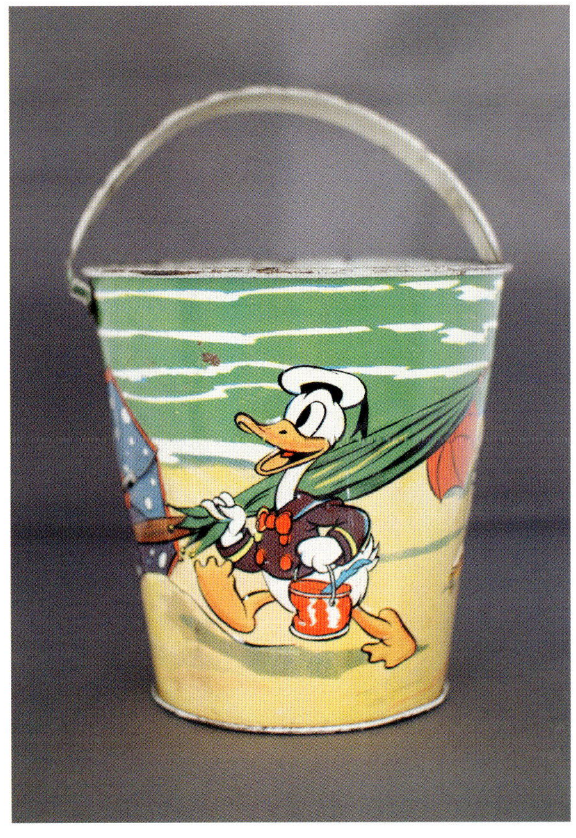

6″ embossed Donald Duck pail by Ohio Art. This is the only embossed Disney pail by Ohio Art that we know of. The three views illustrate how effective embossing can be in improving the looks of a pail. ©Walt Disney Enterprises, Ohio Art Co. Bryan, O. U.S.A. $700-1000

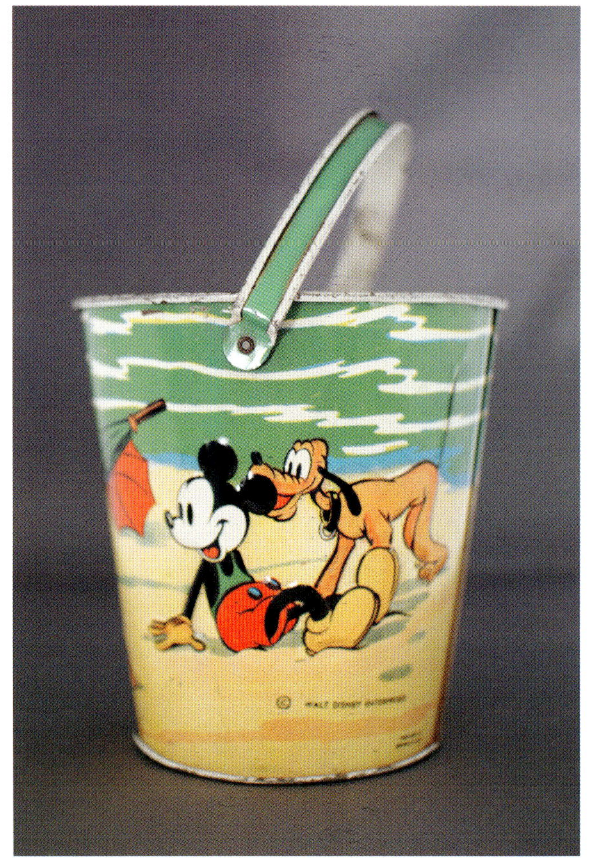

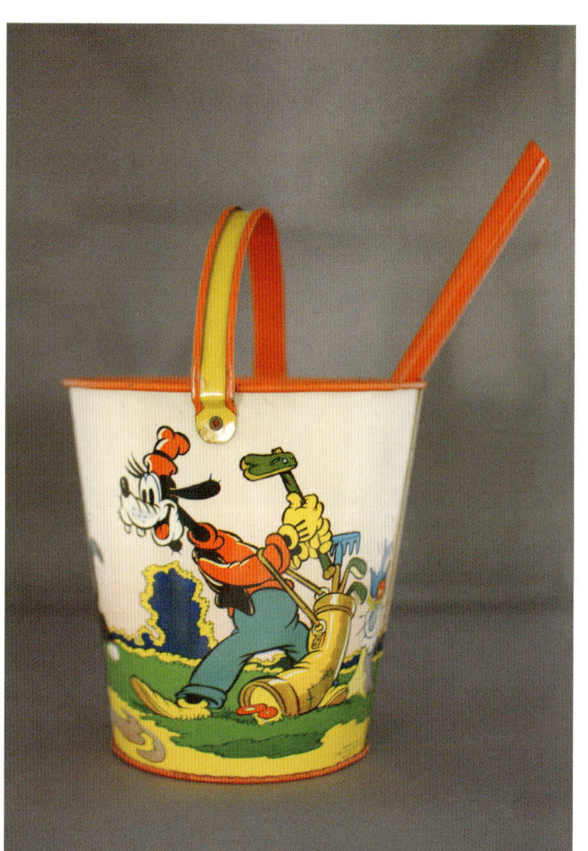

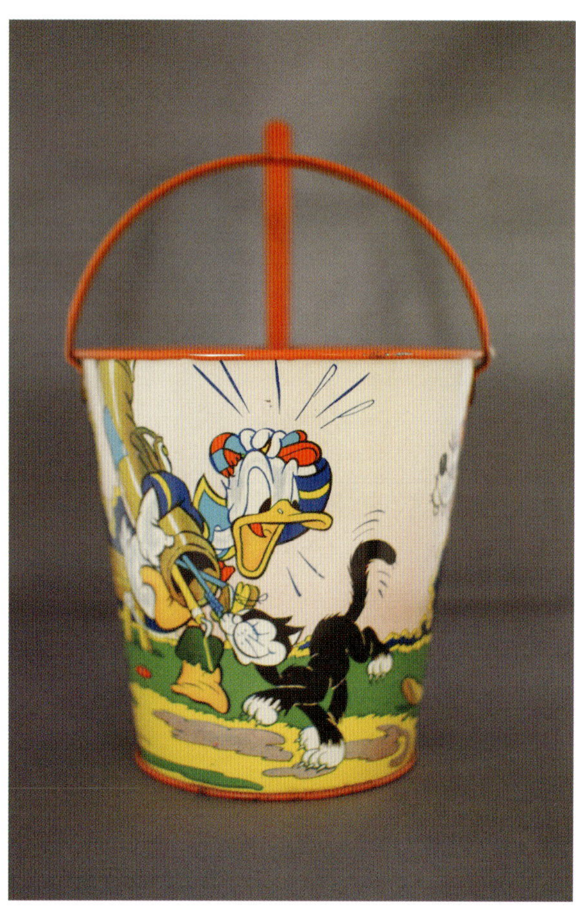

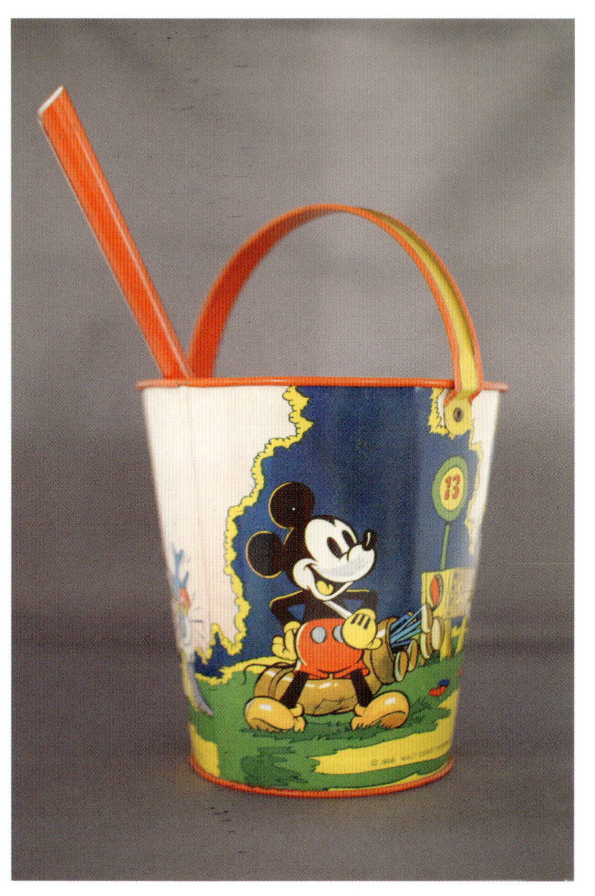

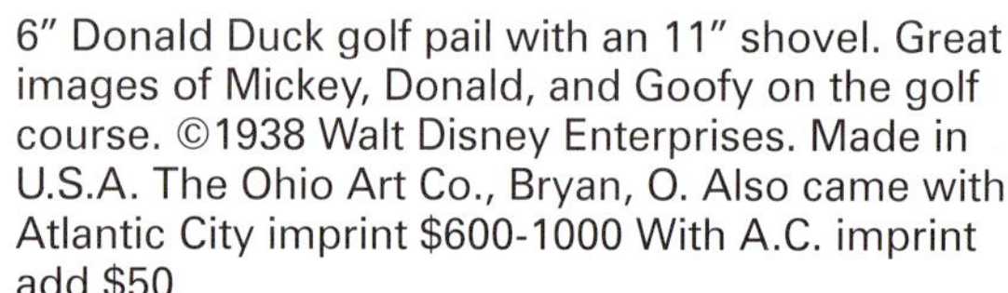

6″ Donald Duck golf pail with an 11″ shovel. Great images of Mickey, Donald, and Goofy on the golf course. ©1938 Walt Disney Enterprises. Made in U.S.A. The Ohio Art Co., Bryan, O. Also came with Atlantic City imprint $600-1000 With A.C. imprint add $50

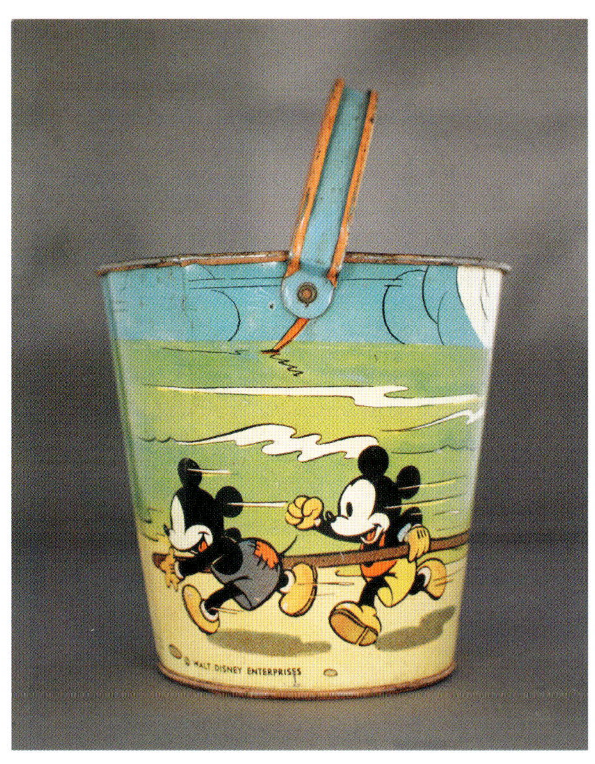

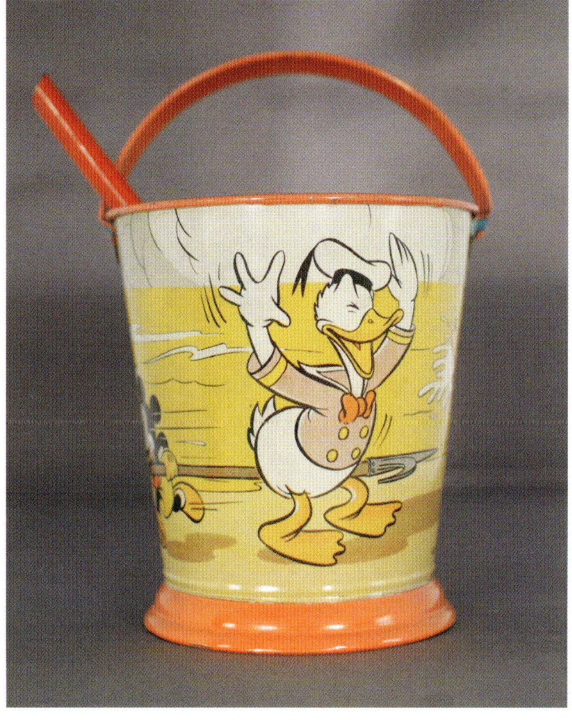

5″ and 5.5″ Donald Duck pails. The 5.5″ bucket has a raised bottom and an 8.5″ shovel. The images show Donald having a belly laugh as Pluto is being dunked by Goofy while Mickey's nephews play on the beach. Although the raised bottom pail is mint, a problem during manufacturing caused most of the blue color to be missing from the pail. ©Walt Disney Enterprises, Ohio Art Co., Bryan, O., U.S.A. $400-700

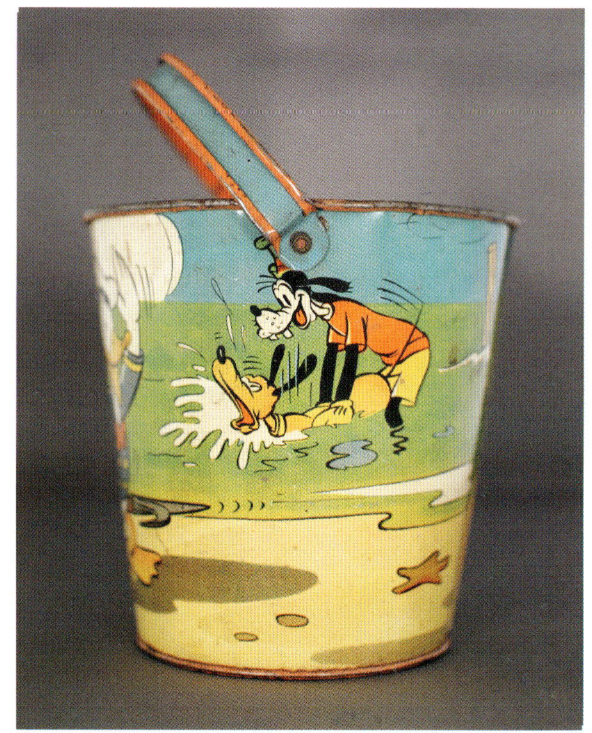

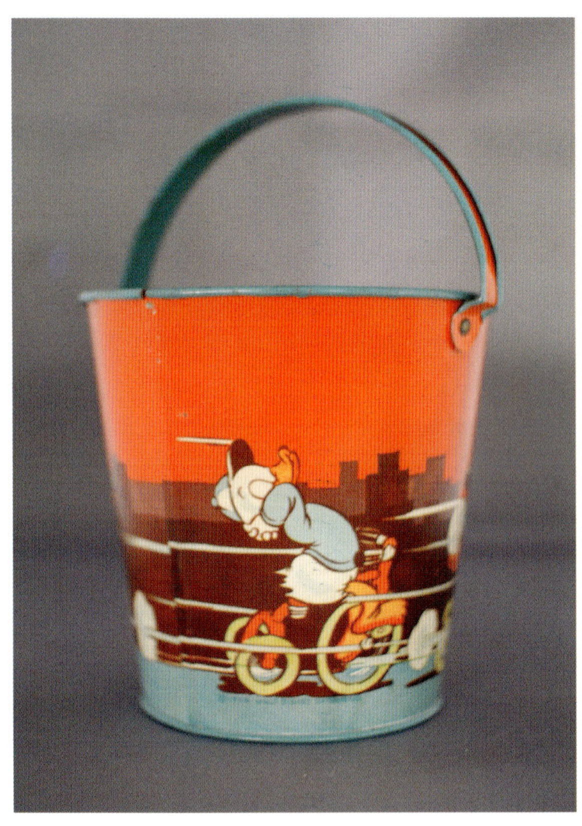

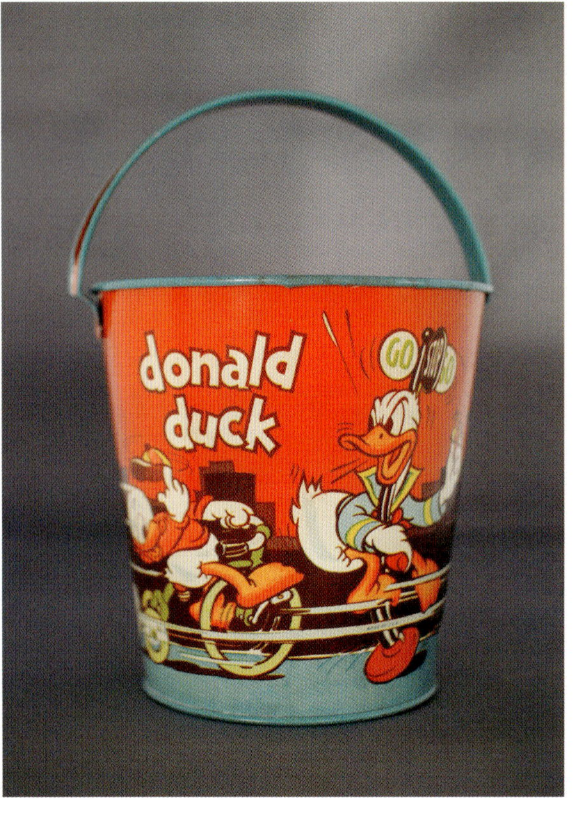

5" Donald Duck pail featuring Donald as a traffic cop, trying to control Huey, Dewey and Louie as they are speeding along. One of the pails with a rare red background. ©1938 Walt Disney Enterprises, Ohio Art Co., U.S.A. *Bernabe collection* $300-500

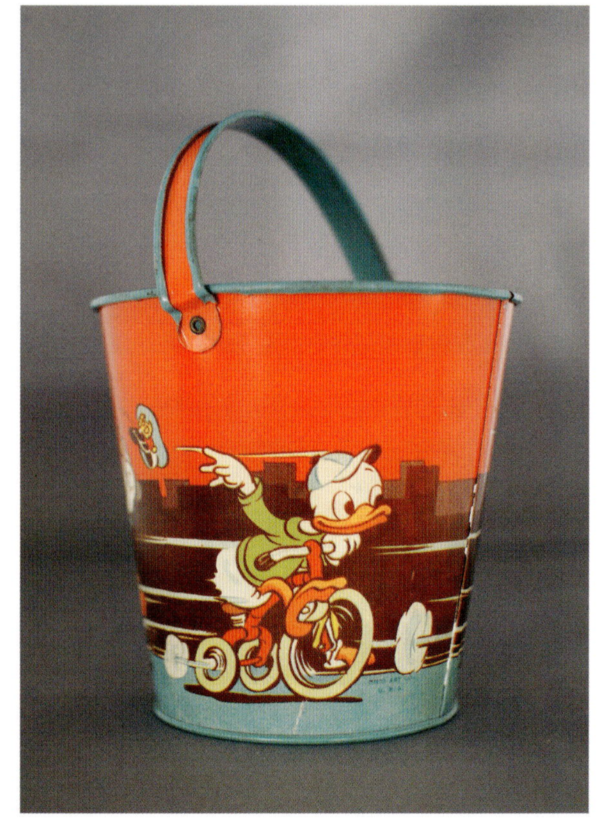

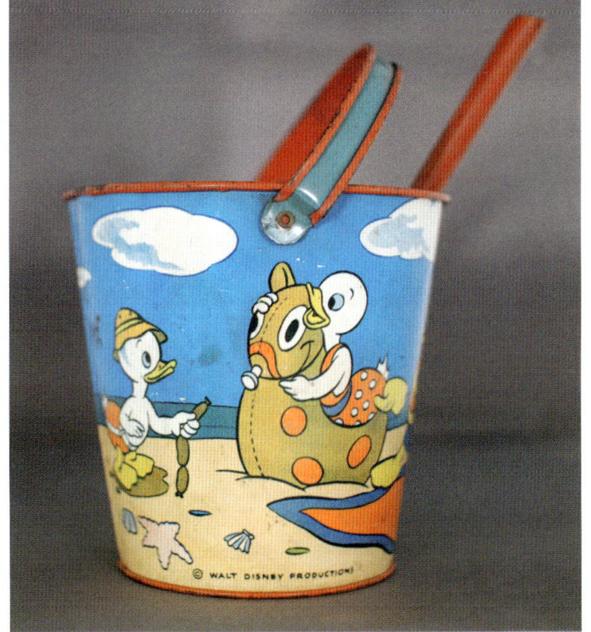

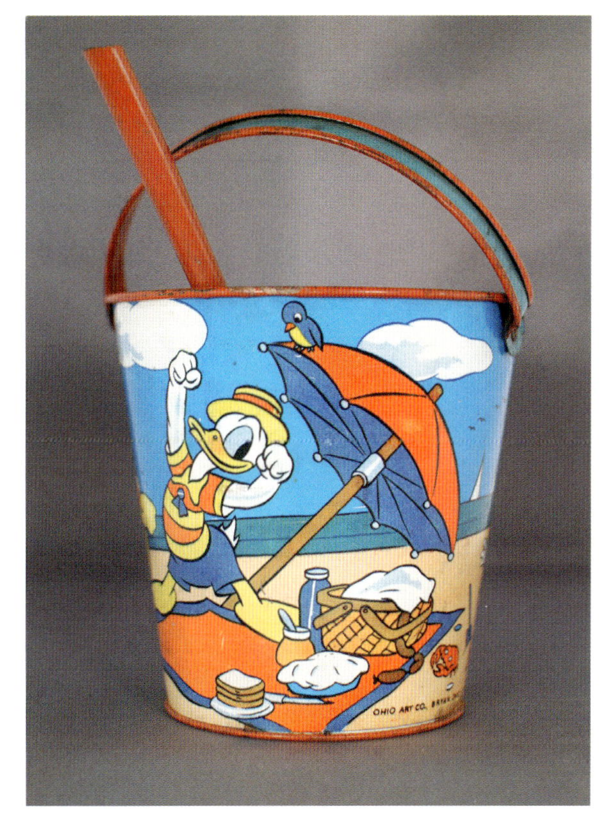

5″ Donald Duck pail with an 8.5″ shovel. The pail shows Donald very proud of his biceps. His nephews are playing on the beach nearby. © Walt Disney Productions, Ohio Art Co., Bryan, Ohio 72 Made in U.S.A. $300-500

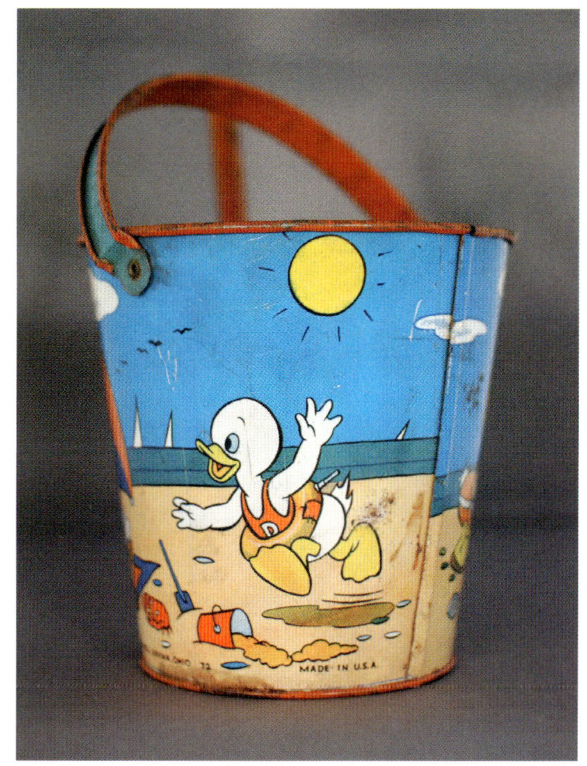

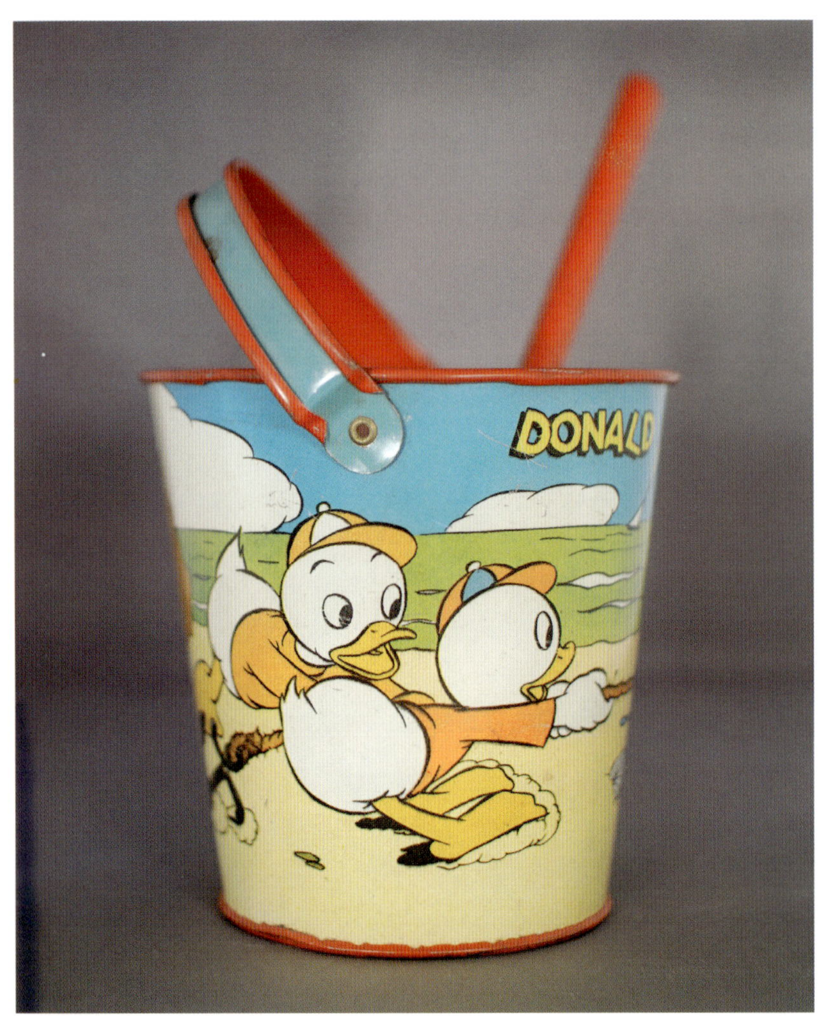

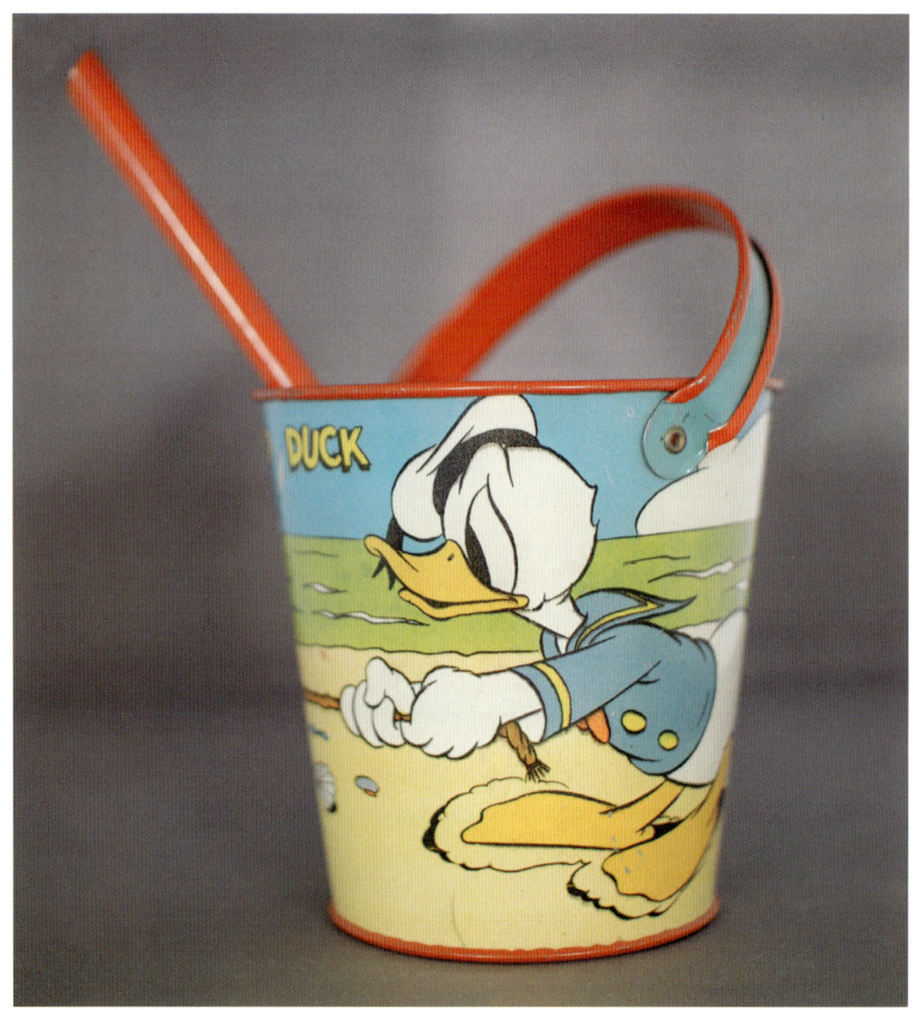

4.25" Donald Duck pail with 8.5" shovel. Donald is having a tug of war with two of his nephews. ©1939 W.D.P., Ohio Art Co., Bryan, Ohio Made in U.S.A. $250-450

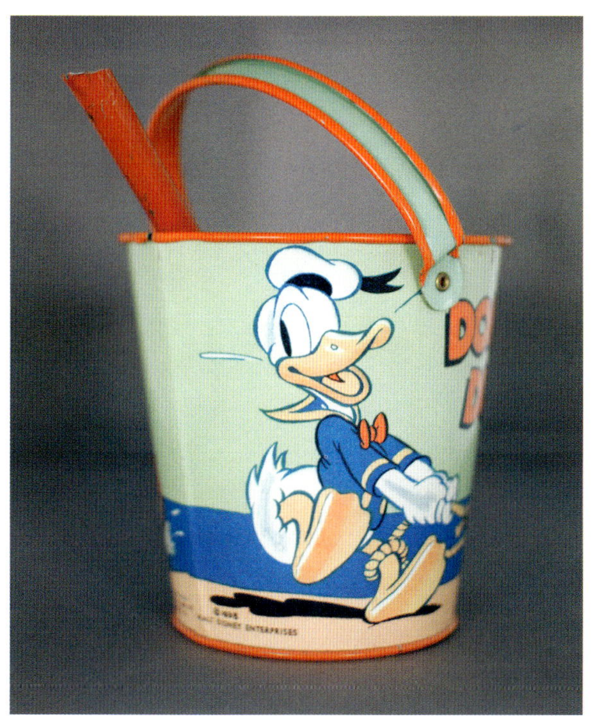

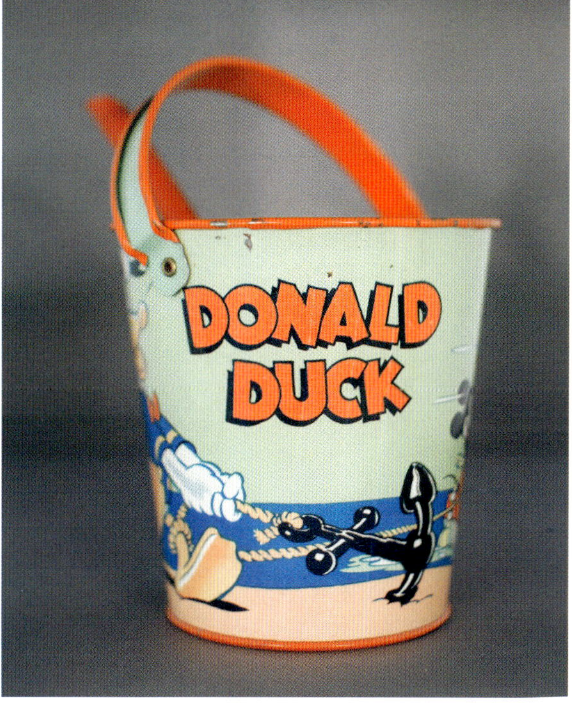

4.25" Donald Duck pail with a 7" shovel. Donald is pulling on an anchor while Mickey, Minnie and Goofy are zipping along in a boat. ©1938 Walt Disney Enterprises. Made in U.S.A. The Ohio Art Co. Bryan, O. $300-500

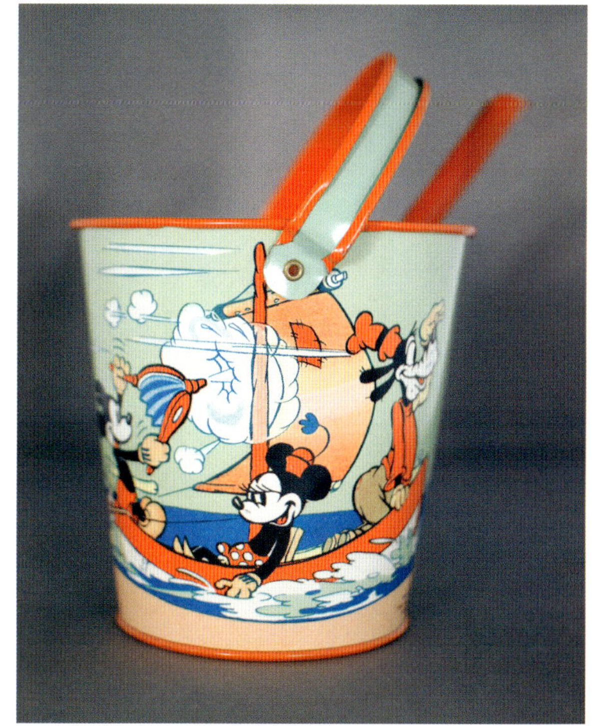

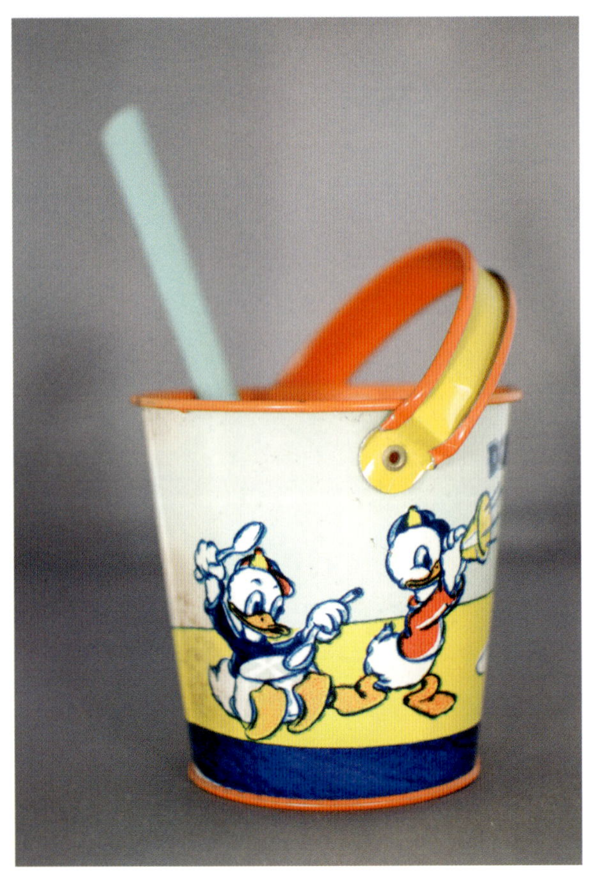

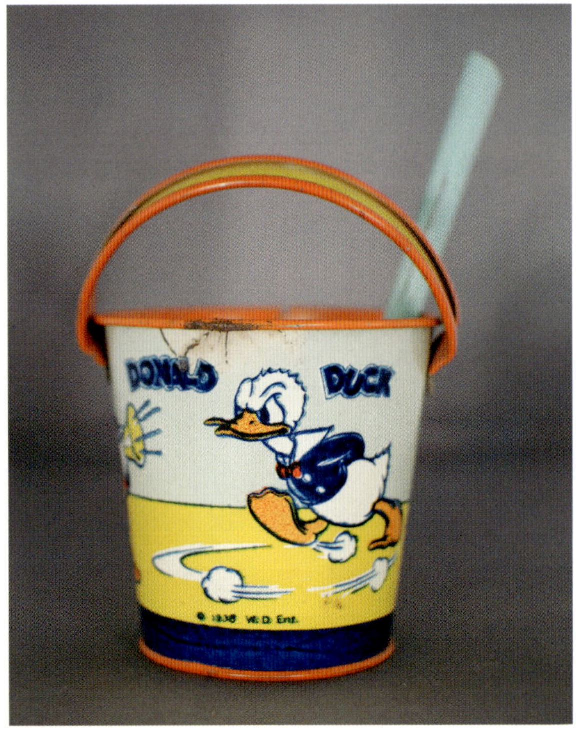

3.5" Donald Duck pail with a 6.25" shovel. A frustrated Donald walking in a circle having to listen to his nephews' music playing. ©1938 W.D.Ent, Made in U.S.A. $200-400

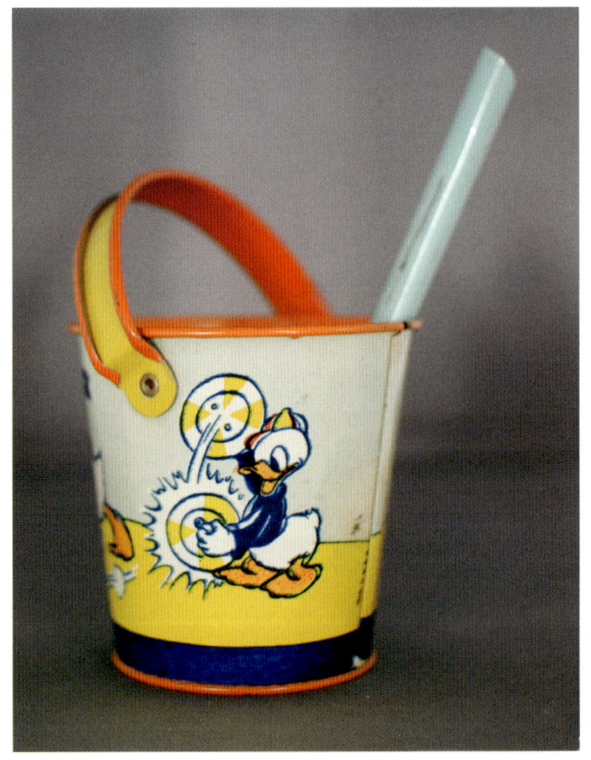

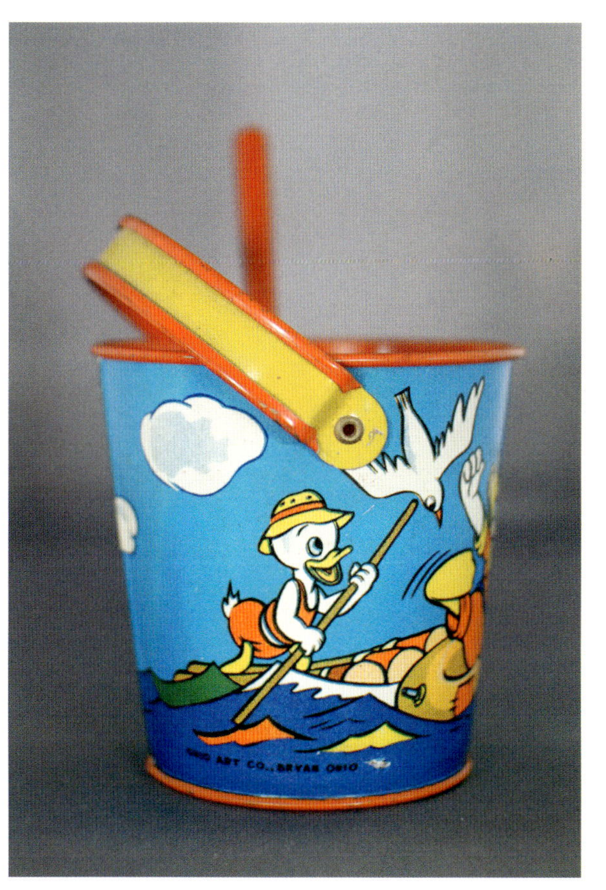

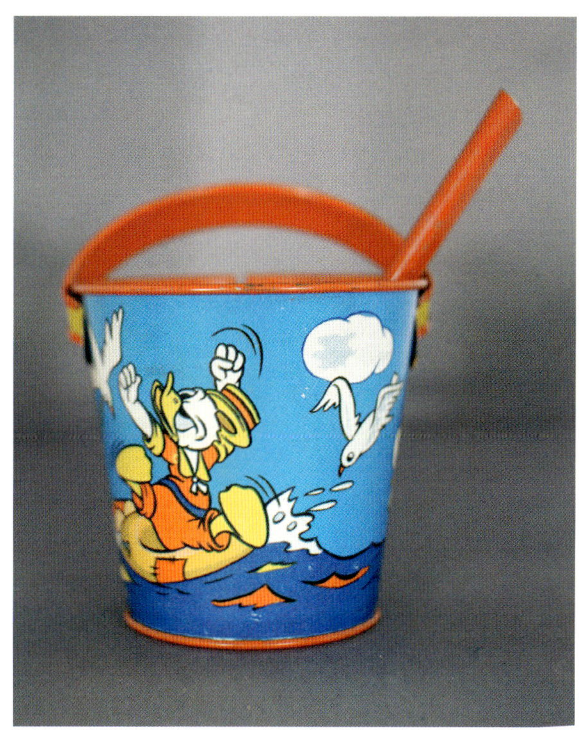

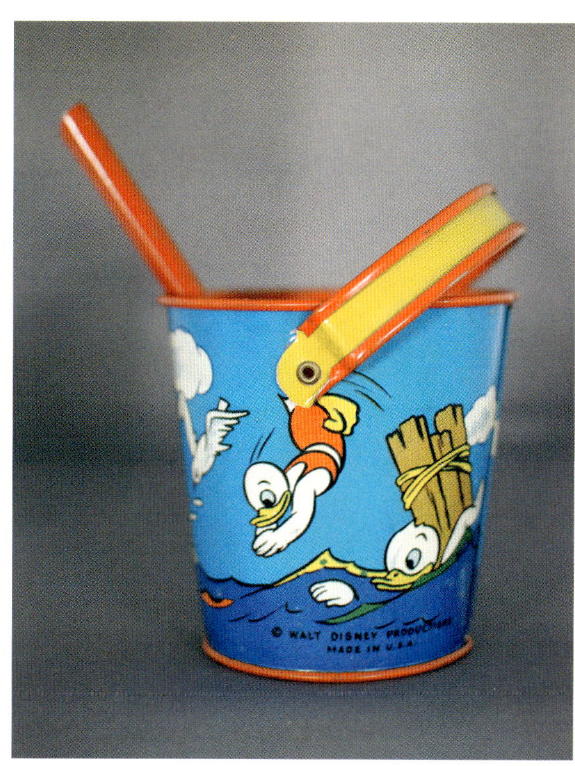

3.5" Donald Duck pail with a 6" shovel. Features Donald in a raft having problems with birds while his nephews enjoy the water. ©Walt Disney Productions Made in U.S.A. Ohio Art Co. Bryan, Ohio $200-300

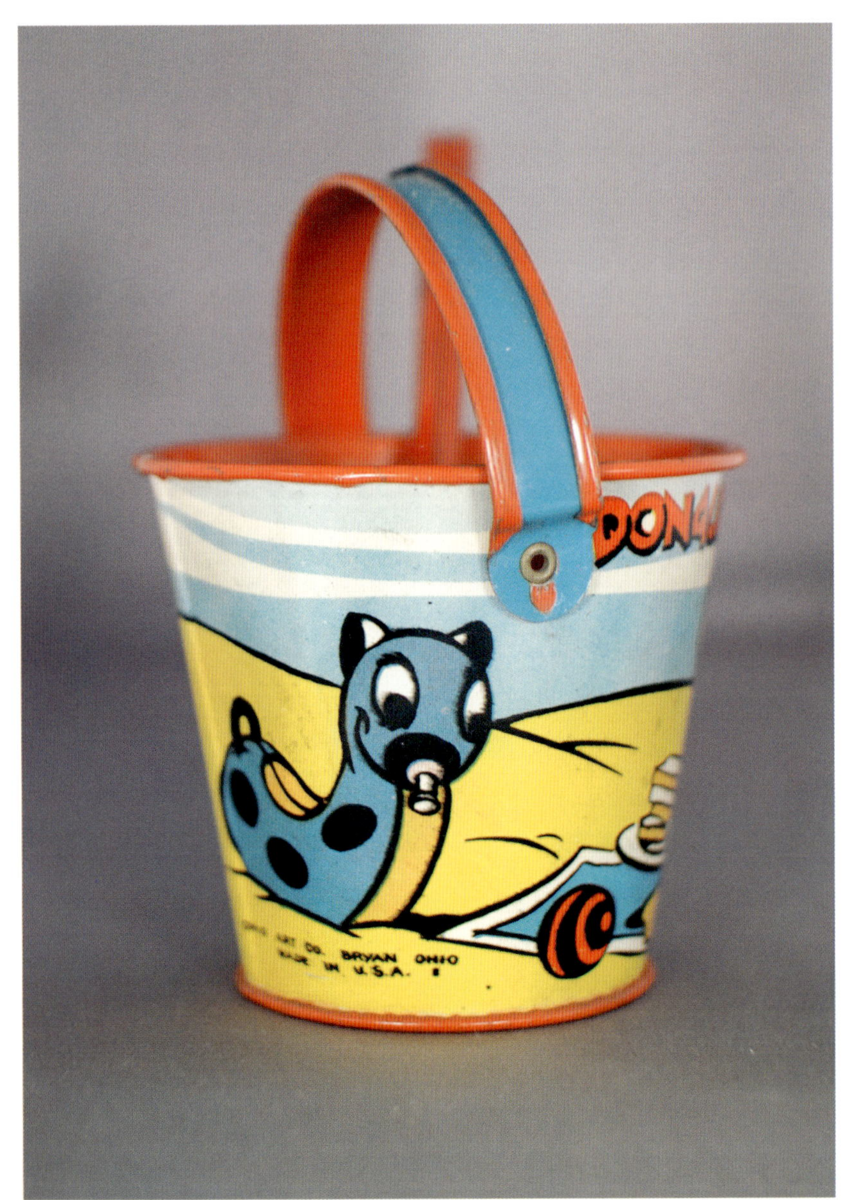

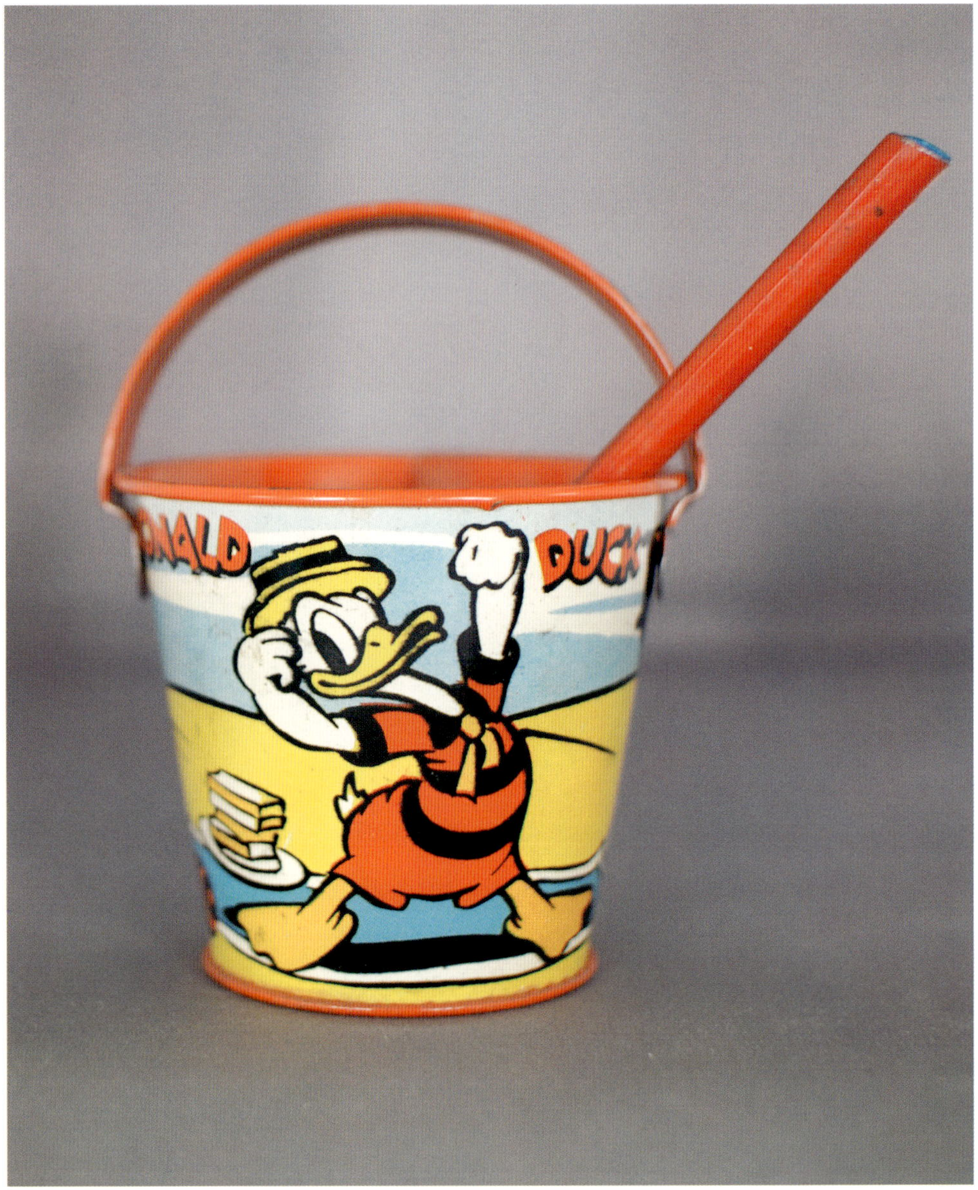

3″ Donald Duck pail with a 6″ shovel. Donald is showing his muscles on the beach. ©1939 W.D.P. Ohio Art Co. Bryan, Ohio Made in U.S.A. $200-350

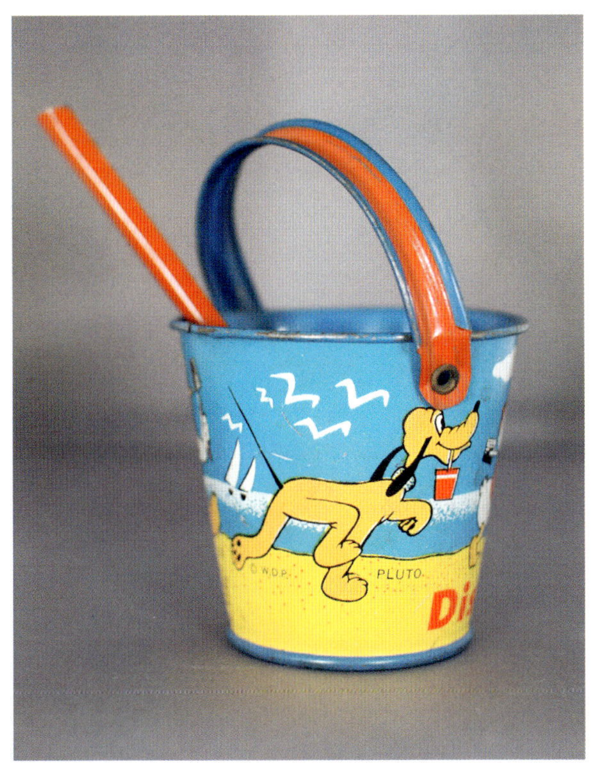

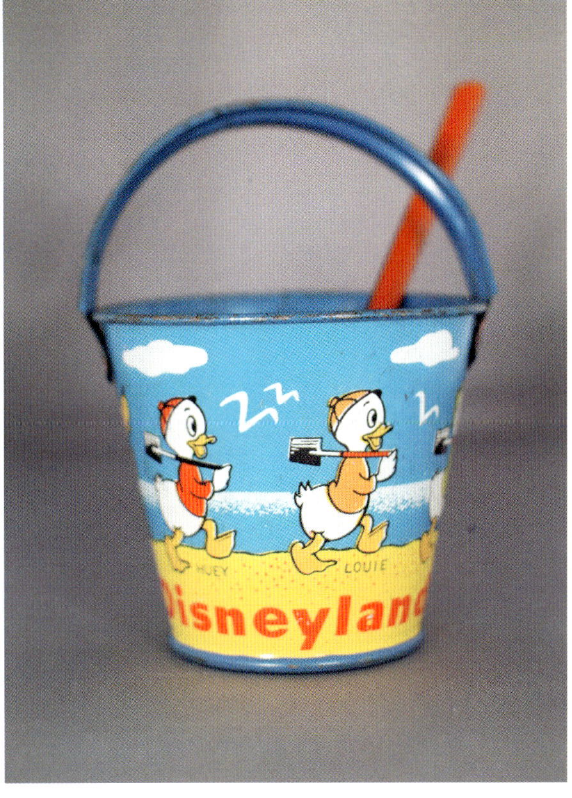

3″ Disneyland candy pail with a 6″ shovel. Believed to have been produced by Ohio Art for the Overland Candy Co. All the characters pictured are named ©W.D.P. Net Wt. 2.75 oz. Ingredients: sugar, corn syrup, citric acid, natural and artificial flavors. Mfg by Overland Candy Co., Chicago, Ill. ©1949 $150-250

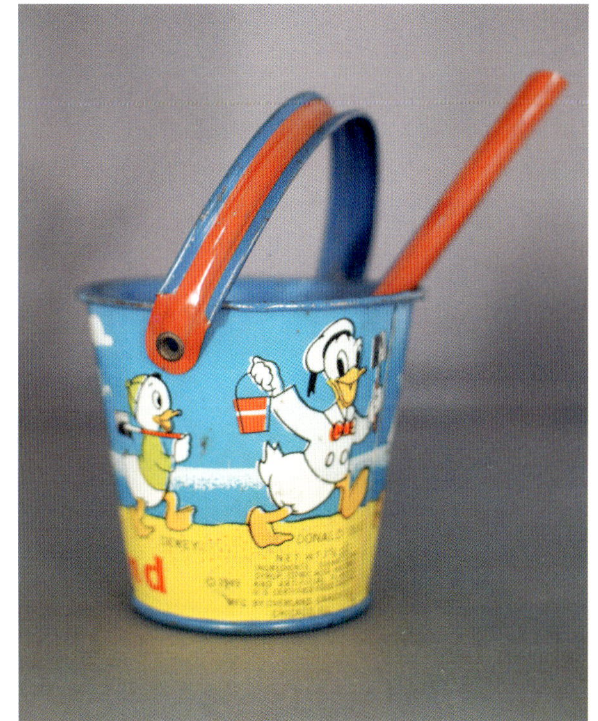

Pinocchio

Taken from a story by Collodi, *Pinocchio* was the second feature animated film by Disney. From an artistic viewpoint it is considered the best of the Disney animated films largely due to the lavish use of the multi-plane camera. The timing of the release was unfortunate because it coincided with the outbreak of World War II, which basically eliminated income from Europe for the movie.

The story involves Geppetto's wooden puppet Pinocchio becoming a real boy with the help of his conscience Jiminy Cricket. His adventures include being under water which is the scene shown on the one Ohio Art Pinocchio sand pail.

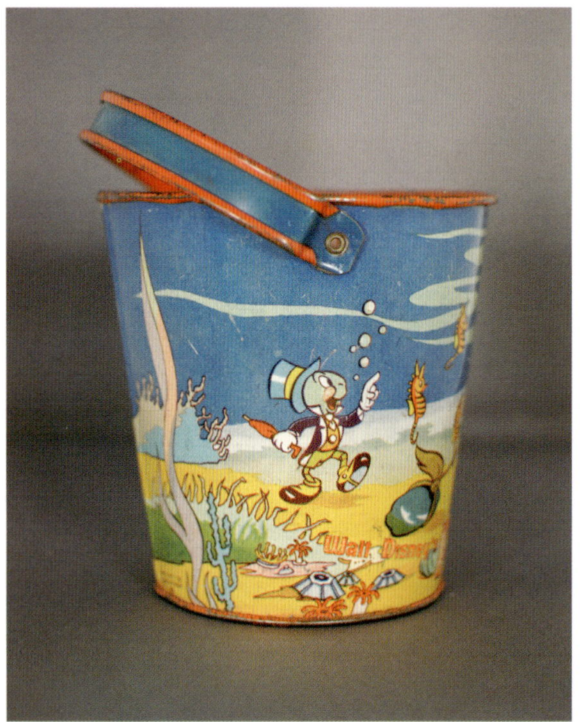

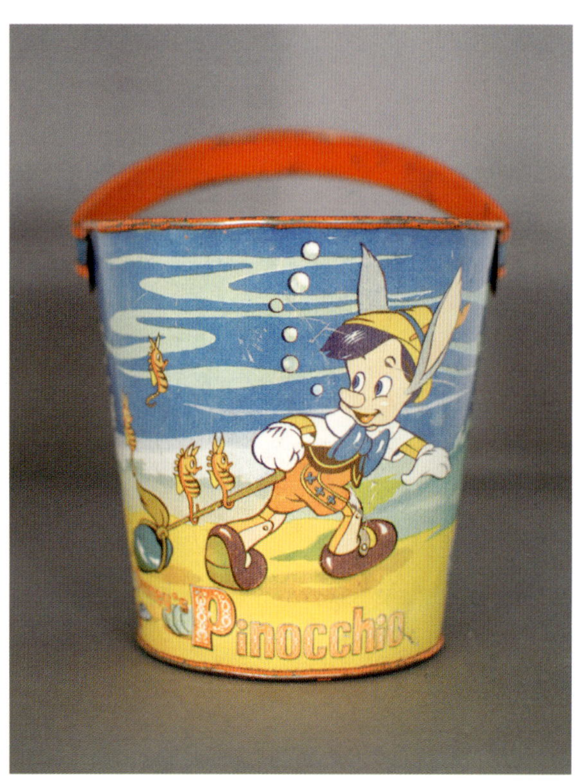

Three images of a 4.25" Pinocchio sand pail showing Pinocchio and Jiminy Cricket. ©1940 Walt Disney Productions, Ohio Art Co., Made in U.S.A. 29 $350-600

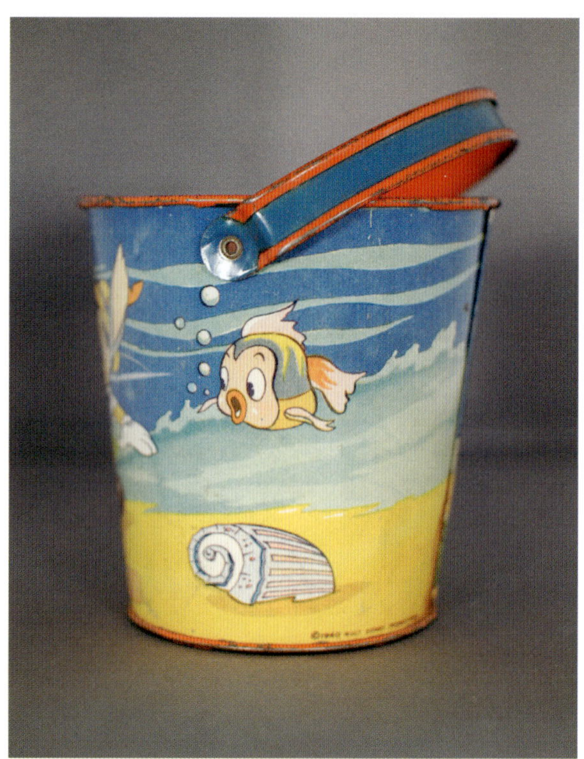

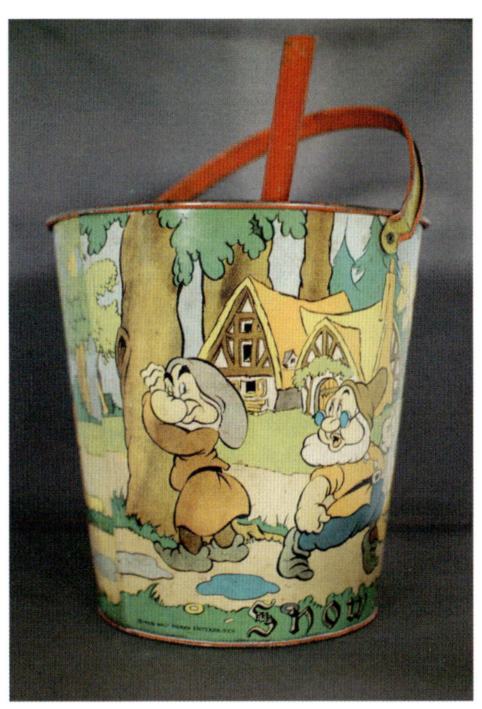

Snow White and The Seven Dwarfs

Snow White and the Seven Dwarfs was the first full-length animated feature ever produced. The original story was a Grimms' fairy tale. Starting in 1934 Walt Disney lavished an amazing amount of loving care on the film. Critics were enthusiastic and ecstatic! It premiered on December 21, 1937 and after 70 years is still one of the landmark films of all times. Those attending the premiere included: Charlie Chaplin, Marlene Dietrich, Shirley Temple, Douglas Fairbanks, Jr., Milton Berle, Jack Benny, George Burns, and Mary Pickford. The Disney Studio won an Academy Award for *Snow White and the Seven Dwarfs*. The highlight of the awards evening was Shirley Temple presenting Walt Disney with an Oscar that consisted of one large Oscar along with seven small ones, all on one base.

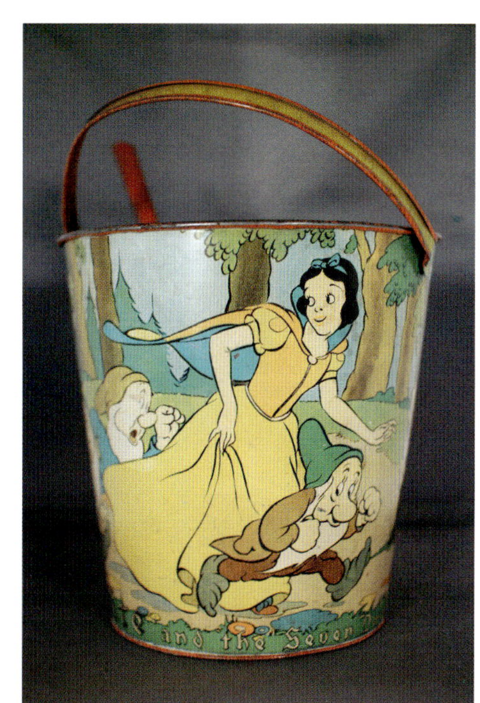

8" Snow White pail with an 11.5" shovel. The four views show Snow White and all of the dwarfs hurrying in front of the dwarfs cottage. Marked ©1938 Walt Disney Enterprises Ohio Art Co. U.S.A. $750-1000

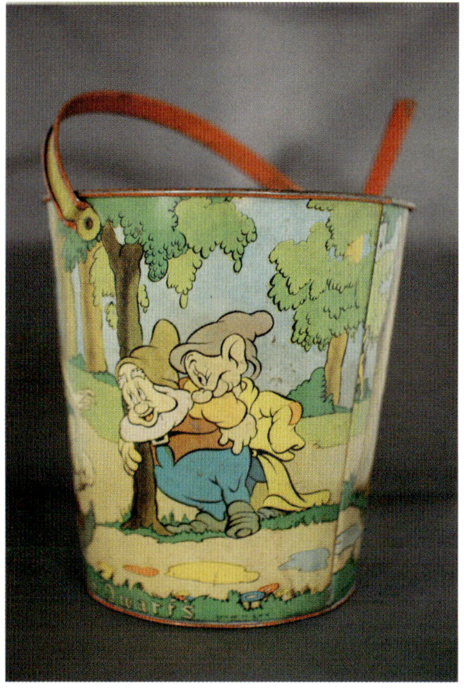

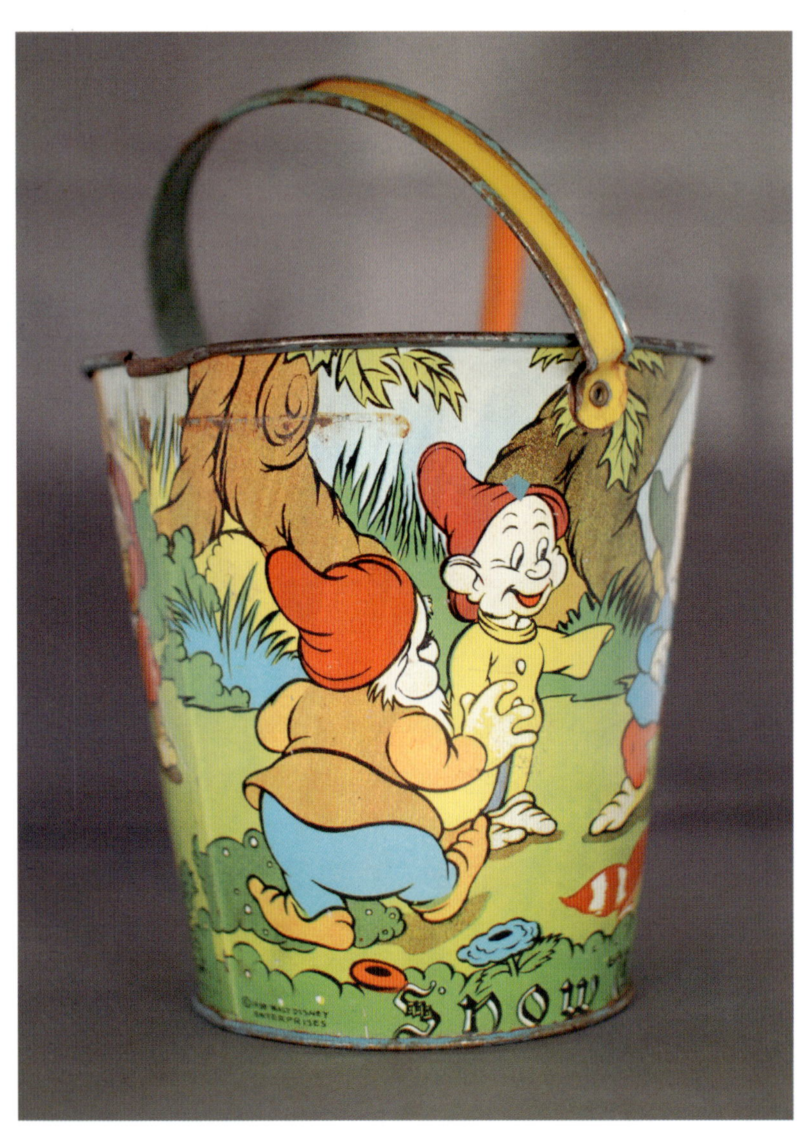

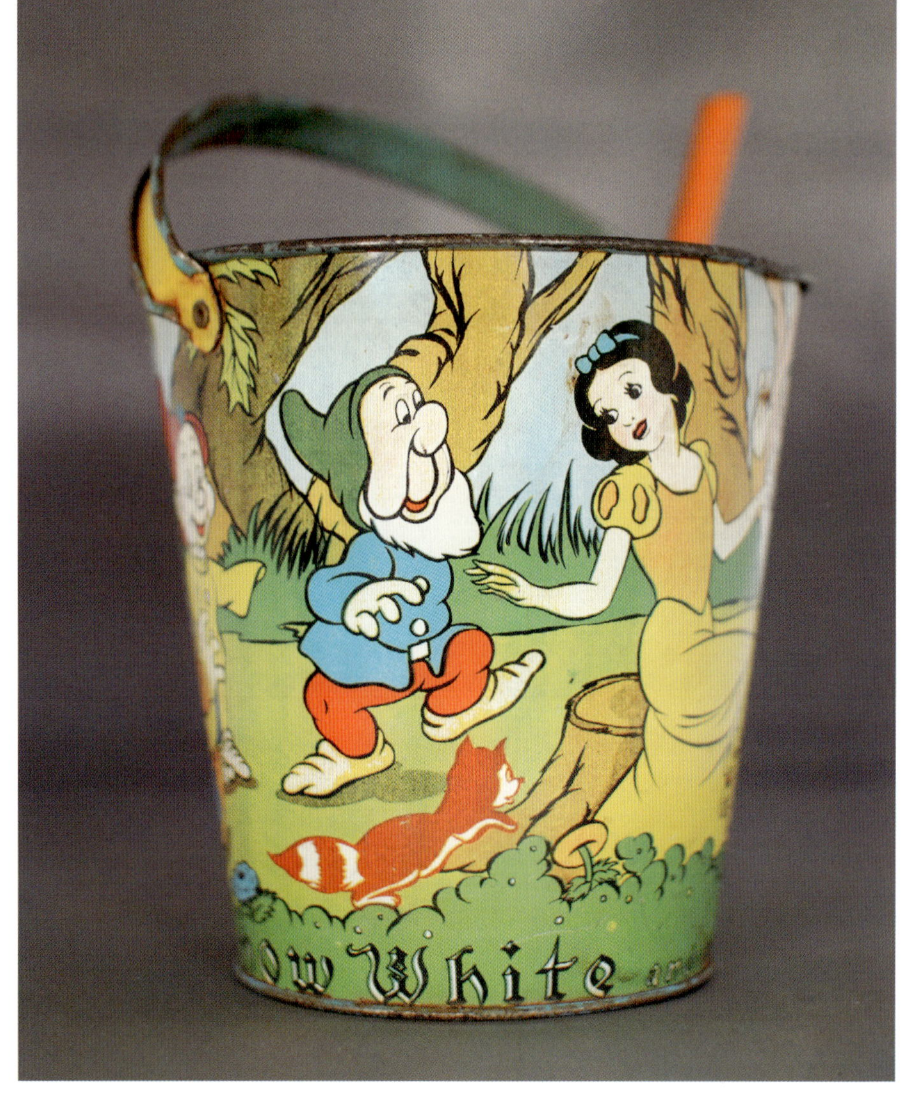

6″ Snow White pail with an 8.5″ shovel. The four views show Snow White sitting among the dwarfs. Marked ©1938 Walt Disney Enterprises Ohio Art Co., U.S.A. $500-800

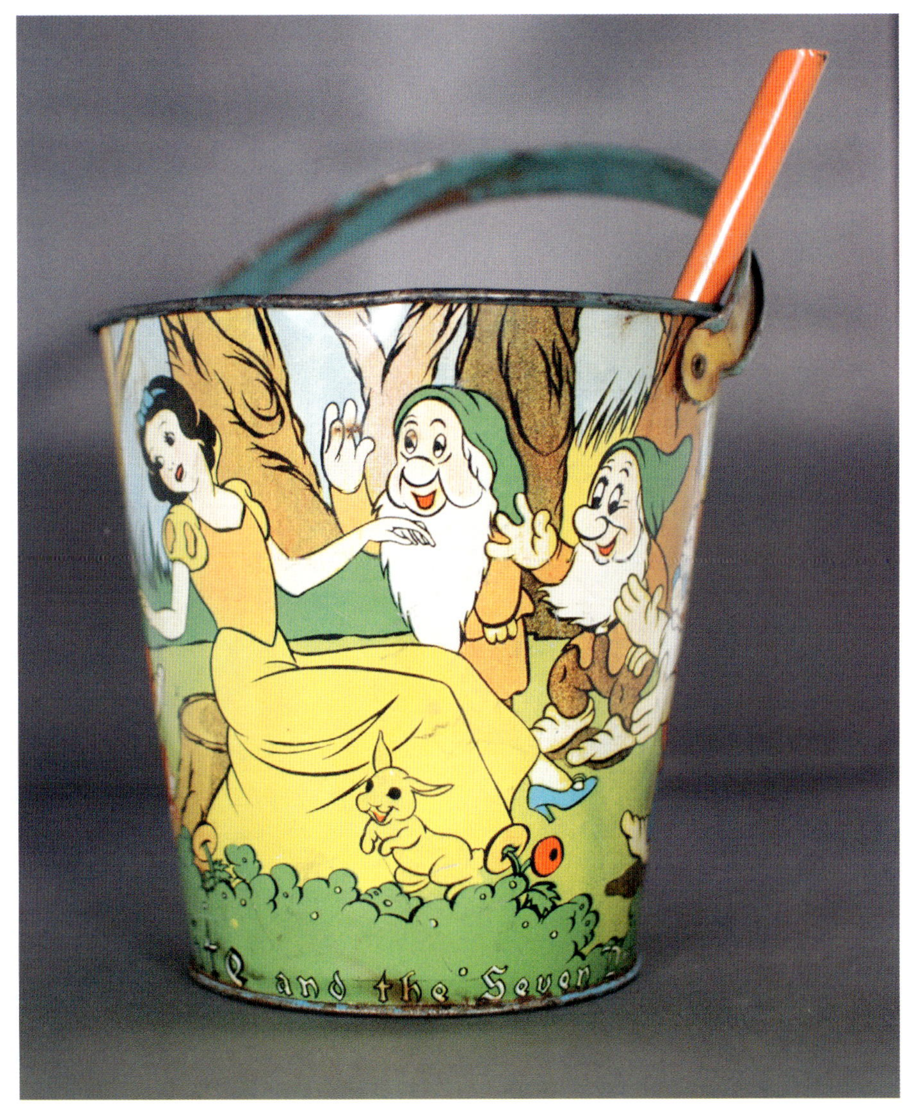
and the Seven
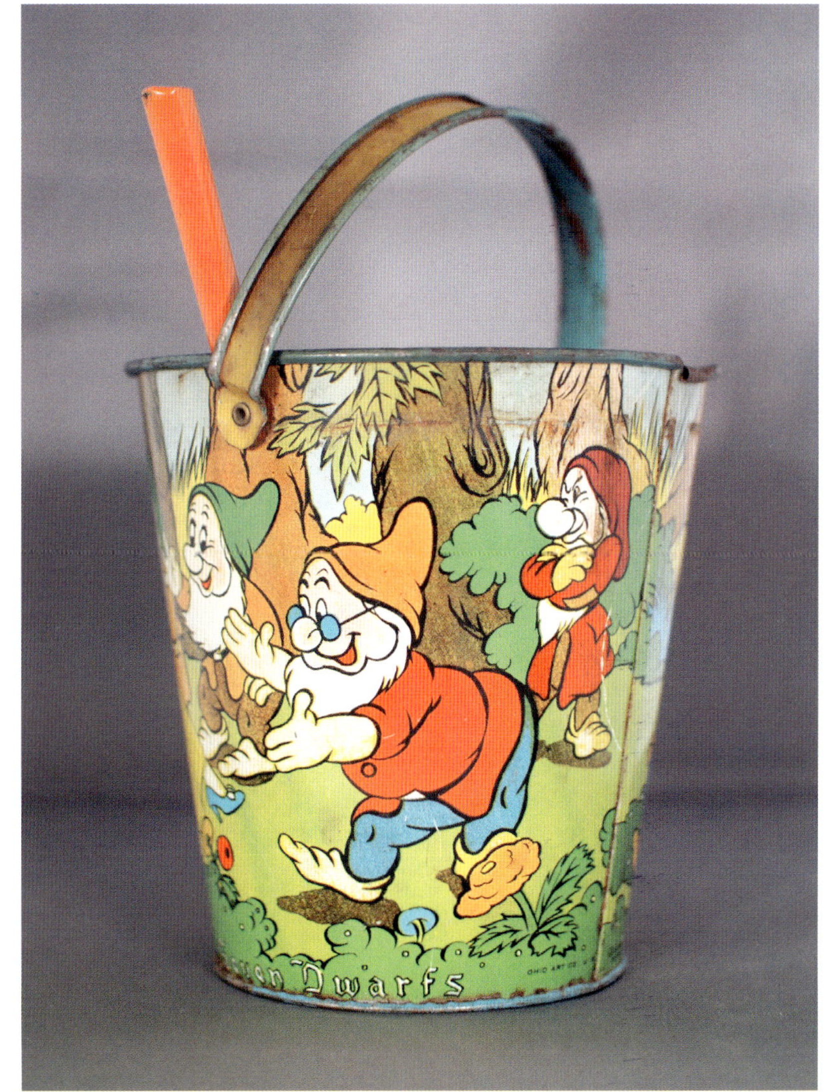
Dwarfs

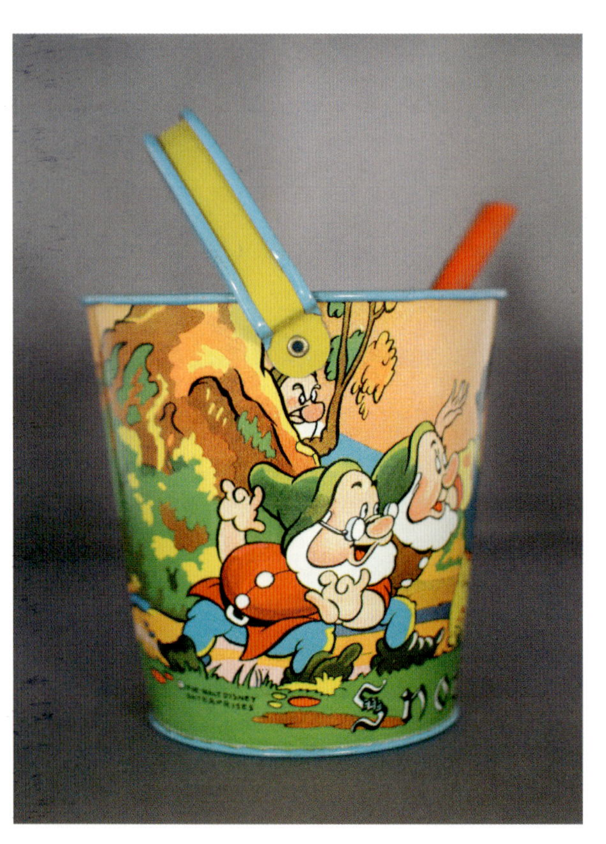

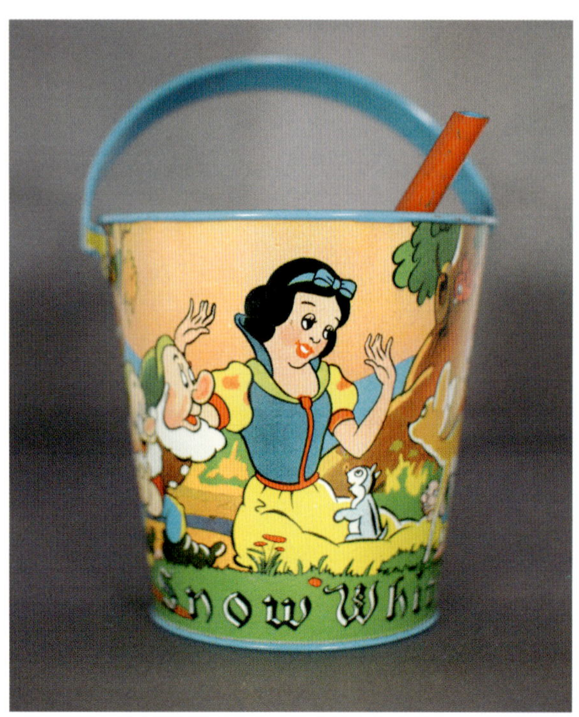

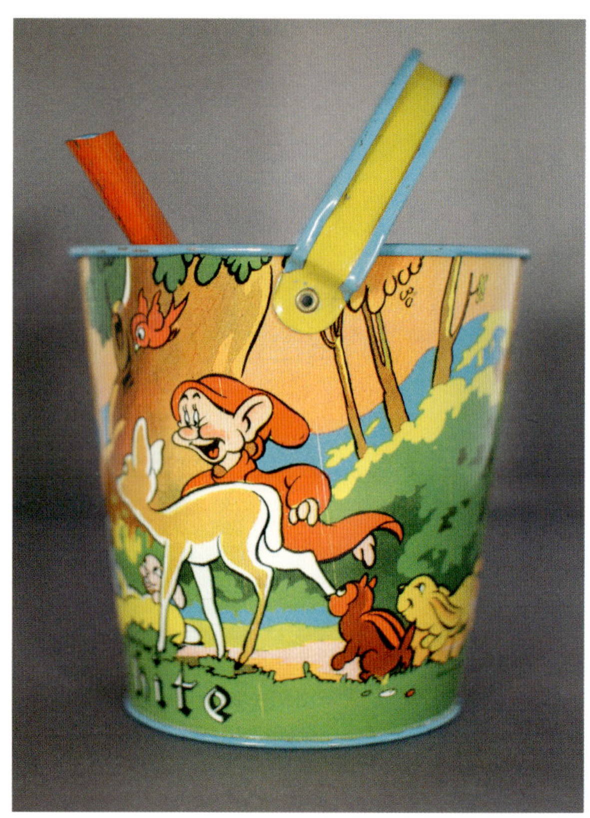

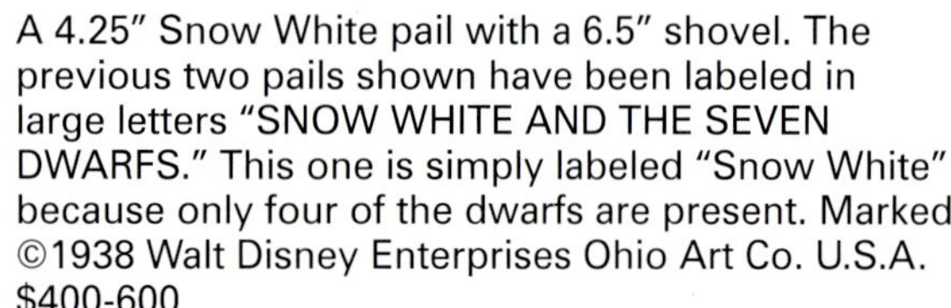

A 4.25" Snow White pail with a 6.5" shovel. The previous two pails shown have been labeled in large letters "SNOW WHITE AND THE SEVEN DWARFS." This one is simply labeled "Snow White" because only four of the dwarfs are present. Marked ©1938 Walt Disney Enterprises Ohio Art Co. U.S.A. $400-600

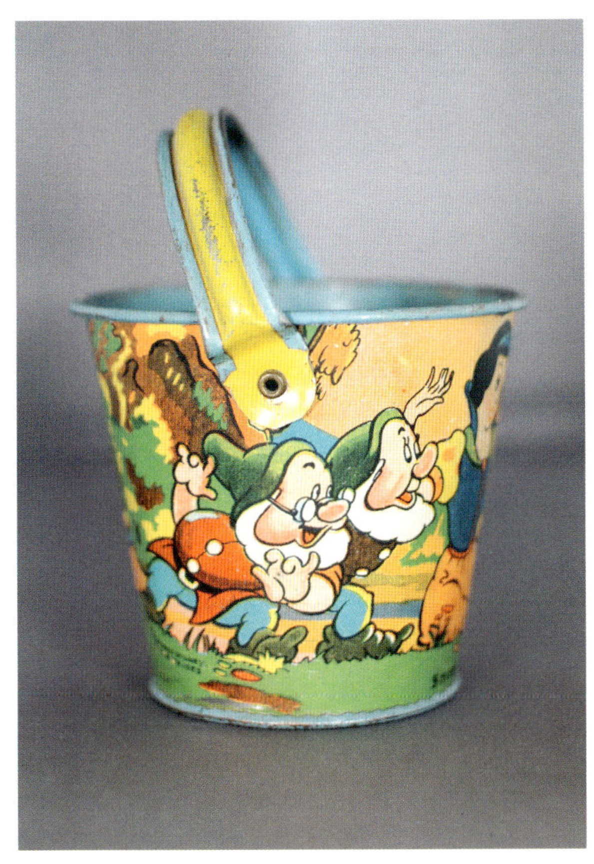

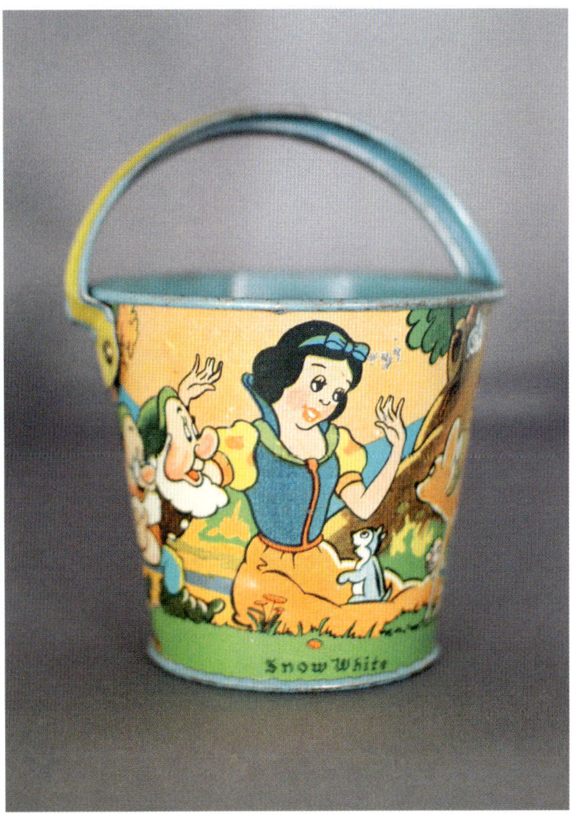

3″ Snow White pail. She is sitting with some animals while three dwarfs look on. Same image as 4.25″ pail. ©Walt Disney Enterprises Ohio Art Co. U.S.A. *Bernabe collection* $150-300

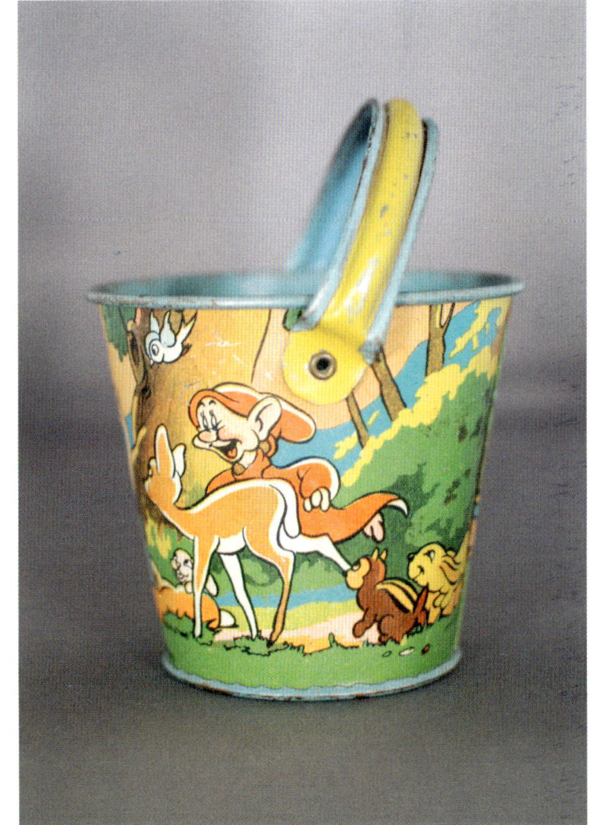

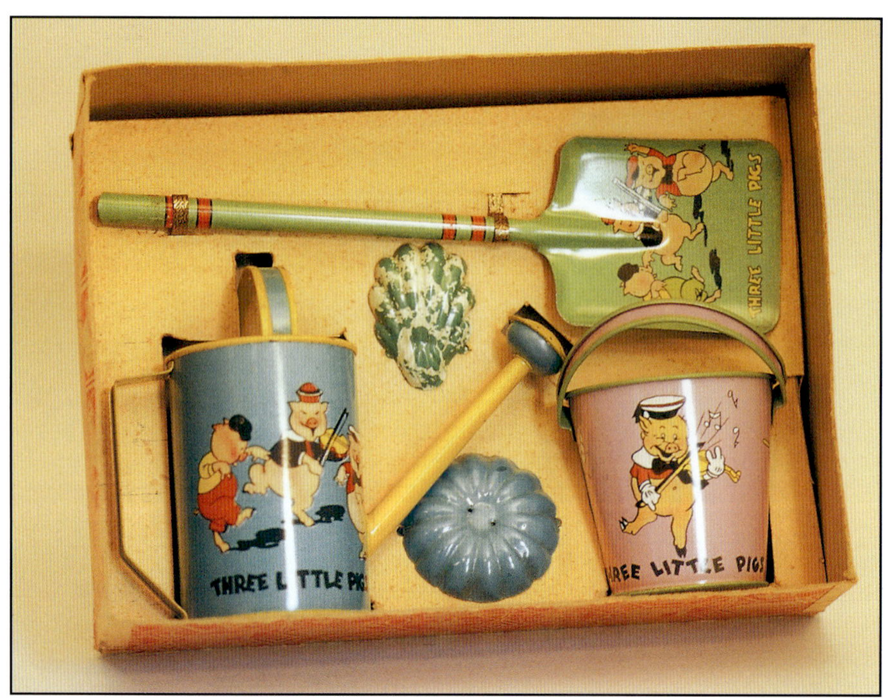

The Three Little Pigs

Big Bad Wolf

Little Red Riding Hood

The Three Little Pigs, a Silly Symphony, had its first showing on May 27, 1933. It was the most popular of Disney's early cartoon shorts. It was also their most profitable. Other shorts in the series were *The Big Bad Wolf* (1934), *Three Little Wolves* (1936), and *The Practical Pig* (1939.) The wolf was always the Pigs' wily foe. He could always fool Fiddler and Fifer pig, but never Practical pig. Ohio Art produced several wonderful pails, shovels and watering cans using these images.

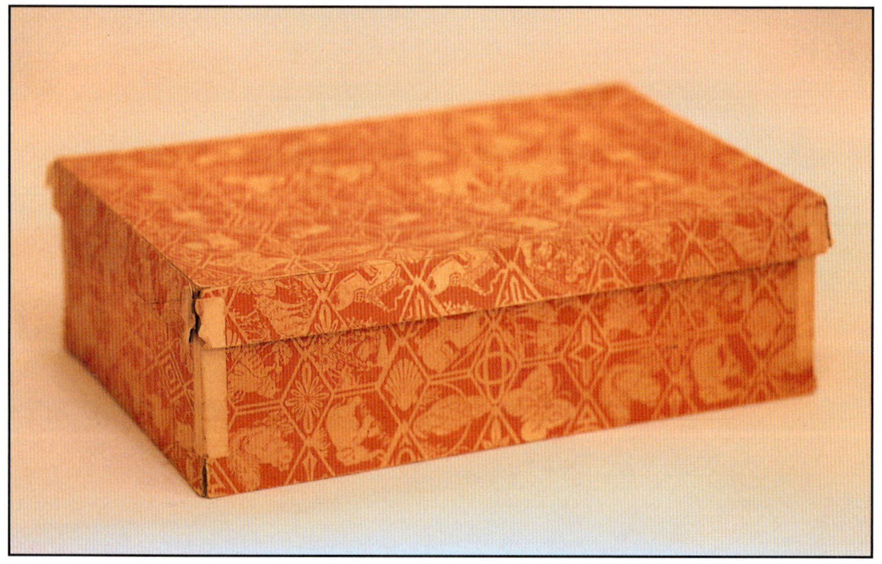

This wonderful Three Pigs sand kit set by Ohio Art contains a 3" pail, a 10" shovel and a 5.75" watering can, all with Three Pigs design plus two shell molds in a generic box. *Collection of Carl Lobel, Photographer Craig Keown.* $1,250-1,750

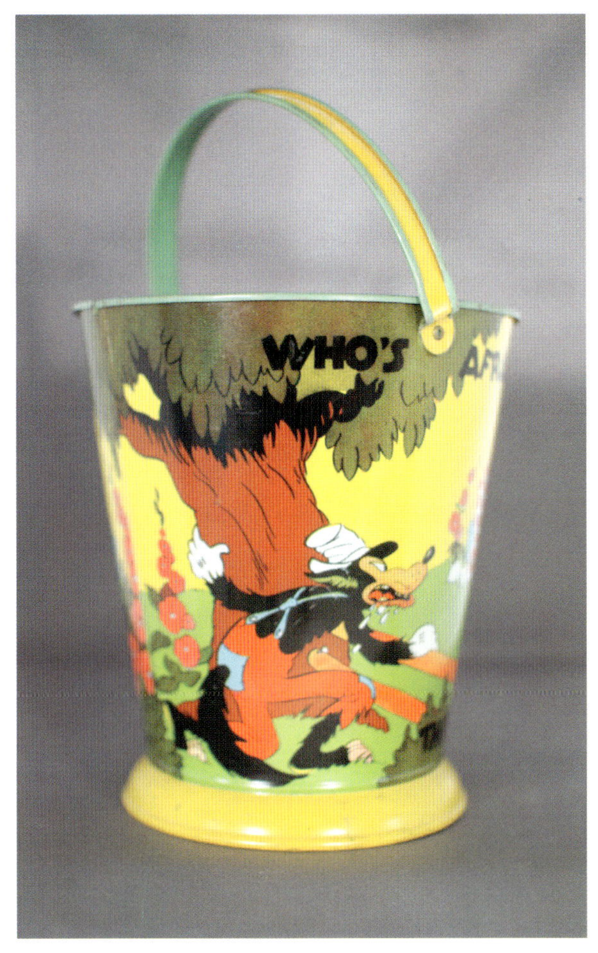

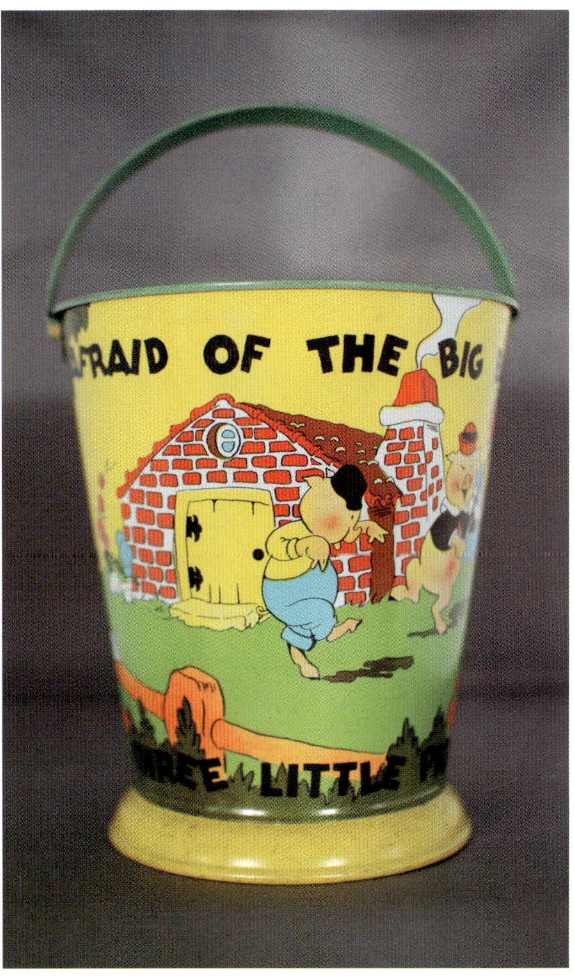

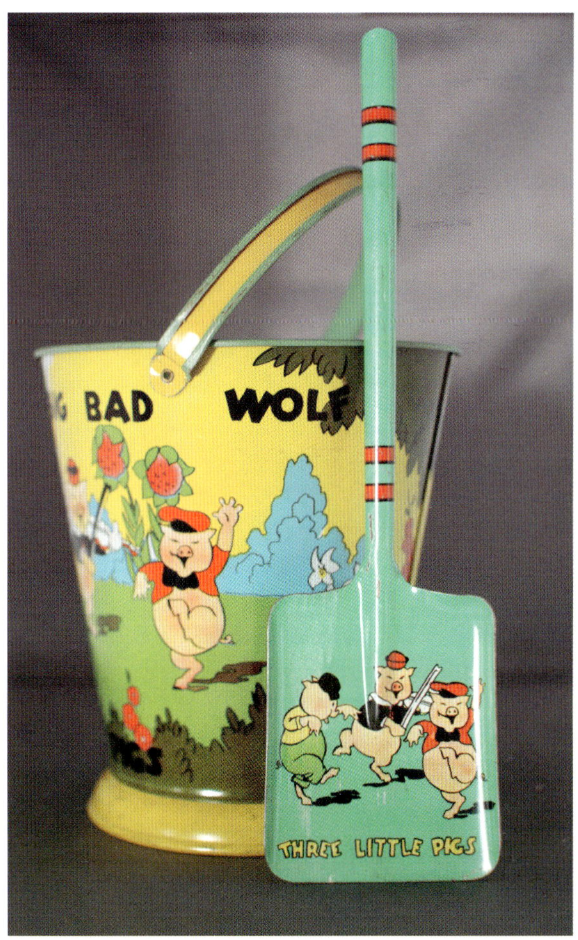

A 7.25" Who's Afraid of the Big Bad Wolf pail together with an 11.25" Three Pigs shovel. ©Walt Disney Ent. Ohio Art Co. Bryan, O. U.S.A. Pail and shovel combination $1,500-1,750 Without shovel $1,200-1400

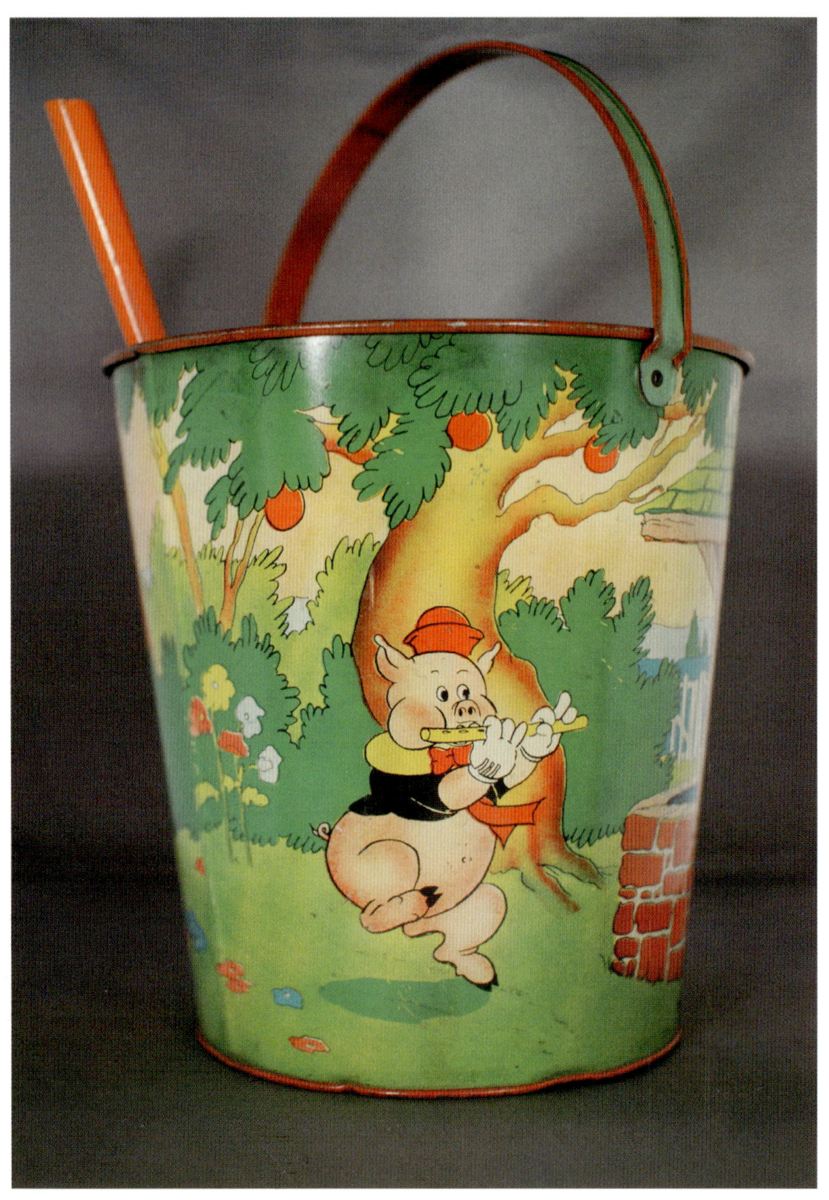

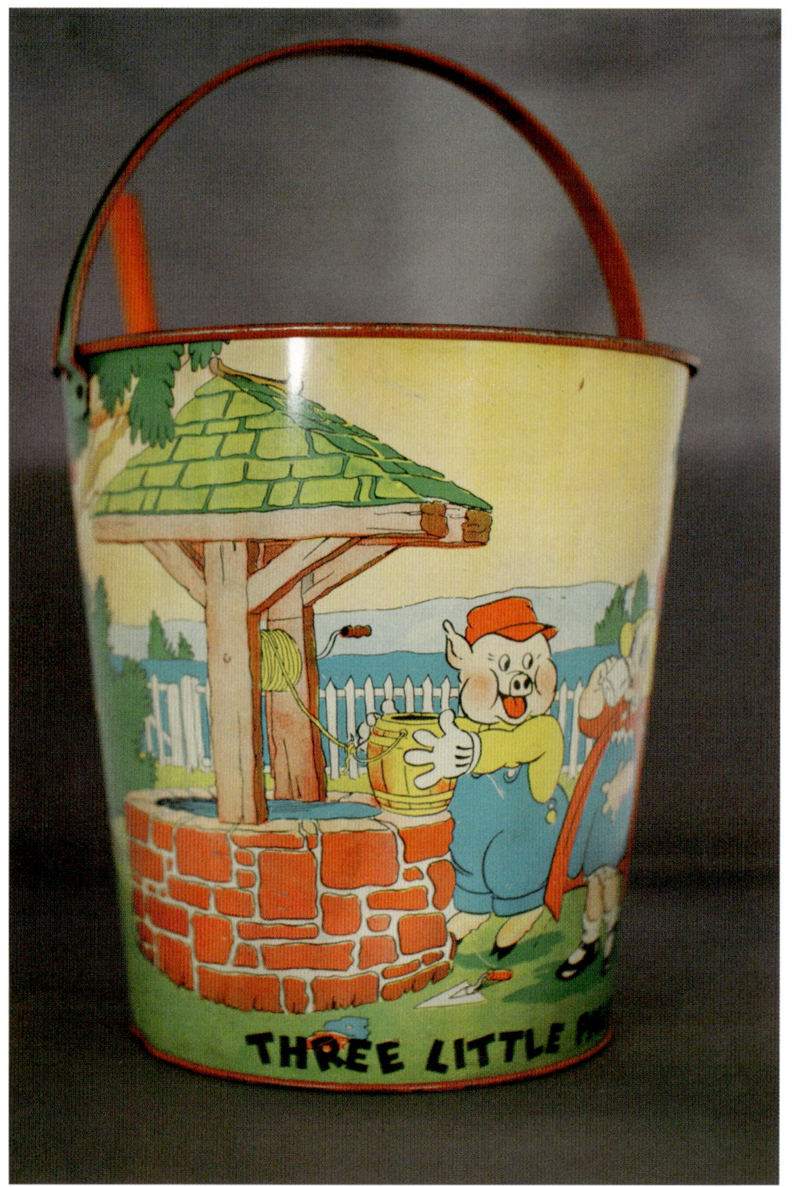

The 8″ Three Little Pigs and Red Riding Hood pail with an 11″ shovel. The four images feature Fifer Pig and Practical Pig at the well. Red Riding Hood and her grandmother together with Fiddler Pig. $900-1,200

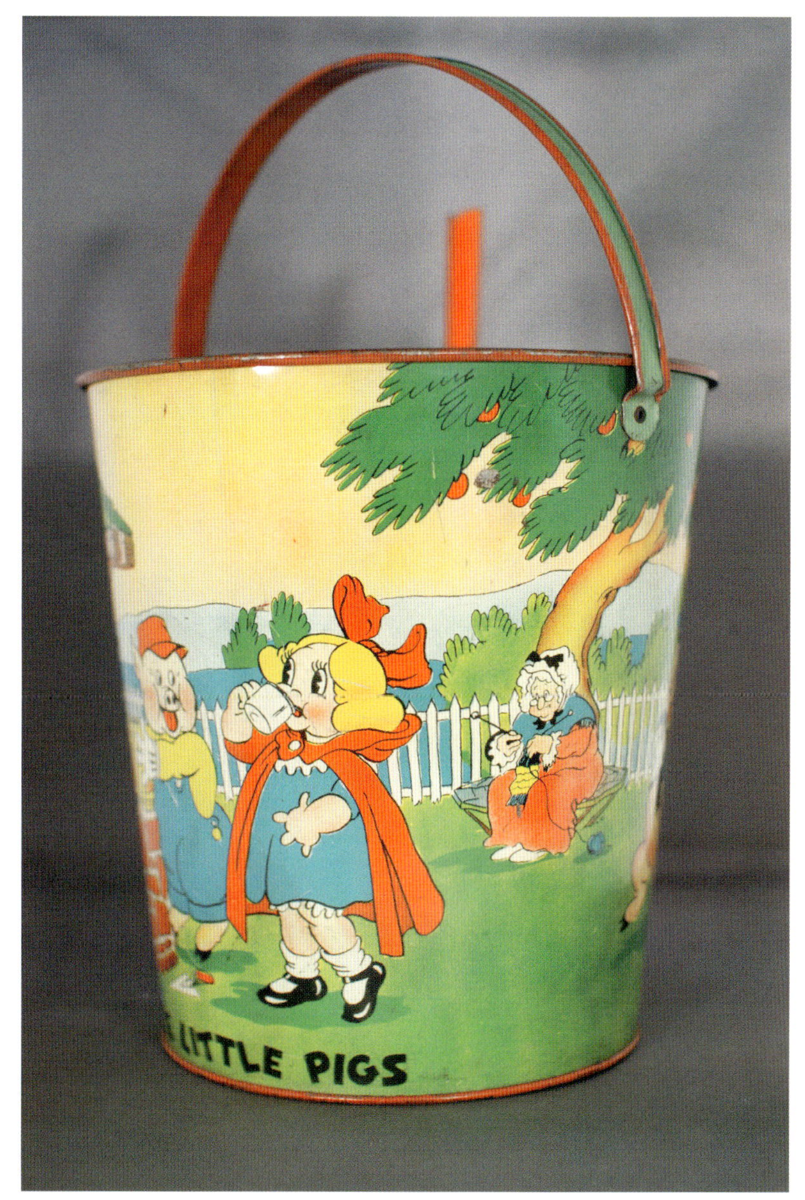
LITTLE PIGS

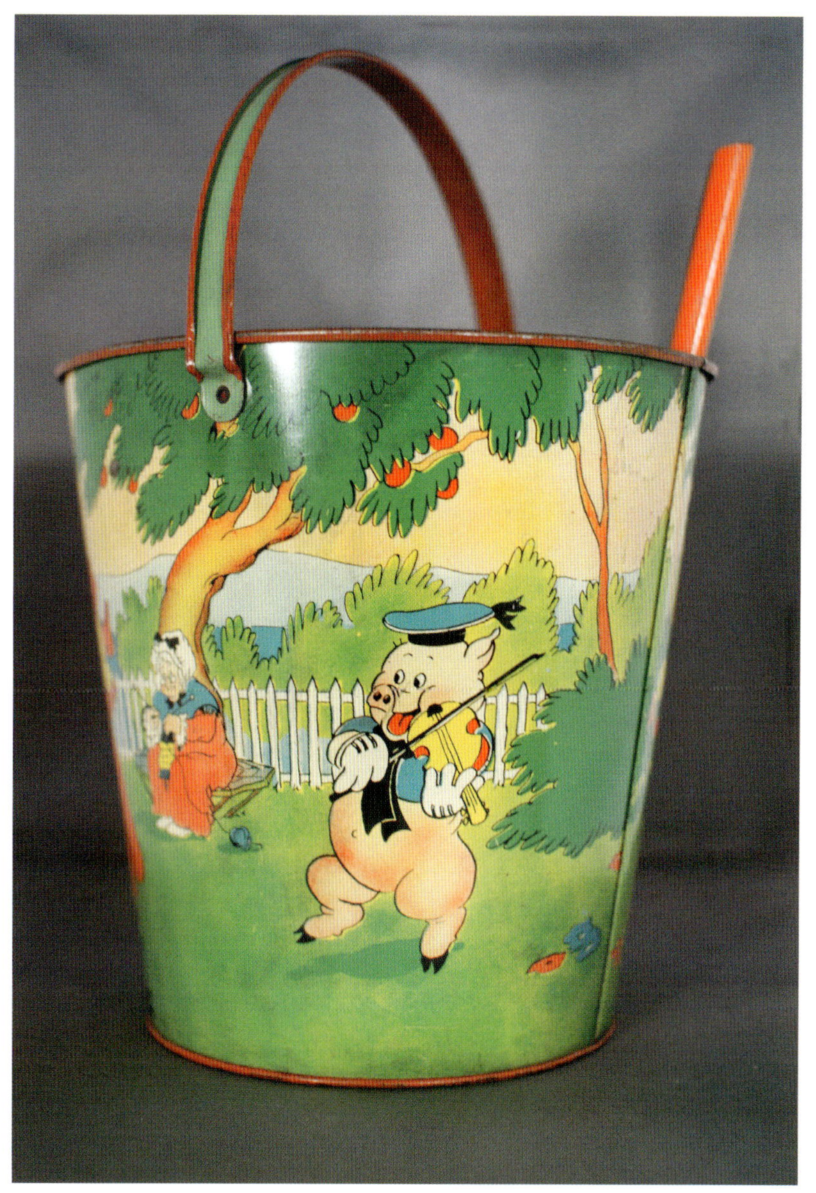

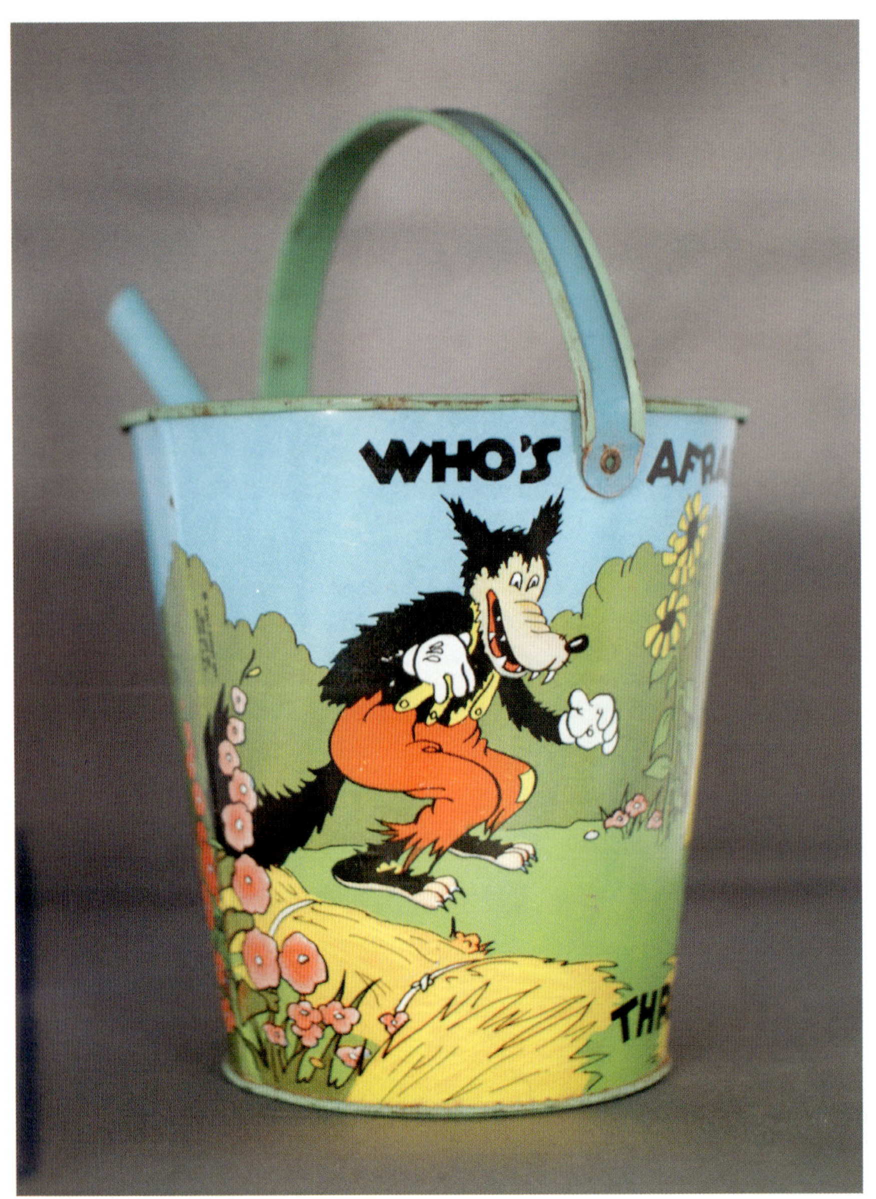

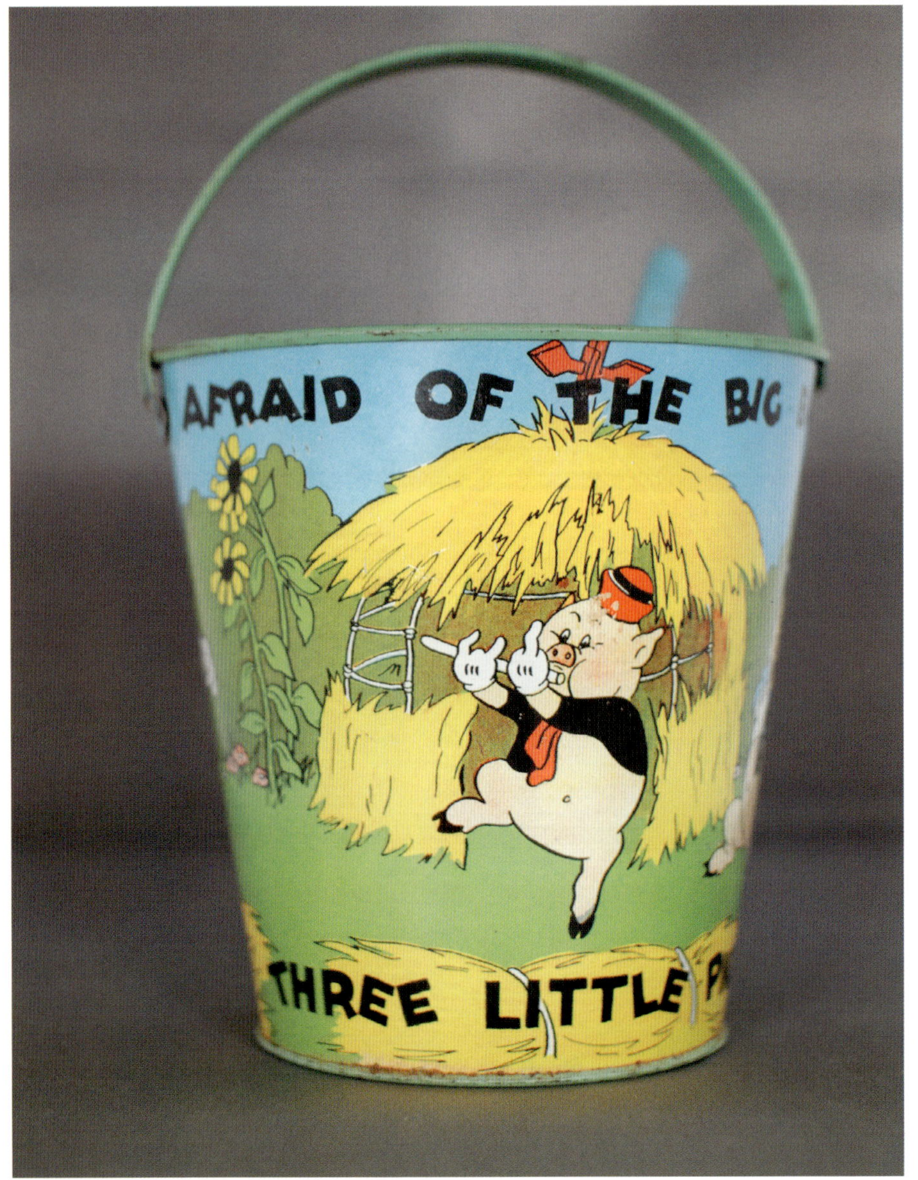

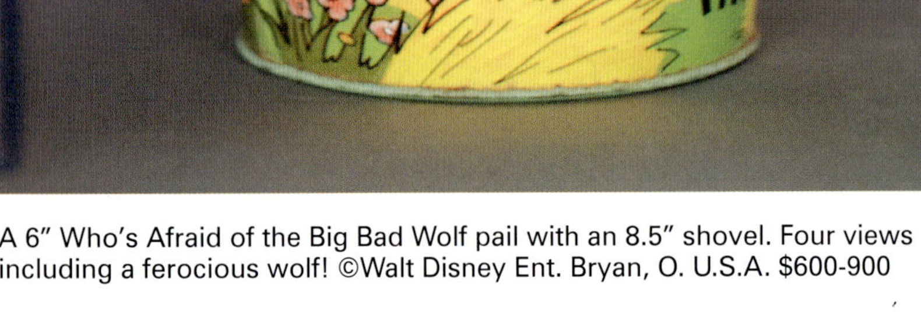

A 6″ Who's Afraid of the Big Bad Wolf pail with an 8.5″ shovel. Four views including a ferocious wolf! ©Walt Disney Ent. Bryan, O. U.S.A. $600-900

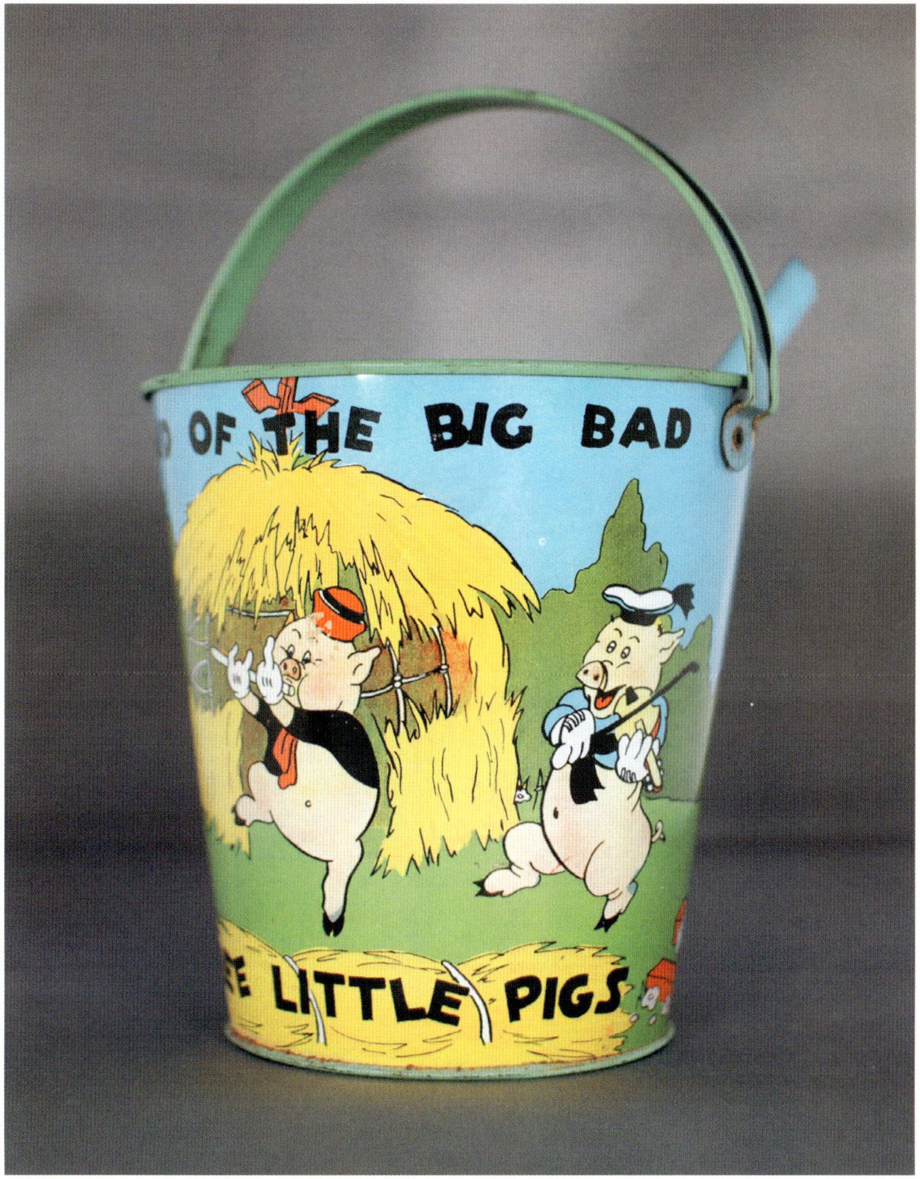

OF THE BIG BAD
LITTLE PIGS

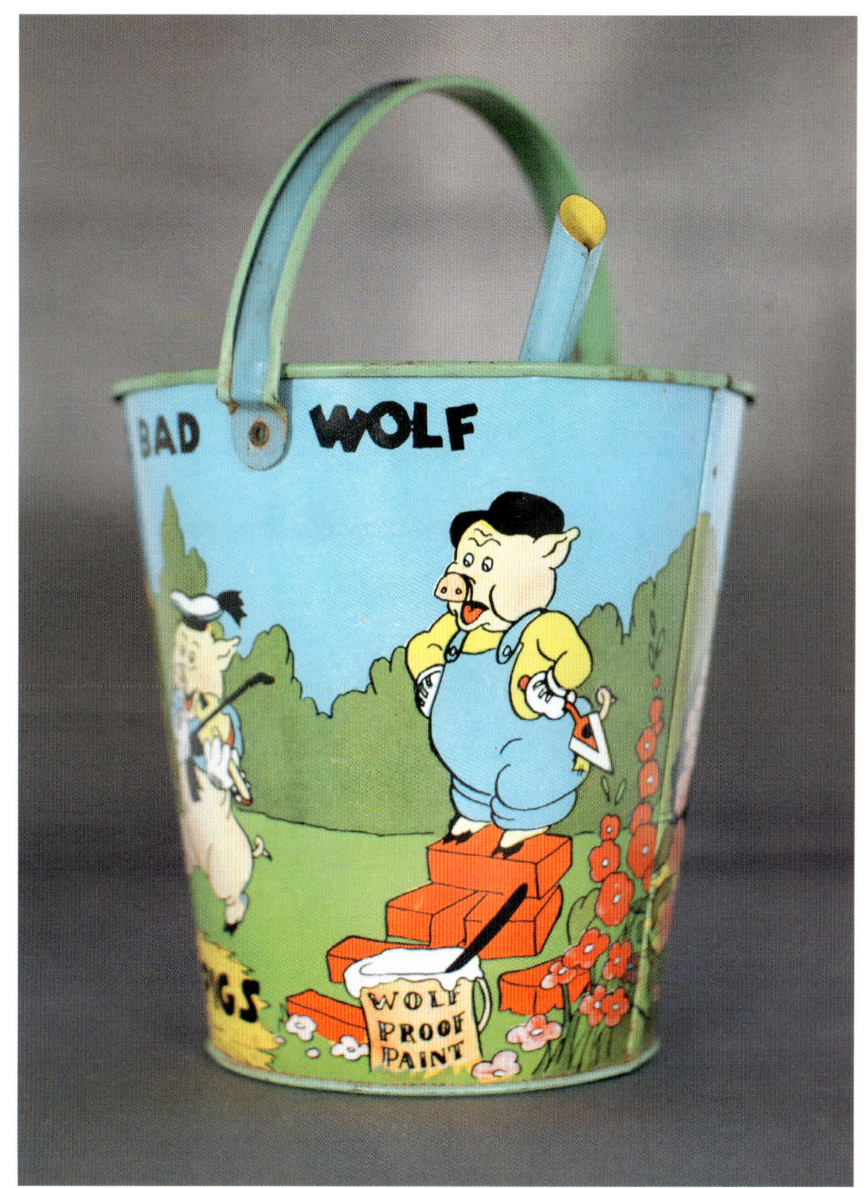
BAD WOLF
WOLF PROOF PAINT

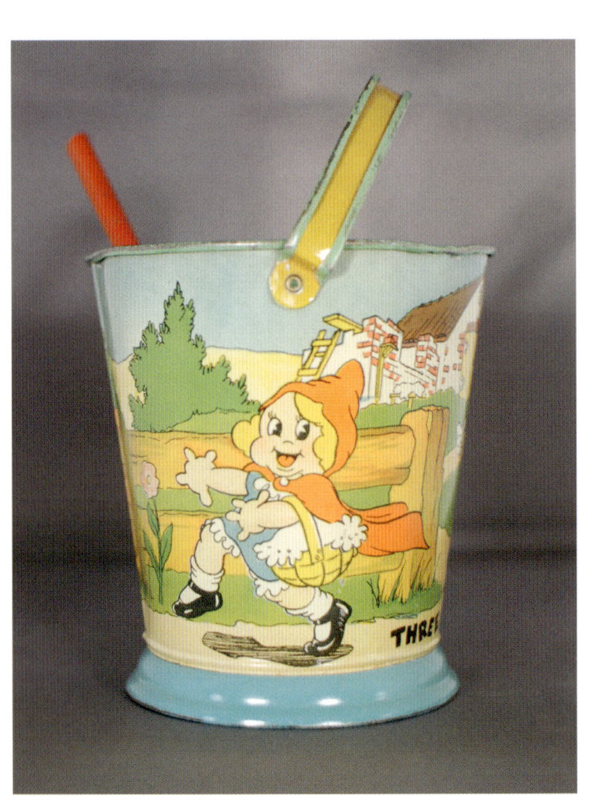

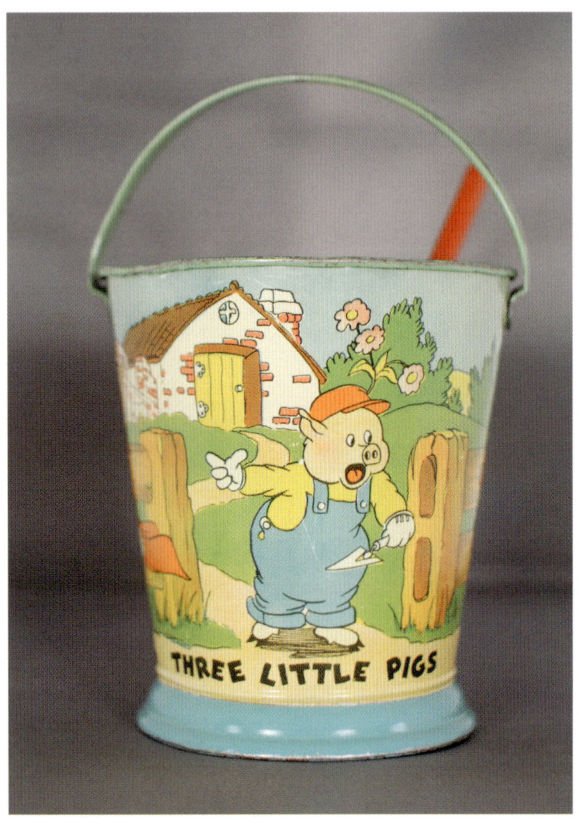

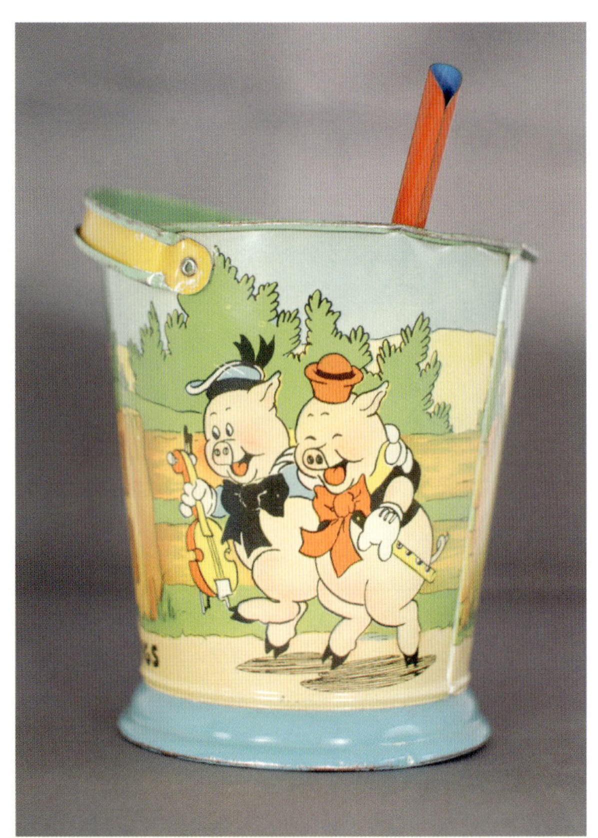

The 5.5" Three Pigs and Red Riding Hood pail with an 8" shovel. Three views of this marvelous sand pail. $450-750

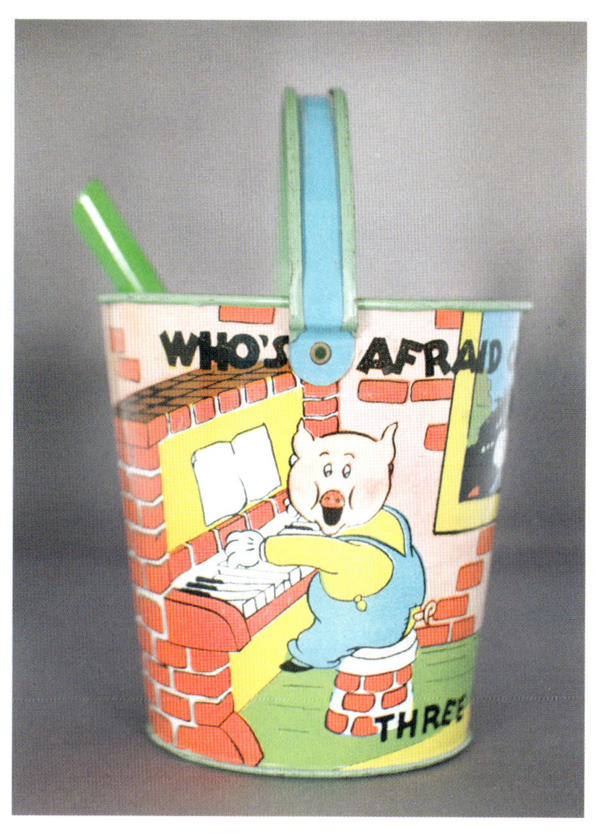

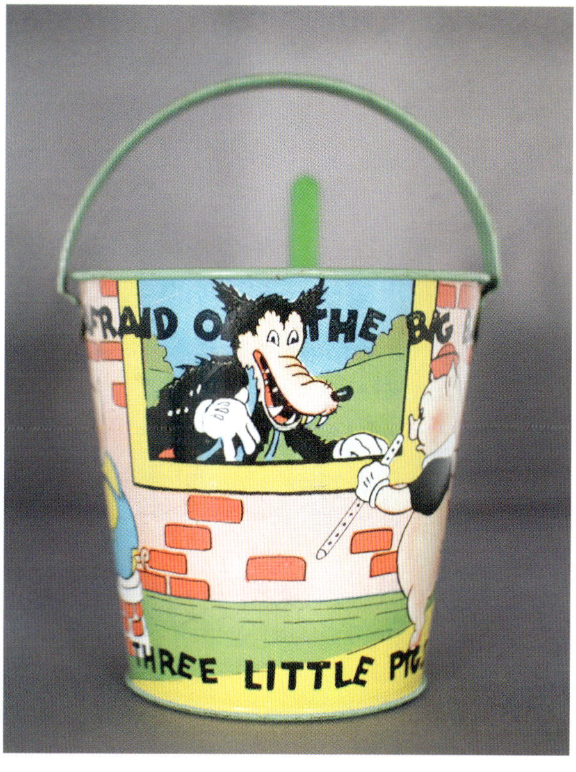

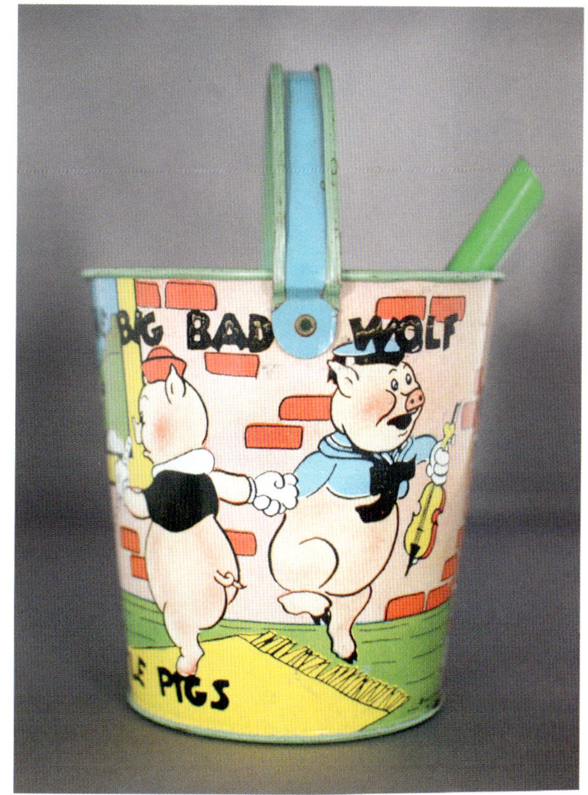

A 4.25" Who's Afraid of the Big Bad Wolf sand pail with a 6.25" shovel. Three views show a menacing wolf looking into the Three Pigs' room. ©Walt Disney Ent. Ohio Art Co. $450-750

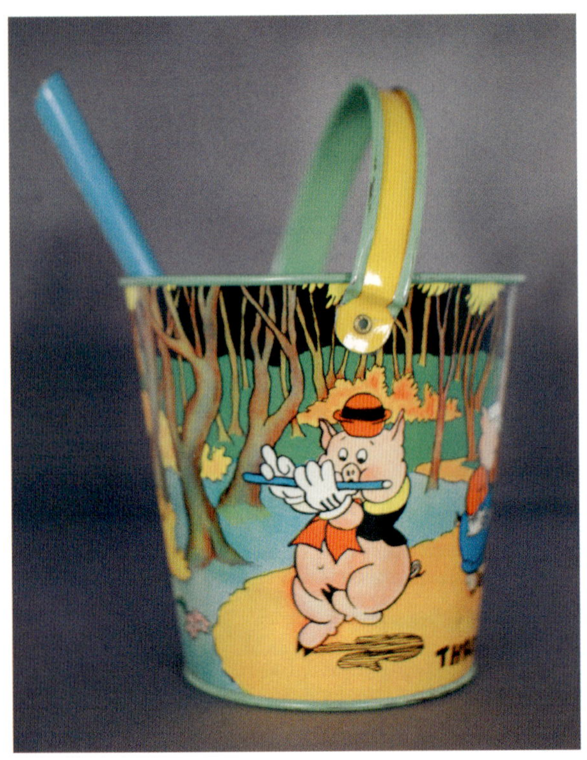

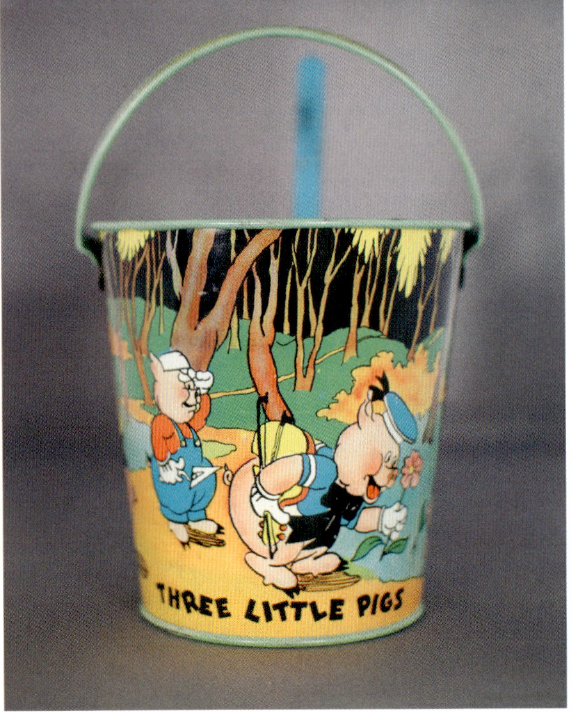

A 4.25″ Three Pigs pail with a 7″ shovel. Note the wolf lurking in the bushes. Due to seams, some Three Pigs pails are missing the copyright and Ohio Art logo $350-650

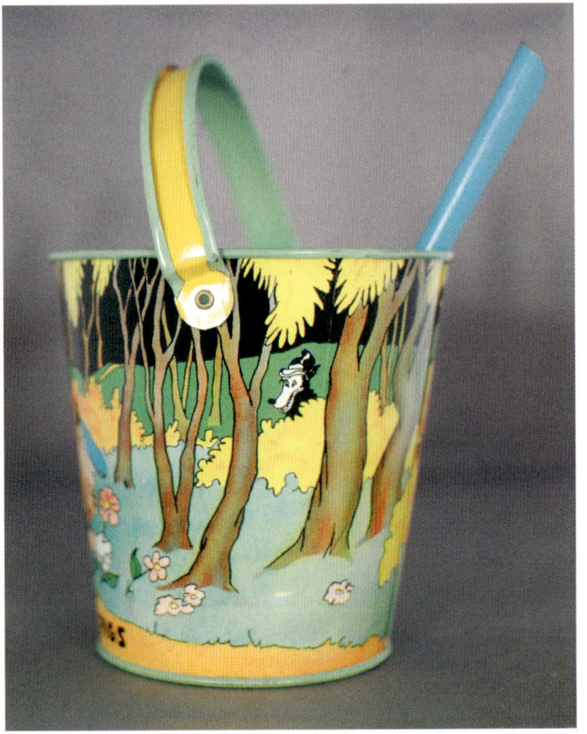

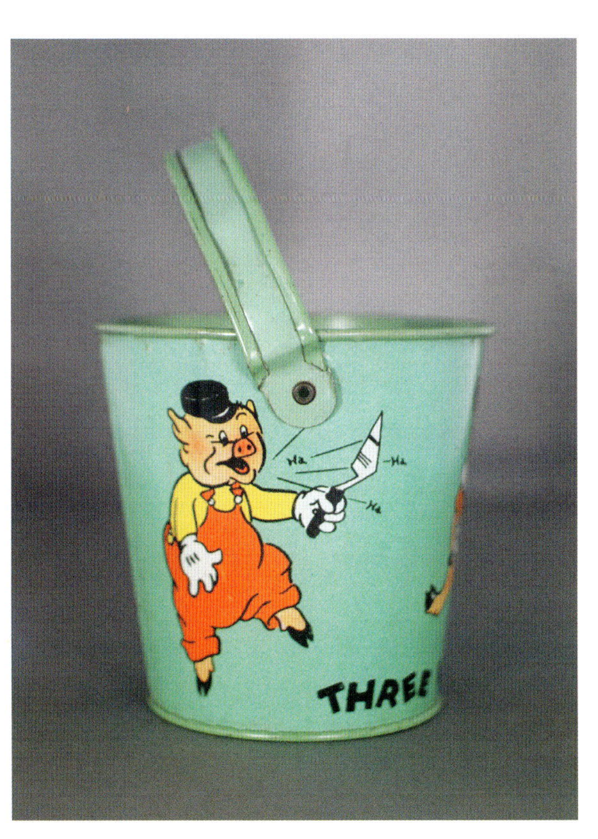

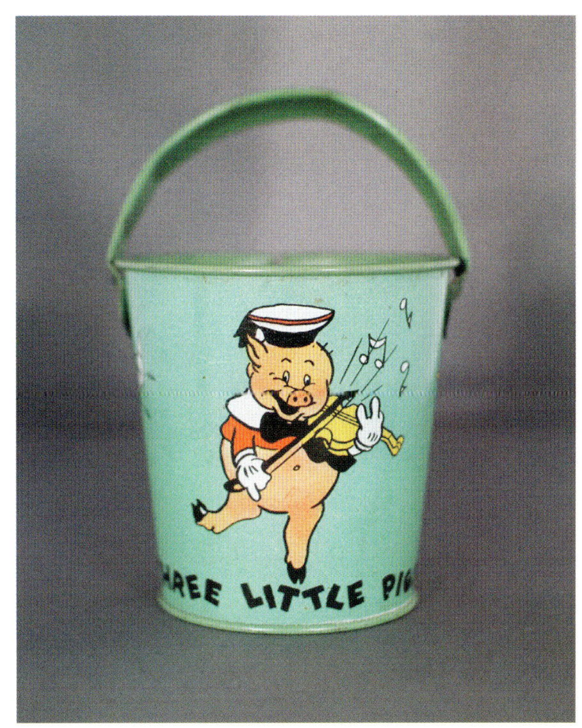

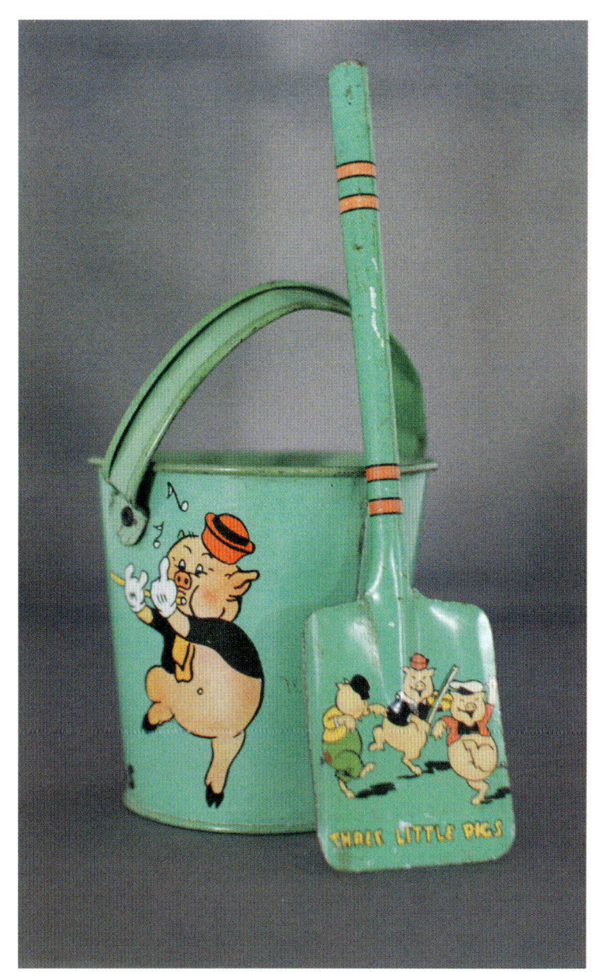

A 3.5″ Three Little Pigs pail with a 7″ Three Pigs shovel. Three views each showing one of the pigs and one includes the shovel. They also made a 3″ version of the same pail.©Walt Disney Enterprises Ohio Art Co. Bryan, O. U.S.A. The copyright appears on both pail and shovel $550-750 Pail only $300-500

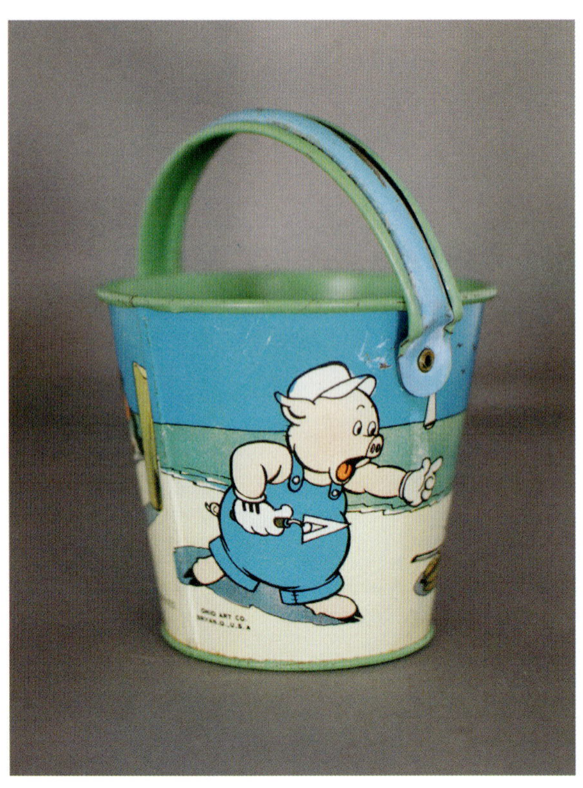

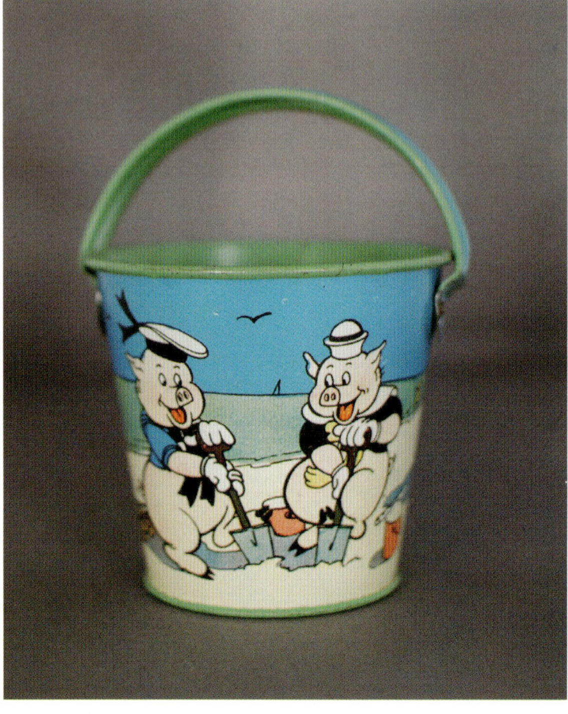

A 3" Three Little Pigs sand pail. Three views showing the pigs on the beach with the Big Bad Wolf lurking. ©Walt Disney Enterprises Ohio Art Co. Bryan, O. U.S.A. $325-550

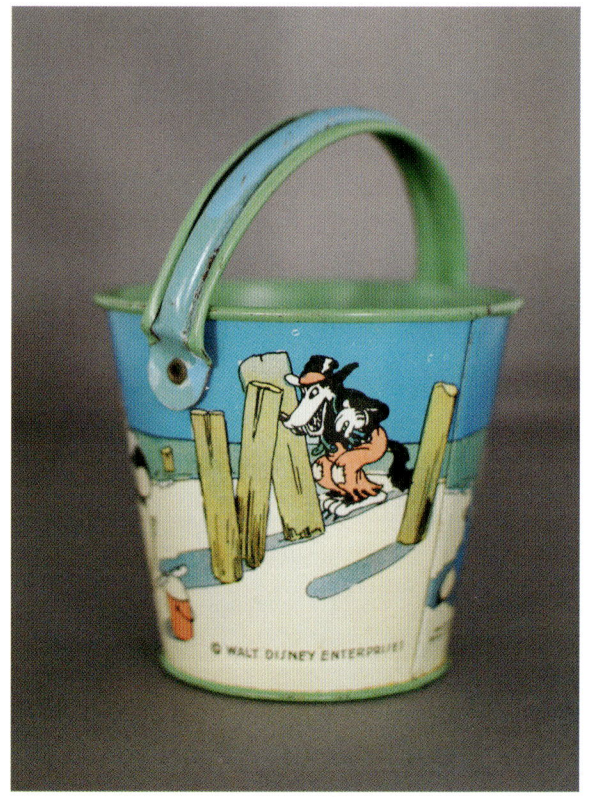

Disney Shovels

Ohio Art

Disney illustrated shovels are among the most difficult sand toys to find. The Mickey Mouse series of sand shovels came in six sizes. The four smaller ones were all of tin and were parts of sets, either boxed kits, sieve sets, or with pails. The two large shovels had wood handles and were sold separately.

There are two Donald Duck sand shovels. Each has a wood handle and each was sold separately. Each sand shovel depicted a beach scene. Ohio Art also made two snow shovels and each pictured a snow scene. Ohio Art produced three sand shovels depicting the Three Pigs. Each was a different size, but featured the same image of the pigs dancing.

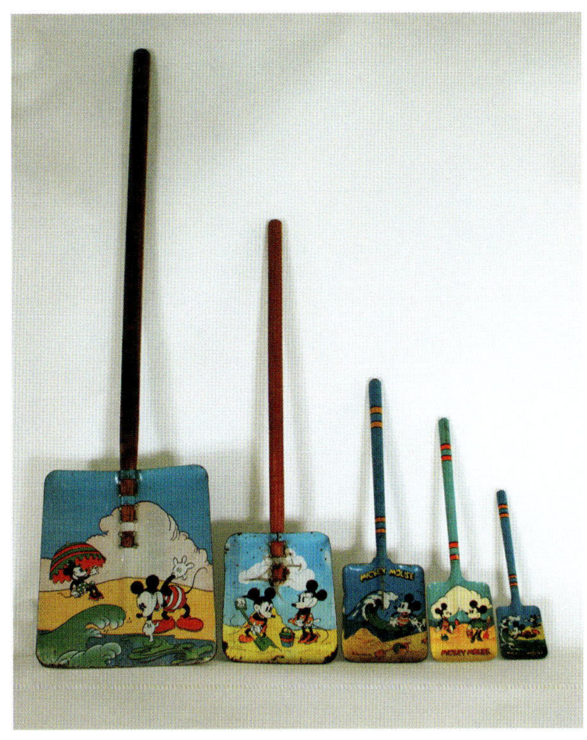

A picture of five Mickey Mouse sand shovels showing relative size. Total heights including handles are: 7″, 10″, 11.5″, 17.5″ and 25″. There is also a 6″ all tin shovel. All five pictured shovels feature scenes at the beach. The three smallest shovels have tin handles. The detail views highlight the great graphics. All shovels ©Walt Disney Ent. Value varies $200-500

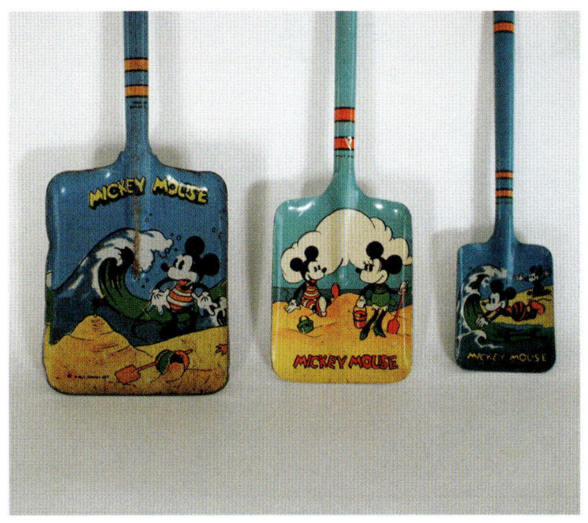

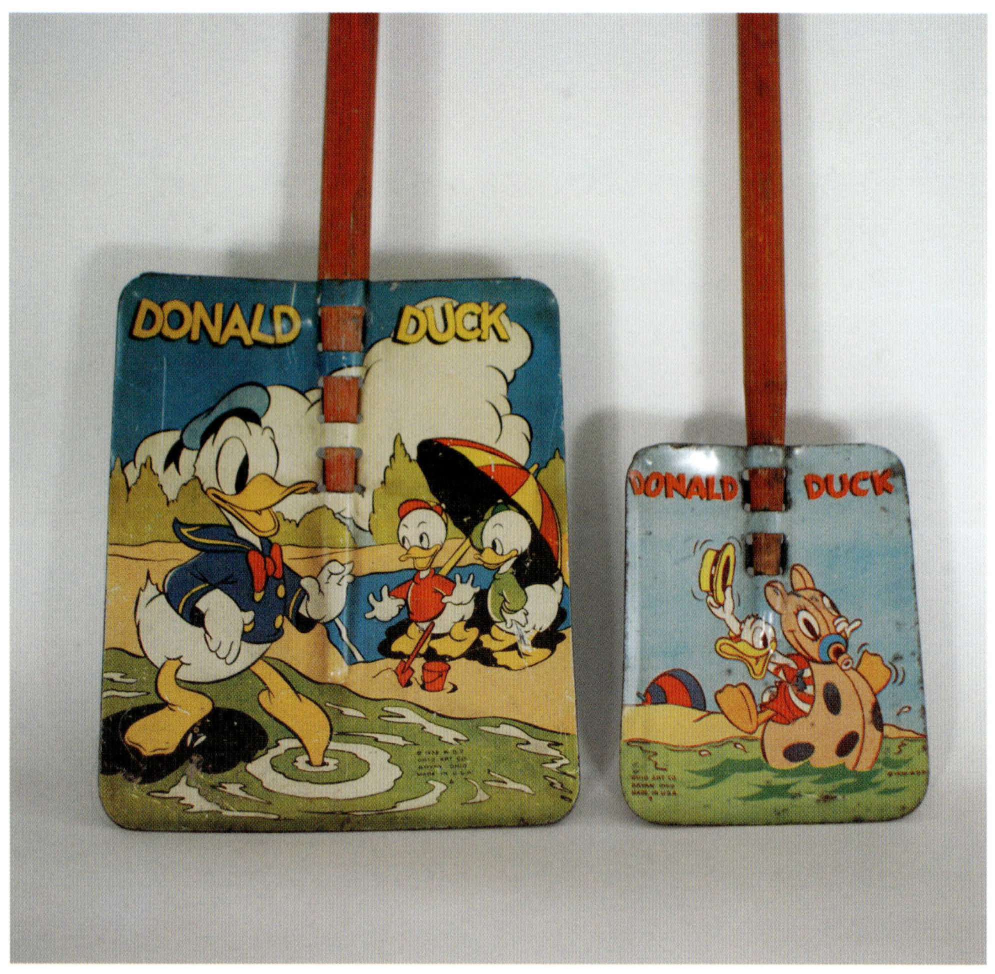

Detail of two Donald Duck shovels with wood handles. One is 17.5″ tall, the other 28″ tall. Both ©W.D.P. Ohio Art Co. Bryan, Ohio Made in U.S.A. $250-500

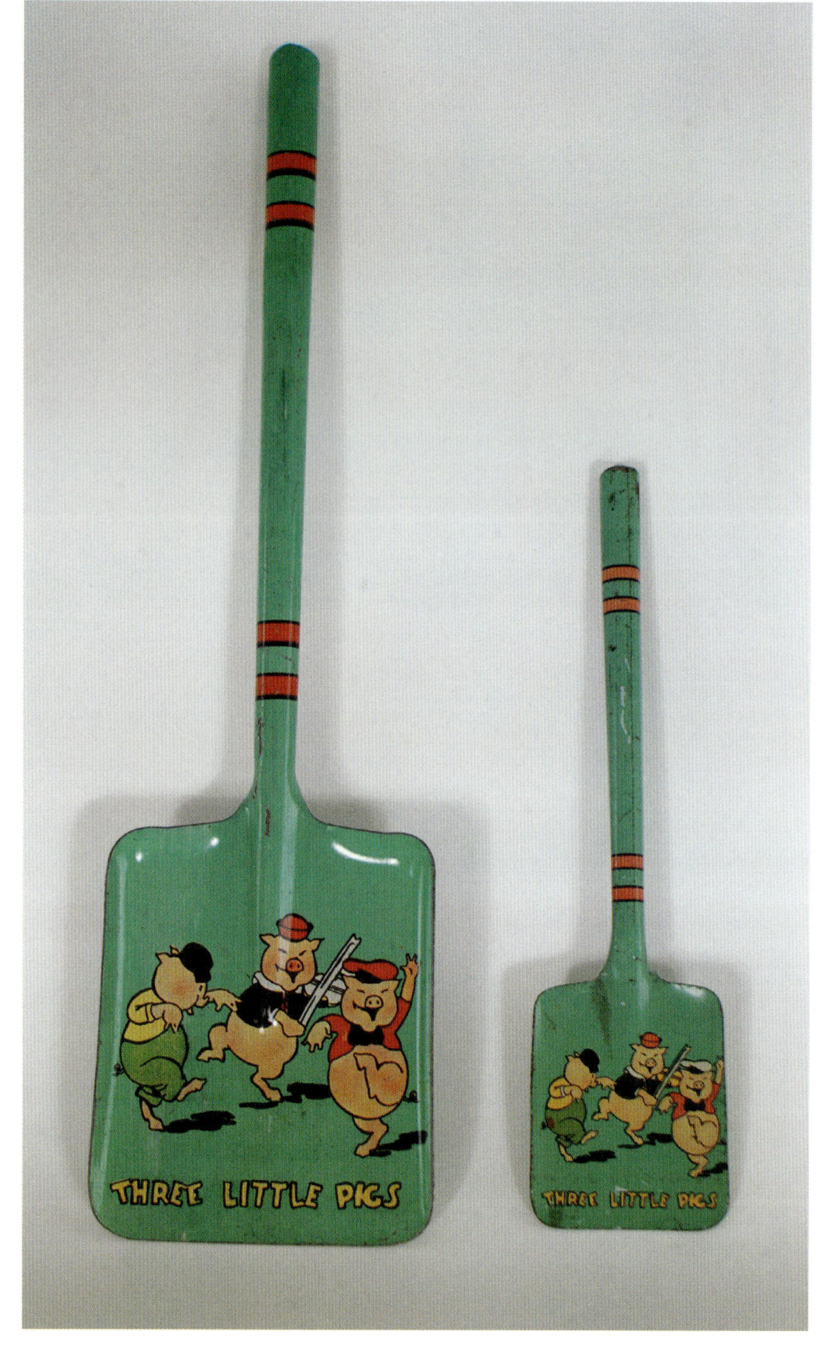

The all tin Three Little Pigs shovels came in three sizes: 7″, 10″ and 11.5″. They each had the same image. The 7″ and 11.5″ are pictured here. Each has a copyright on back of the handle: ©Walt Disney Ent. Ohio Art Co. Bryan, O. U.S.A. $200-300

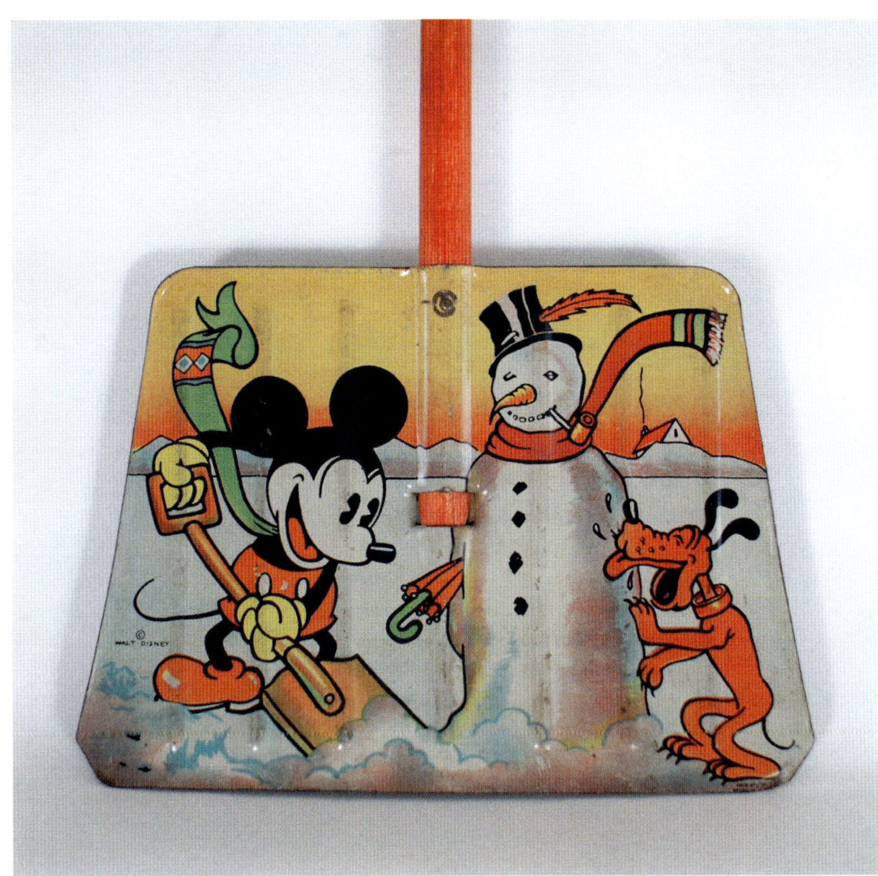

Mickey Mouse snow shovel. The shovel is 26" tall and features Mickey and Pluto building a snowman. Unlike the sand shovels, the snow shovels have a wooden cross piece at the top of the handle. ©Walt Disney $350-700

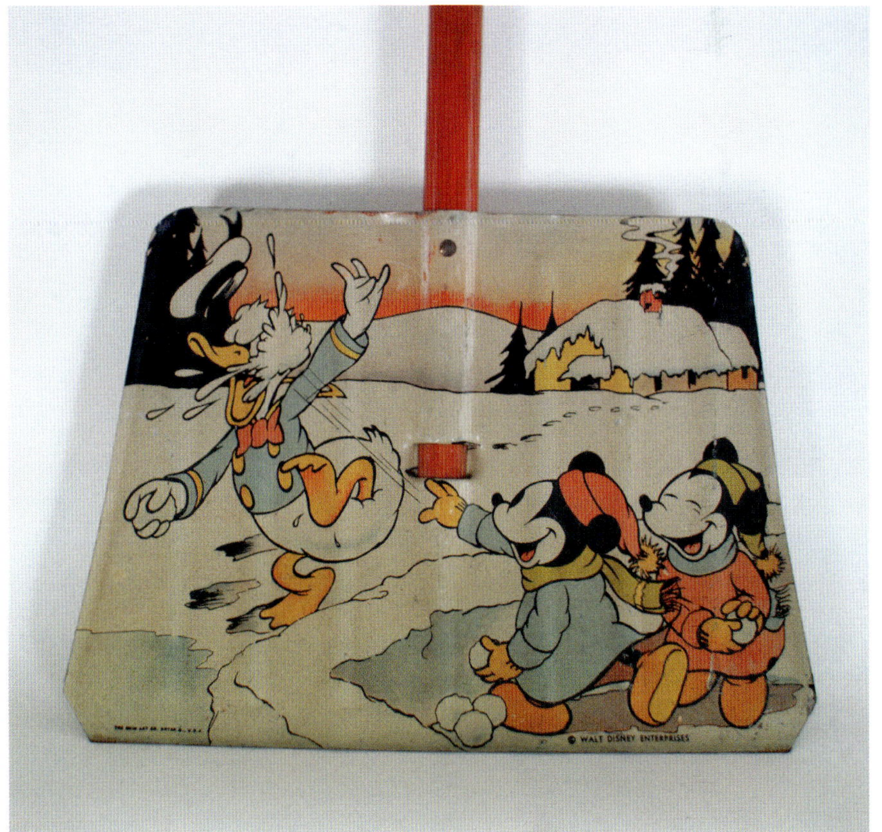

The Donald Duck snow shovel shows Donald being pelted with snow balls by Mickey's nephews. 27" tall. ©Walt Disney Enterprises The Ohio Art Co., Bryan, O. U.S.A. $300-600

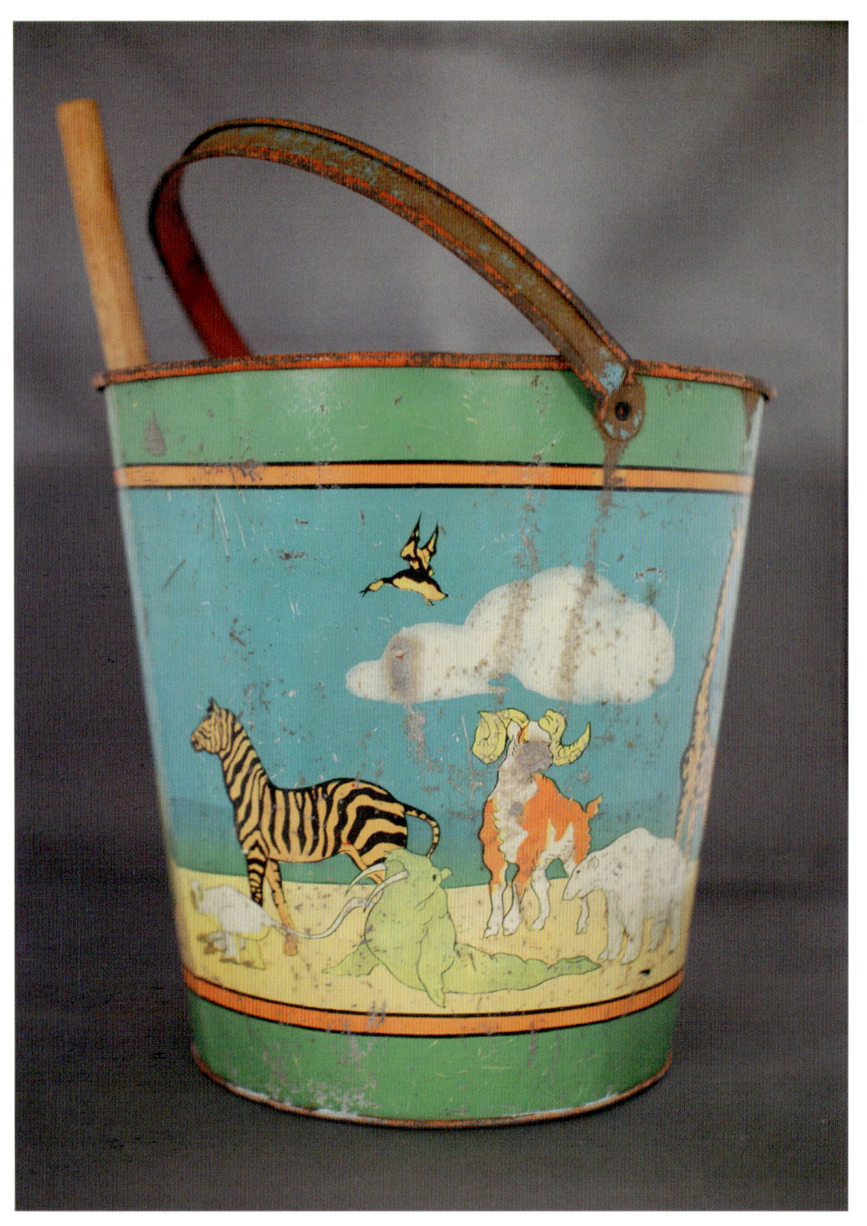

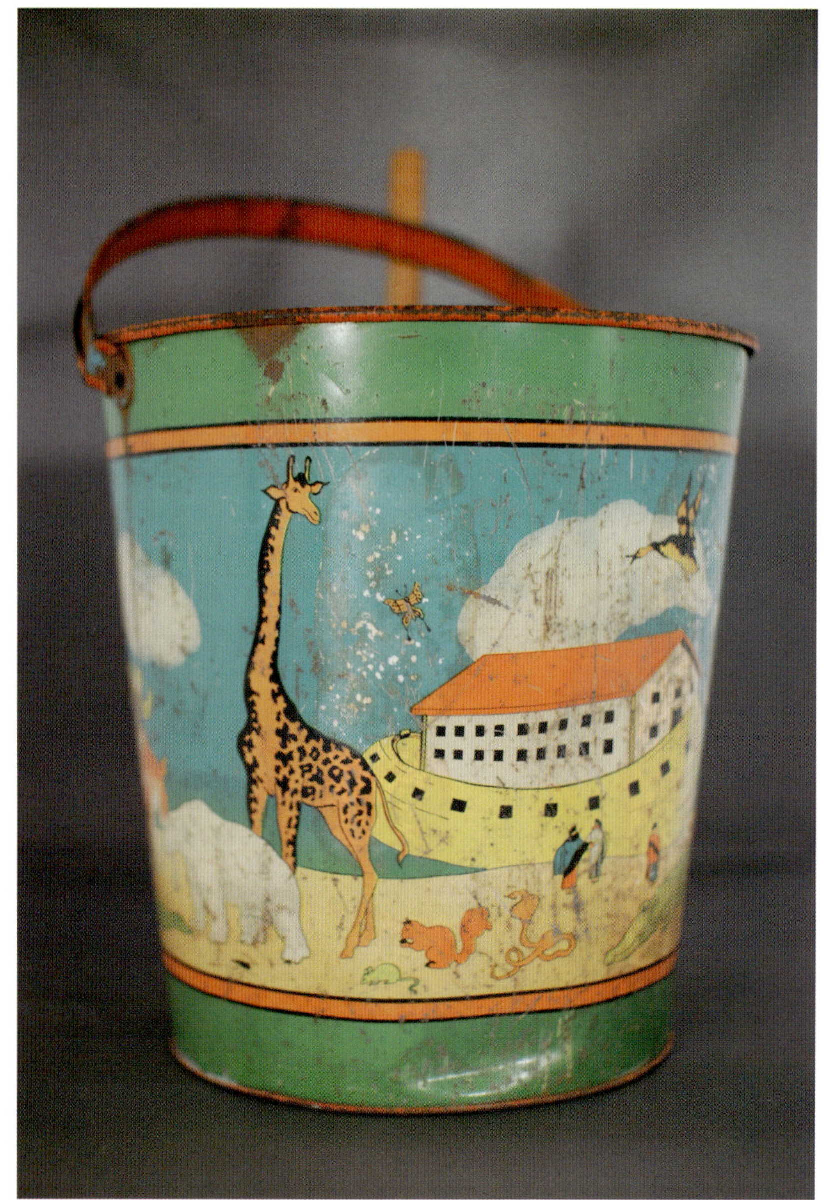

Four views of the 8″ Disney Noah's Ark pail. Extremely rare and difficult to find in good condition. ©Walt Disney Enterprises Mfg by Ohio Art Co., Bryan, O. U.S.A. $250-750

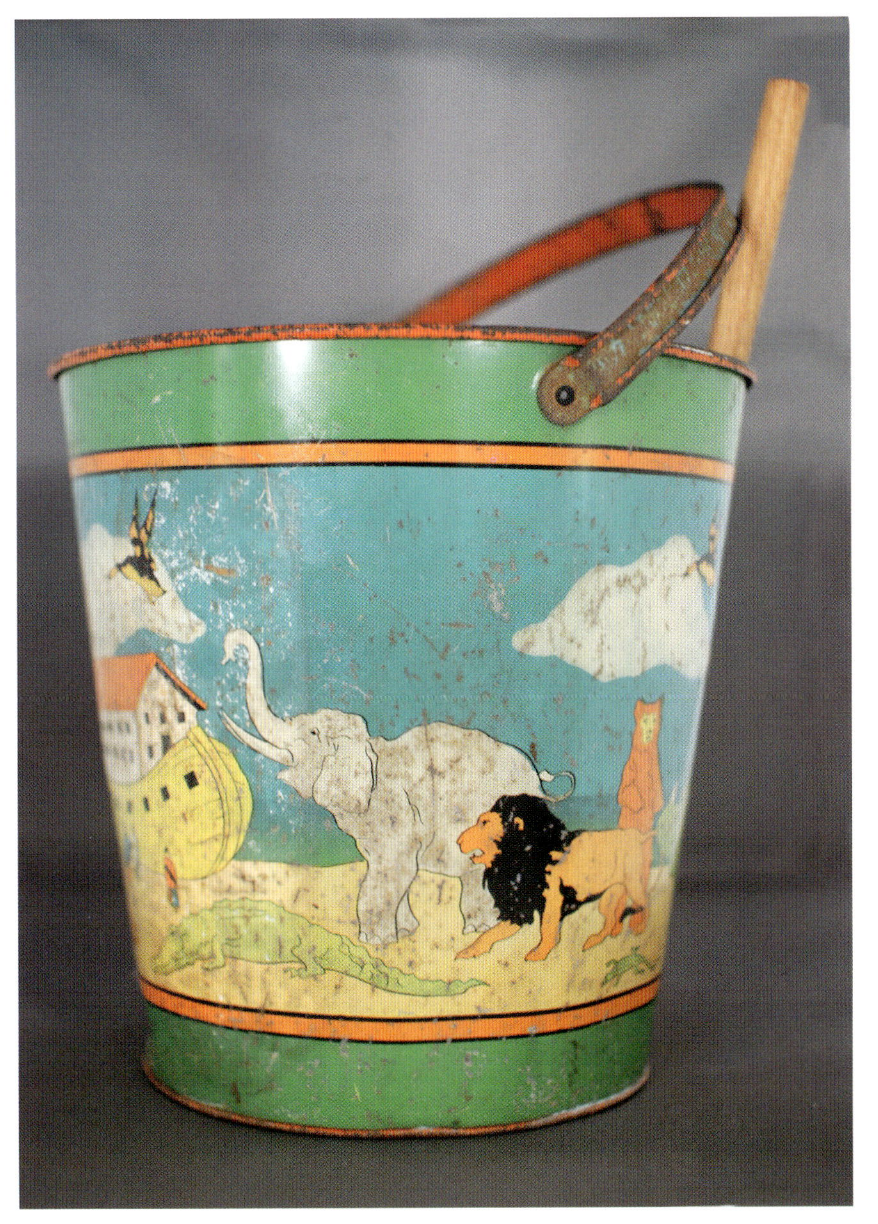

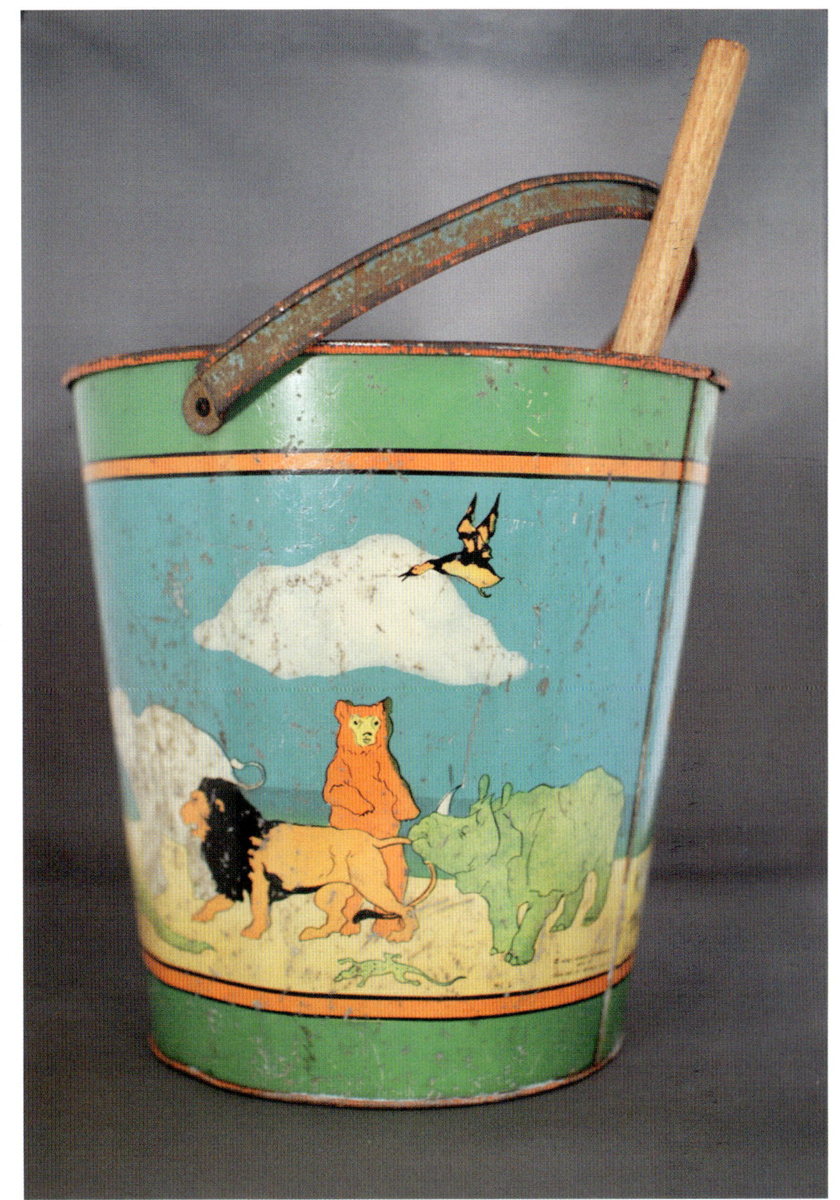

Disney Sieves

Ohio Art

To our knowledge, the Ohio Art Company was the only company anywhere in the world that produced character sieves (or sifters). Their sieves featured Disney characters. The sieves always included sand molds and either a shovel or a spoon. Sometimes, when not sold with a boxed set, they included a Mickey shovel as in the example on this page. They came in two sizes, either 6.5" in diameter or 7.75"

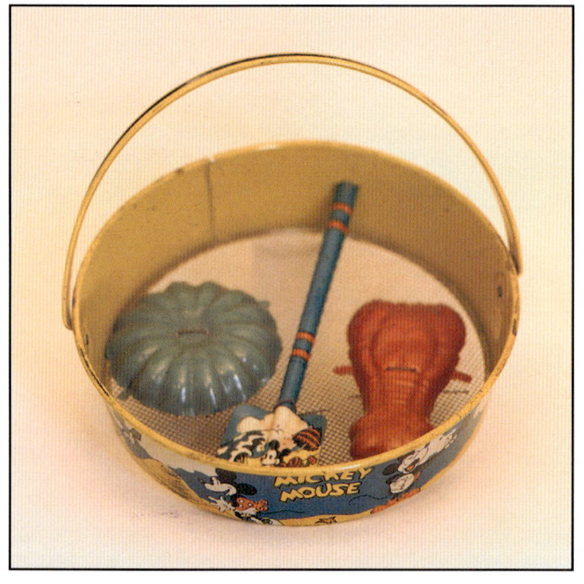

This rare 6.50" Mickey sifter came with two sand molds and a 6" Mickey shovel. *Lobel Collection; Keown Photograph.* $550-650

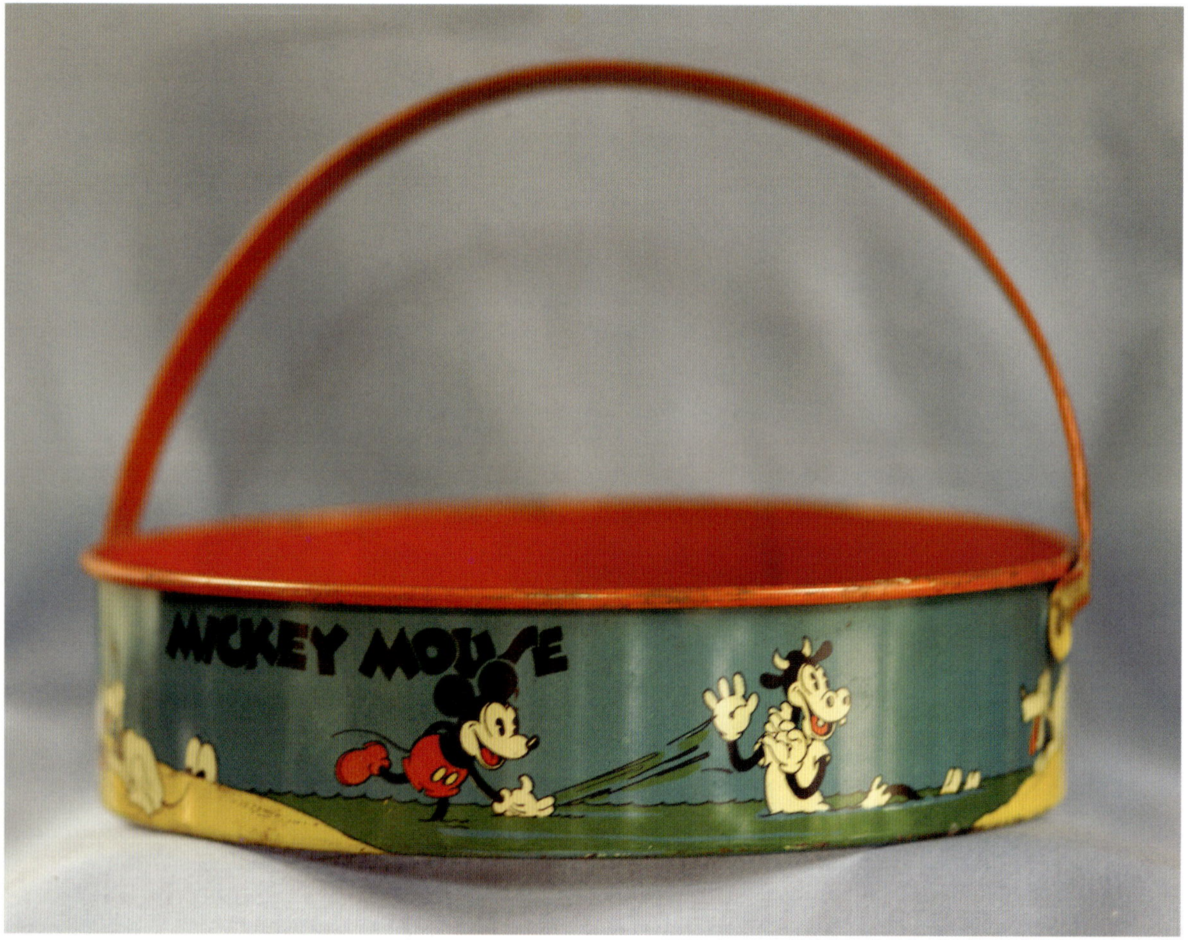

A view of the 7.5" Mickey Mouse sieve featuring all the early characters. ©Walt Disney Enterprises Ohio Art Co. Bryan, Ohio U.S.A. $150-275

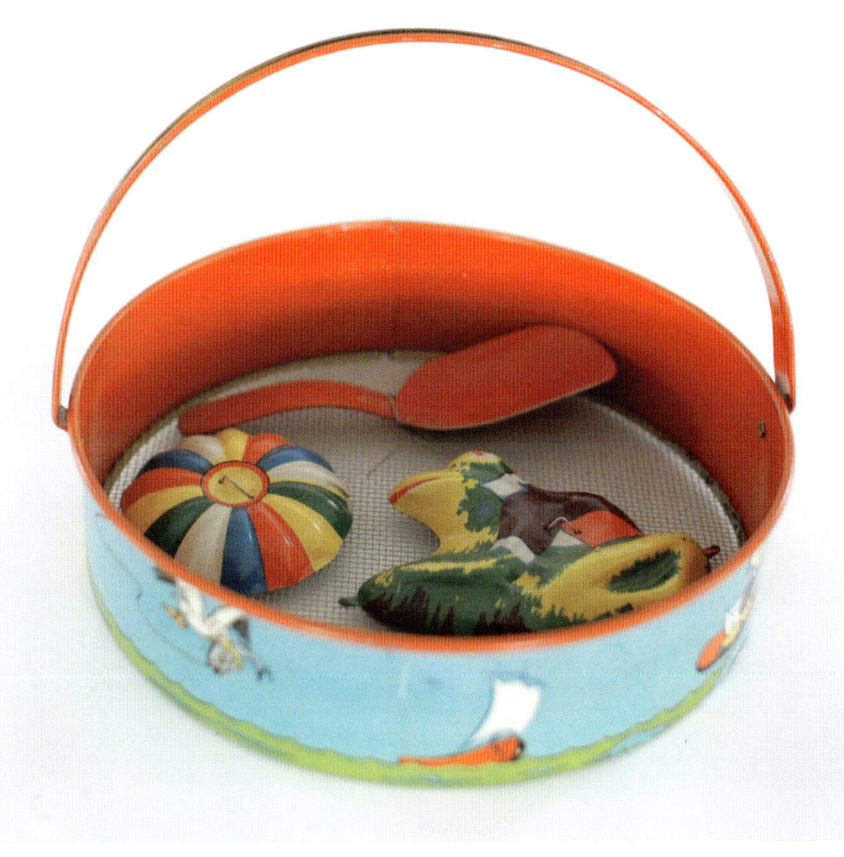

Two views of a 7.75" Donald Duck sieve with a spoon and two molds, one of a frog and one of a shell. ©1938 Walt Disney Enterprises Made in U.S.A. Ohio Art Co. $250-400

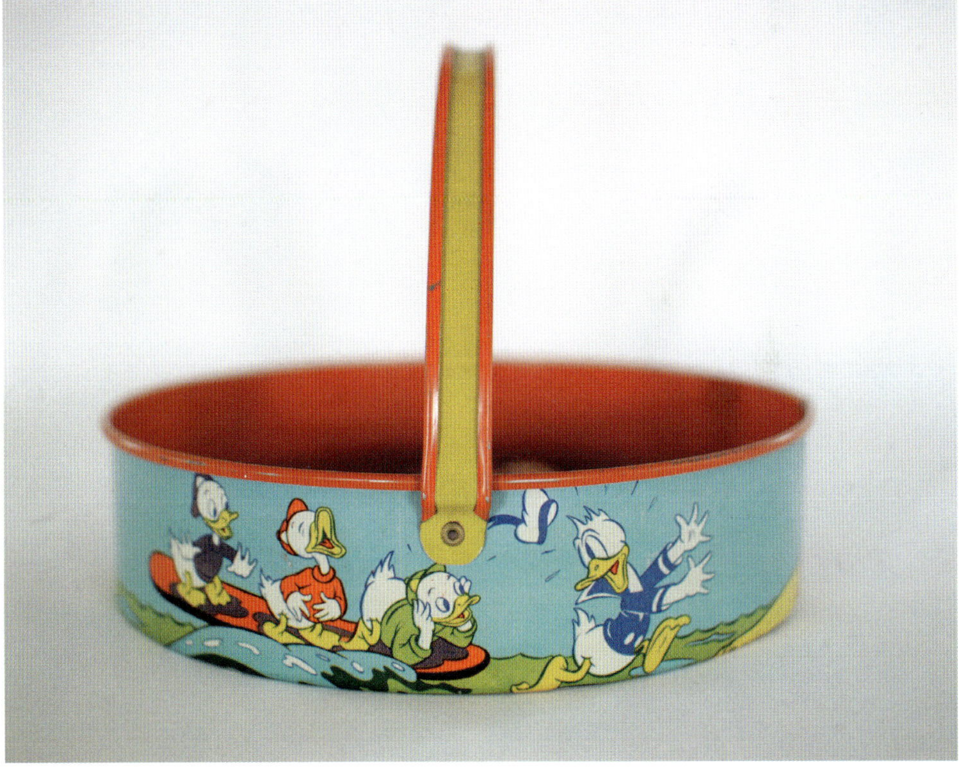

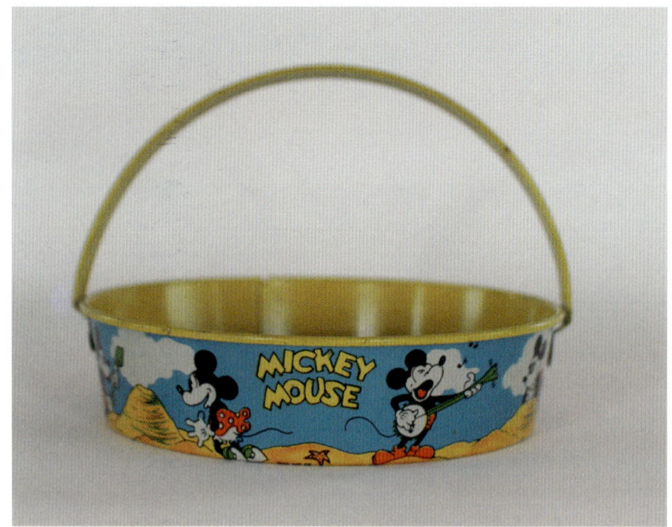

The 6.5″ Mickey Mouse sieve. ©Walt Disney Ent. Ohio Art Co. $200-300

Disney Watering Cans

Ohio Art

Ohio Art also made several watering cans featuring Disney designs. They were sometimes referred to as "sprinklers." Unlike pails, shovels, and sieves, the size of watering cans is measured differently. The height is measured from the base of the can to the tip of the fixed handle. Rather than the diameter or width, the measure is of the distance between the end of the spout and the end of the handle.

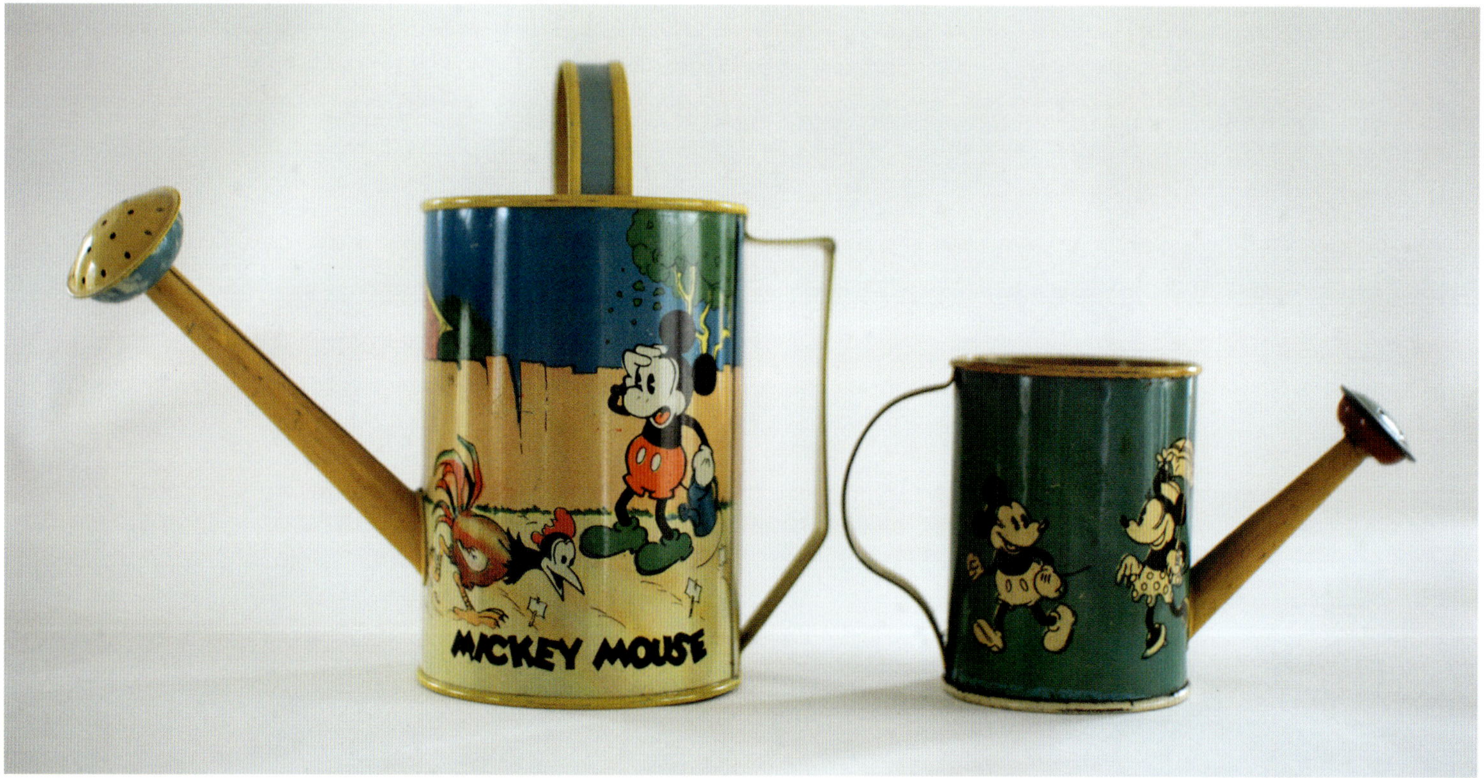

A 5.75″ high x 7.5″ Mickey with rooster watering can together with a 3″ high x 5.5″ Mickey and Minnie watering can which was the smallest Ohio Art made. Small can marked ©Walt Disney and rooster one marked ©Walt Disney Ent. Ohio Art Bryan, O. Small watering can $100-125; Rooster $175-300.

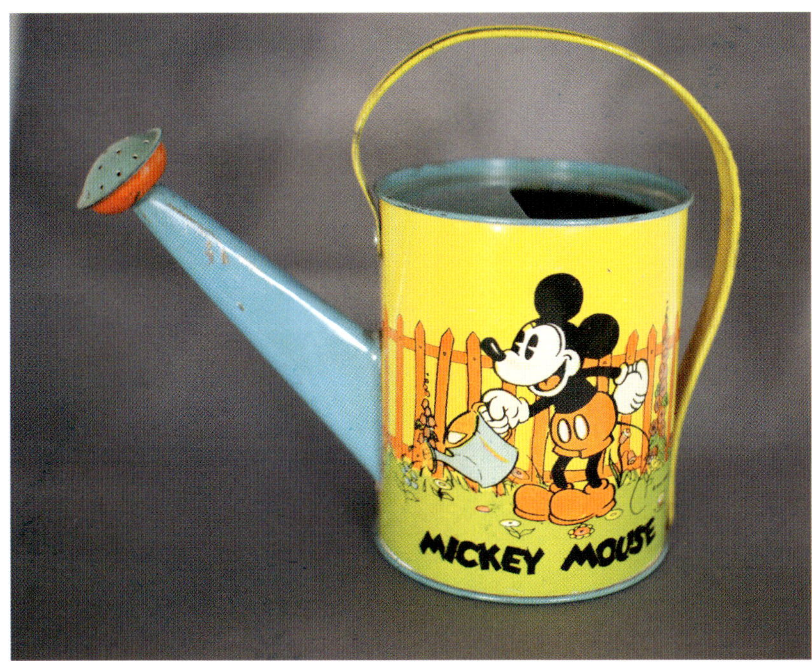

A 6.5″ x 8.5″ Mickey Mouse watering can. Both sides have an image of Mickey watering his flowers. ©Walt Disney Ent. Ohio Art Co. Bryan, O. U.S.A. $350-600

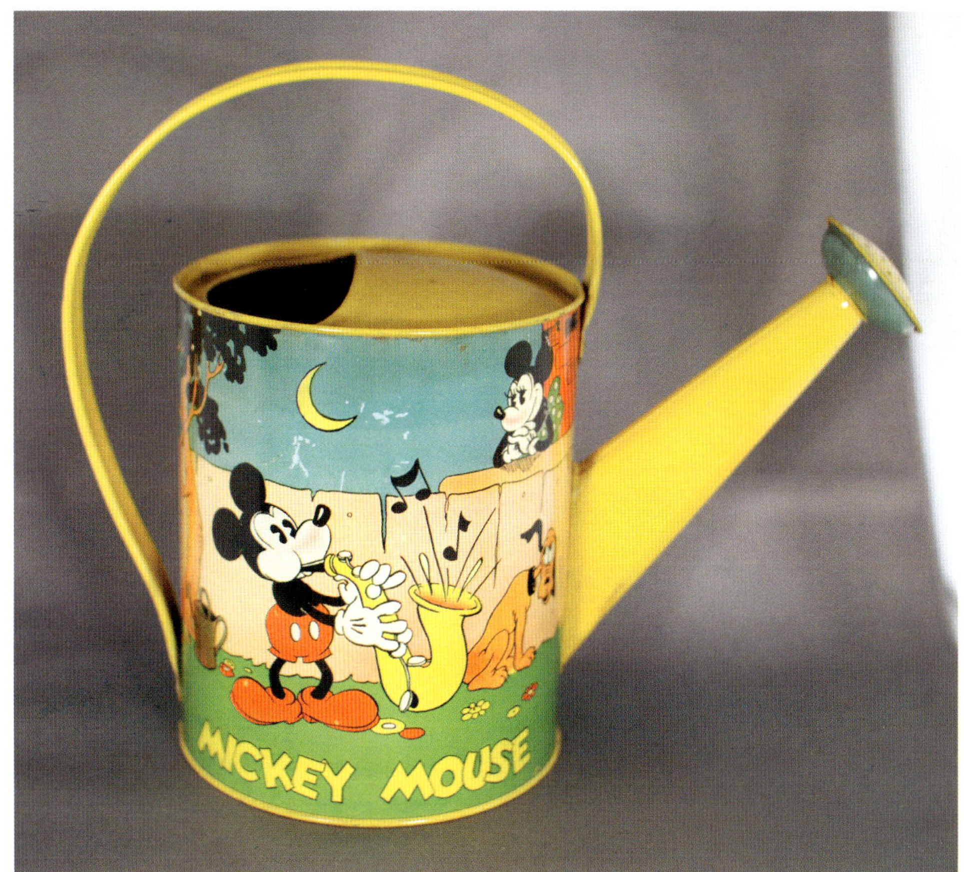

A 9″ high x 11″ Mickey Mouse watering can. Both sides feature Mickey playing the saxophone for a rapt Minnie and a not so rapt Pluto. ©Walt Disney Ent Ohio Art Co., Bryan, O. U.S.A. $350-750

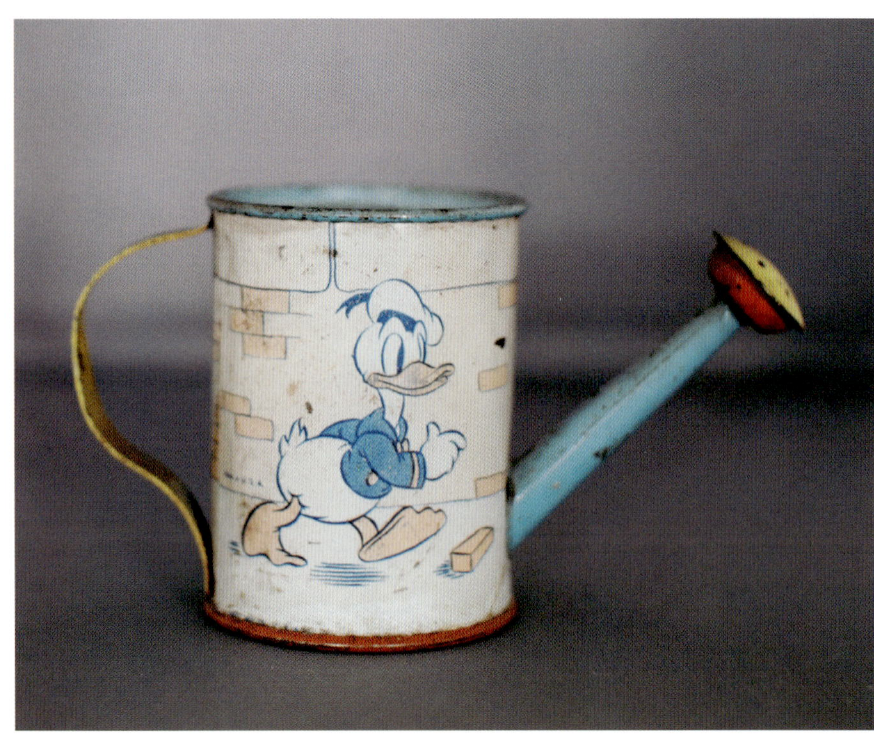

A 3" high x 5.5" Donald Duck watering can. The first side shows Donald about ready to trip over a fallen brick. The other side shows an upset Donald, having tripped and fallen. ©W.D.Ent Made in U.S.A. *Collection of John Reynolds* $150-250

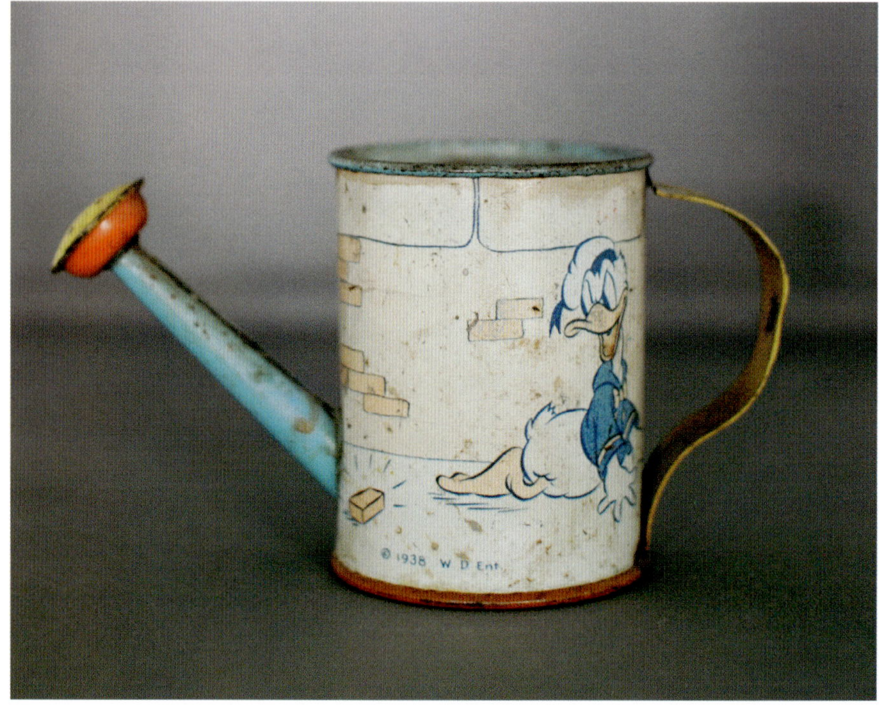

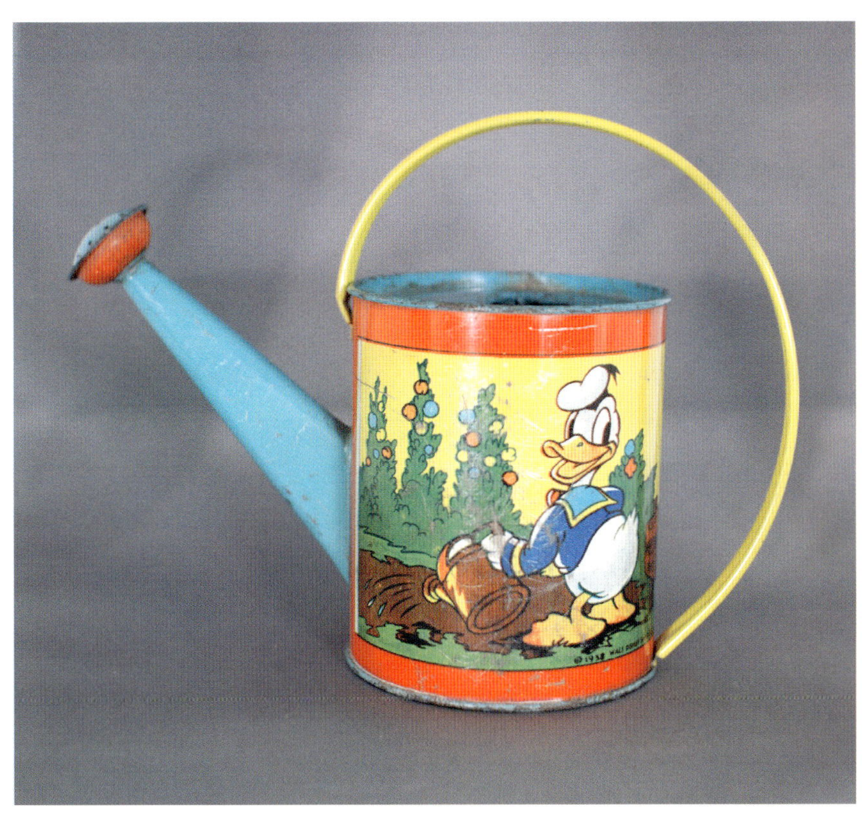

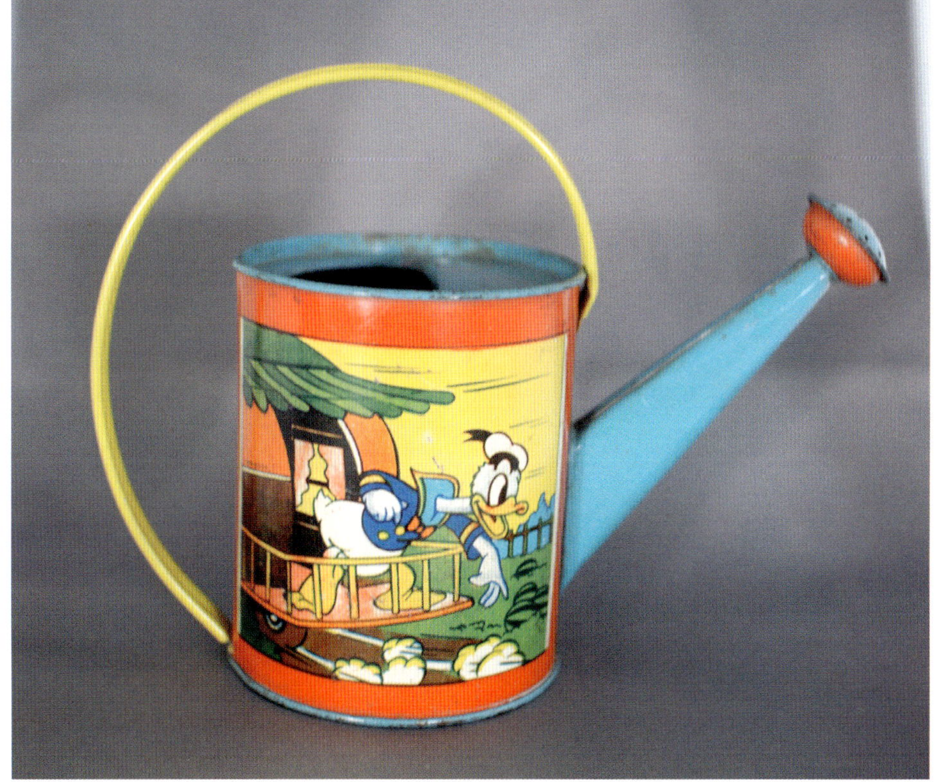

A 6.5" high x 9" Donald Duck watering can. One side features Donald watering his garden and the other shows Donald in a trailer. ©Walt Disney Enterprises The Ohio Art Company $250-500

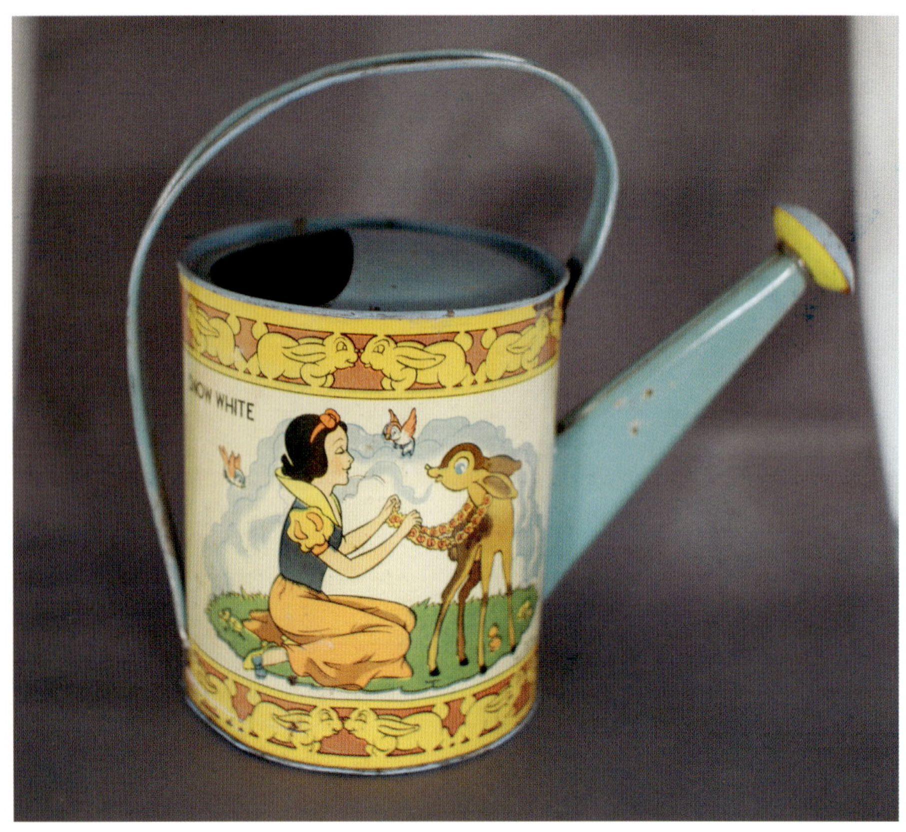

The front and back of the 9″ high x 10″ Snow White and Seven Dwarfs watering can. Snow White and each dwarf is named. ©1938 Walt Disney Enterprises Ohio Art Co. U.S.A. $400-600

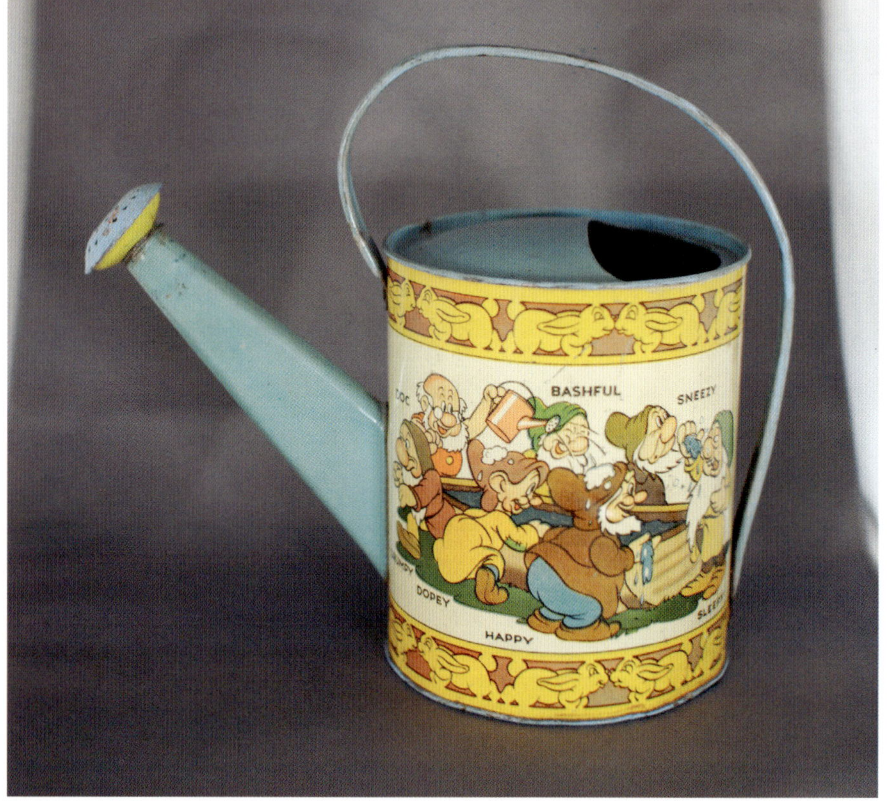

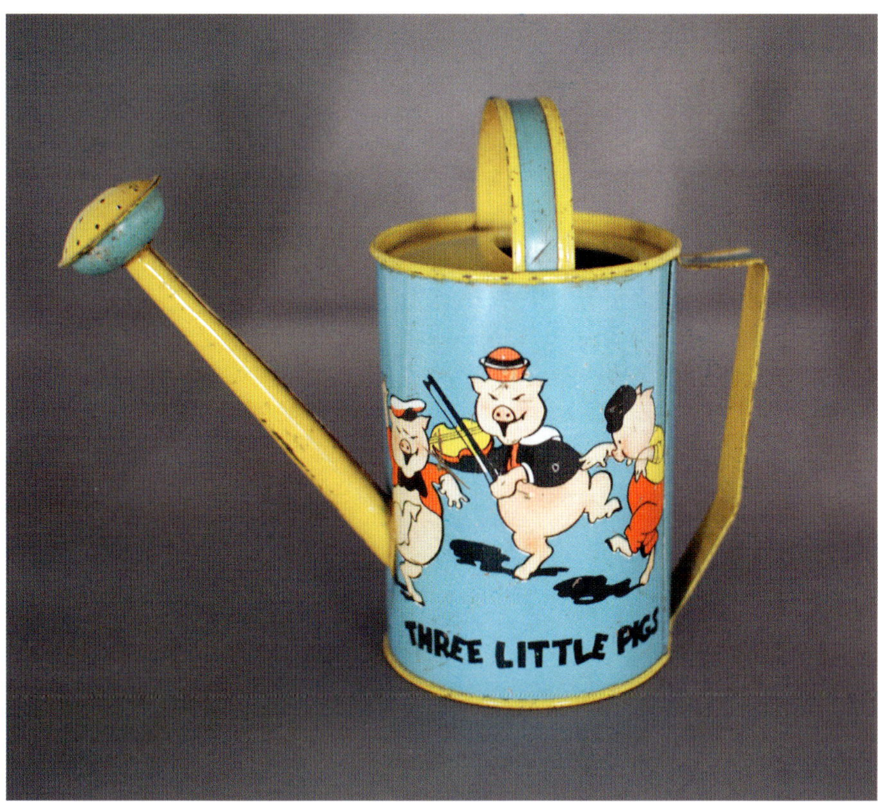

A 5.75″ high x 7.5″ Three Little Pigs sprinkler. The image is the same on both sides. ©Walt Disney Ent. Ohio Art Co. Bryan, O. U.S.A. $150-250

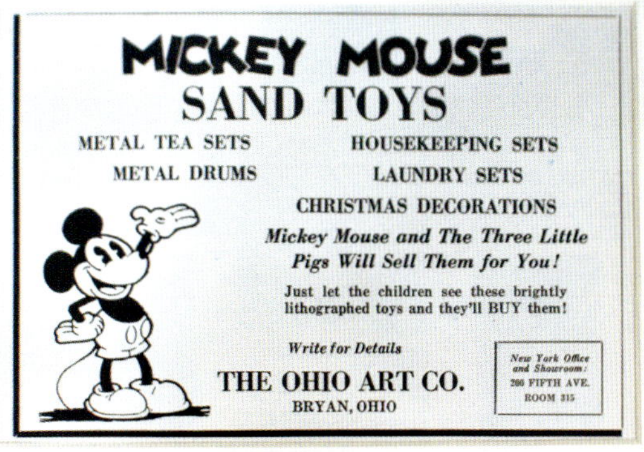

We end the Ohio Art Disney section with this Ohio Art ad from 1935 advertising their toys. No other company even comes close! *Bernabe Collection*

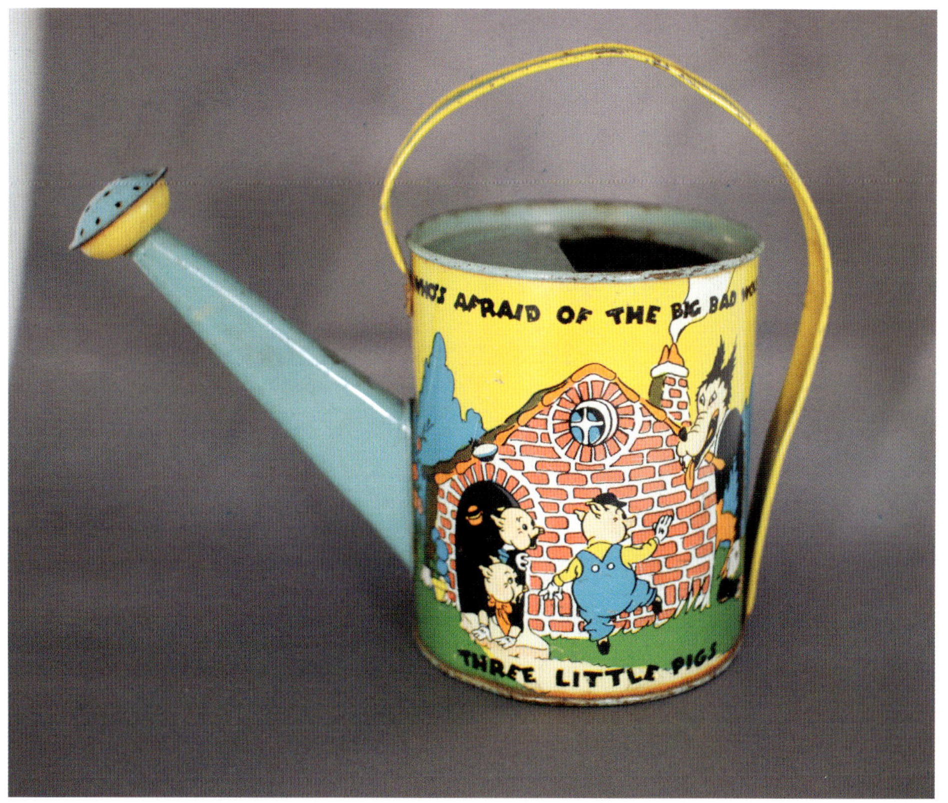

A 6.5″ high x 8.5″ Three Little Pigs watering can. Very colorful sprinkler with "Who's Afraid of the Big Bad Wolf" at the top. Both sides are the same ©Walt Disney Ent. Ohio Art Co. Bryan O. U.S.A. $250-450

J. Chein & Co.

Founded in 1903 by Julius Chein and three others, including his wife, J. Chein & Co. was an important American toy maker of the 20th century. In the 1930s Chein received a Disney license to produce novelty toys. The license did not include sand toys for which Ohio Art had an exclusive license. However the Disney characters and particularly sand toys were so popular that Chein started producing sand pails with images that looked very much like Mickey and other Disney characters. To help protect themselves, they included images of Krazy Kat-type figures. Because of their trouble with Universal over Oswald, Disney was very careful to have all of their merchandise include their copyright. You will never find a Disney copyright on the early Mickey look-a-like Chein pails. Later in the 1960s Chein obtained a license to produce sand pails and all their later pails include the Walt Disney Productions copyright, usually with a date.

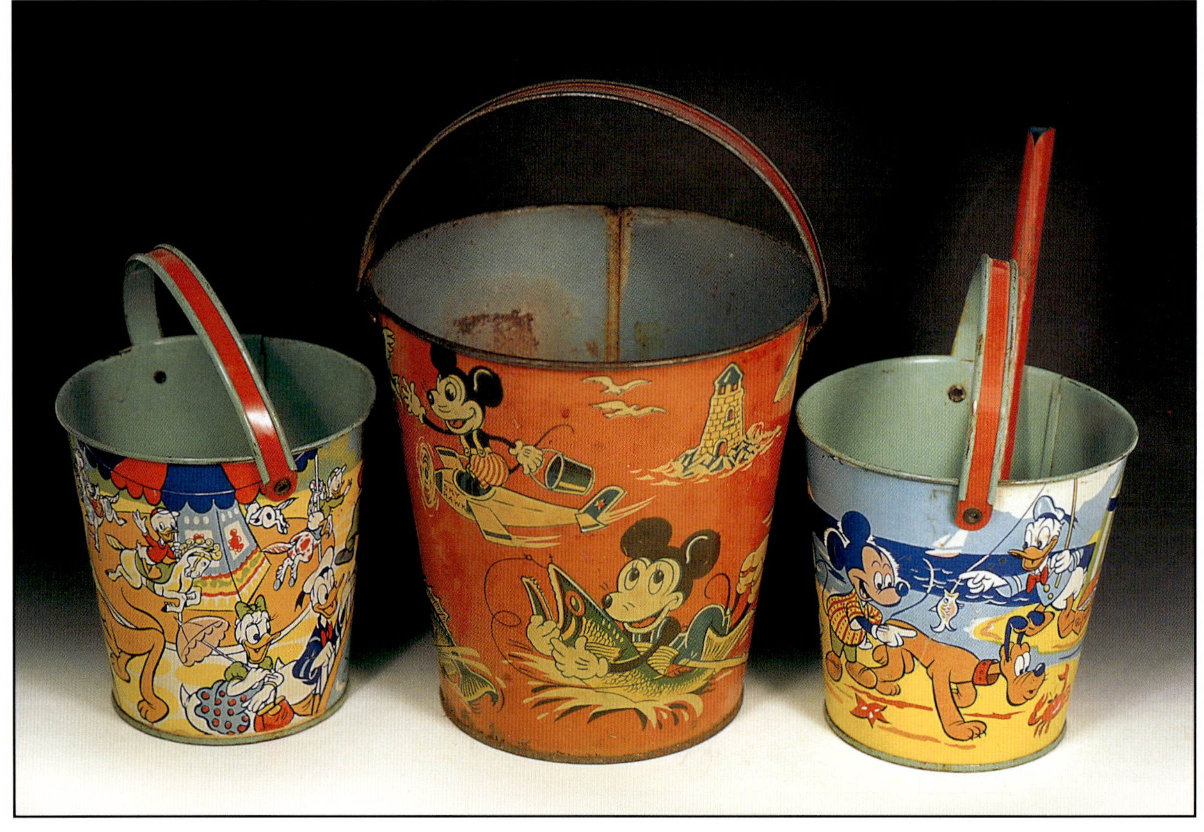

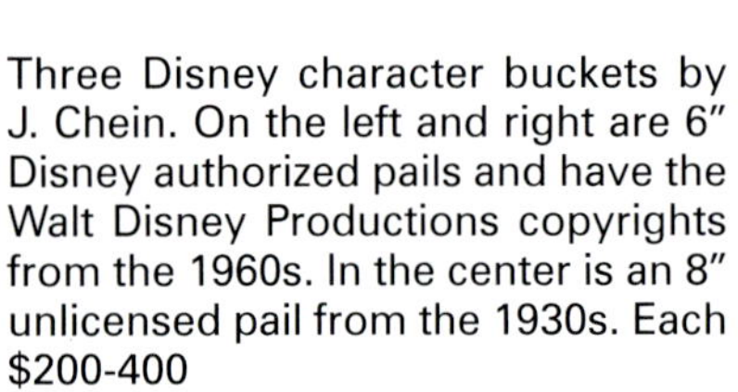

Three Disney character buckets by J. Chein. On the left and right are 6" Disney authorized pails and have the Walt Disney Productions copyrights from the 1960s. In the center is an 8" unlicensed pail from the 1930s. Each $200-400

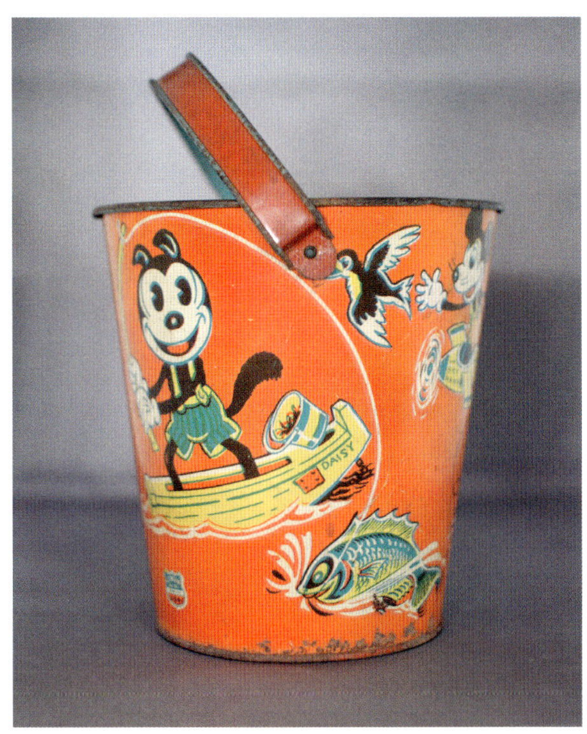

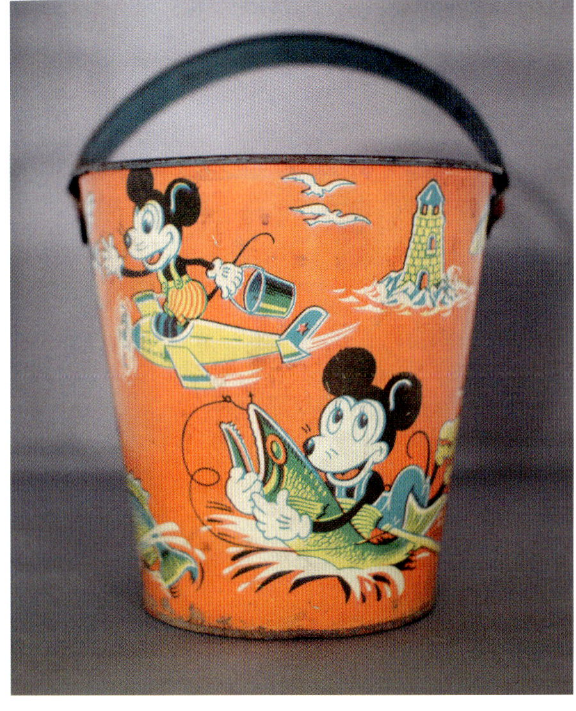

Three views of 6″ unauthorized Disney character pail from 1930s by J. Chein. $200-450

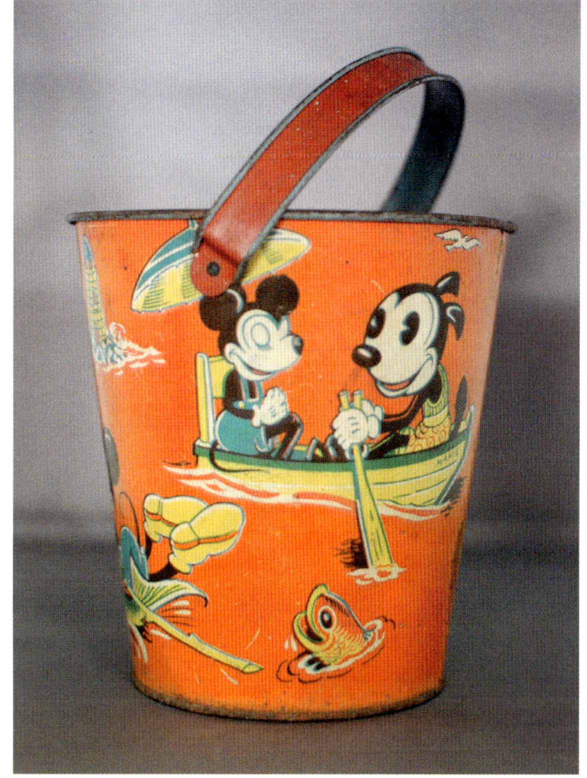

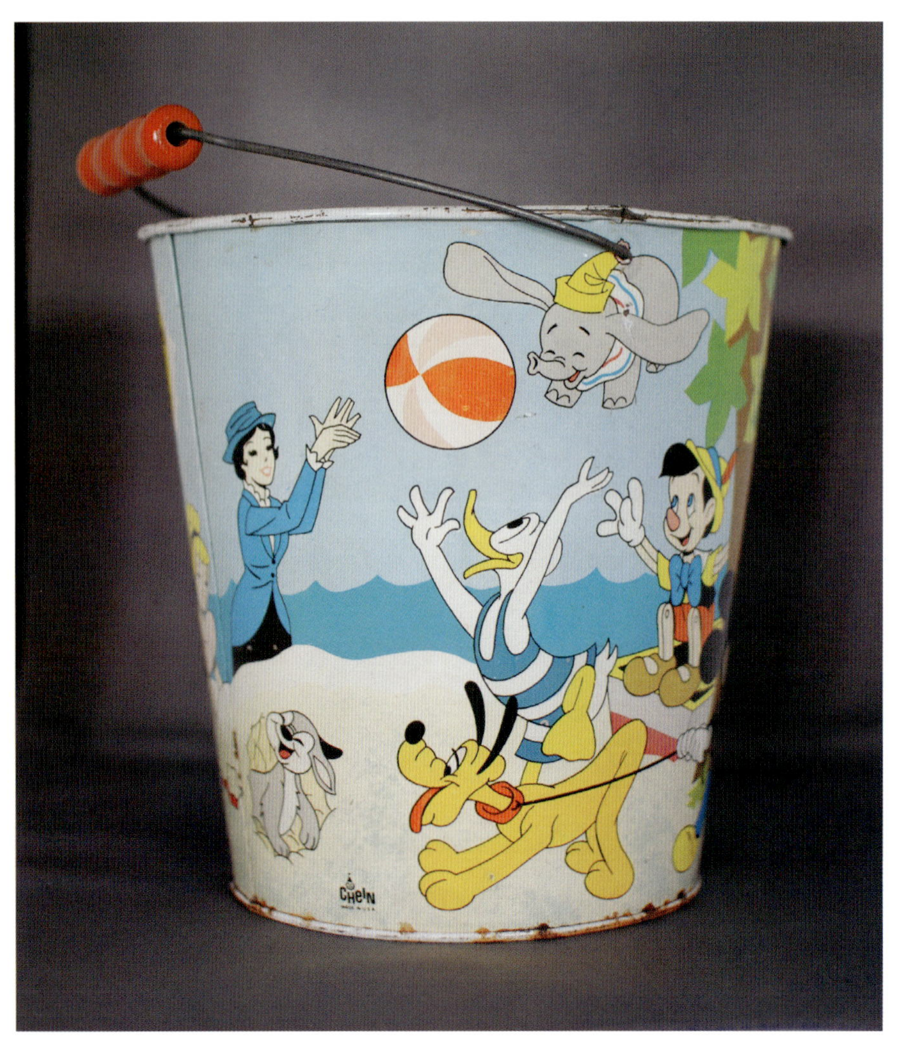

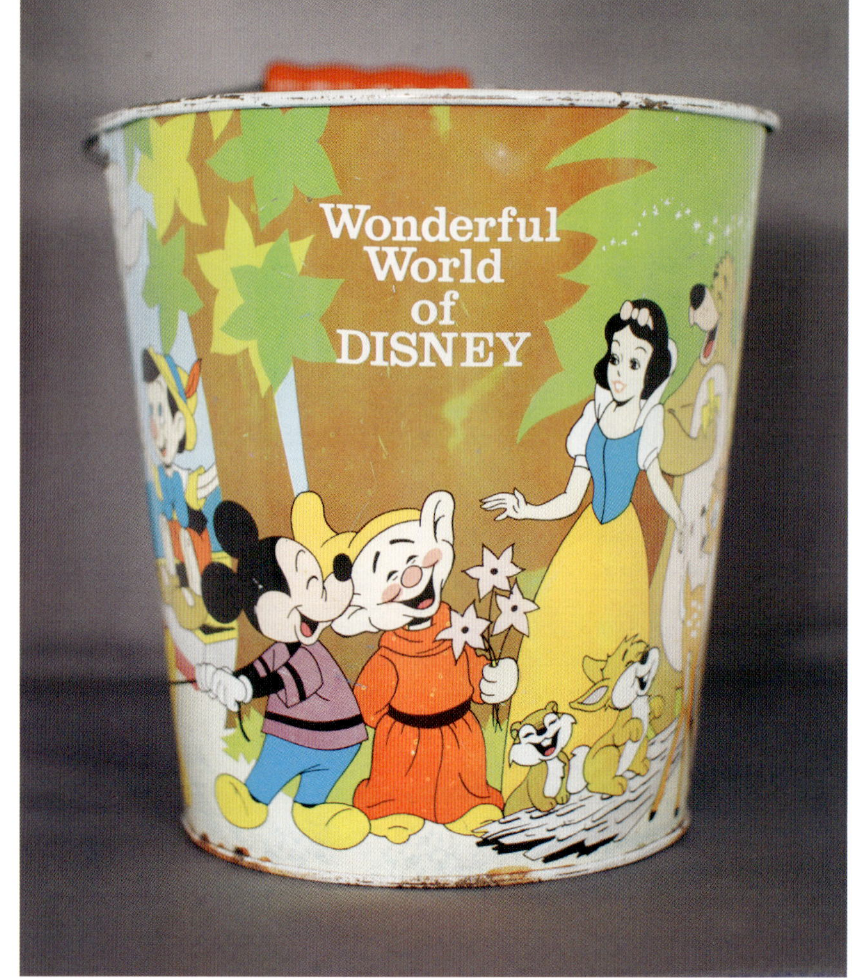

Four views of an authorized 8" Wonderful World of Disney pail by J. Chein. Many of the favorite Disney characters from Mickey and Donald to Mary Poppins are included. ©MCMLXVI Walt Disney Productions Chein logo Made in U.S.A. $150-250

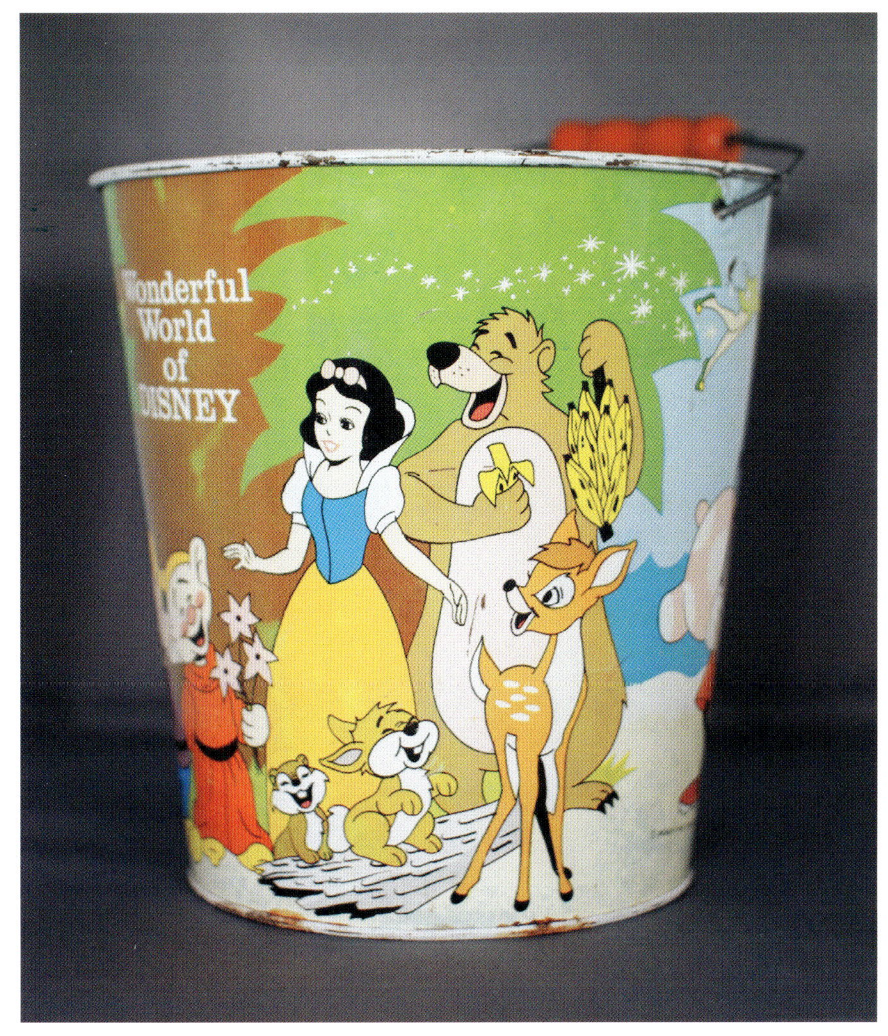
Wonderful
World
of
DISNEY

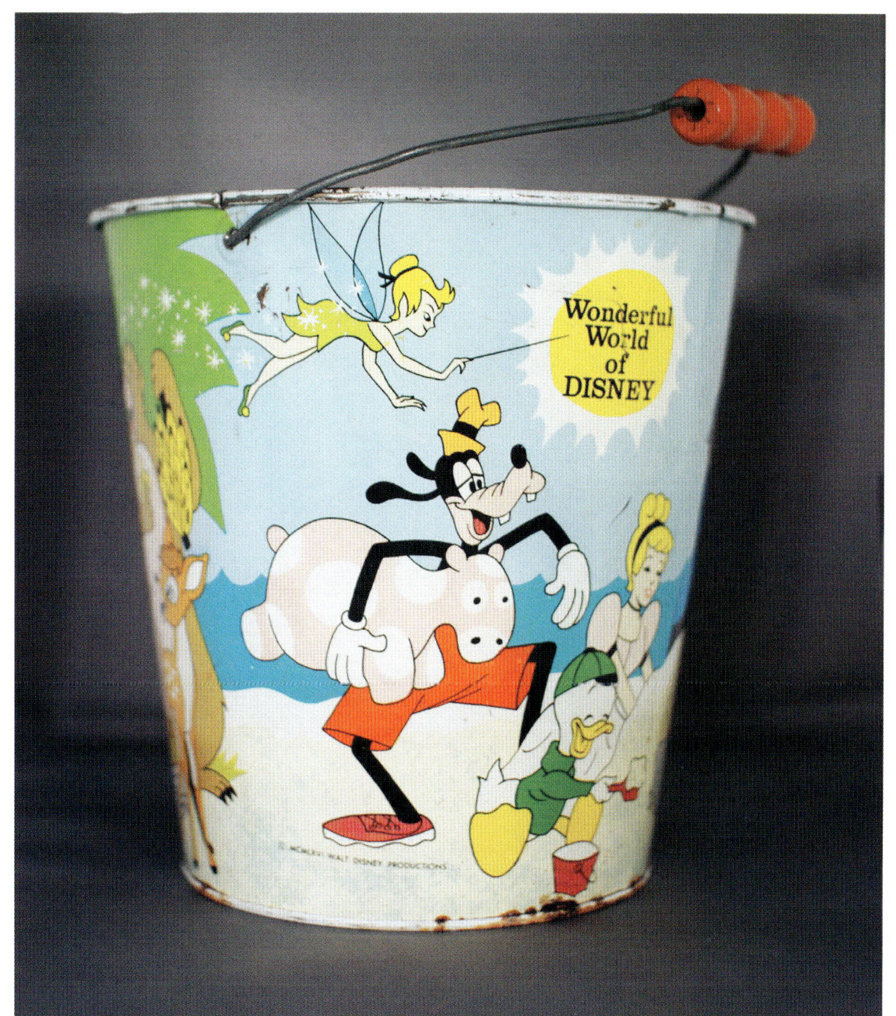
Wonderful
World
of
DISNEY

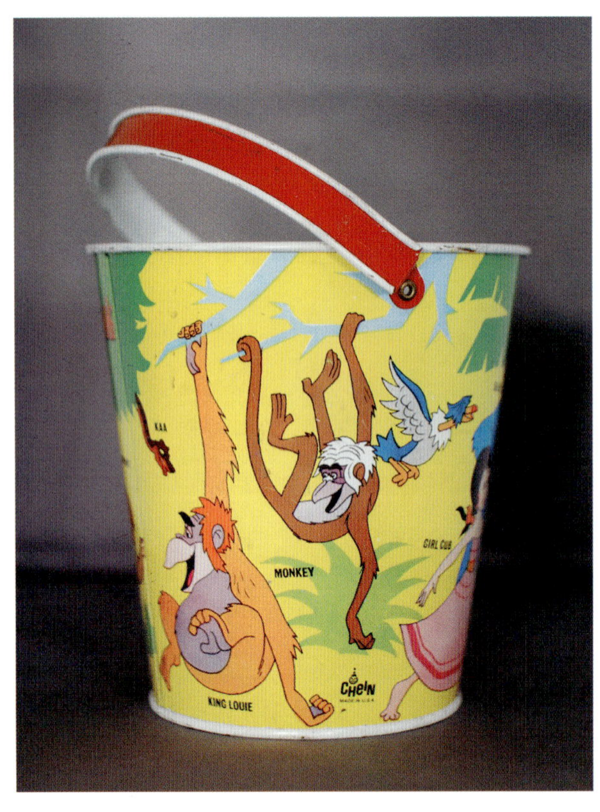

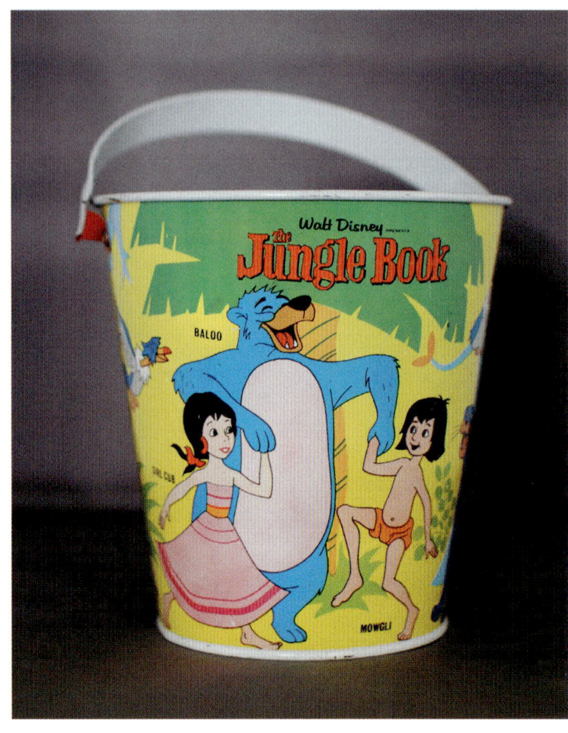

Four views of "Walt Disney Presents the Jungle Book" 6" pail by Chein. 0169 ©MCMLXVI Walt Disney Productions Chein logo Made in U.S.A. $150-$250

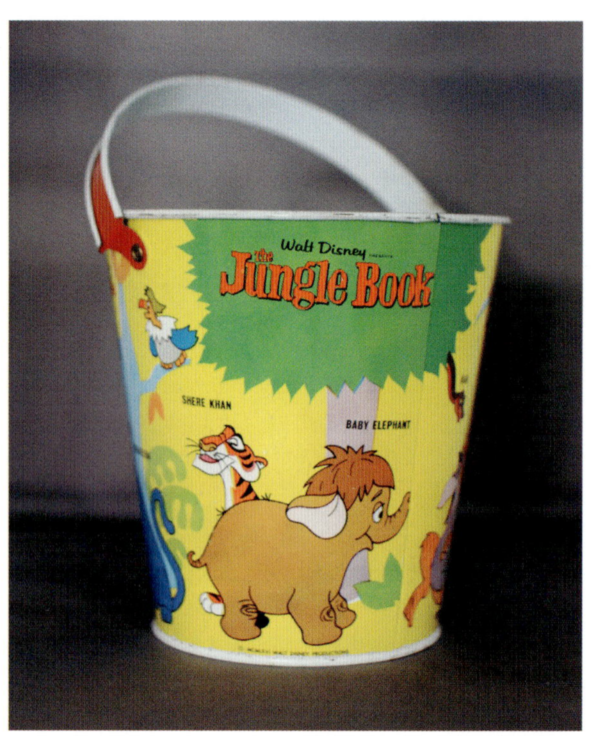

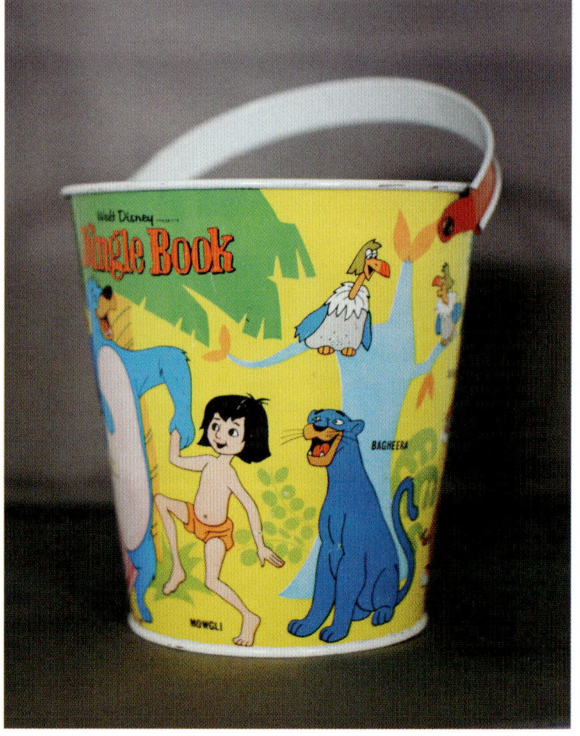

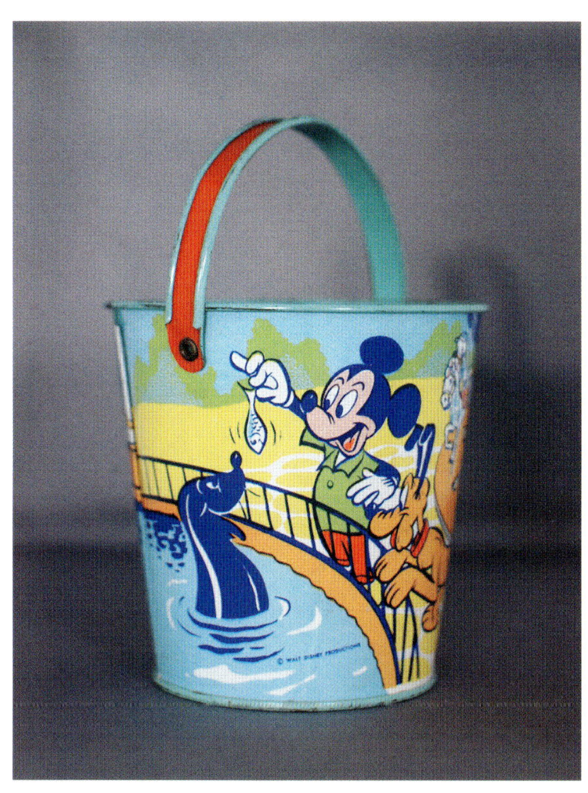

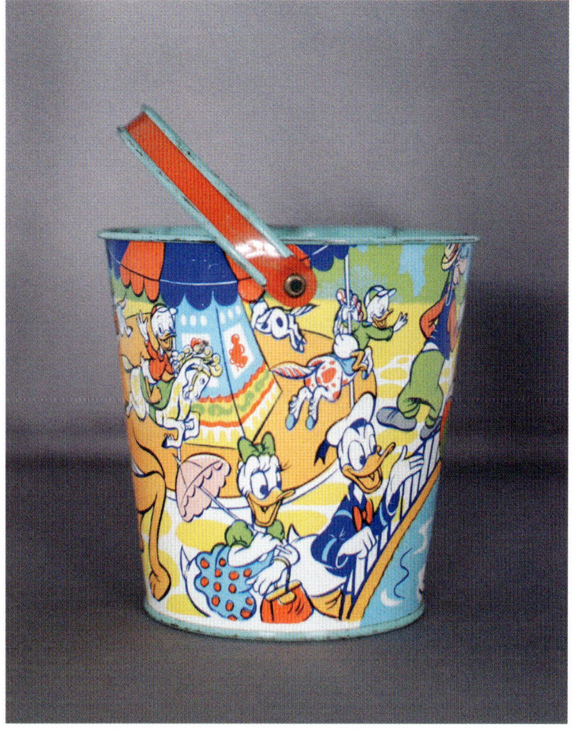

Three views of a 4.25" pail showing Disney characters at the zoo. The scenes feature Mickey, Pluto, Daisy and Donald with seals, Donald's three nephews on a merry-go-round and Goofy watching monkeys. ©Walt Disney Productions with J. Chein & Co. Made in U.S.A. logo $250-350

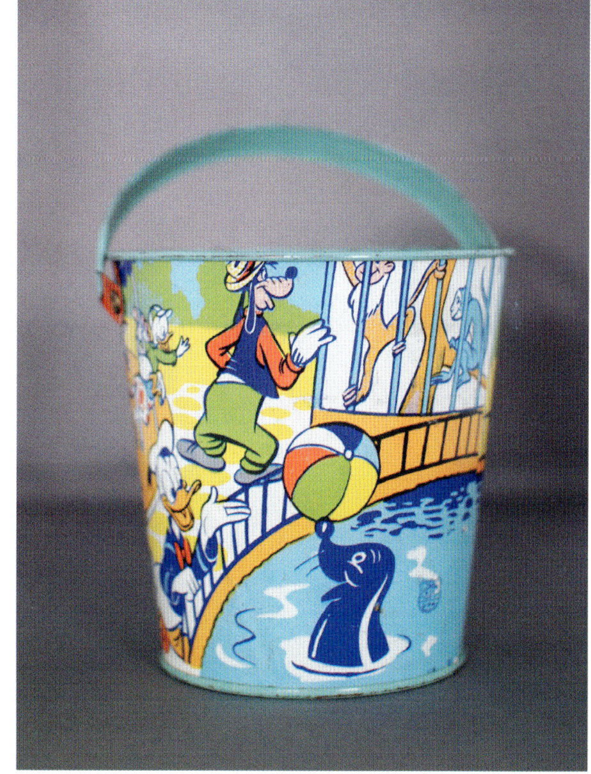

Recent Disney Pails from U.S.A.

Over the past decade or so several companies have produced sand pails with some featuring old, established characters such as Mickey, Felix, Betty Boop, and Popeye as well as some new creations from children's television. These include Disney Princesses, Dora the Explorer, and SpongeBob SquarePants. Often the pails contained treats or Easter goodies and could be used in the sand or for decoration when the treats were gone. The main companies doing the distributing were: American Specialty Confections, Inc. (A.S.C.) Lancaster, Pennsylvania; Schylling, Ipswich, Massachusetts; and the Tin Box Company of Farmingdale, New York.

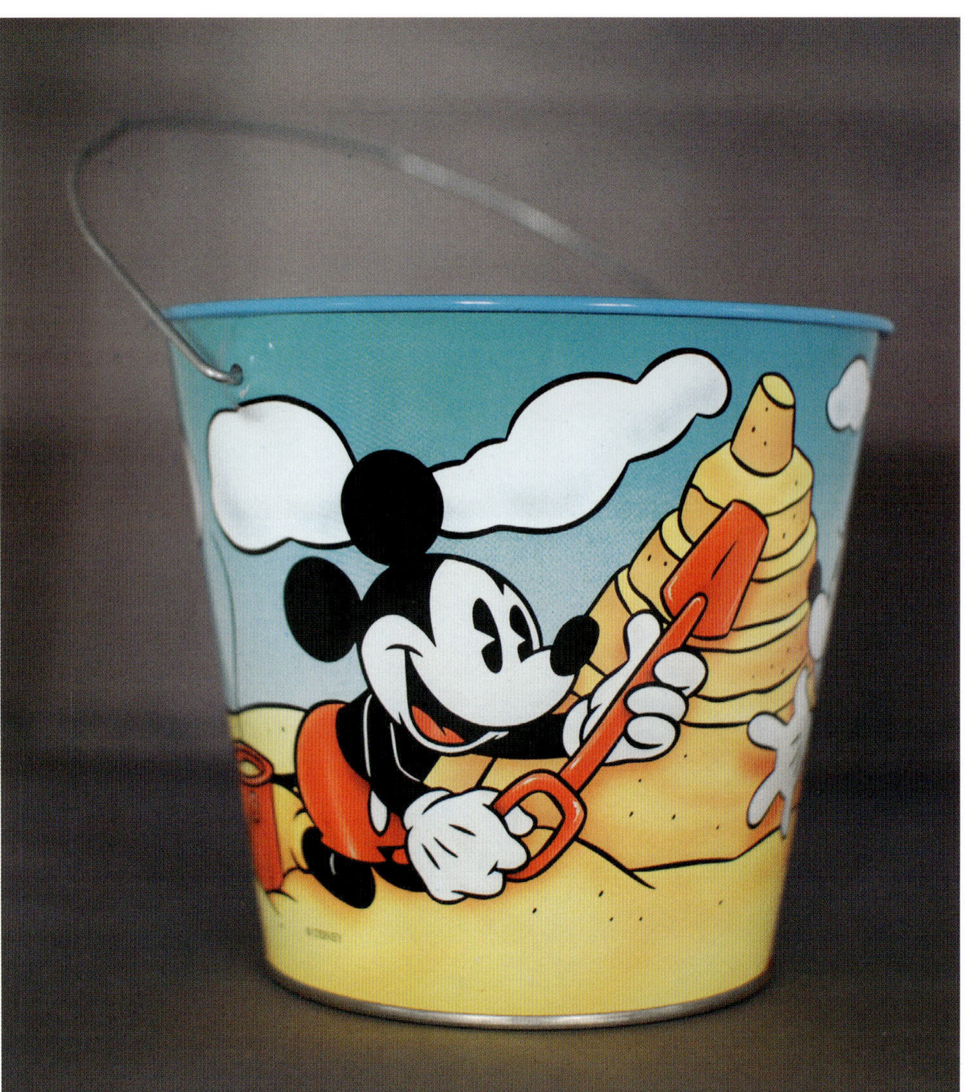

This 5.5" Mickey Mouse pail by A.S.C. is almost an exact duplicate of a 4.25" Ohio Art pail from the 1930s. It originally contained confections and counted on Mickey Mouse to help market the treats. ©Disney 1996 Series #1 A.S.C. Lancaster, PA 17601. ©Disney indicates it was produced in the last decade or so. This is not to be confused with ©Walt Disney which indicated it was made prior to 1934. $5-15

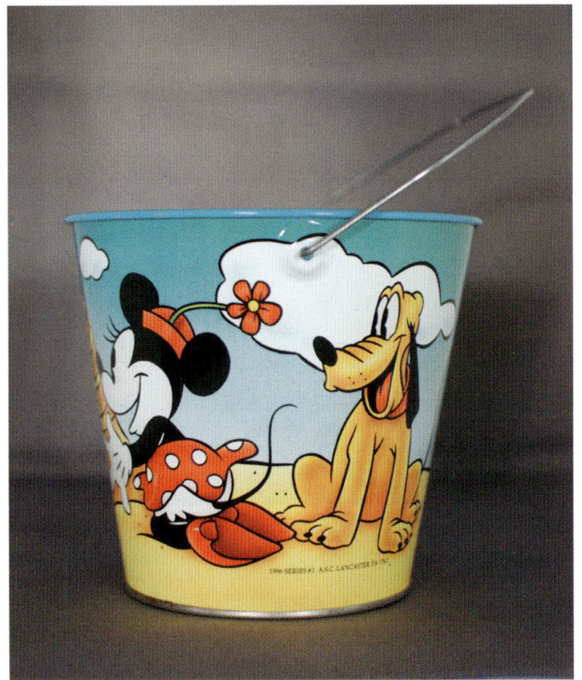

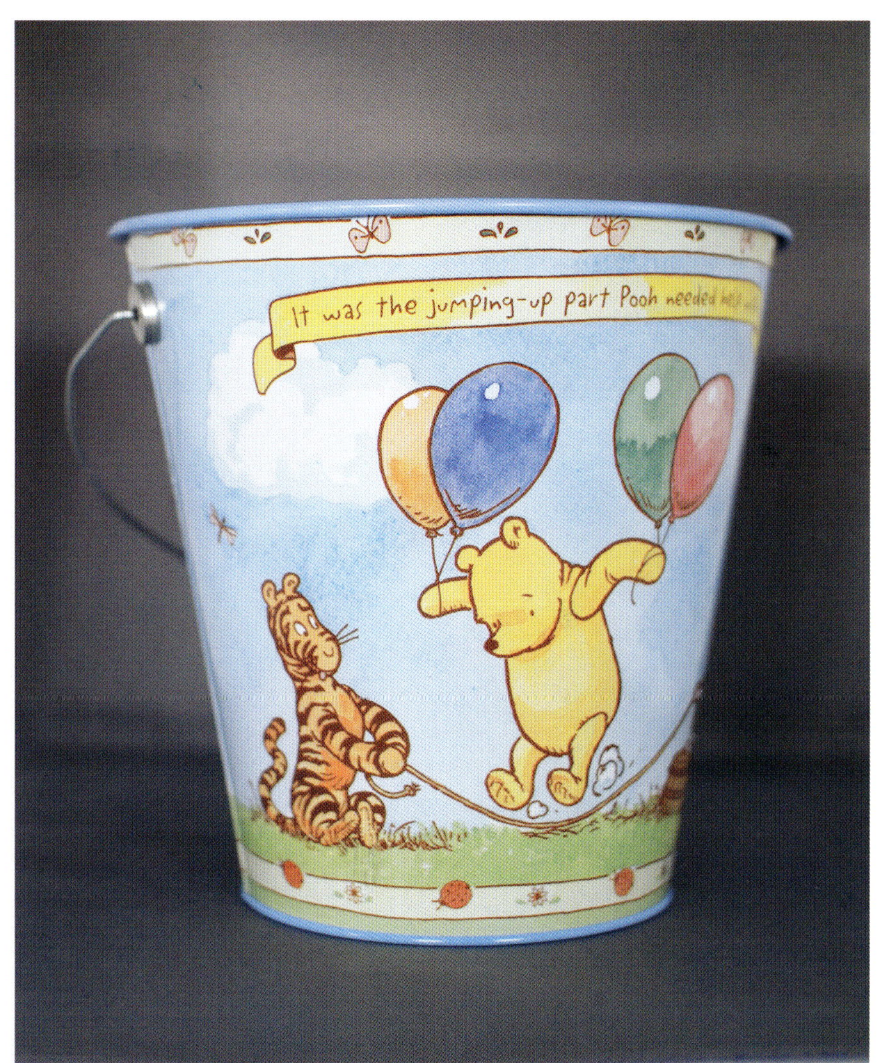

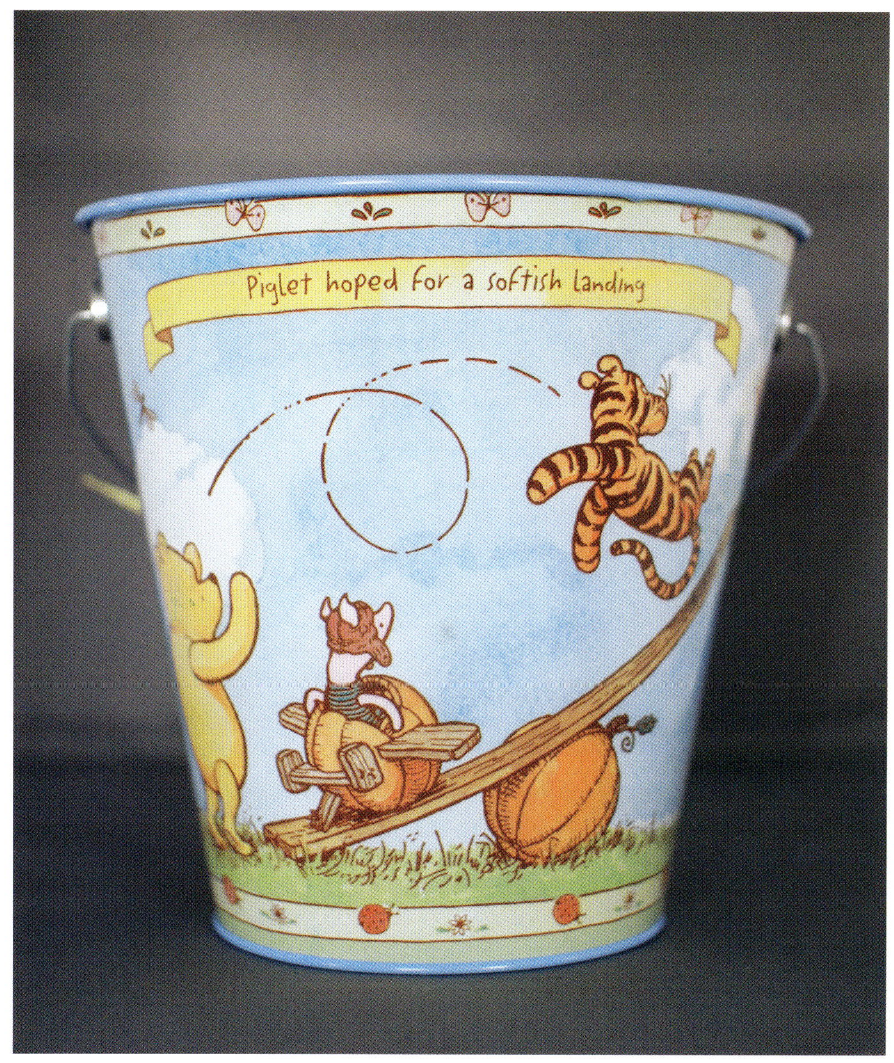

Two views of a 7" Winnie the Pooh pail. Winnie, Tigger and friends are jumping rope and playing on the seesaw ©Disney Based on the Winnie the Pooh works, ©A.A. Milne and E.H. Shepard. More fun from Schylling, Ipswich, MA 01938 Made in China $5-15

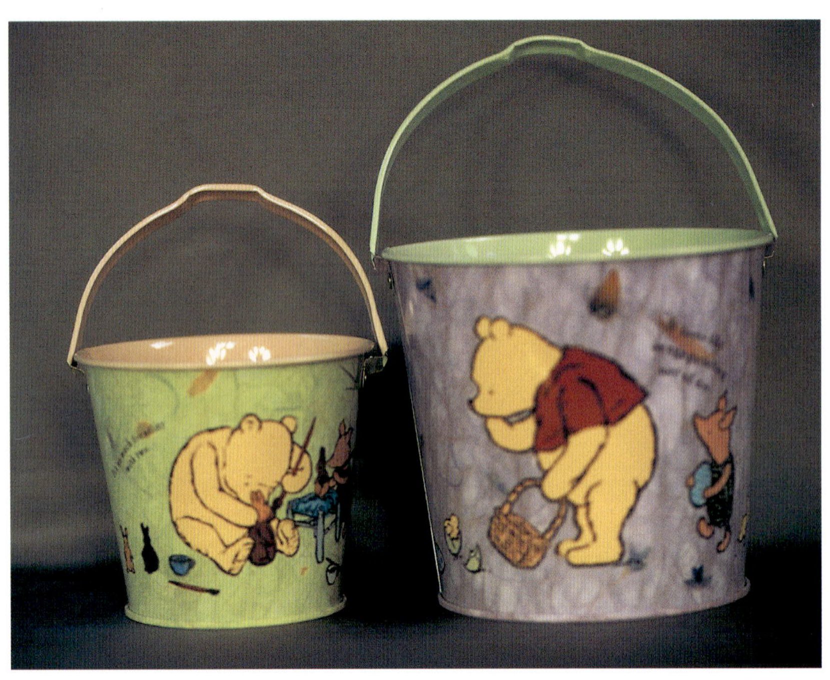

Two views of two contemporary Pooh pails. The first is 3.5" tall and the second is 4.5" tall. Both are marked: ©A.A. Milne and E.H. Shepard, CHARPENTE ©Disney, Made in Taiwan. Small is code 50030, large is 50031. Each $5-15

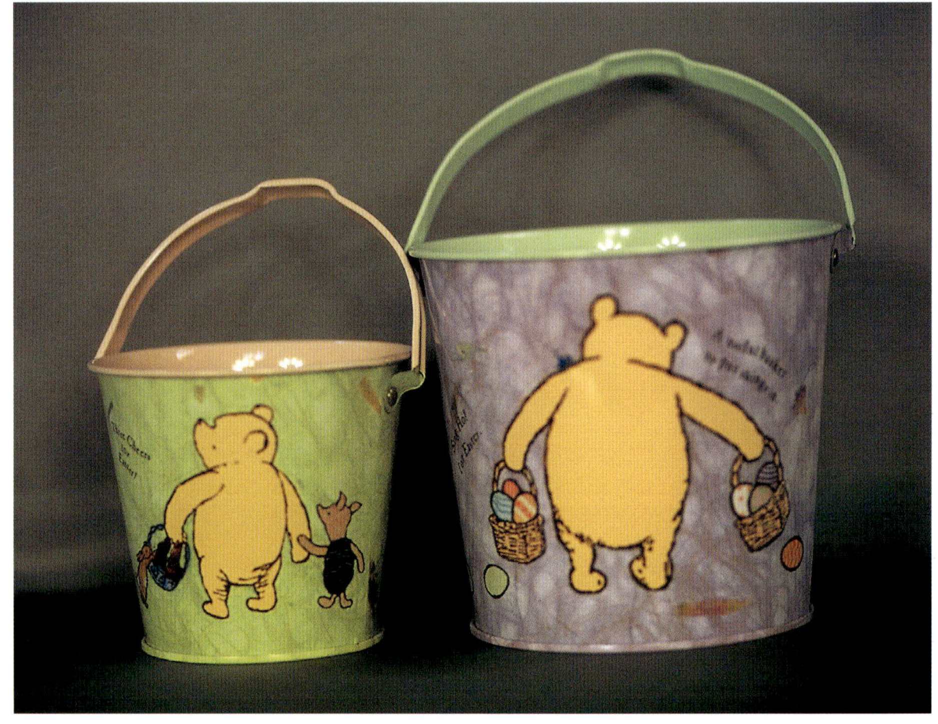

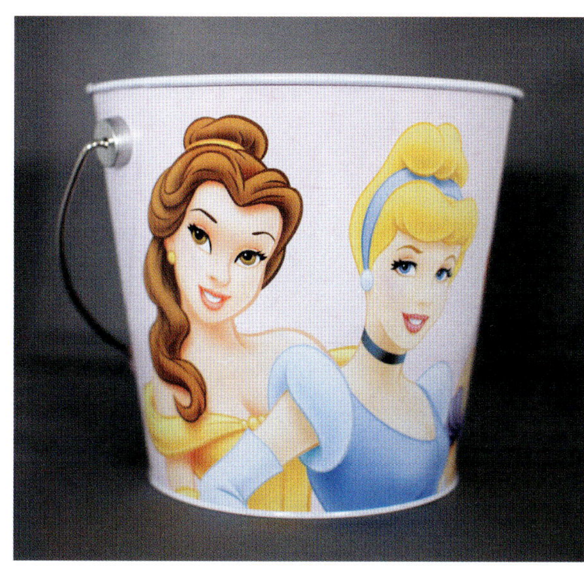

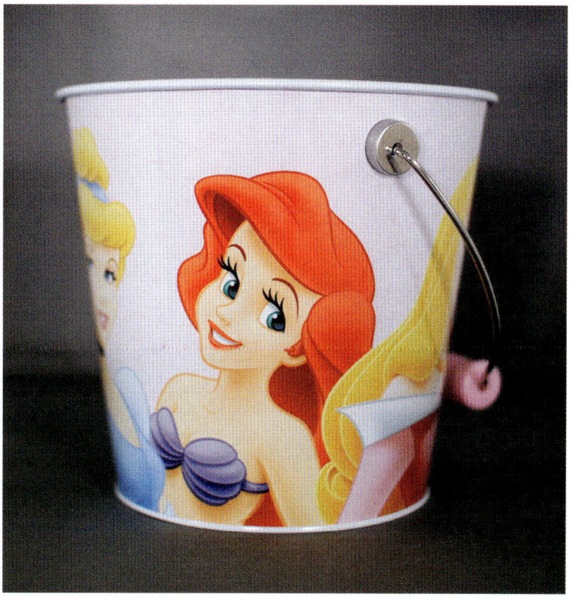

Perhaps no characters in recent years have stolen the hearts of little girls as have the Disney Princesses. Here, the three views around the pail show Belle, Cinderella, Ariel, Sleeping Beauty and Snow White. Made in China, this 6" pail is imported and distributed by the Tin Box Co. of Farmingdale, NY, probably the leading distributor in the world of this type of product. ©Disney *Courtesy of the Tin Box Company.* $5-15

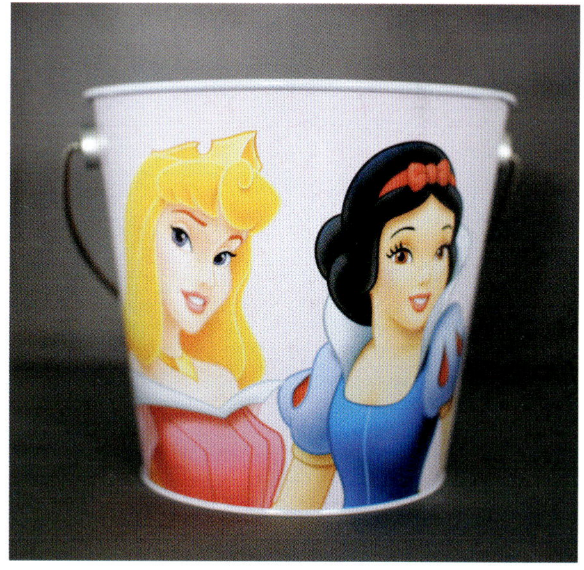

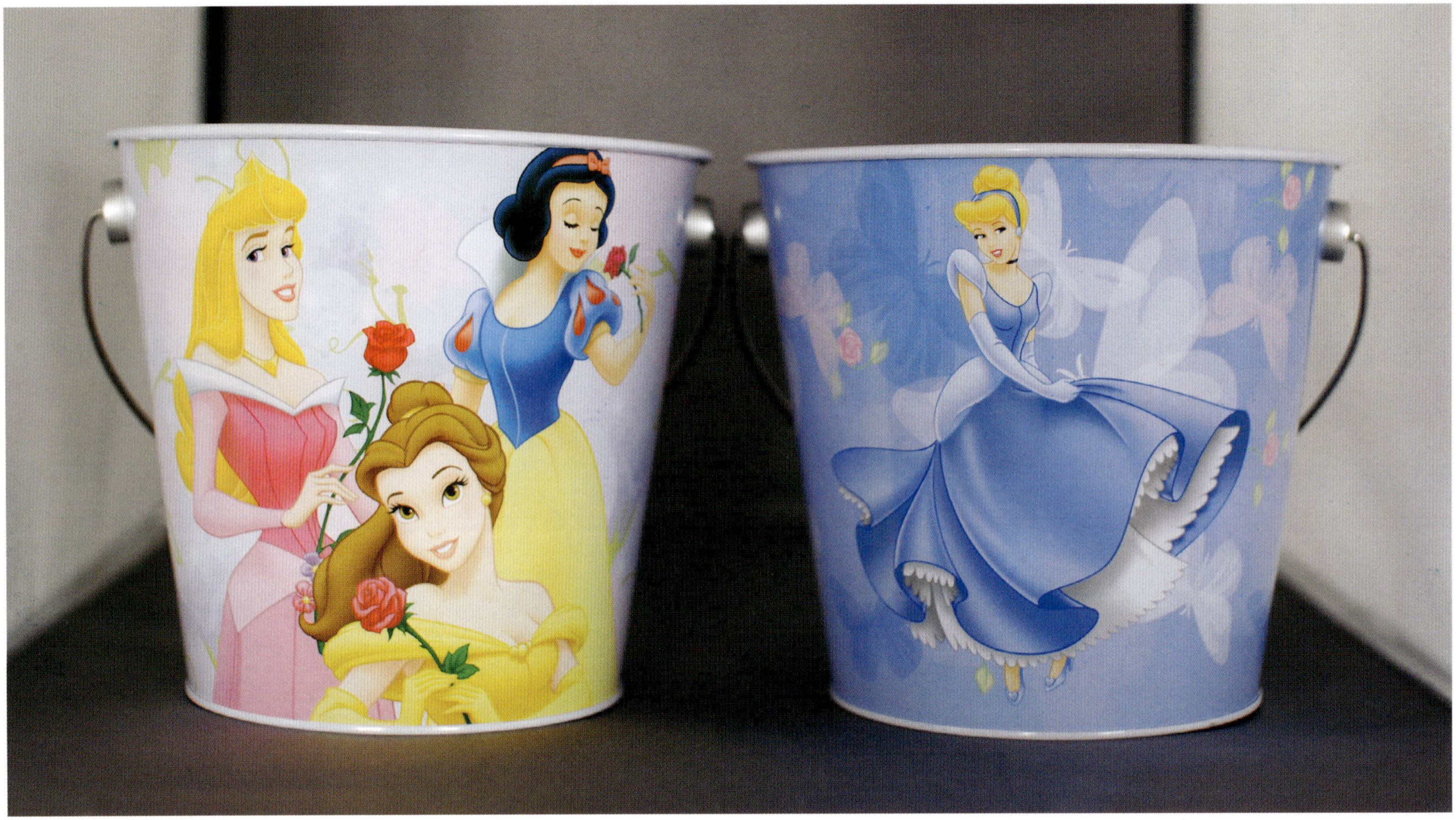

Two more Princess pails together with label on bottom. *Courtesy of the Tin Box Co.* $5-15

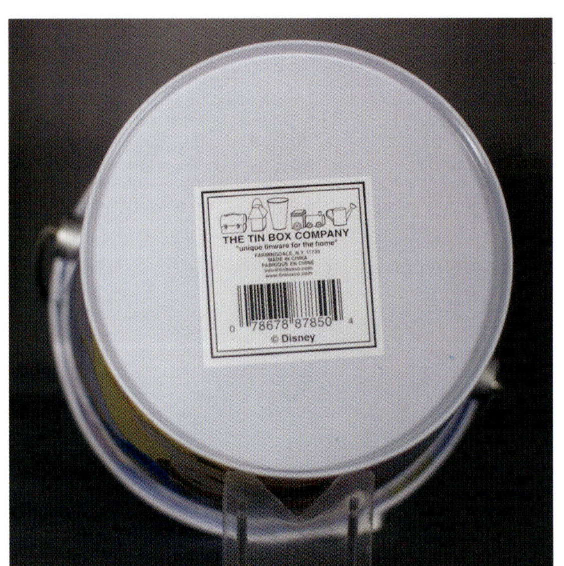

Chapter 8:

Disney Metal Sand Toys from Other Countries

Argentina

Toymakers in other countries quickly realized that profits could be made from the popularity of the Disney characters. Most did not concern themselves with obtaining a license to produce the items. They simply sent their artists to the local cinemas to watch the cartoons and then come back to design the toys. That is why, although Mickey Mouse always had three fingers and a thumb, the artists never counted and invariably assumed there were four fingers and a thumb.

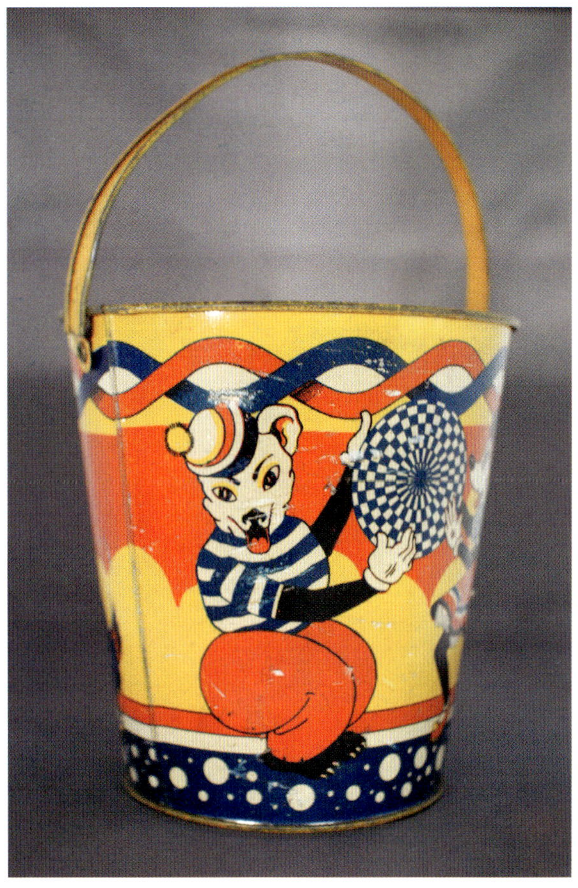

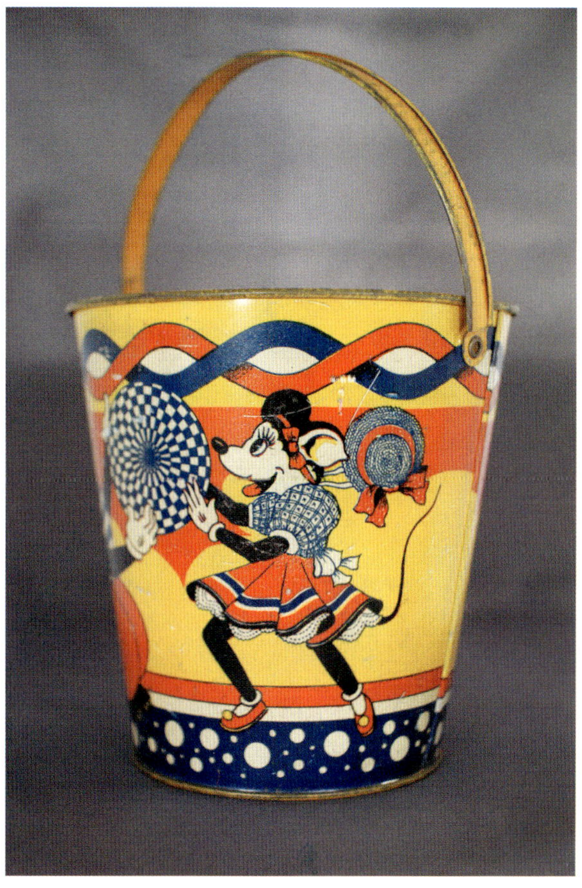

This 7" pail from Argentina really makes us wonder whether the artists ever saw the cartoons. Mickey, Minnie and Donald are really primitive. Note the five fingers. Marked OMA Industria Argentina $200-300

Australia

In 1934, Kay Kaman, responsible for the licensing of all Disney merchandise, appointed his nephew George Kamen to handle merchandising outside of the Americas. George set up his offices in London and during the next three years set up offices in 11 countries, signing 285 licensees and doing over $20,000,000 per year of sales. The Willow Co. was the licensee to produce sand toys. We believe they were licensed by George Kamen about 1938. The pail designs were provided by Disney for Willow. Willow is one of the few companies to make square pails for which they had a registered design, although they did produce some round pails too.

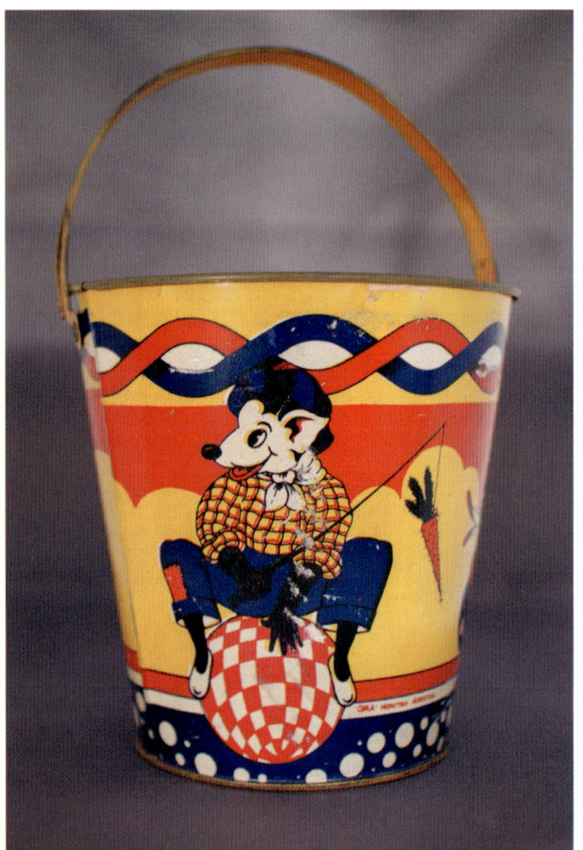

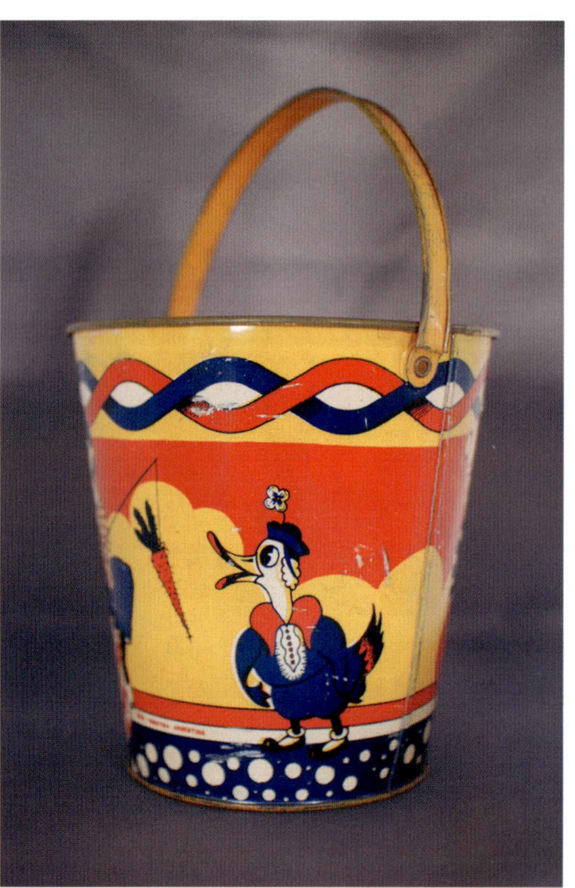

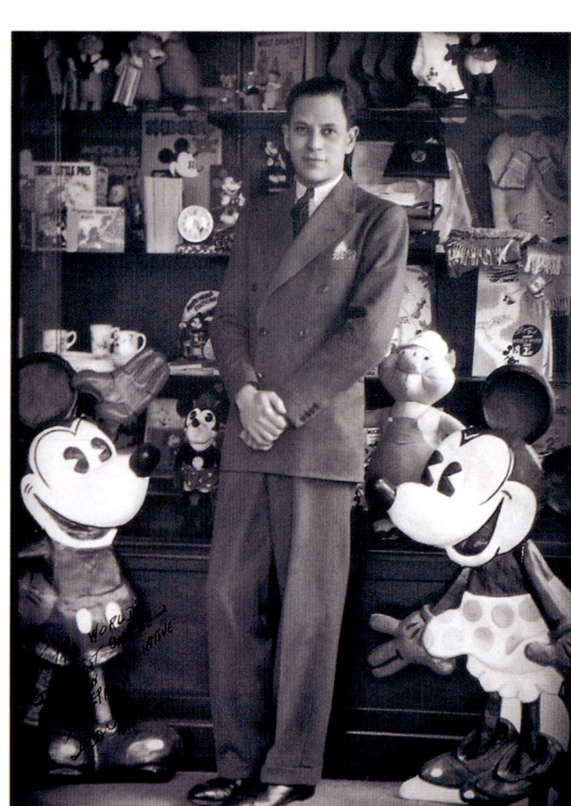

A photograph of George Kamen that he sent to his Uncle Kay. Inscribed "To the world's greatest uncle – from an appreciative nephew. George" Note the interesting merchandise shown in the photograph.

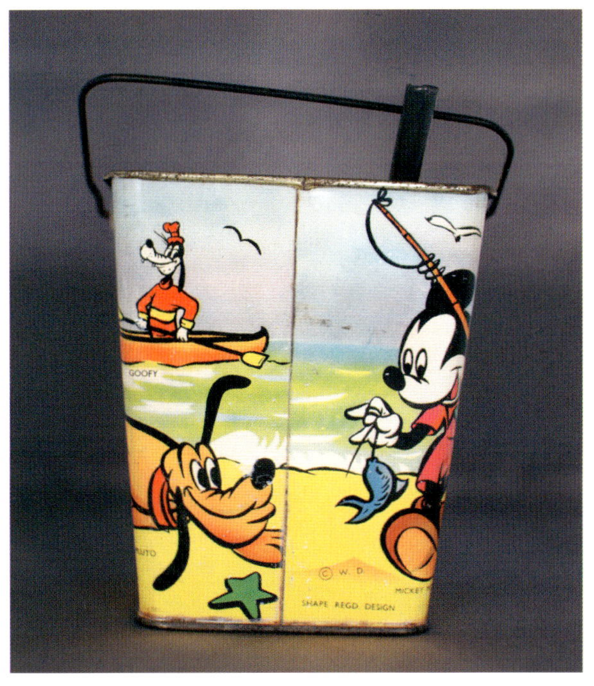

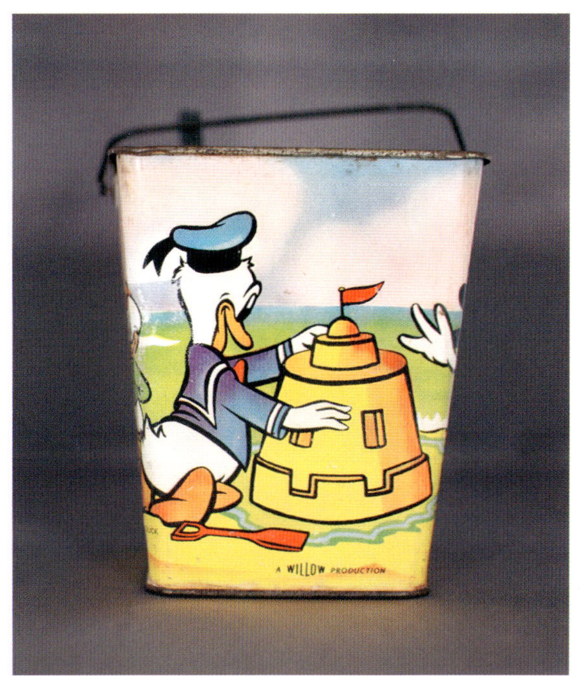

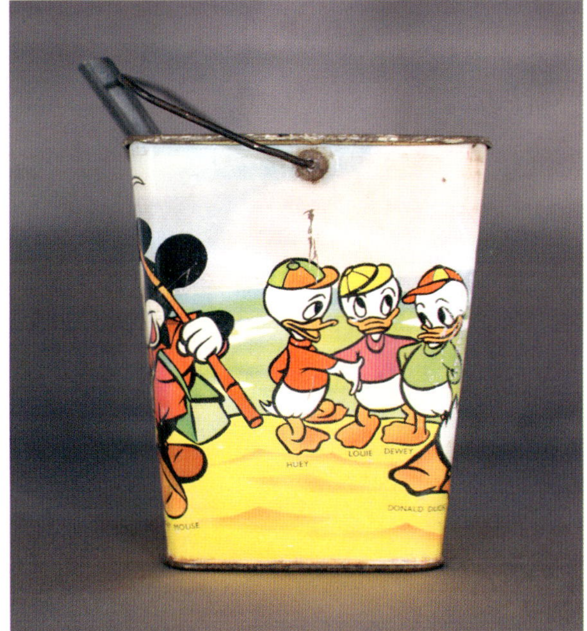

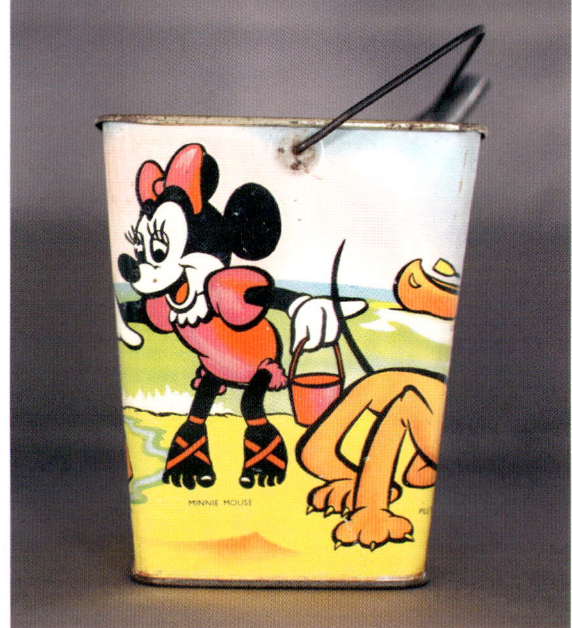

Four sides of a 6" square pail with 8.5" sand shovel featuring the characters building a sand castle. As with most Willow pails, the handle is a wire bail. This is the only time we have seen Minnie with her four toes showing. Embossed on the bottom: Willow Made in Australia Marked ©W.D. Shape Regd. Design A Willow Production. All the characters are named. $125-$300

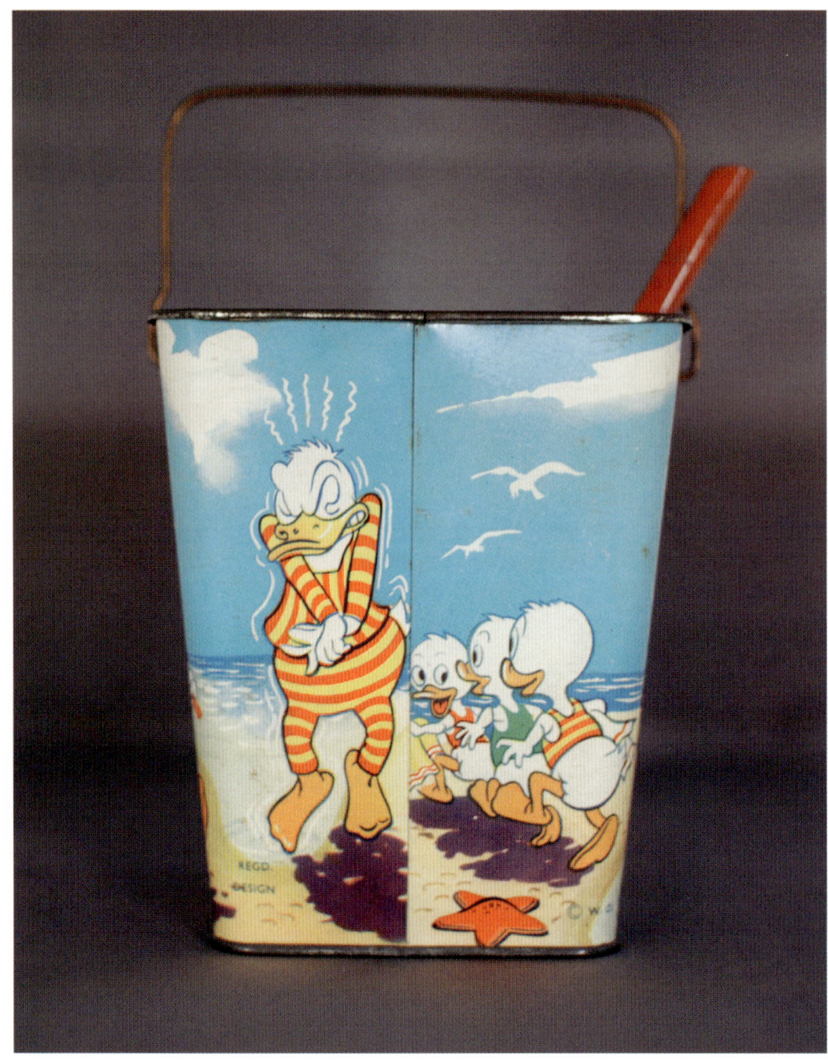

Four sides of a 6″ Donald Duck square bucket with an 8.5″ shovel. Poor Donald caught just a little fish while each of his nephews caught a large one. Also a great image of Donald shivering in a pair of long johns. Same markings as previous pail. $150-350

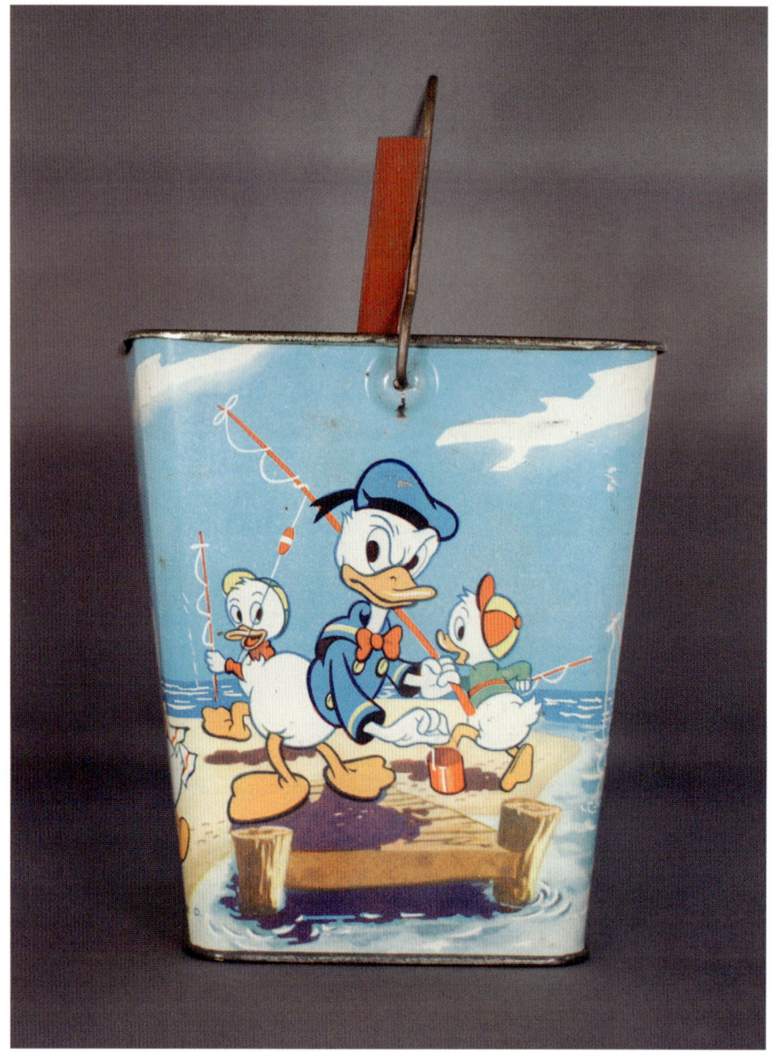

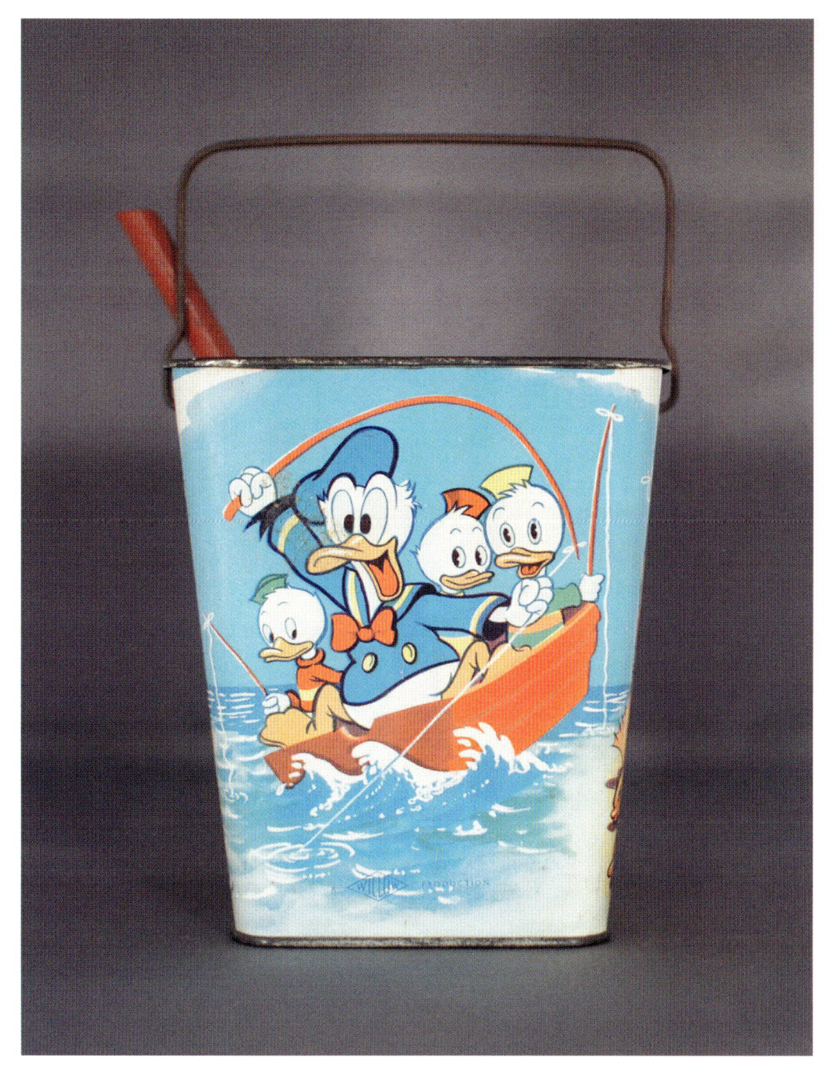

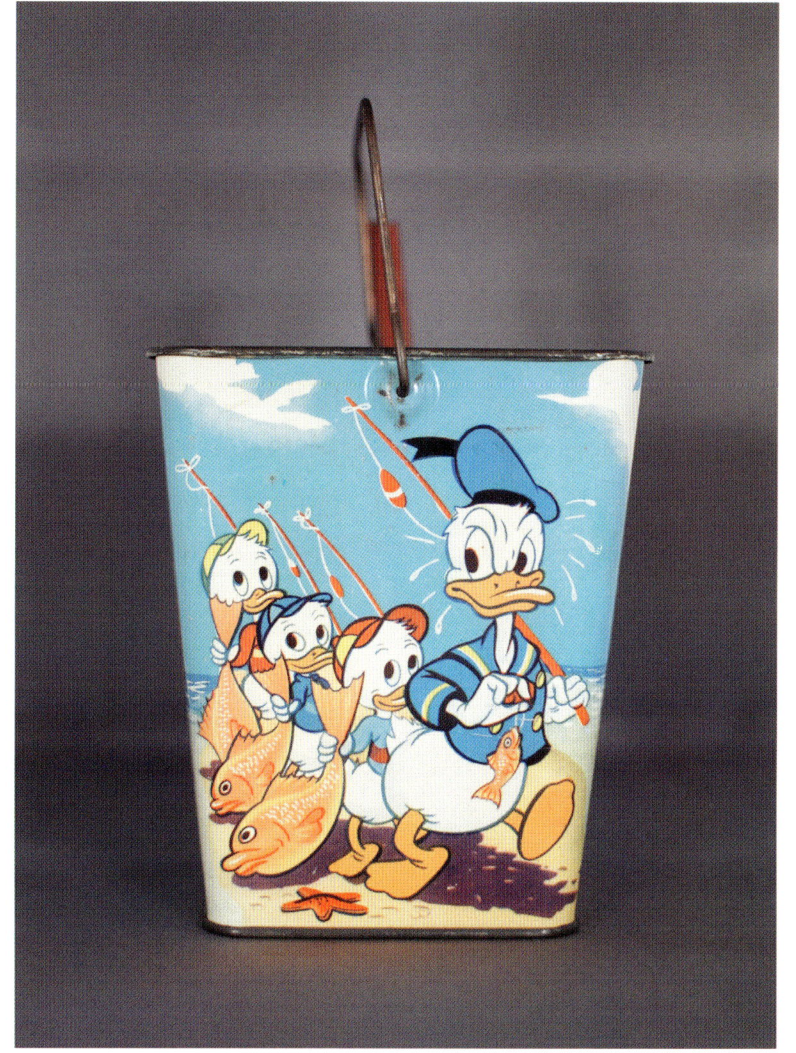

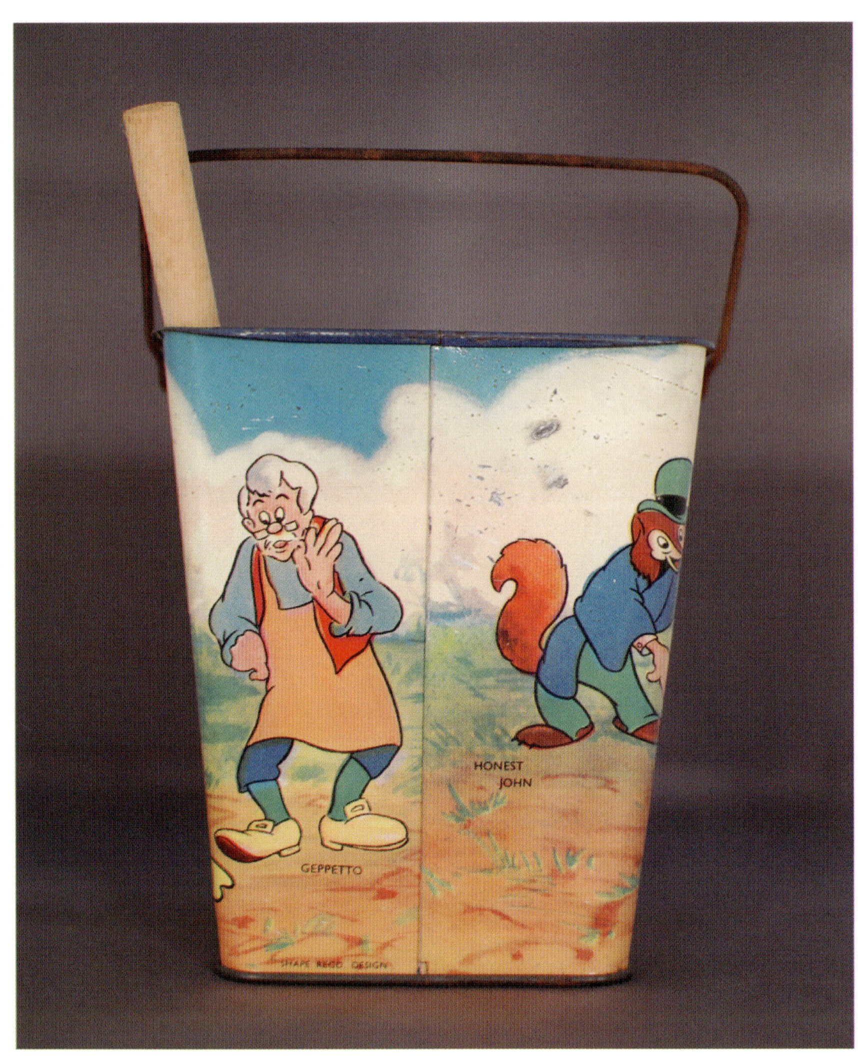

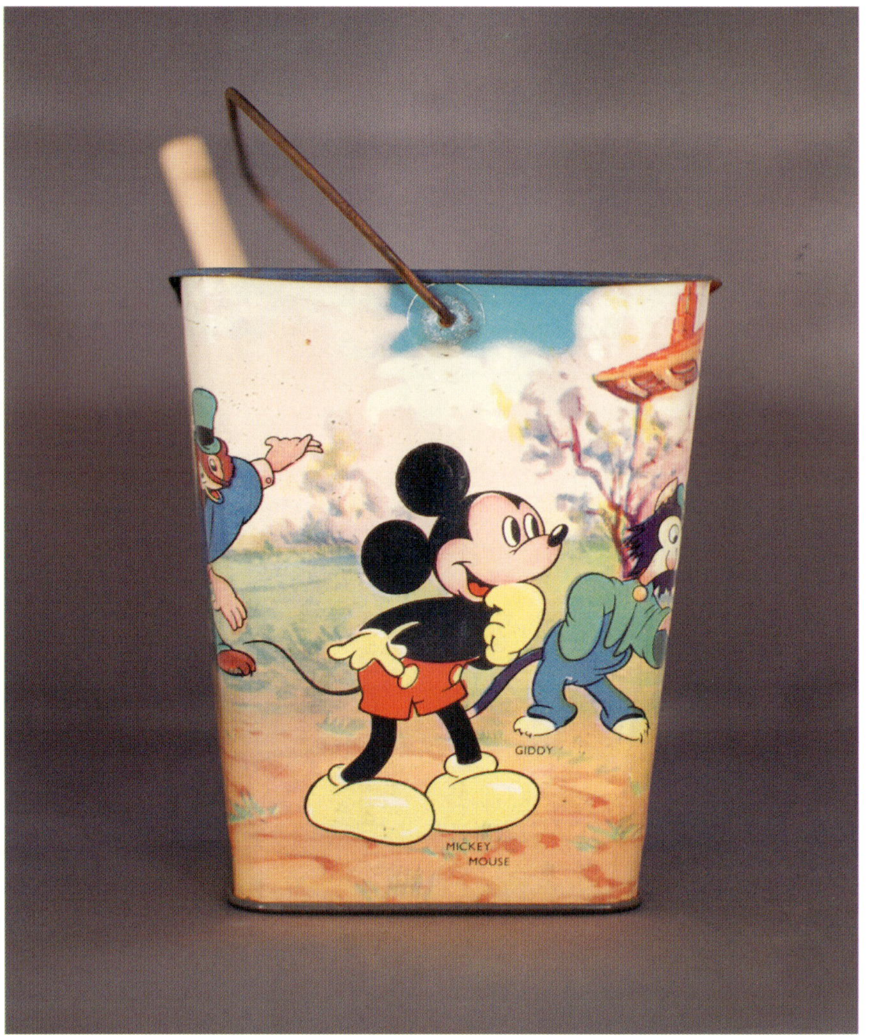

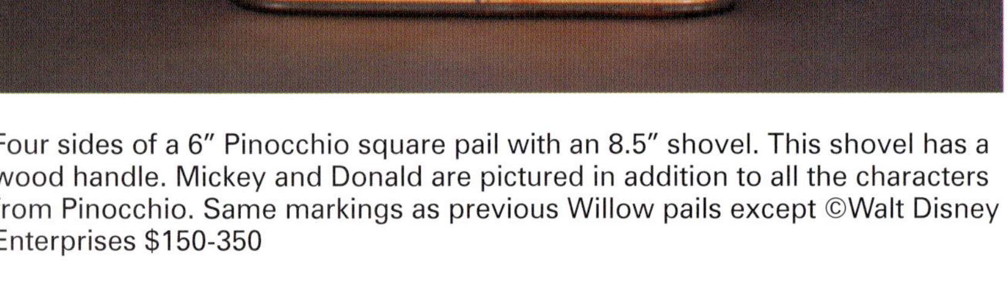
Four sides of a 6″ Pinocchio square pail with an 8.5″ shovel. This shovel has a wood handle. Mickey and Donald are pictured in addition to all the characters from Pinocchio. Same markings as previous Willow pails except ©Walt Disney Enterprises $150-350

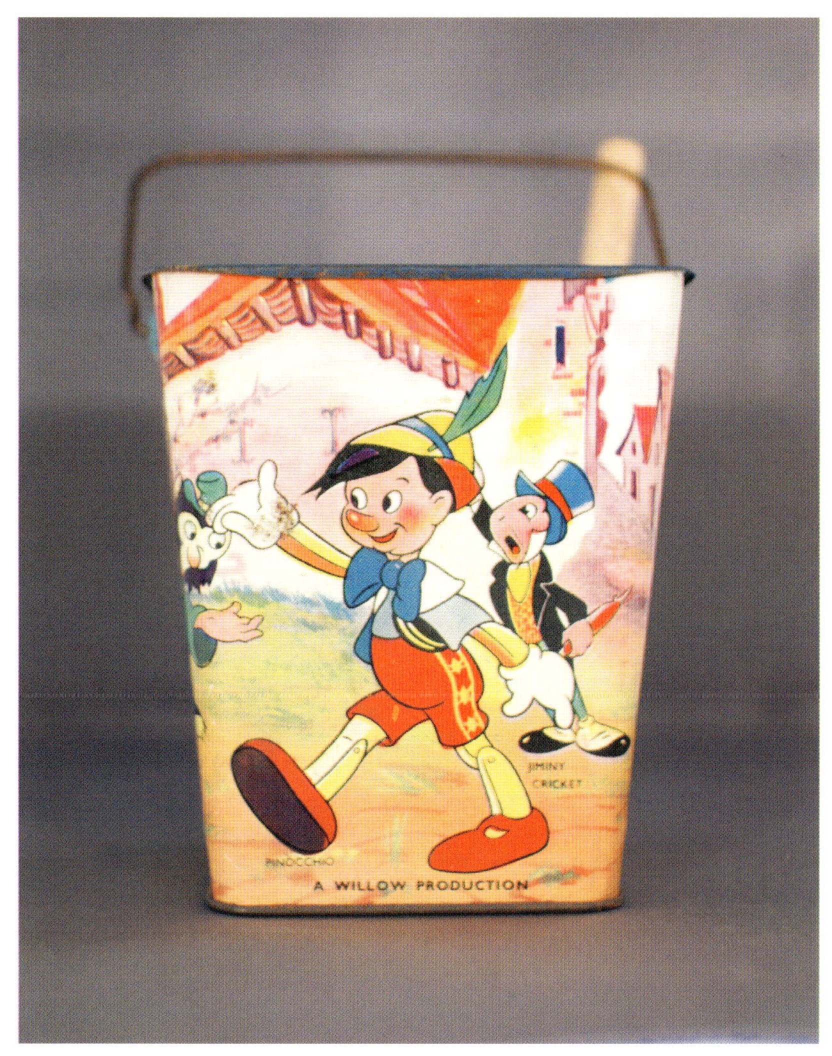
JIMINY
CRICKET
PINOCCHIO
A WILLOW PRODUCTION

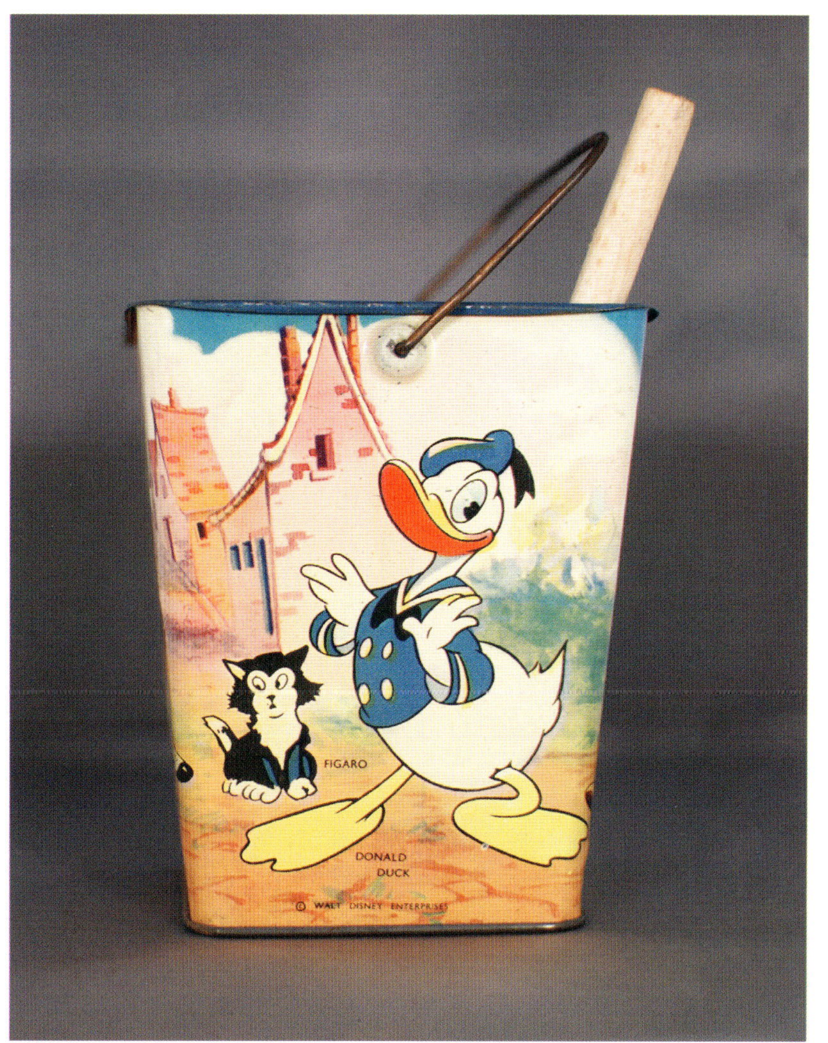
FIGARO
DONALD
DUCK
© WALT DISNEY ENTERPRISES

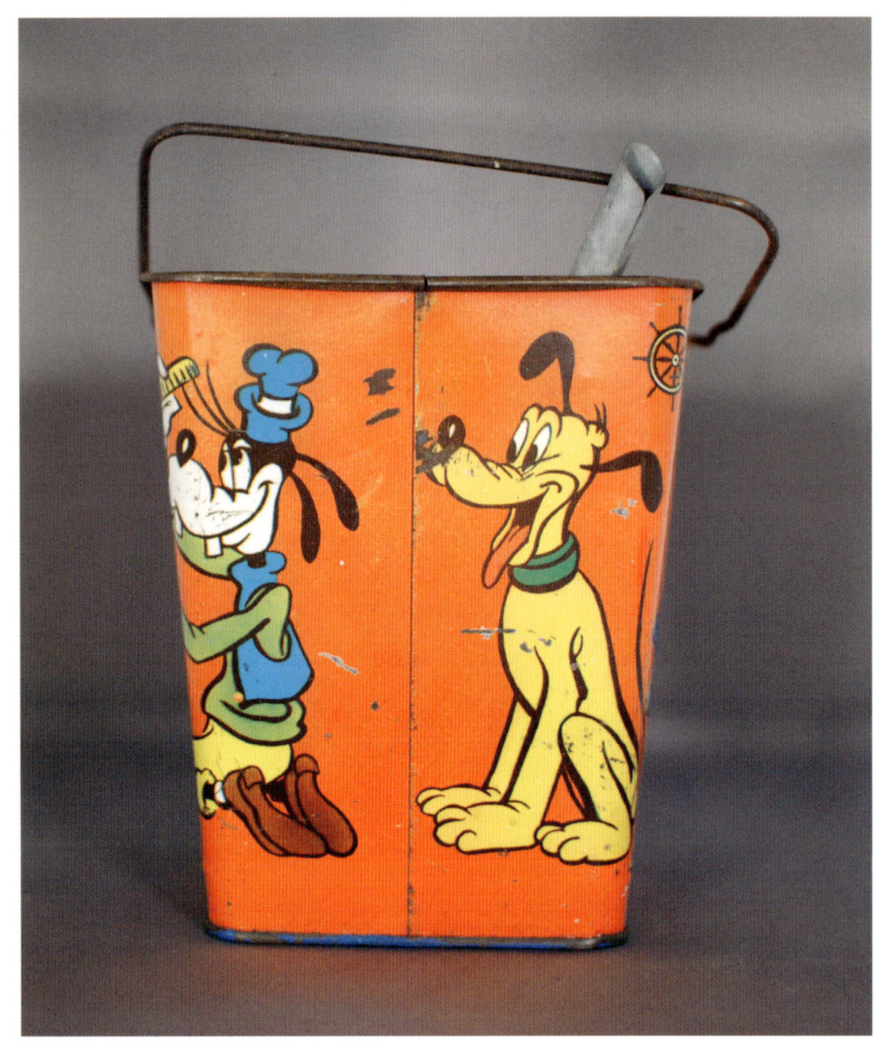

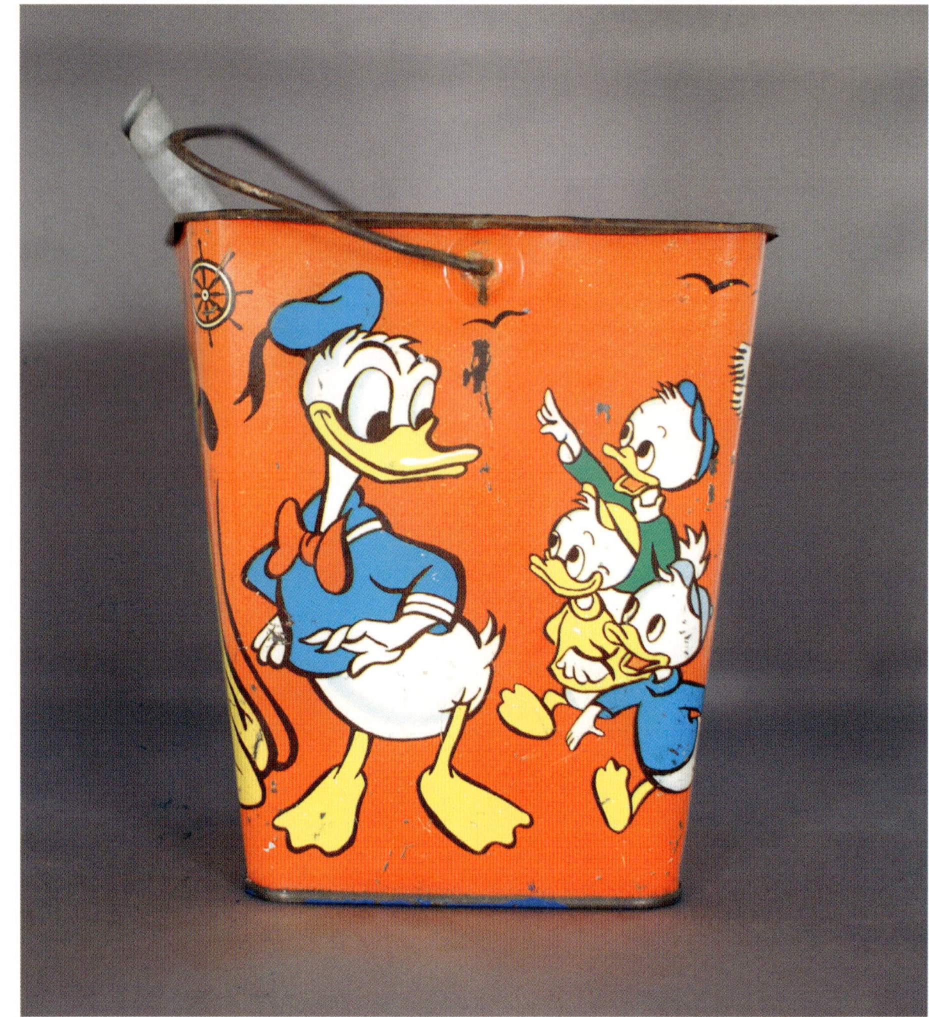

Four sides of a 6″ Disney square pail with an 8.5″ shovel. Mickey, Minnie, Goofy, Pluto, Donald and his three nephews adorn the pail. Same markings as previous pail except ©W.D.P. $100-225

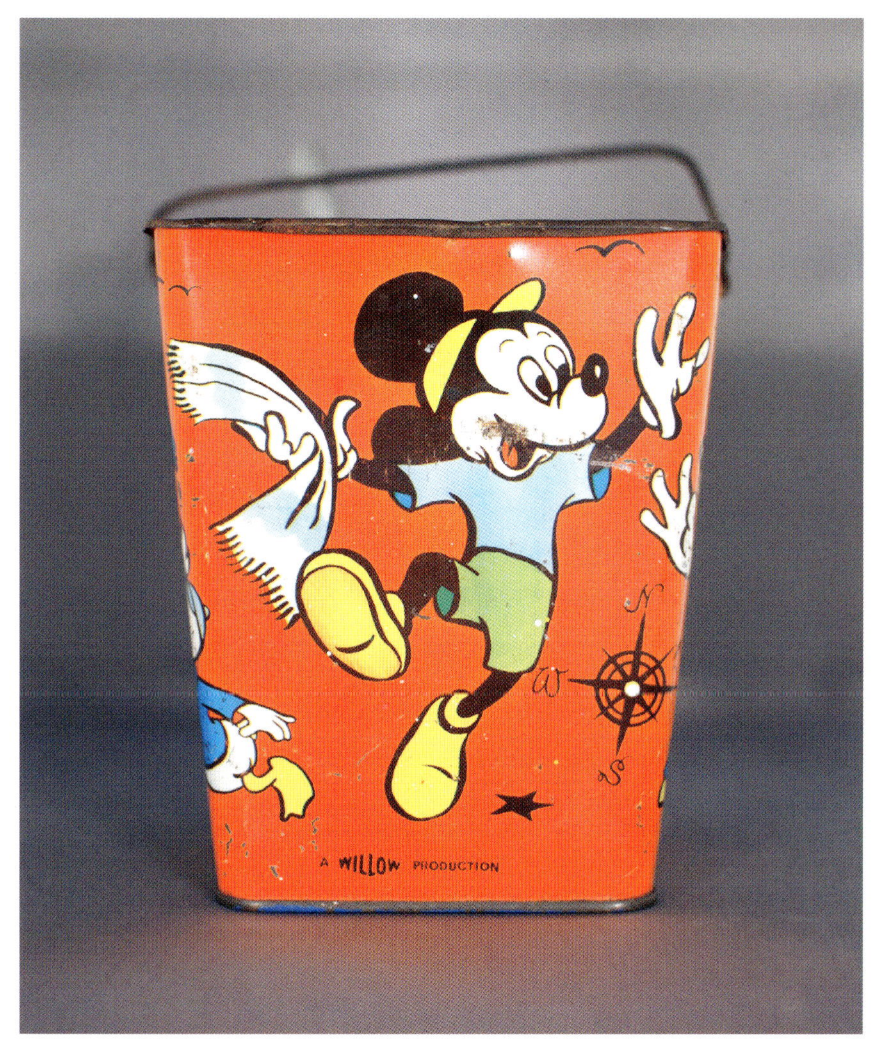
A WILLOW PRODUCTION

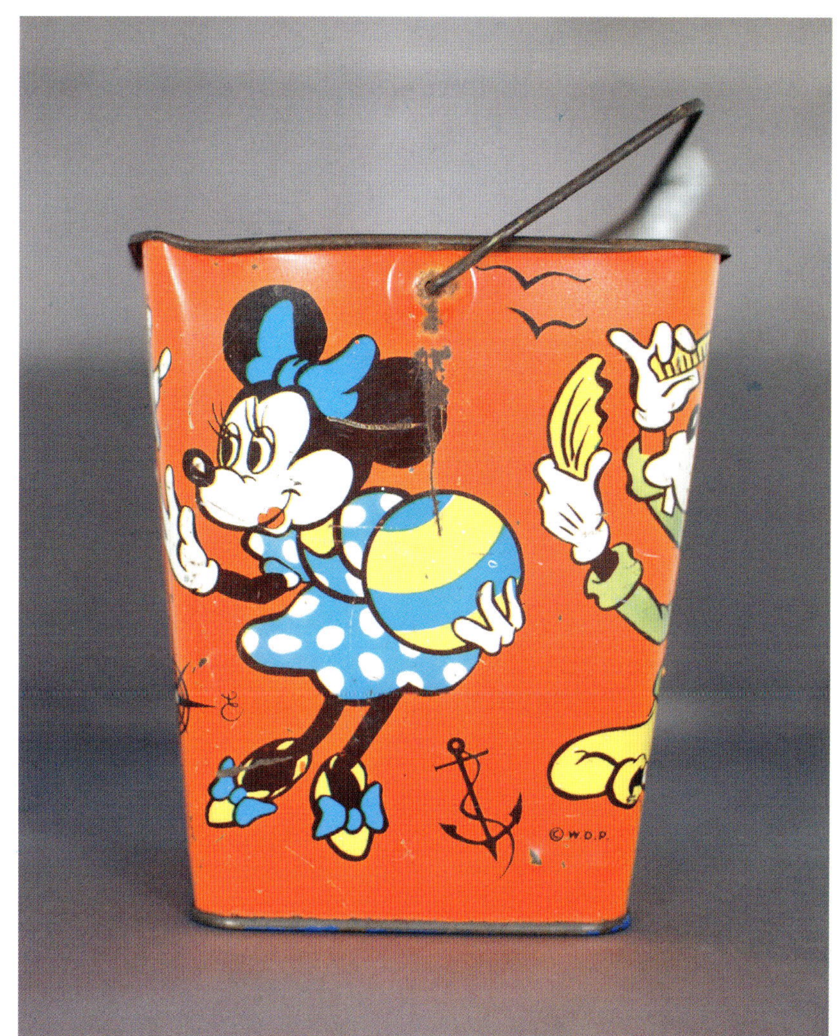
© W.D.P.

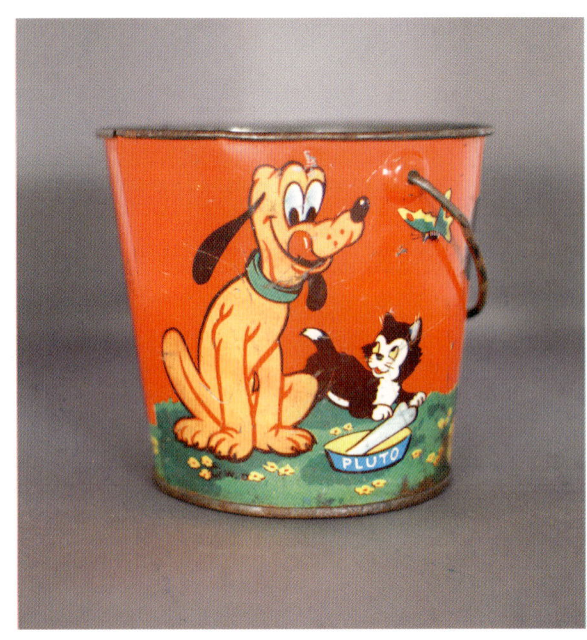

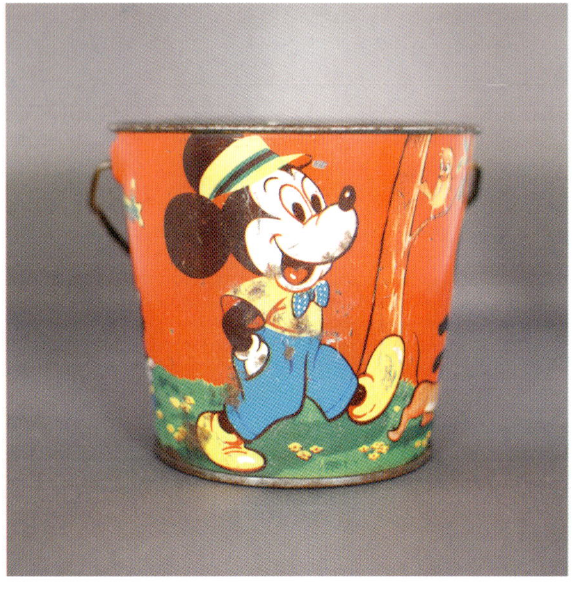

Three views of a 4" Disney round pail by Willow. Markings same as previous. $125-200

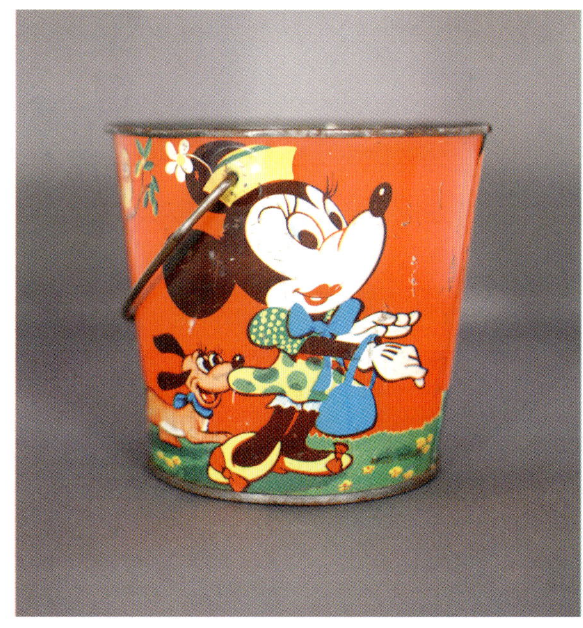

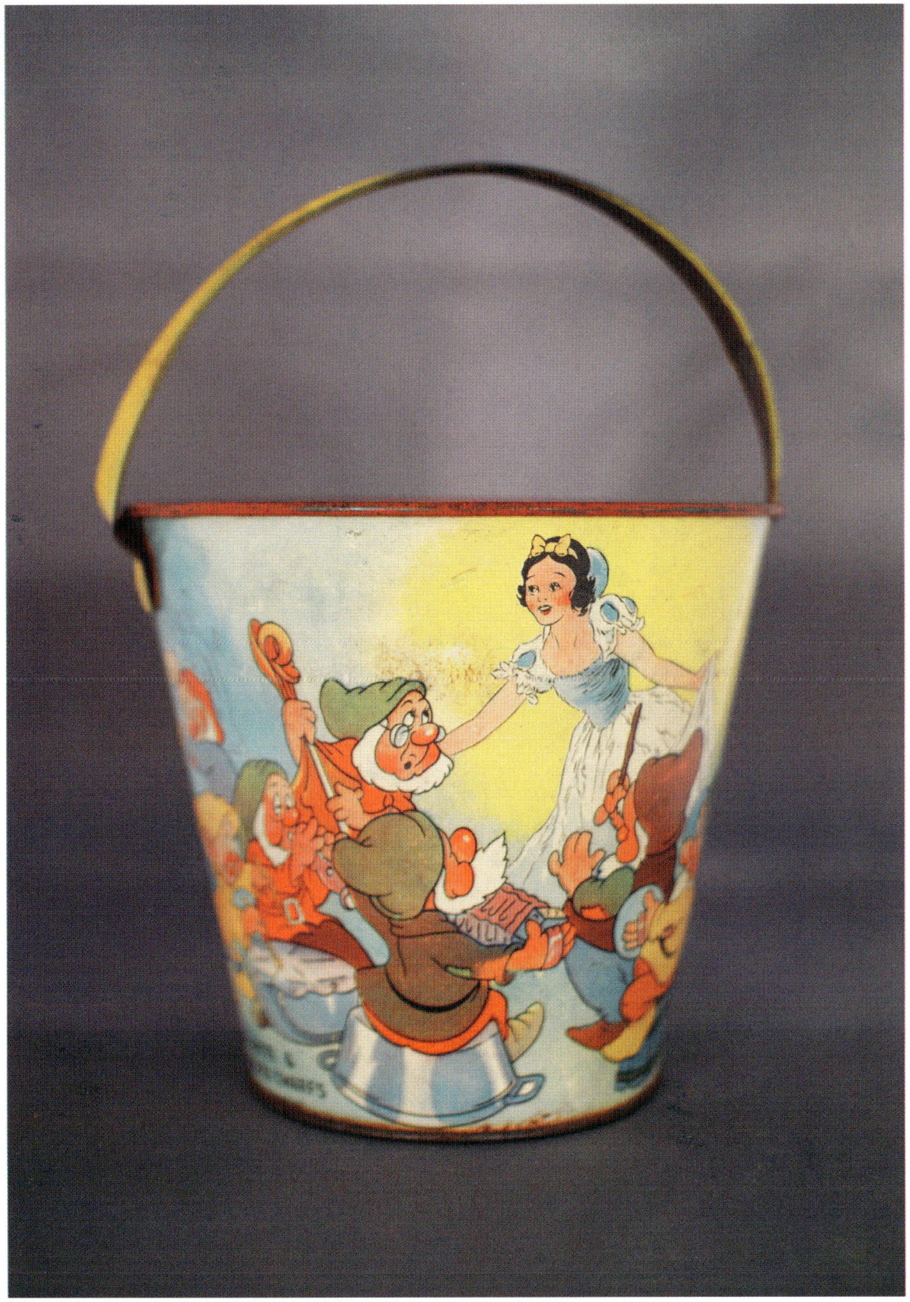

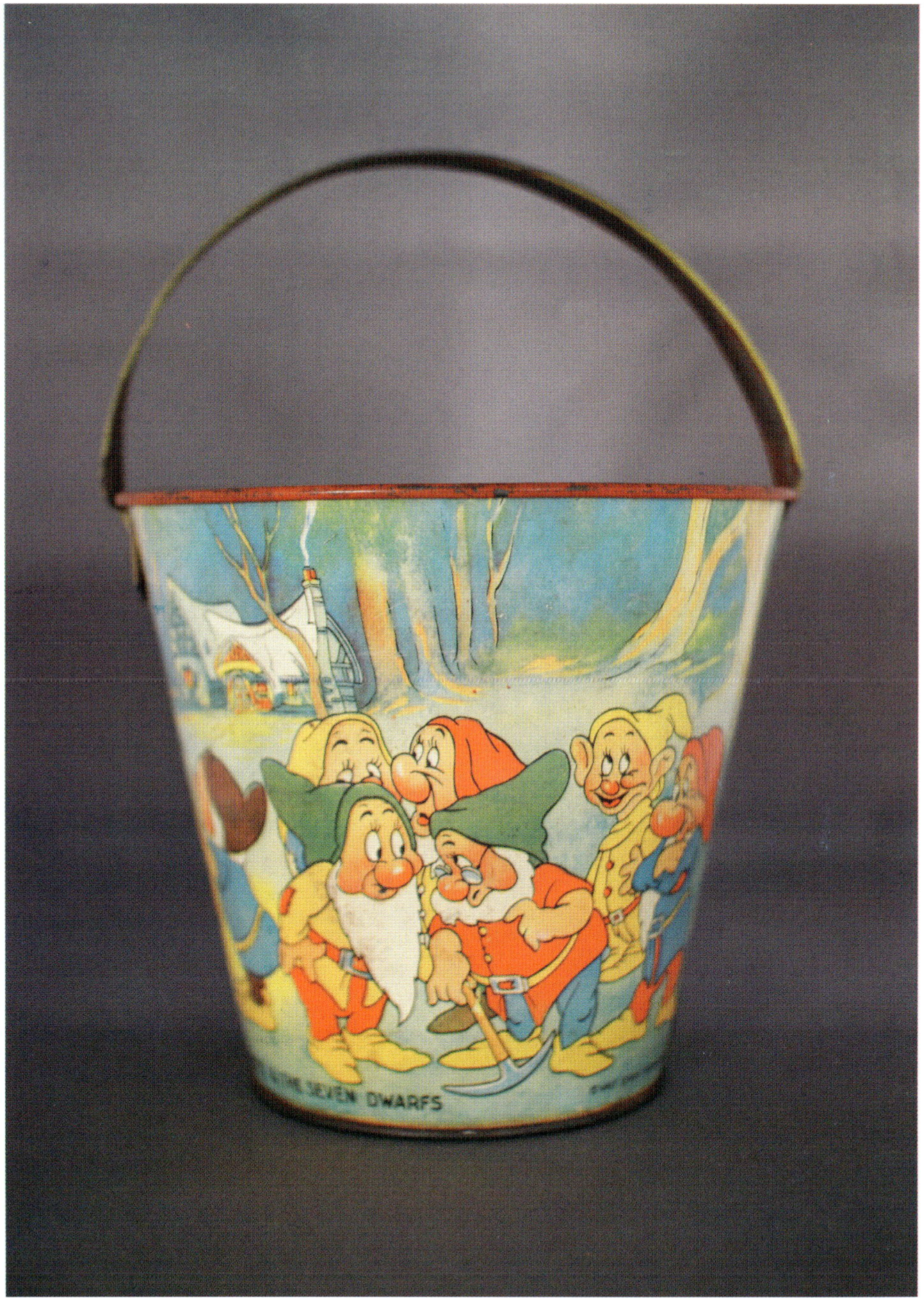

Two views of the 6" Snow White and Seven Dwarfs round sand pail that has a regular handle rather than the bail. Marked ©Walt Disney Enterprises with Willow embossed on bottom.
$300-650

Belgium

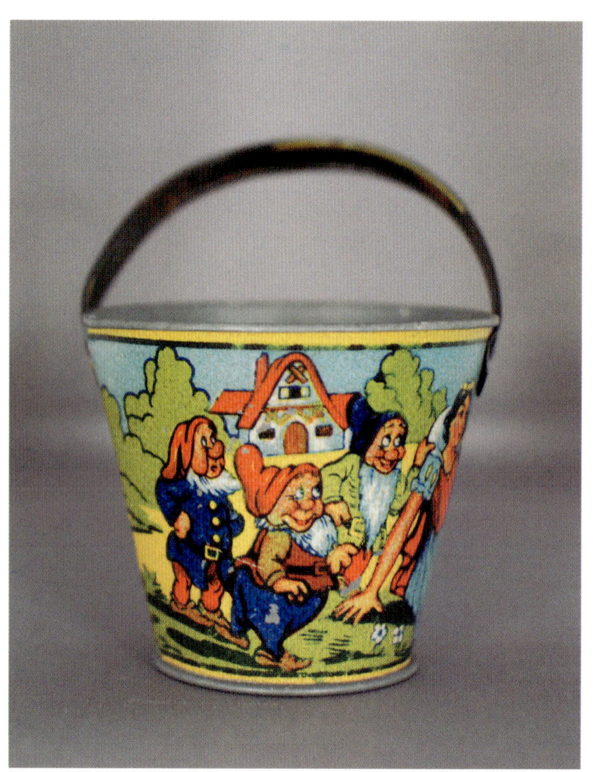

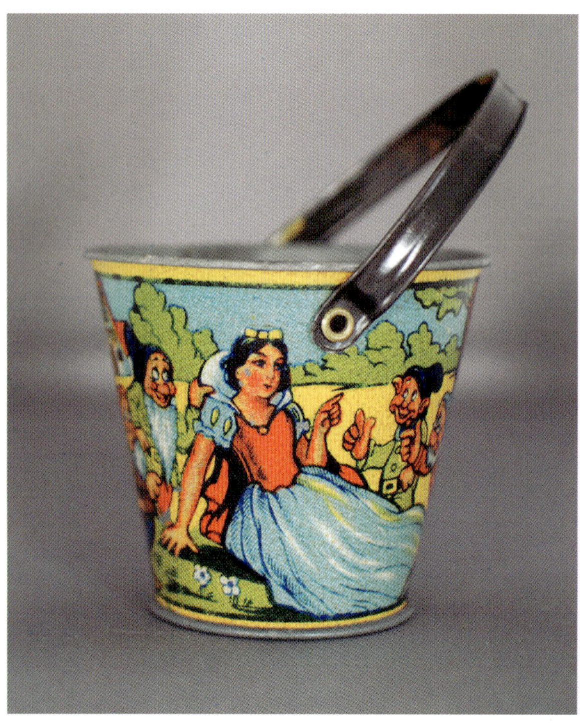

Three views of a 3" Snow White and the Seven Dwarfs pail. It is unmarked but believed to have been made in Belgium. Because it is unmarked, it is probably unauthorized. $75-150

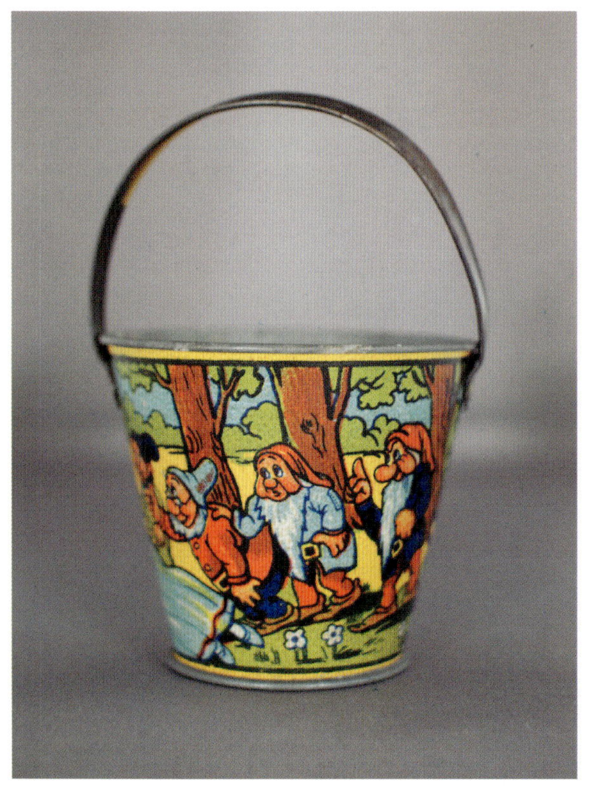

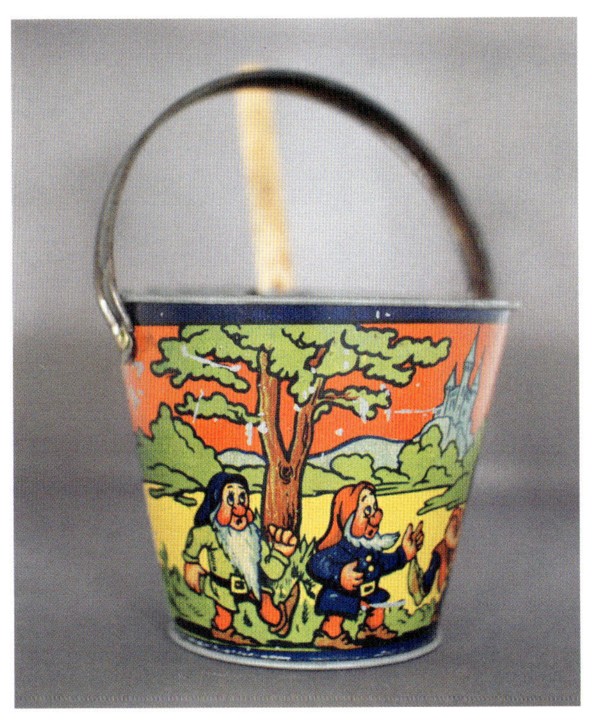

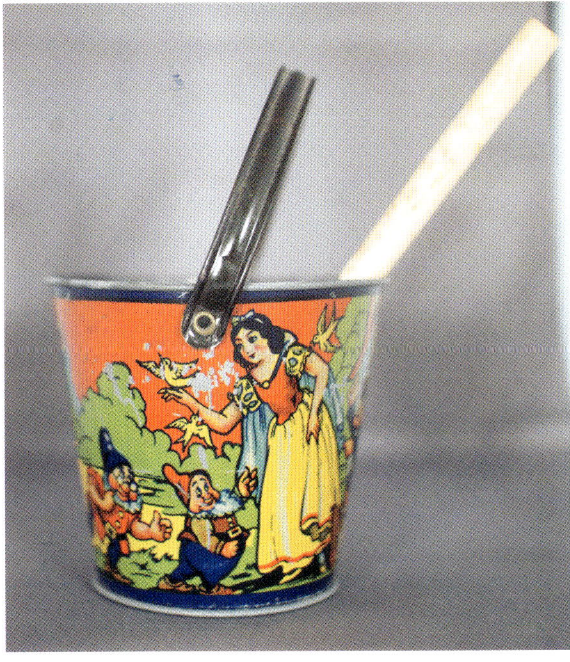

A similar pail to the previous but three different scenes. This is a 5″ pail with its original 8.5″ shovel with a wood handle. *Bernabe collection.* $75-175

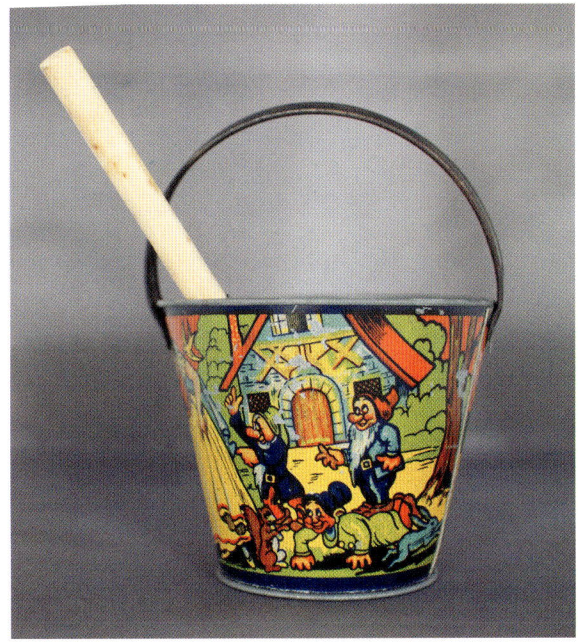

Brazil

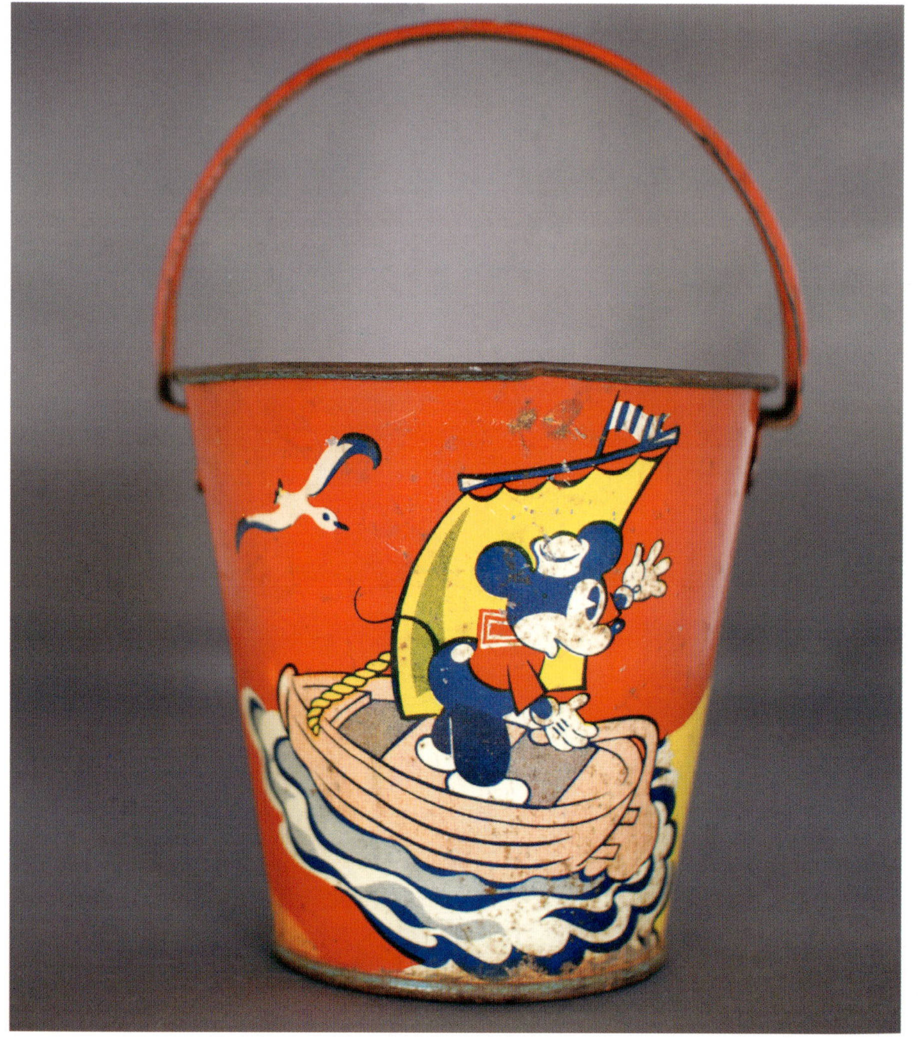

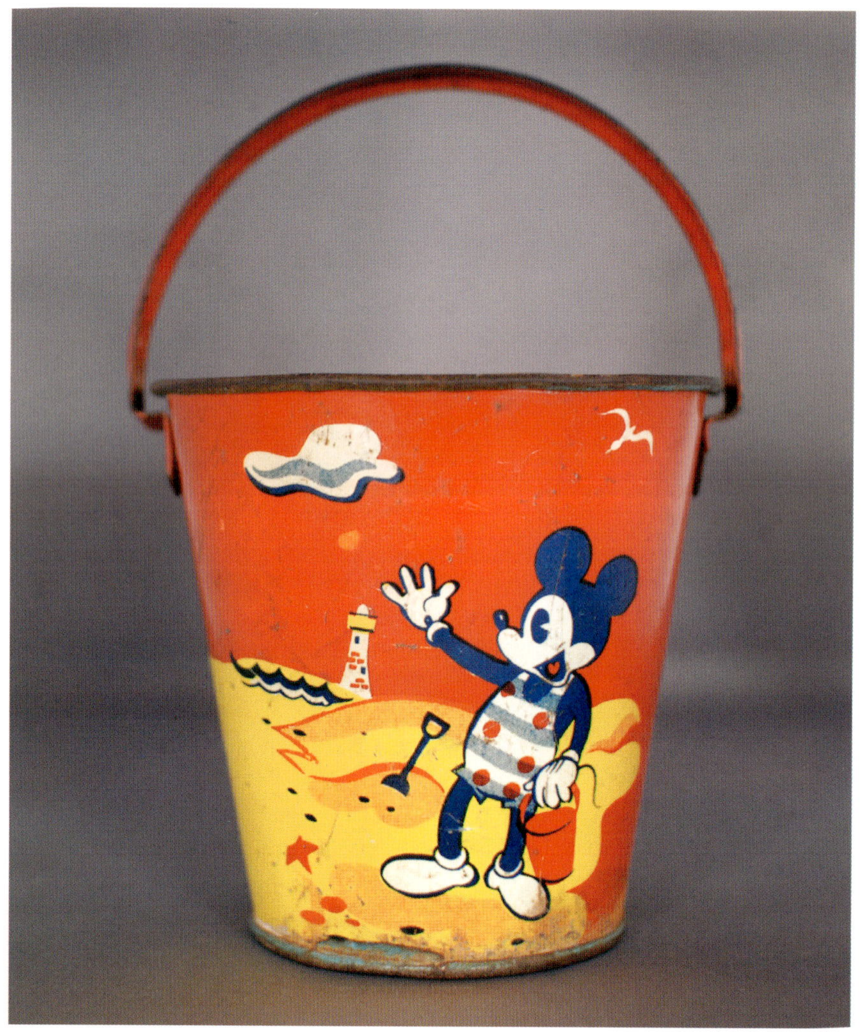

A 4.5" Mickey sand pail. Unmarked, but from South America, probably Brazil. It shows Mickey with sand pail and shovel and a nephew sailing a boat. $125-250

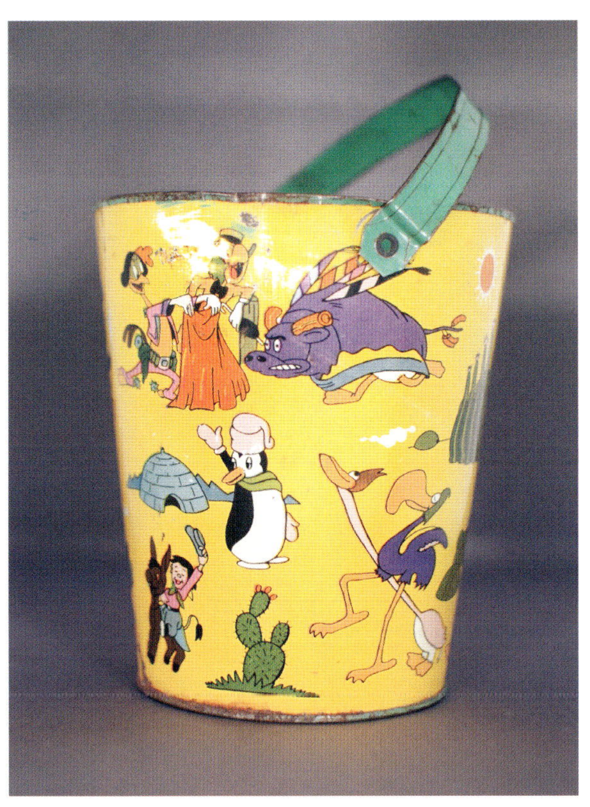

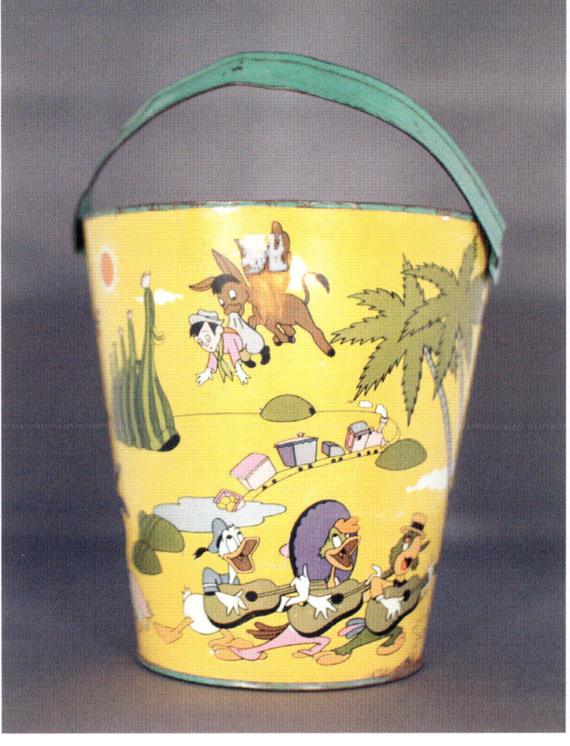

A 6" Three Caballeros pail believed to have been made in Brazil. There are no markings but it is from South America and the film took place in Brazil. $150-250

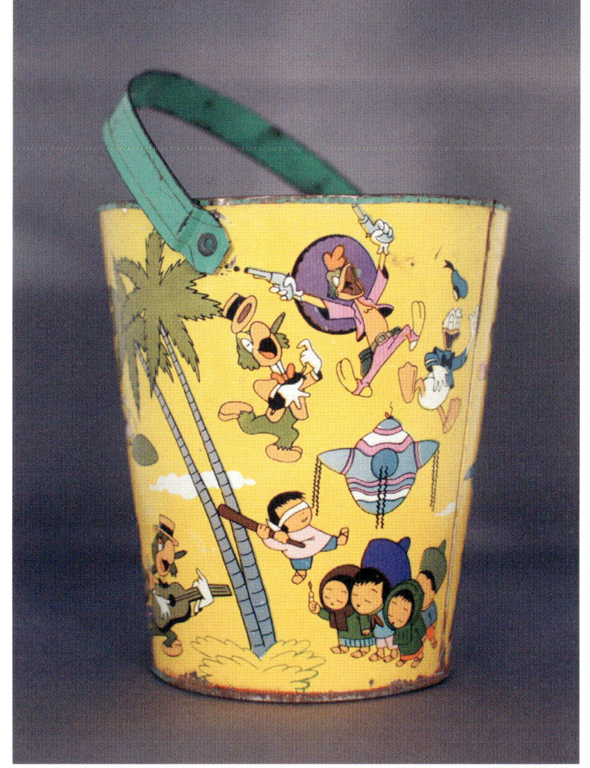

Canada

Canada produced a number of great pieces of Disney merchandise from the 1930s through to the present day. However, few sand pails were produced. The example here is interesting because it relates the story of Mickey Mouse and Donald Duck building a sand castle. Because of its shape, it might have originally held confections.

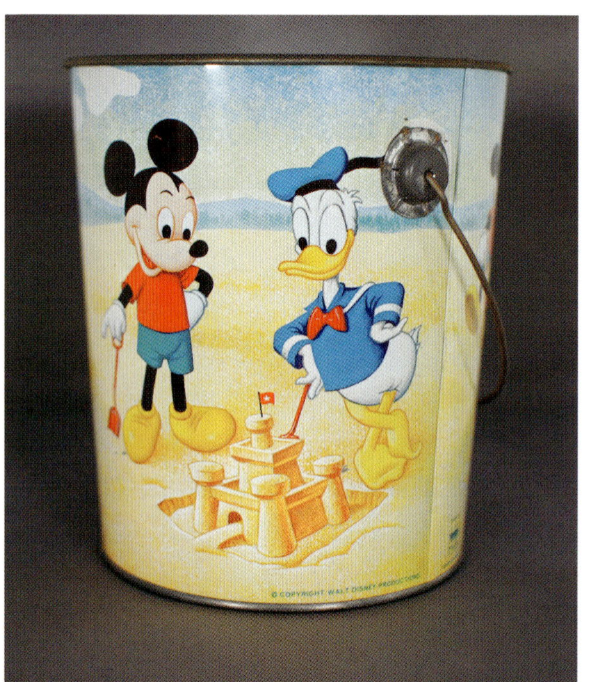

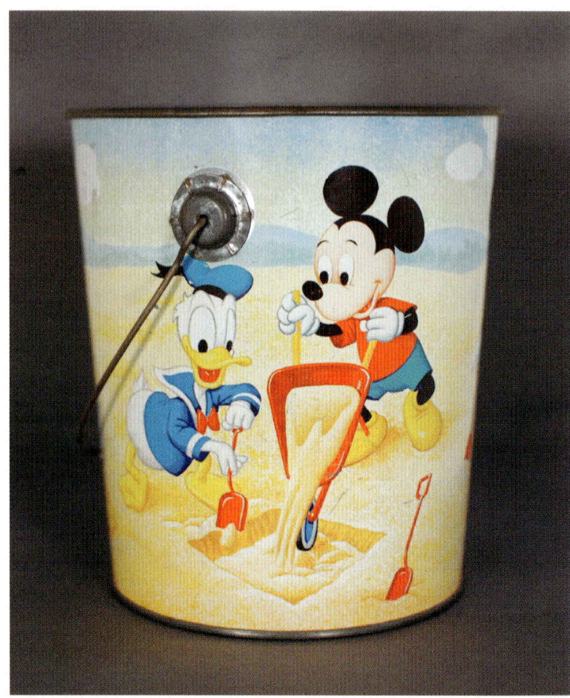

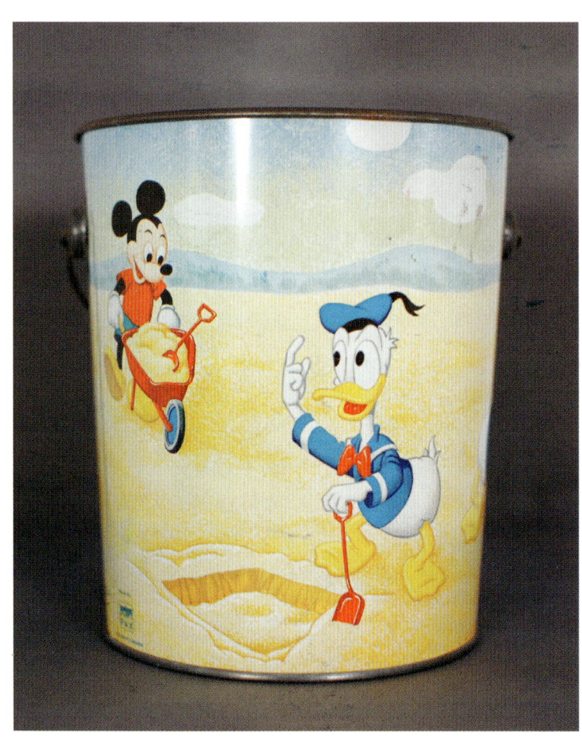

Three views of this 7.25" pail showing Mickey and Donald building a sand castle. Marked © Copyright Walt Disney Productions PAX Toronto Canada $125-200

Chile

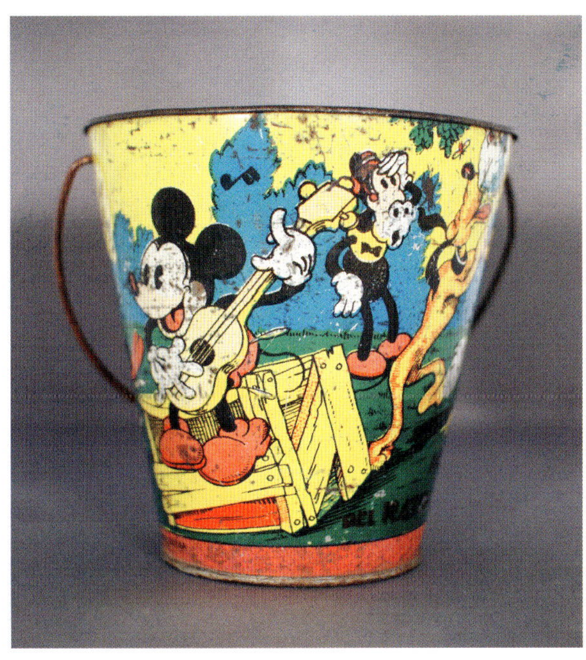

A 6" Mickey's Picnic pail made in Chile. Condition is an issue. Images are identical to Ohio Art pail, although markings say "Picnic del raton Mickey" and Fabricacion chilena. $125-250

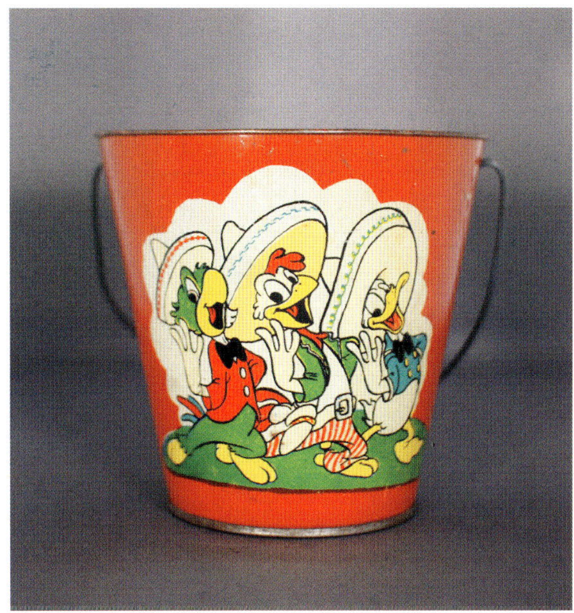

Both sides of The Caballeros 4.5" pail with 6.5" shovel featuring Donald, Panchito and Joe Carioca. All the pails from Chile we have seen have bail handles. Marked "Fabricacion chilena F.E. s.k." $200-400

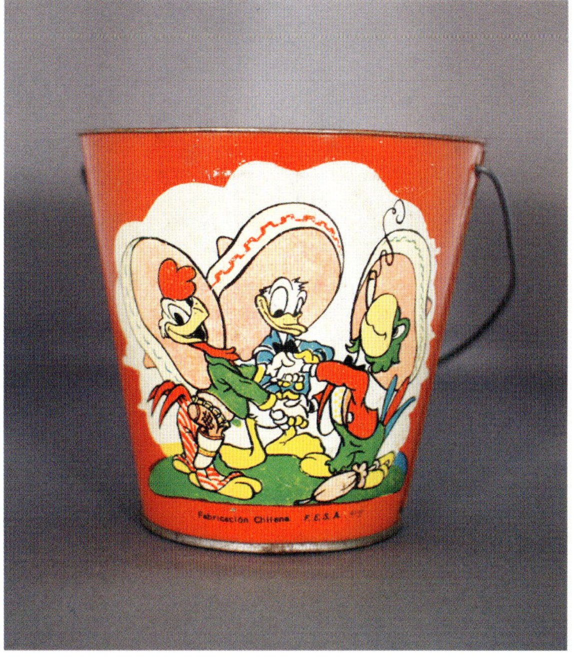

Denmark

Although the Scandinavian countries of Denmark, Finland, Norway, and Sweden produced some great Disney merchandise, they did not make many sand toys because of the lack of beaches and warm water. With 25 licensed vendors by 1937, they did produce many products including some great tin containers. Denmark did produce a beautiful Snow White sand pail which is pictured here.

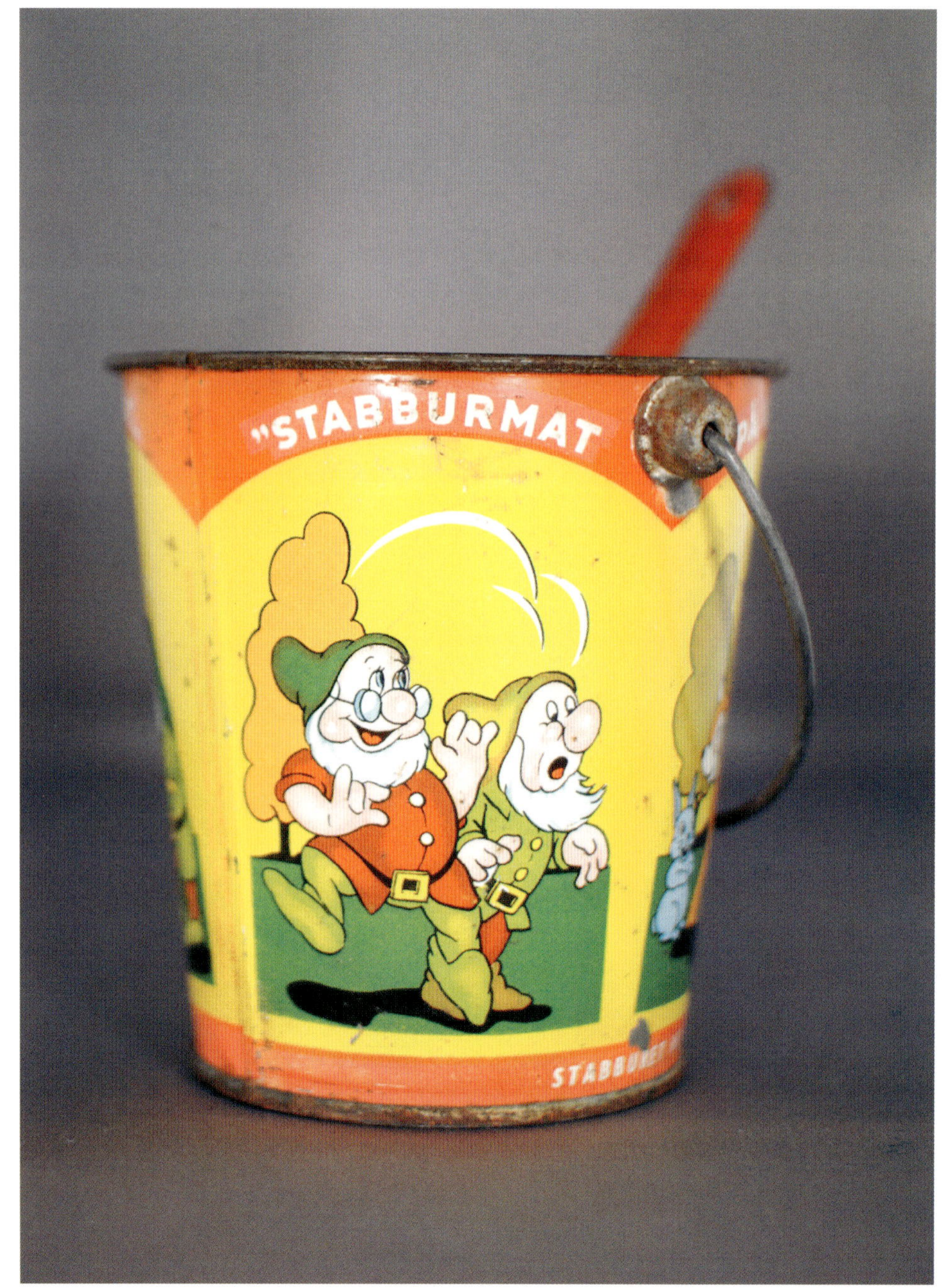

This 4.25" pail with a 6" spoon features Snow White and five of the Dwarfs. Copyright Walt Disney Productions. Med Tihatelse. Av Mickey Mouse Corporation Kobenhavn. $175-300

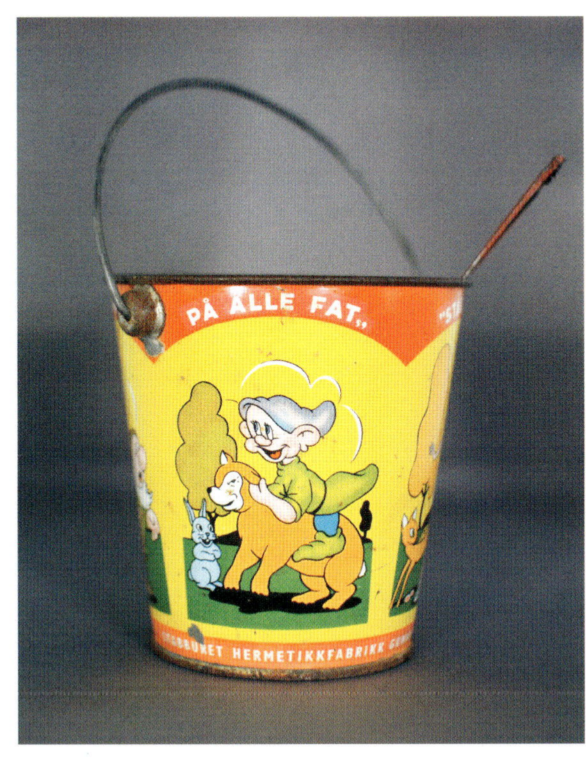
PÅ ALLE FAT„
HERMETIKKFABRIKK

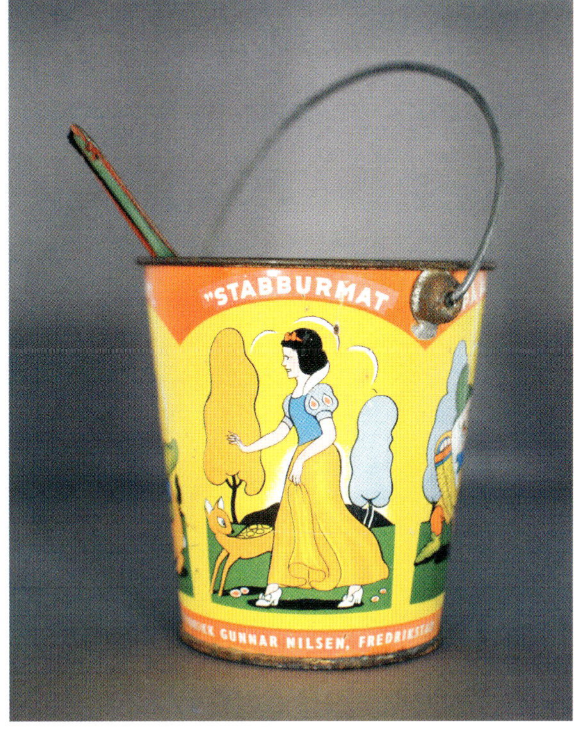
"STABBURMAT
GUNNAR NILSEN,

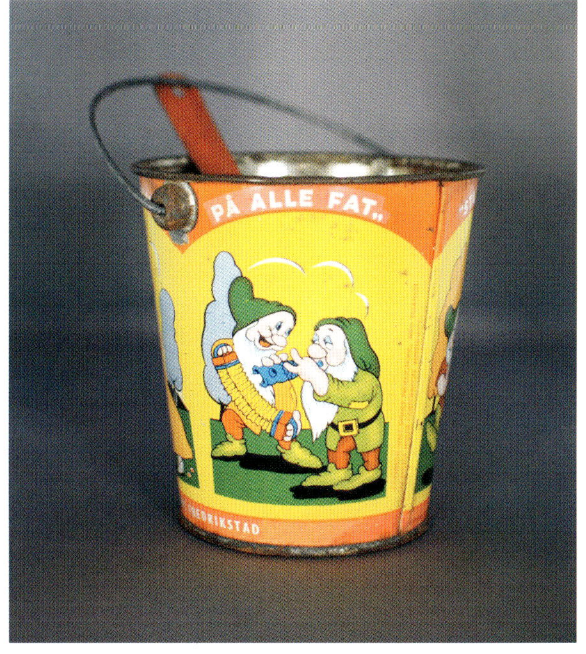
PÅ ALLE FAT„
FREDRIKSTAD

France

Although their production was limited, EGDA (Etablissements G. de Andreis S.A.) produced truly magnificent sand pails. Included are two examples both from the mid-1930s. Each is embossed with bright colors and each has a raised bottom.

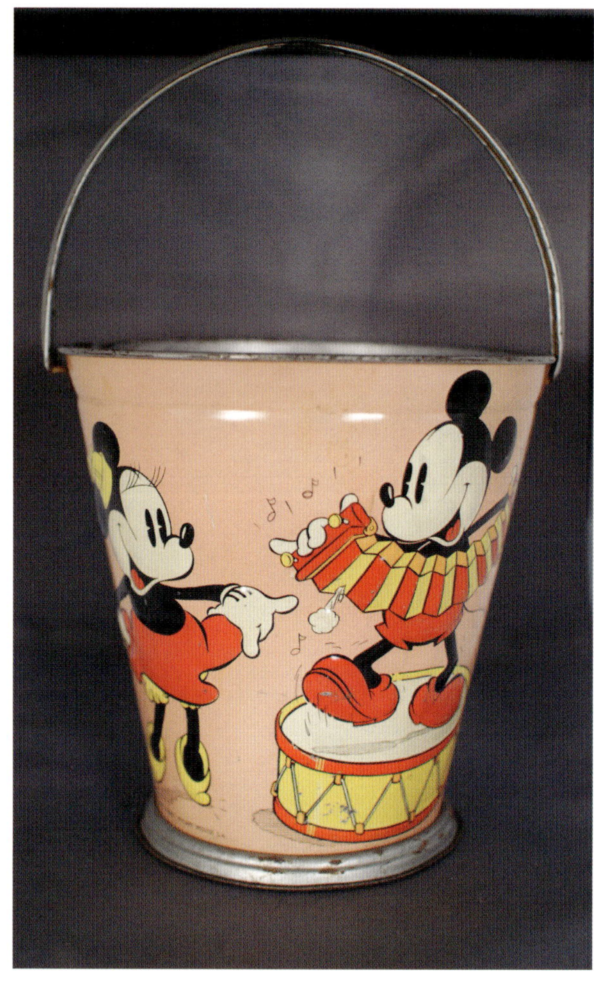

Perhaps the finest Disney sand pail ever produced, this 8.75″ embossed pail features Mickey on a drum playing the concertina while a delighted Minnie looks on. From the mid 1930s, it is marked: EGDA Par Aut. Walt Disney – Mickey Mouse S.A. $2,000-4,000

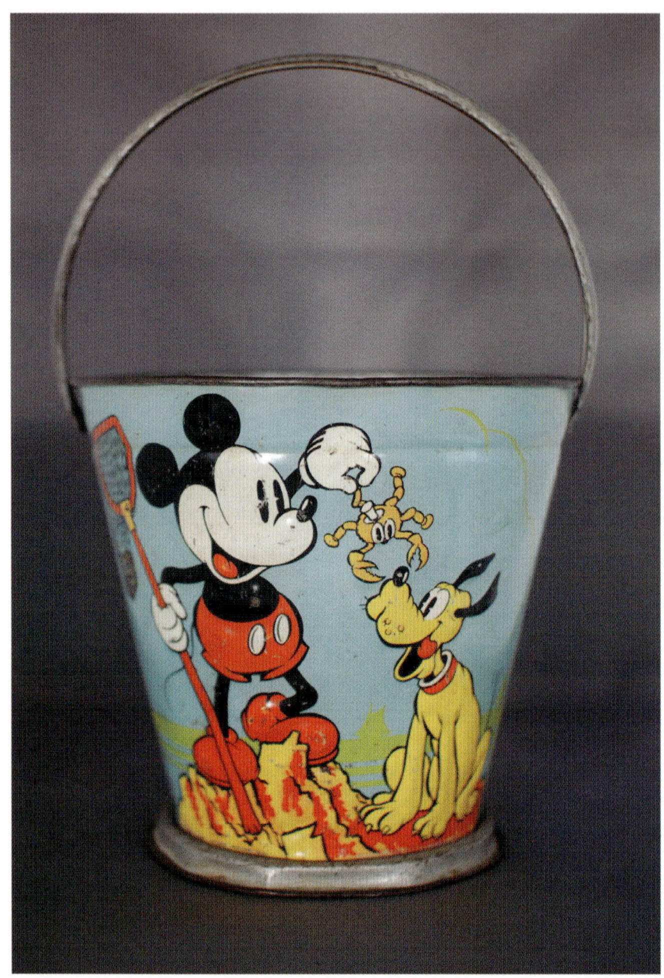

This 6.5″ embossed pail by EGDA features Mickey holding a crab up for Pluto to admire. Marked: EGDA Par Aut. Walt Disney – Mickey Mouse S.A. It also came in a 5″ version. The same image is on both sides. $600-900

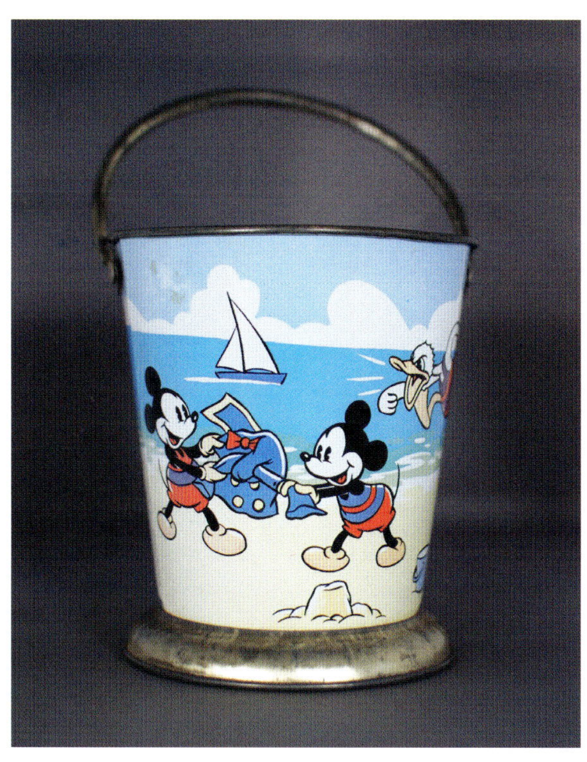

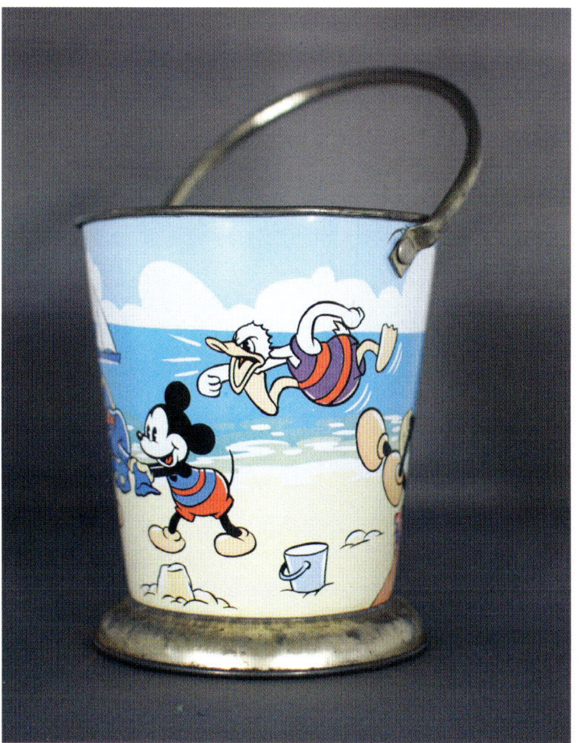

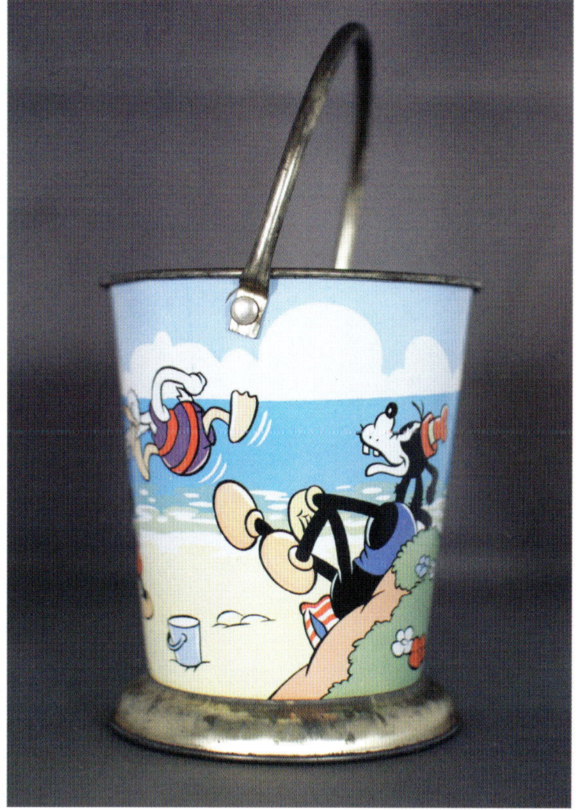

Four views of a 5" French pail featuring Mickey, Donald, Goofy and Mickey's nephews. The pail looks older than it is due to the pie-eyed Mickey and long billed Donald. From the late 1960s or early 1970s. Marked ©Walt Disney Productions Virojanglor-Paris-Made in France. Features a raised bottom. $150-350

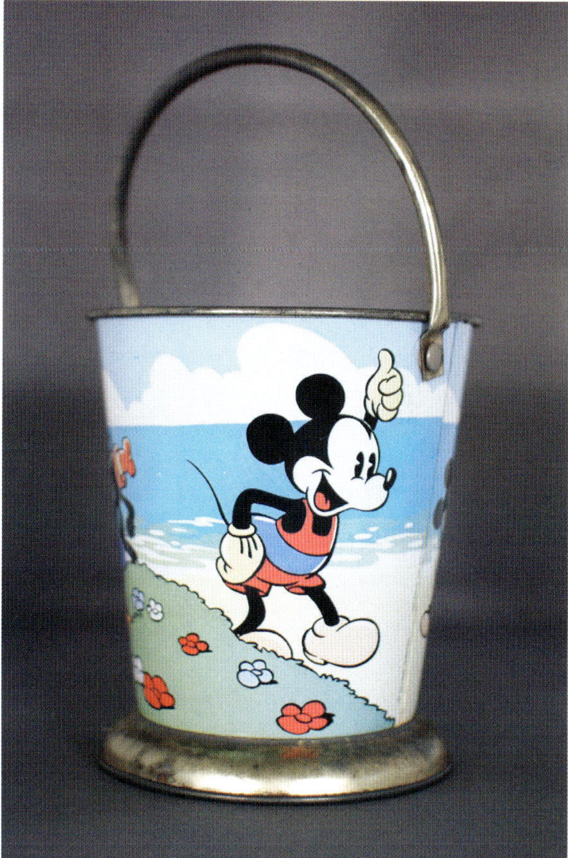

Great Britain

Through the efforts of George Kamen, Great Britain had more licensed products than any other country after the United States. This was particularly true with sand pails and sprinklers as a British company, Paton-Calvert & Co. Ltd. of Liverpool, with their Happynak Series were exceeded only by Ohio Art in the number of metal sand toys they produced. A sampling is shown here. A few were manufactured in the 1930s, having great early images. Most were produced in the late 1940s and 1950s.

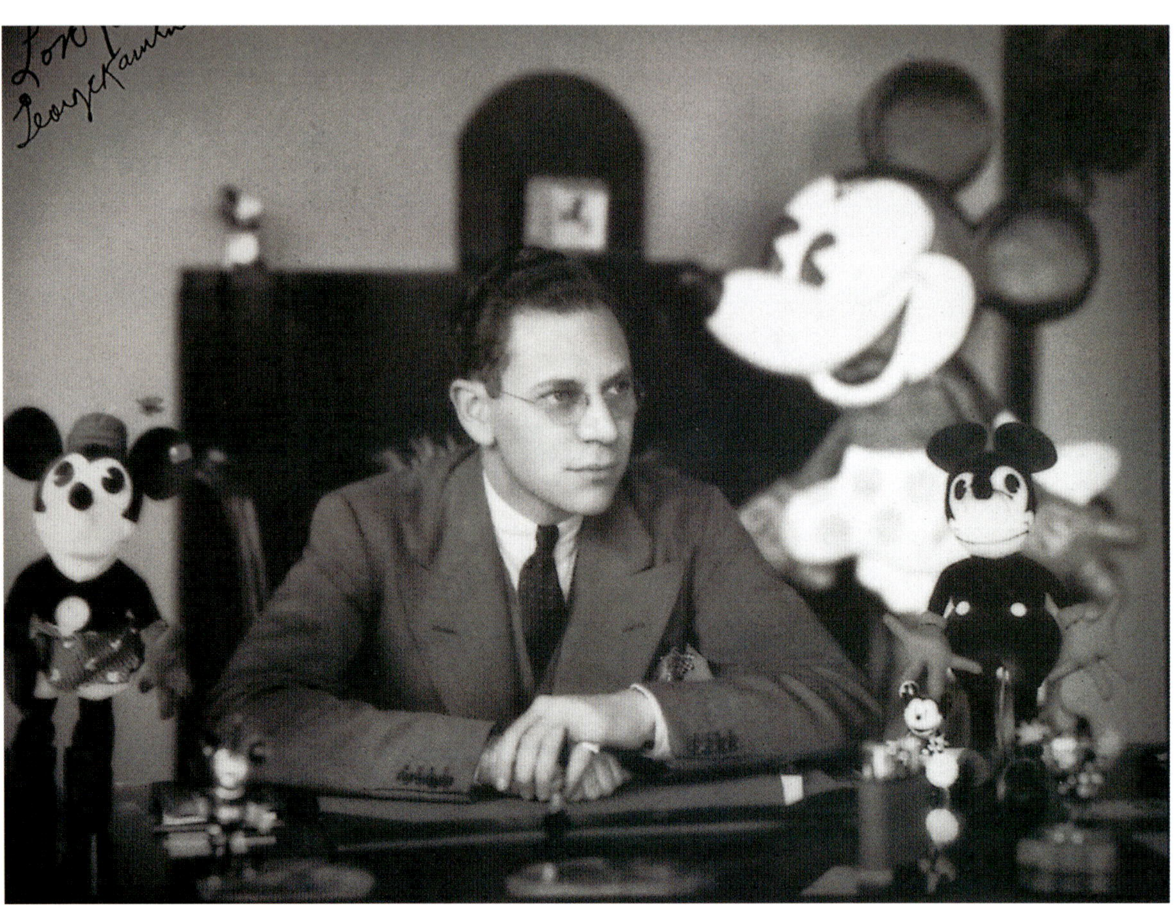

Another photograph of George Kamen with a few of the items he was responsible for licensing.

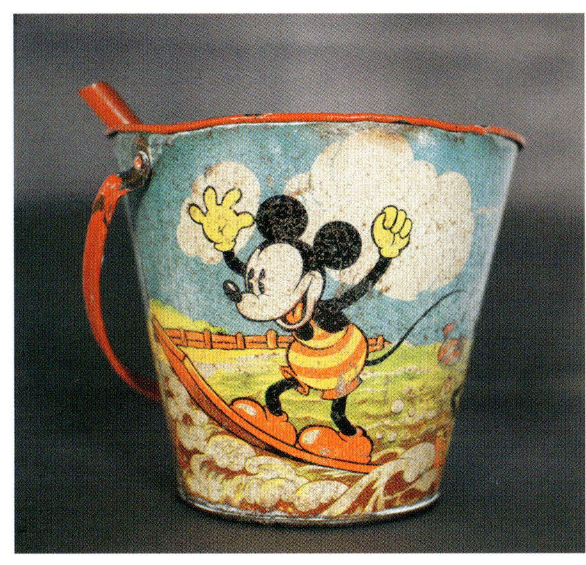

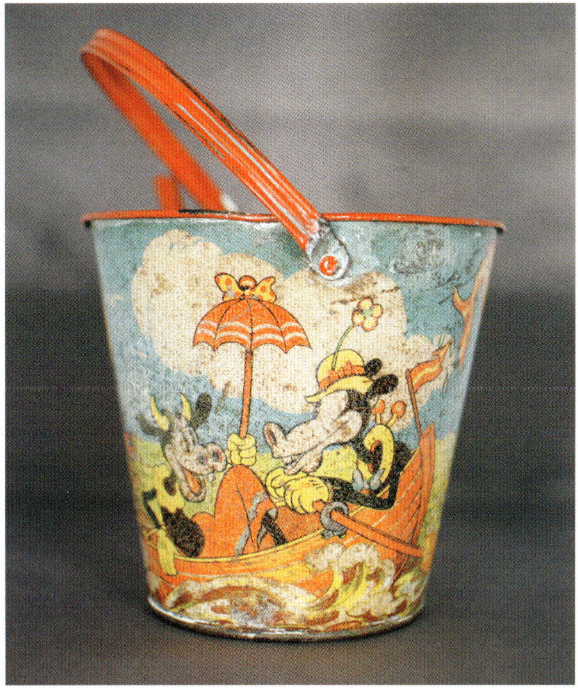

Even with its condition problems, this 6″ Mickey and friends pail with an 8.5″ shovel is the earliest Happynak pail included here. Featuring Mickey riding a surf board, Clarabelle being rowed by Horace and Minnie catching a large fish, the images are as fine as found on any sand pail. Marked: By Permission Walt Disney, Mickey Mouse Ltd Happynak Series Made in Gt. Britain. Pail has a crab embossed on the bottom. In this condition $250-500 Excellent condition about $1,000.

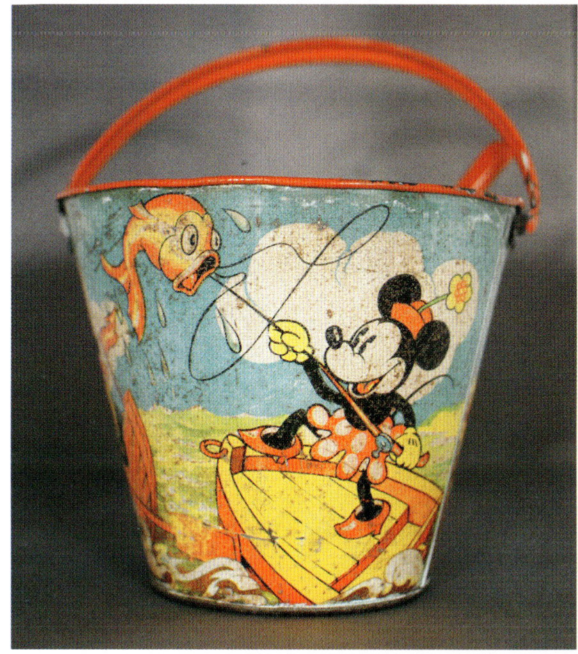

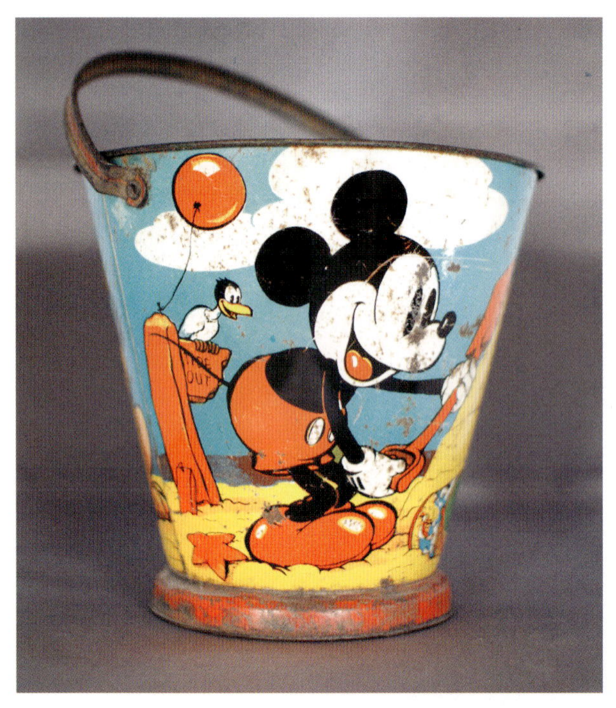

This great Happynak 7" pail features Mickey, a long-billed Donald, Minnie and Pluto building a sand castle. It has a raised bottom. As with many pails, this one features a small pail lying in the sand with the same image as the pail. Same copyrights as the previous pail. The bottom is stamped British Made. *Bernabe Collection* $500-800

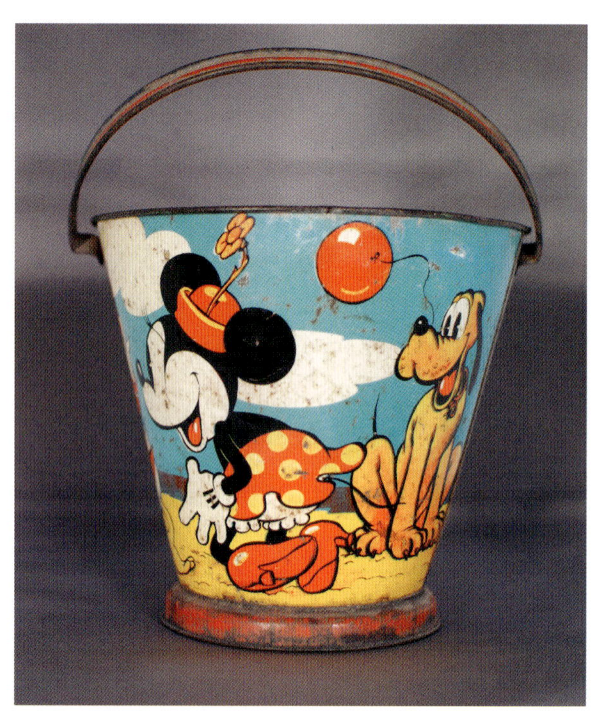

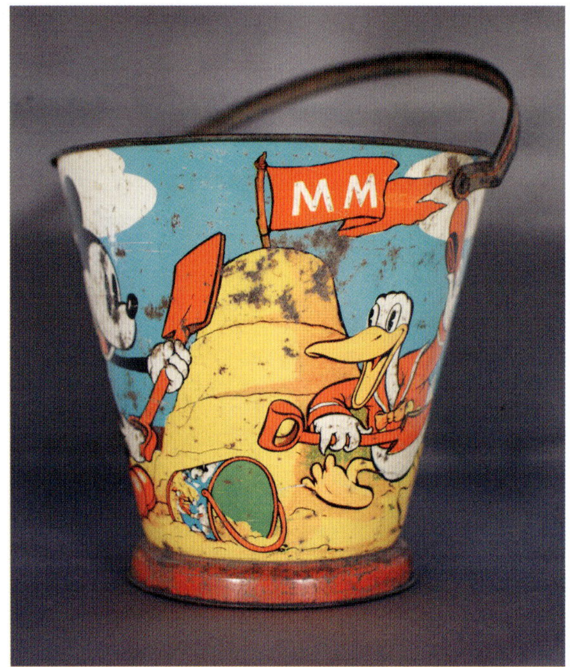

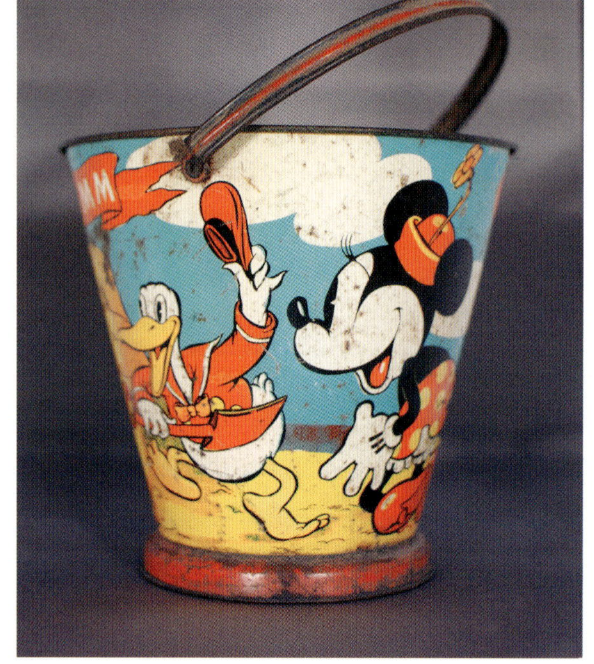

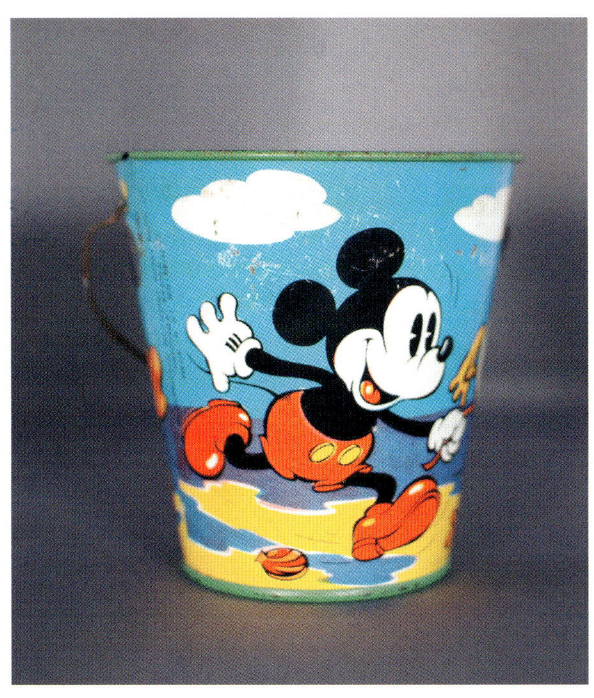

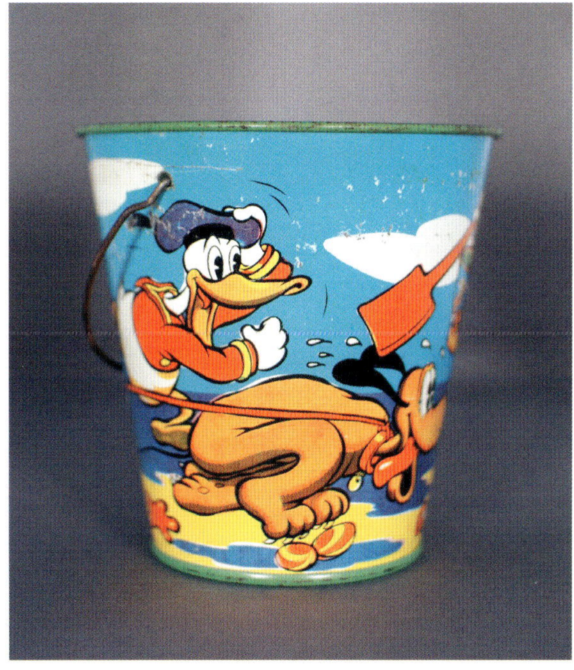

Three images of this marvelous 4.5″ pail featuring early images of Mickey, a long-billed Donald, Pluto, and Minnie on the beach. In great condition, the copyright marks are the same as the previous Happynak pails. Other than concentric circles, nothing is embossed on the bottom. *Collection of Larry Langer* $400-750

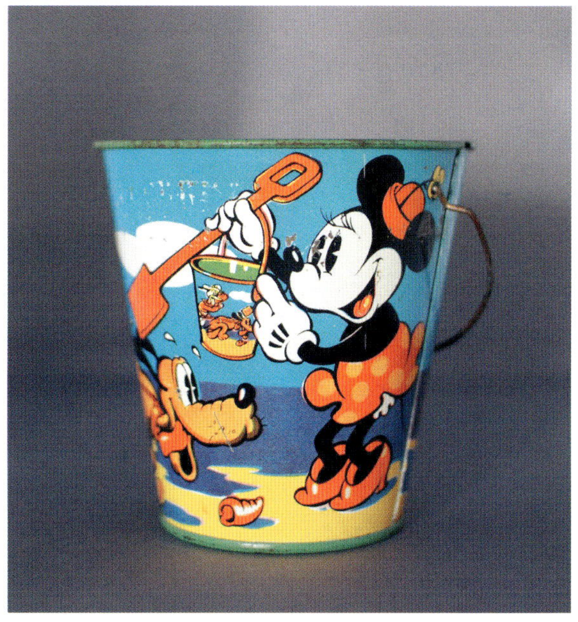

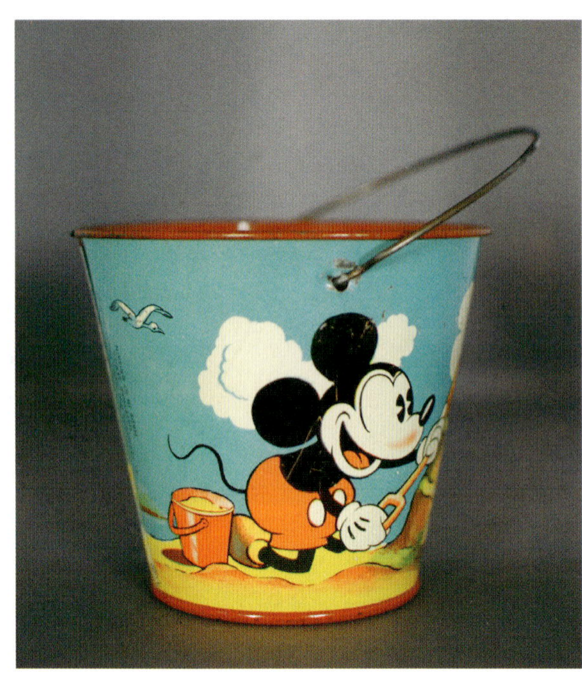

A scarce small 3.75" Happynak pail featuring Mickey, Minnie and Pluto building a sand castle. Although some later pails showed the Disney characters playing in the ocean, this is really the last of the Happynak pails featuring beach scenes. In beautiful condition, the copyright marks are the same as previous pails although this one has a plain bottom. *Bernabe Collection* $300-500

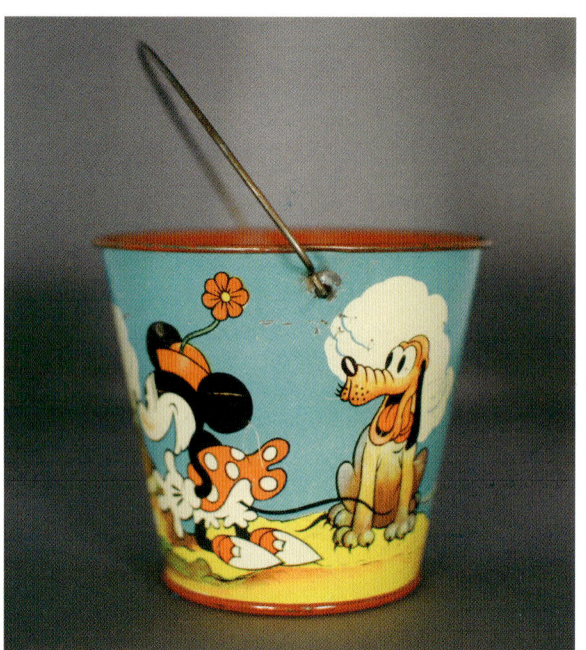

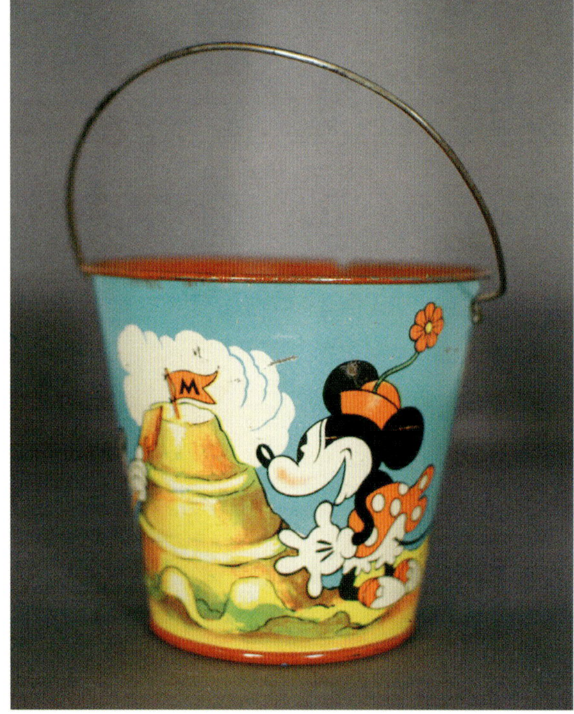

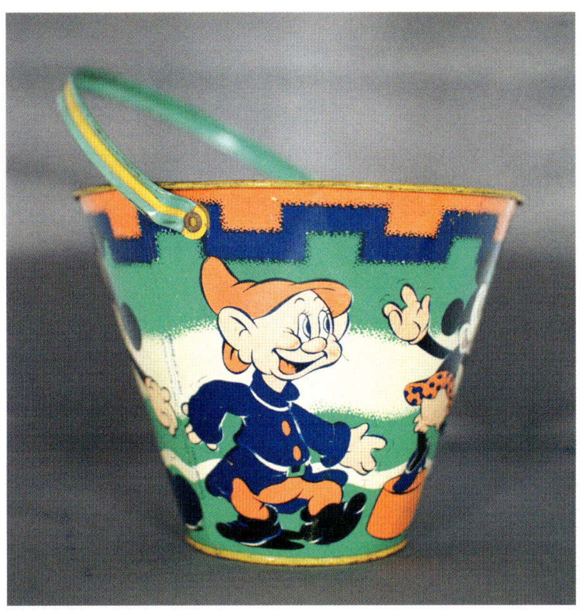

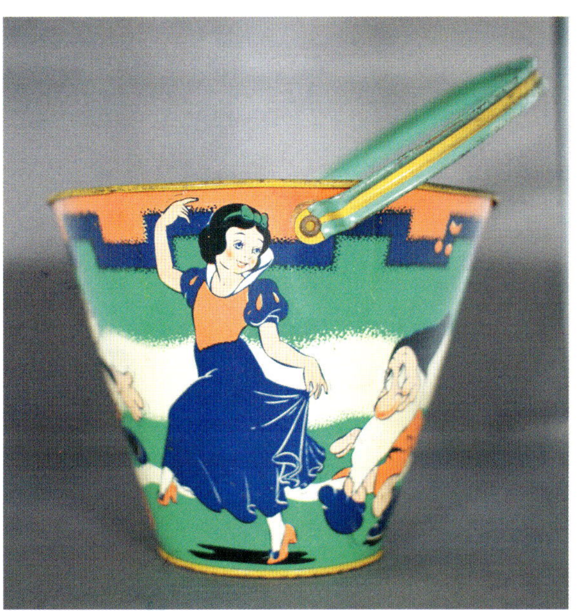

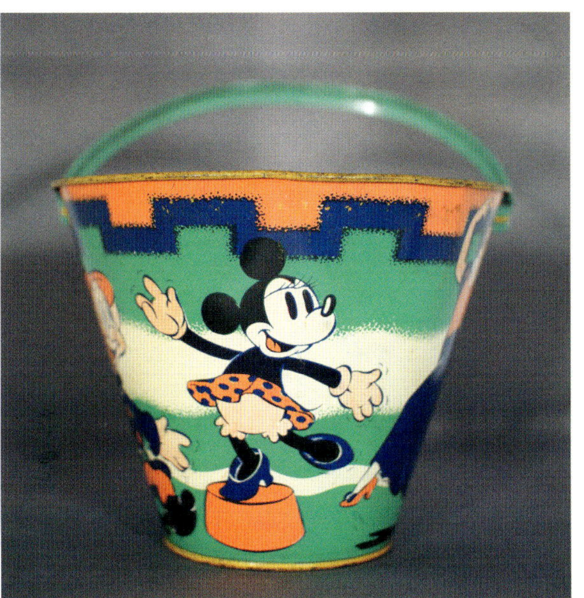

This 5.75" pail features Mickey, Minnie, Snow White, Dopey and Bashful. This combination of lithographed colors is quite limited for Happynak pails. Markings are the same as previous pails. Bottom marked with embossed British Made mark $500-900

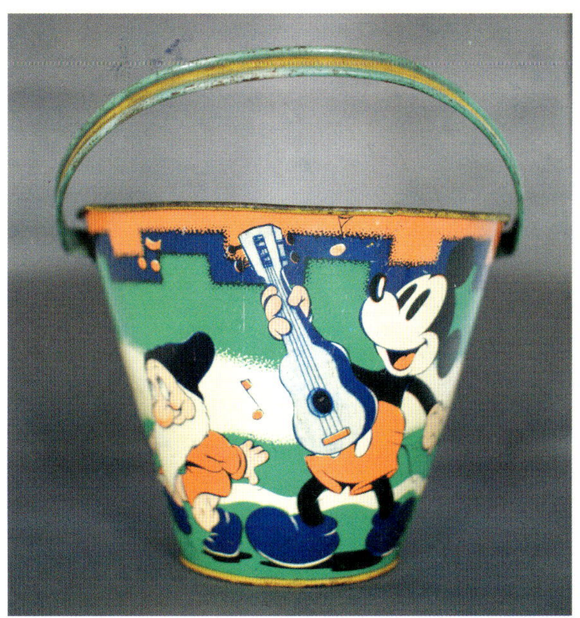

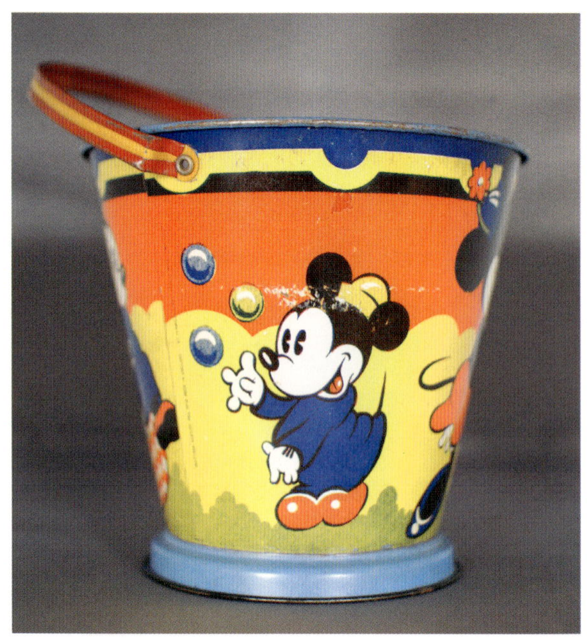

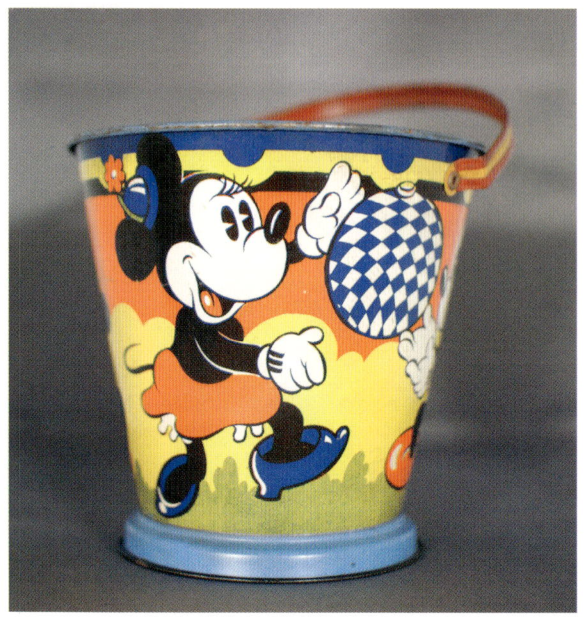

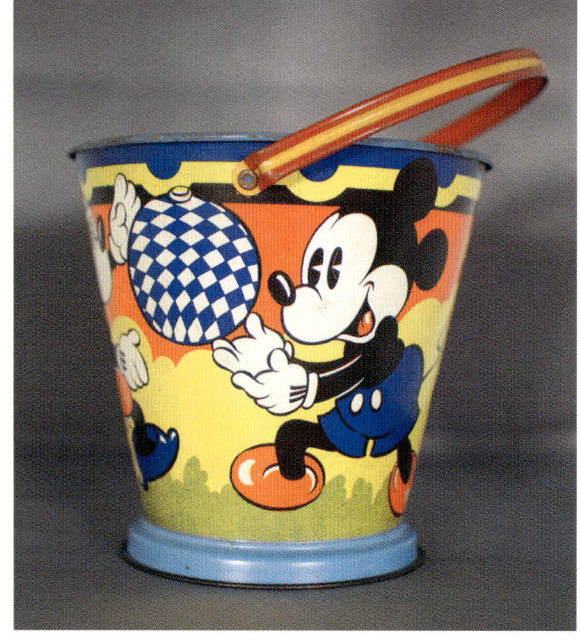

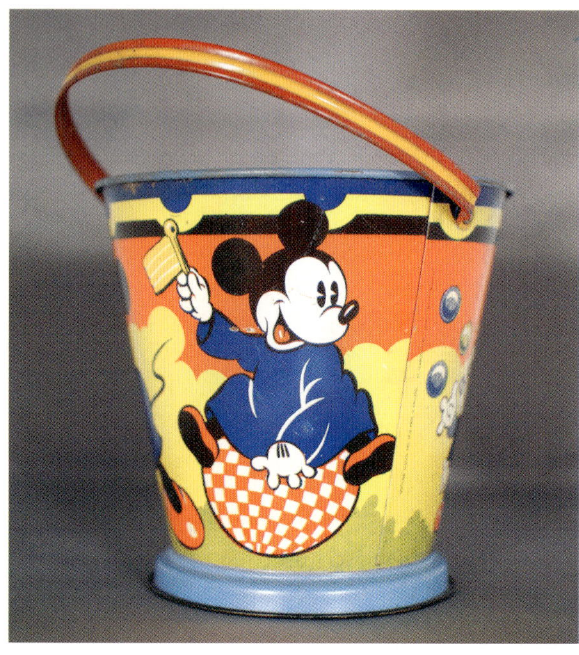

A 6.5" pail with Mickey and Minnie playing with a beach ball while one nephew juggles and the other sits on a ball. The pail features a raised bottom. There is an identical design on another pail but without the raised bottom. Marked Happynak Seaside Pail No. 12 Made in England By Permission Walt Disney – Mickey Mouse Ltd. Embossed British Made on the bottom. $300-500

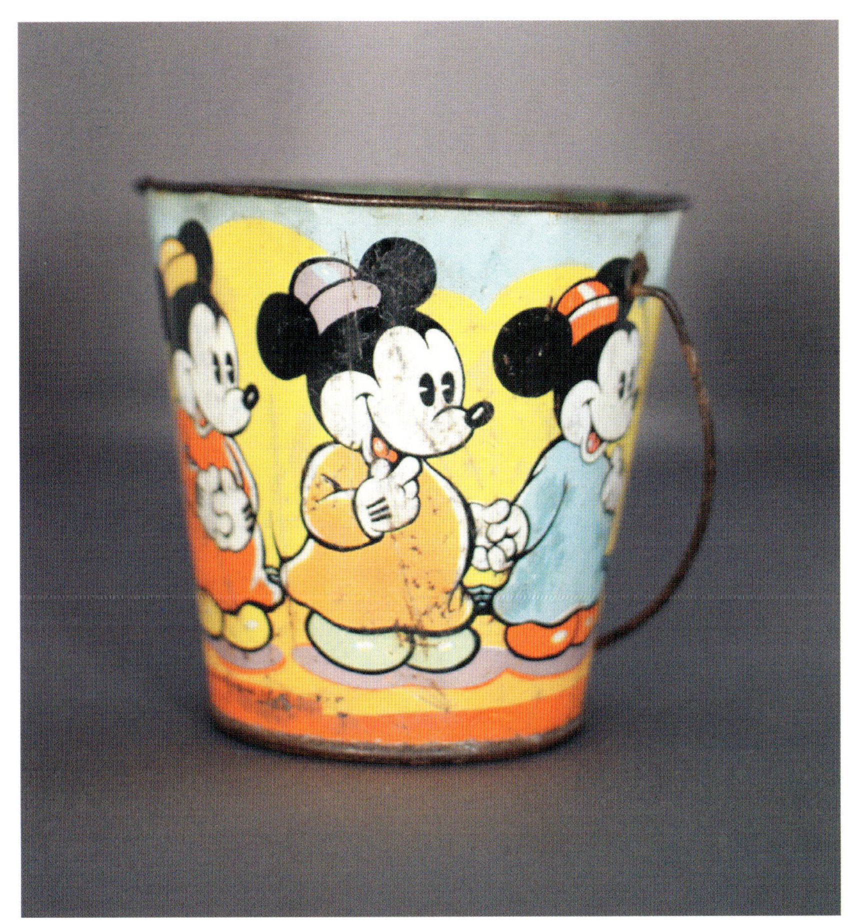

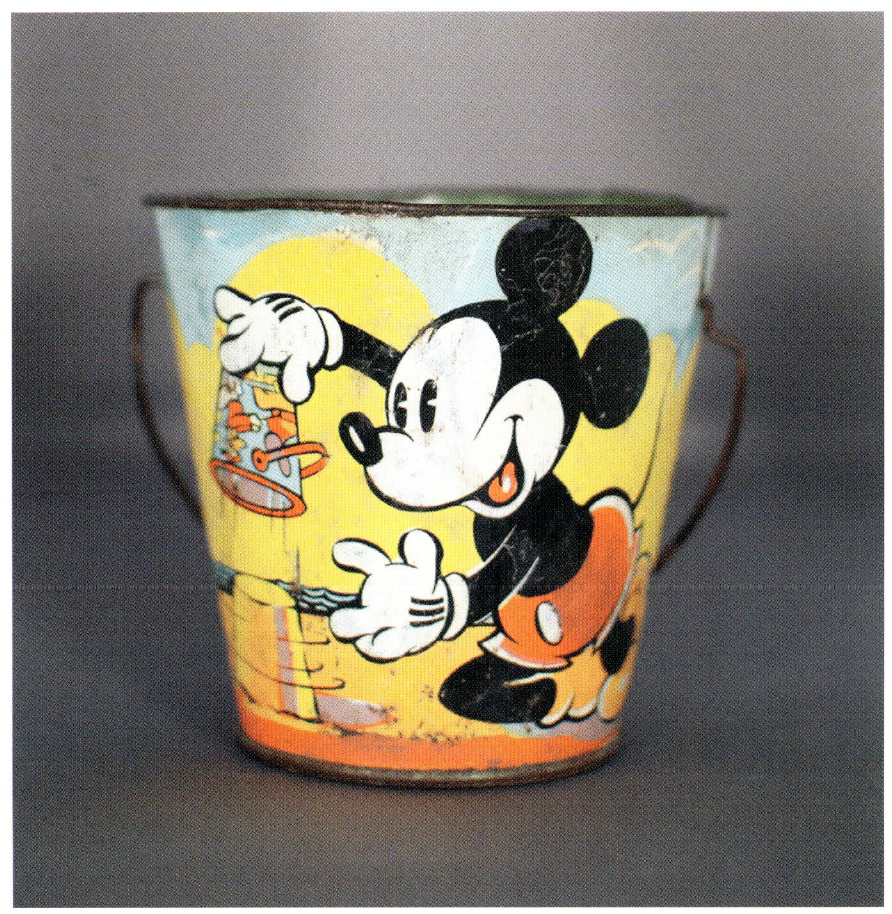

A 3.5" pail with two views of Mickey using a pail as a sand mold. This small size is quite scarce for a Happynak pail. Marked By Permission Walt Disney Mickey Mouse Ltd., Happynak Series, Made in Gt. Britain $175-275

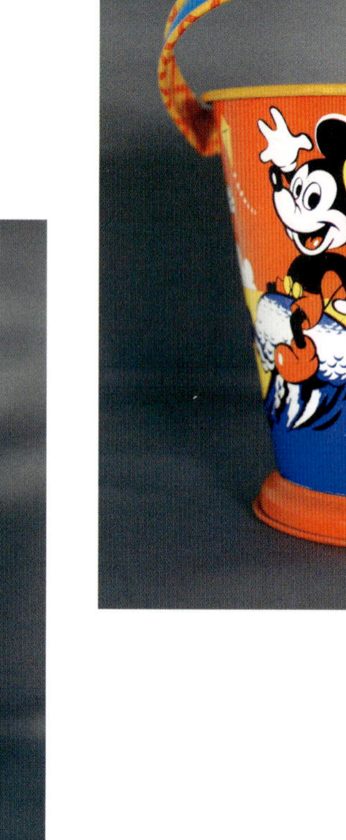

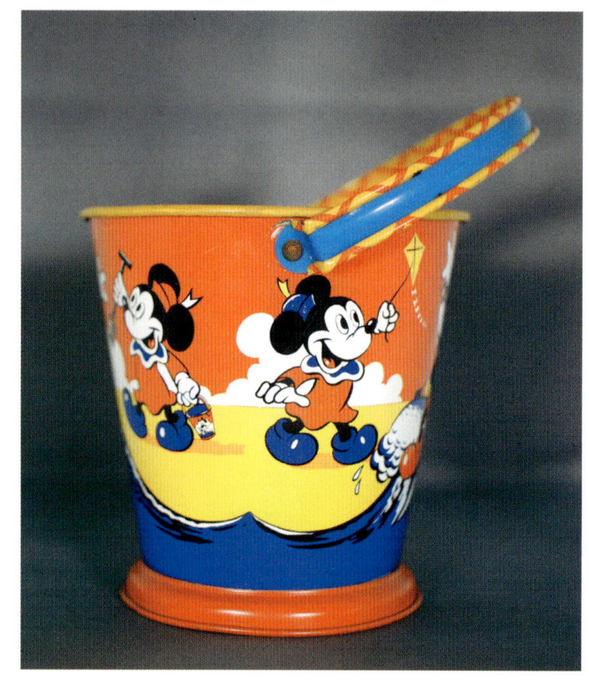

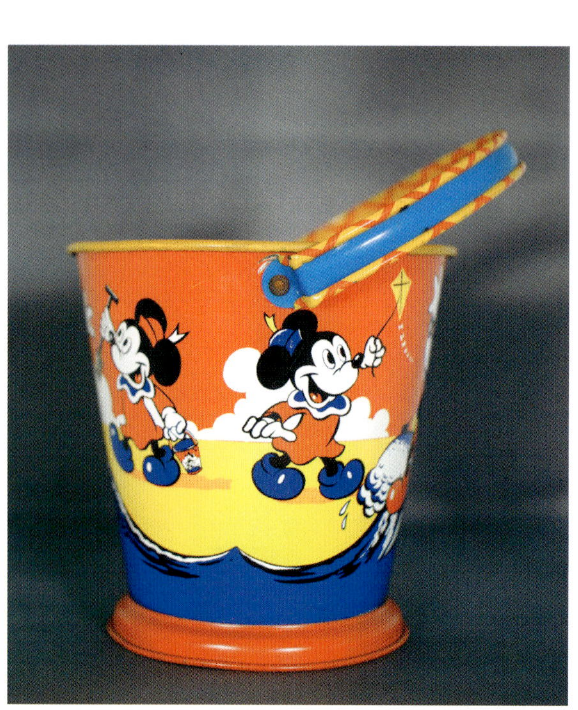

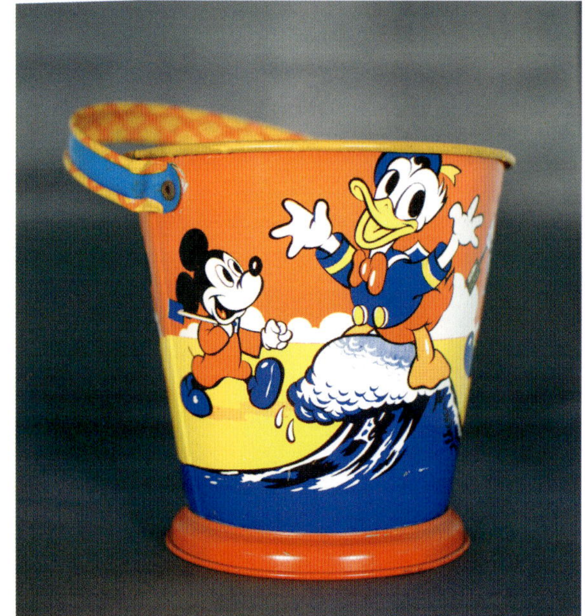

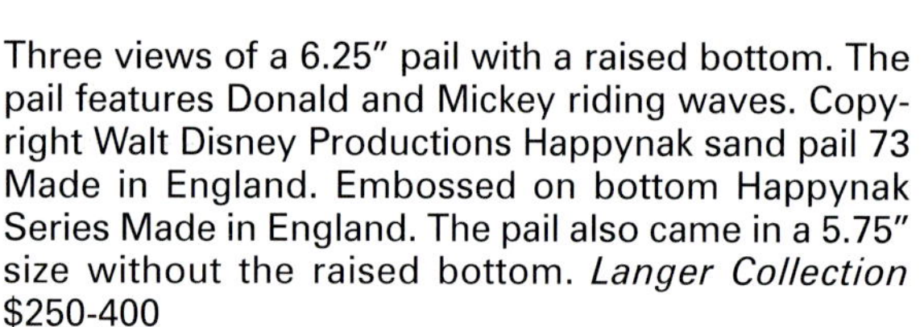

Three views of a 6.25" pail with a raised bottom. The pail features Donald and Mickey riding waves. Copyright Walt Disney Productions Happynak sand pail 73 Made in England. Embossed on bottom Happynak Series Made in England. The pail also came in a 5.75" size without the raised bottom. *Langer Collection*
$250-400

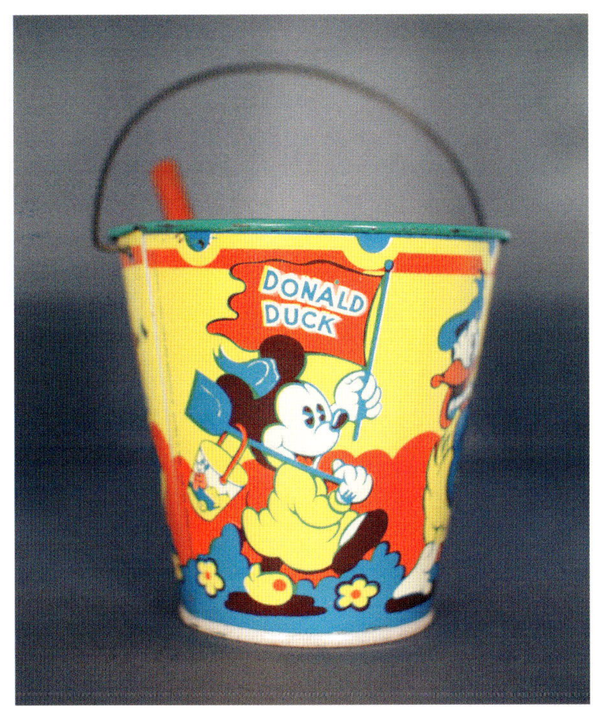

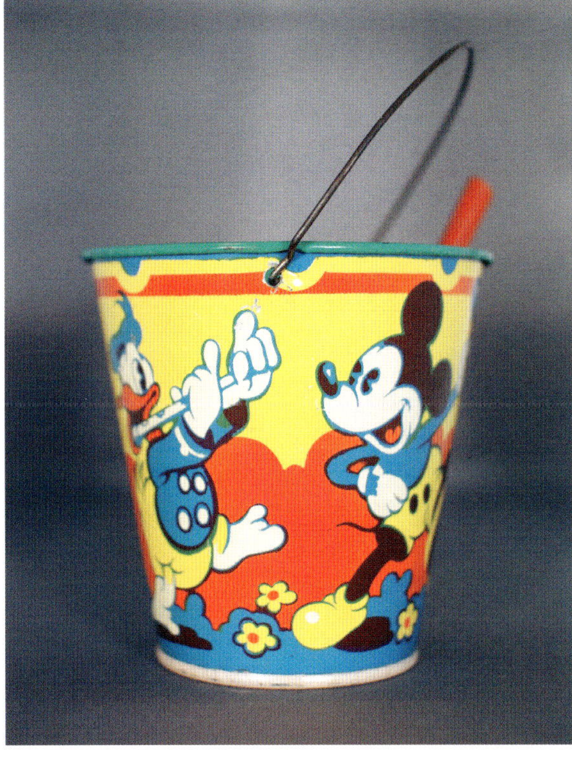

Three views of a 4.5″ pail with 6″ shovel. Marked Happynak Pail No. 7 Made in England by Permission Walt Disney – Mickey Mouse Ltd. $200-300

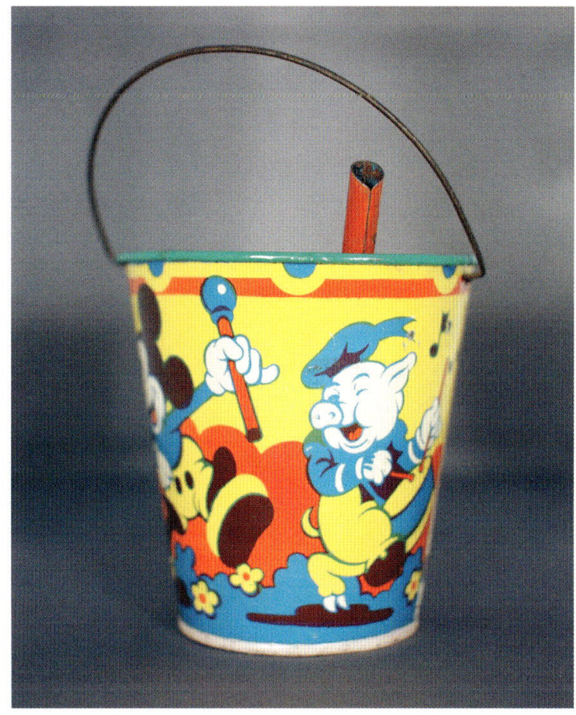

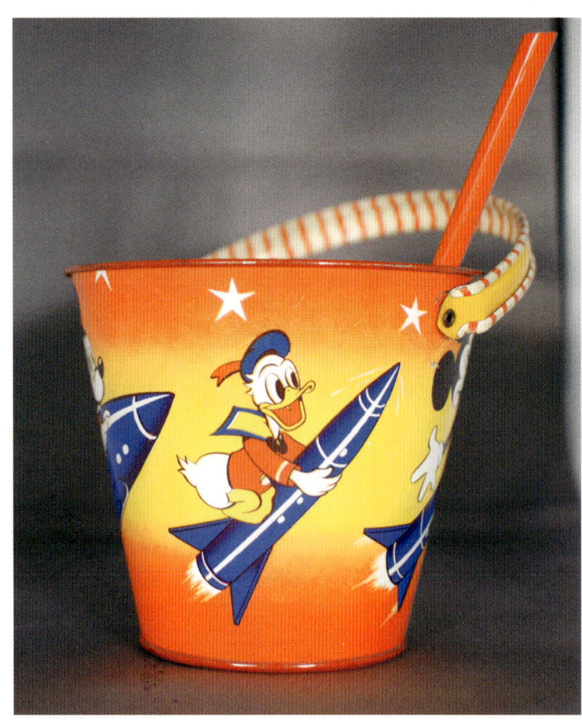

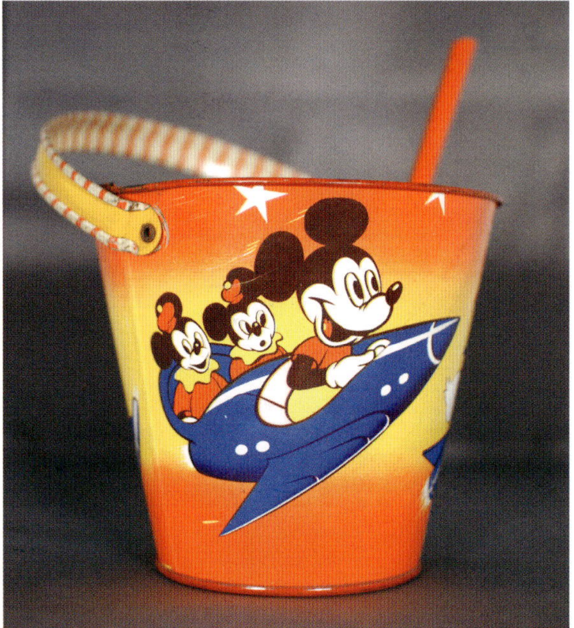

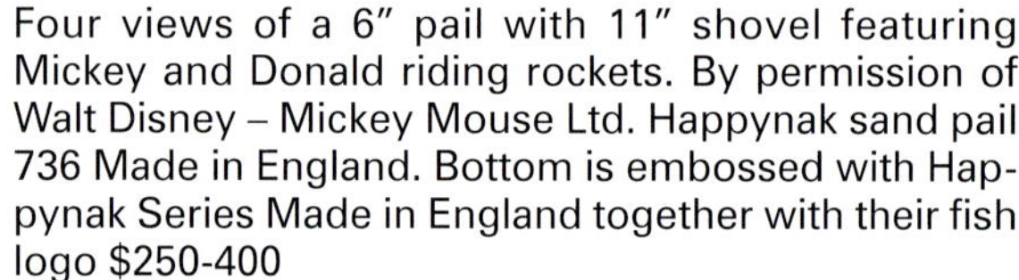

Four views of a 6" pail with 11" shovel featuring Mickey and Donald riding rockets. By permission of Walt Disney – Mickey Mouse Ltd. Happynak sand pail 736 Made in England. Bottom is embossed with Happynak Series Made in England together with their fish logo $250-400

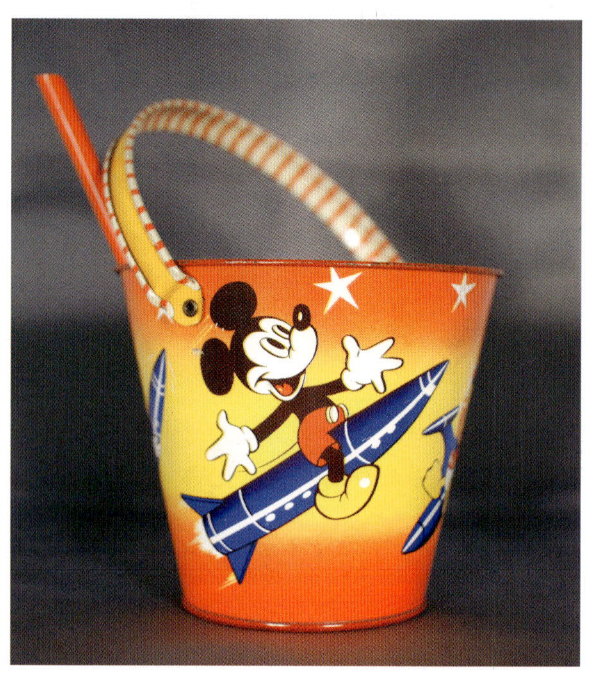

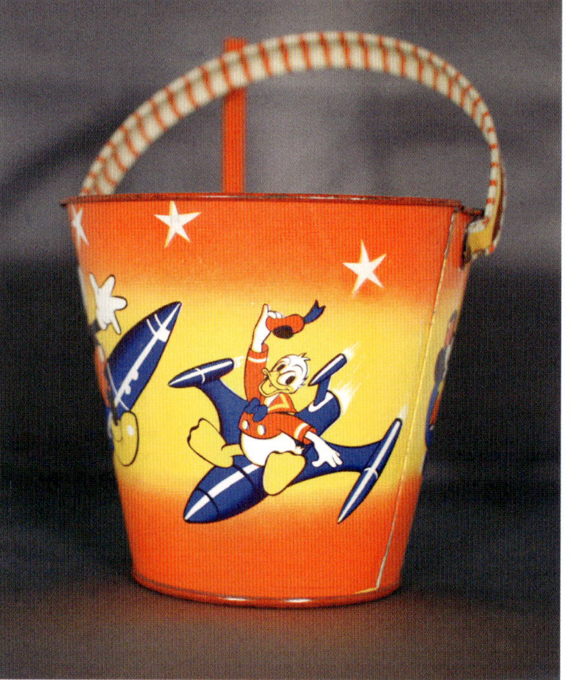

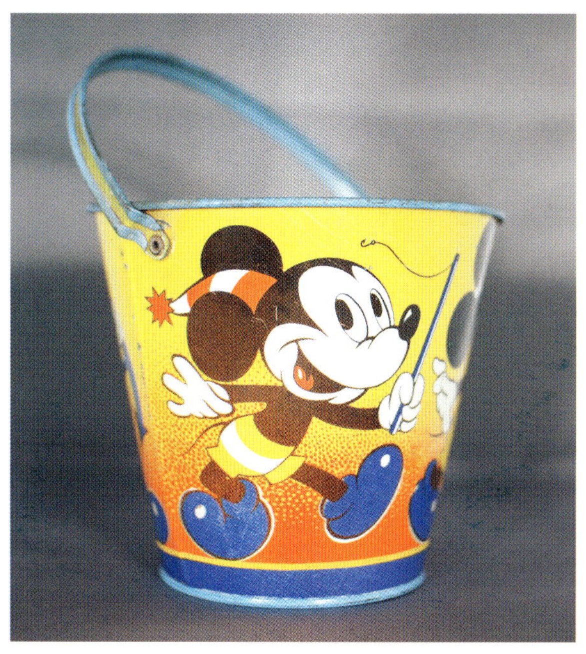

Four views of a 6" pail with Mickey holding an anchor. By permission Walt Disney – Mickey Mouse Ltd. Happynak sand pail 736 Made in England. Bottom embossing same as previous pail. For some reason Happynak used duplicate numbers such as 736 and 725 on their pails. *Langer Collection.* $200-300

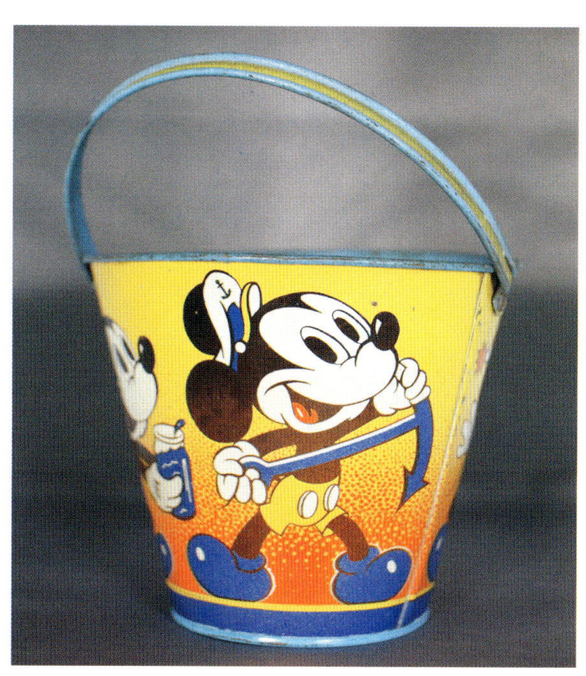

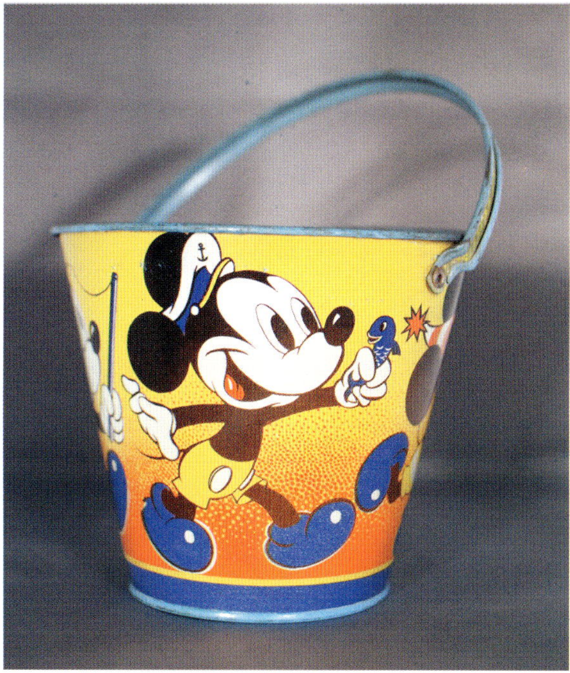

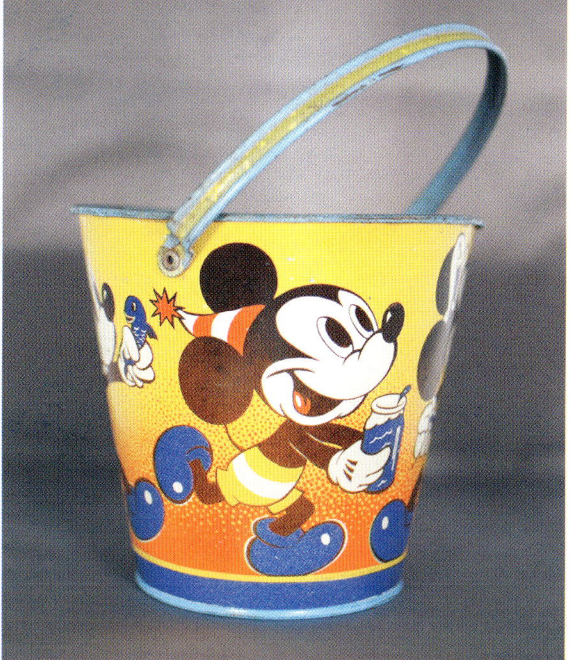

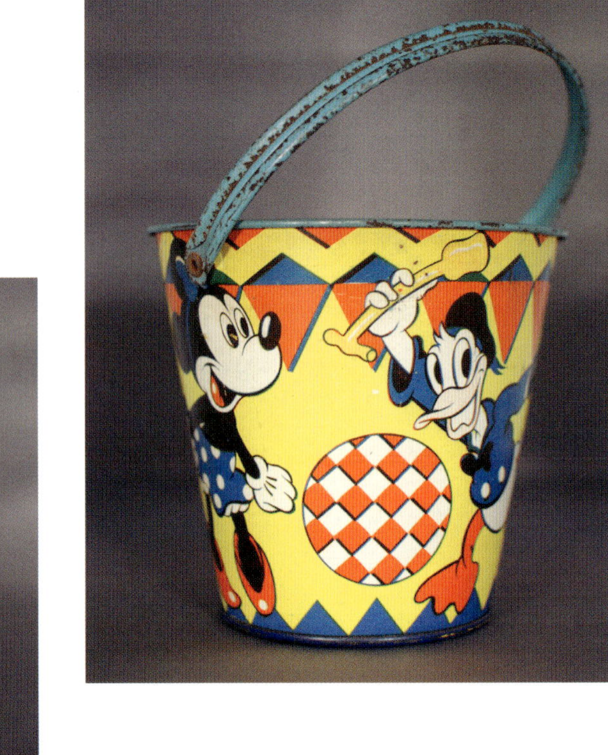

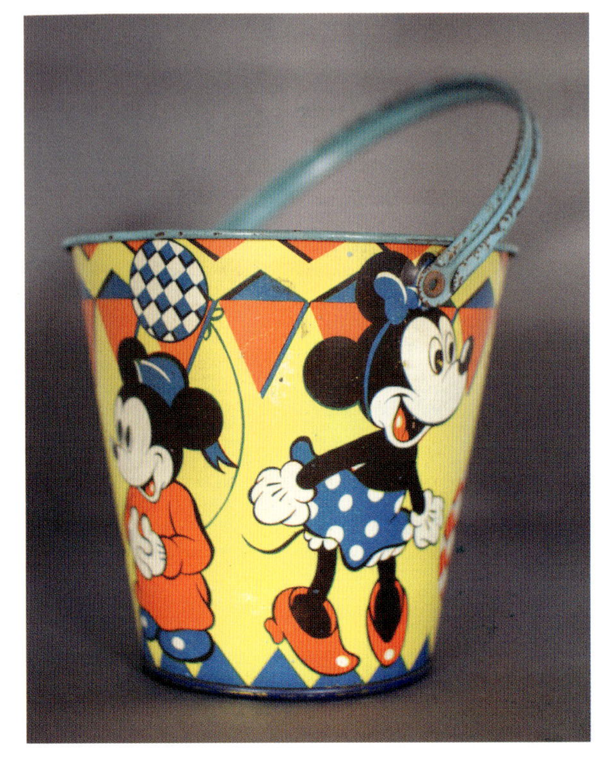

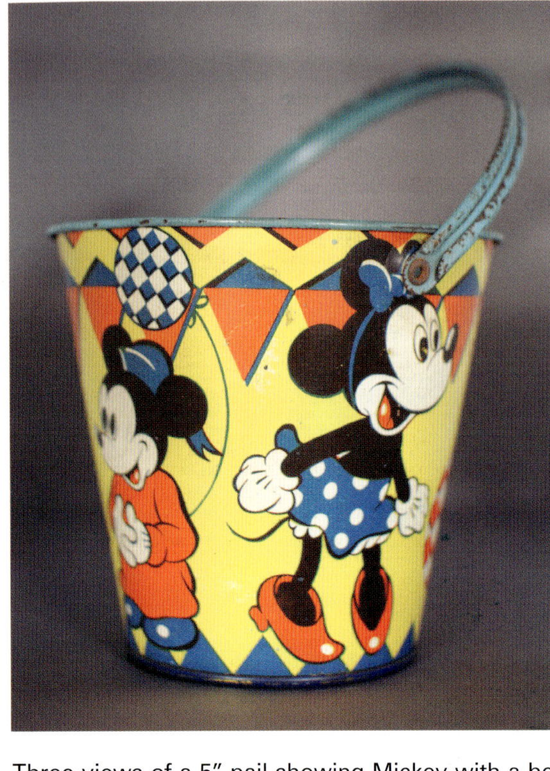

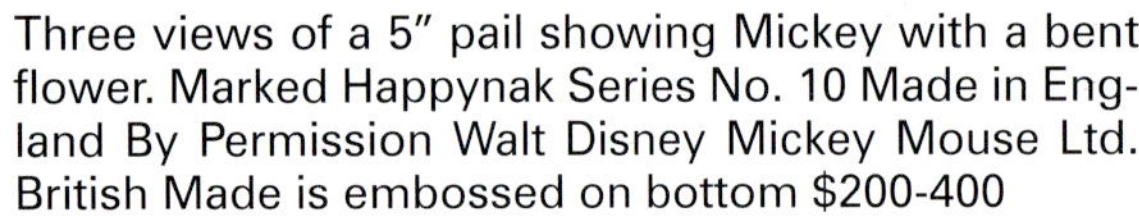

Three views of a 5″ pail showing Mickey with a bent flower. Marked Happynak Series No. 10 Made in England By Permission Walt Disney Mickey Mouse Ltd. British Made is embossed on bottom $200-400

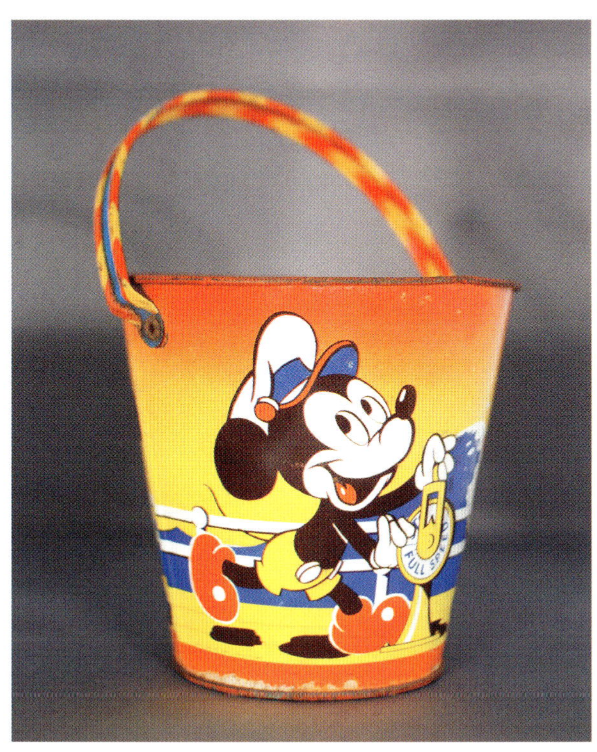

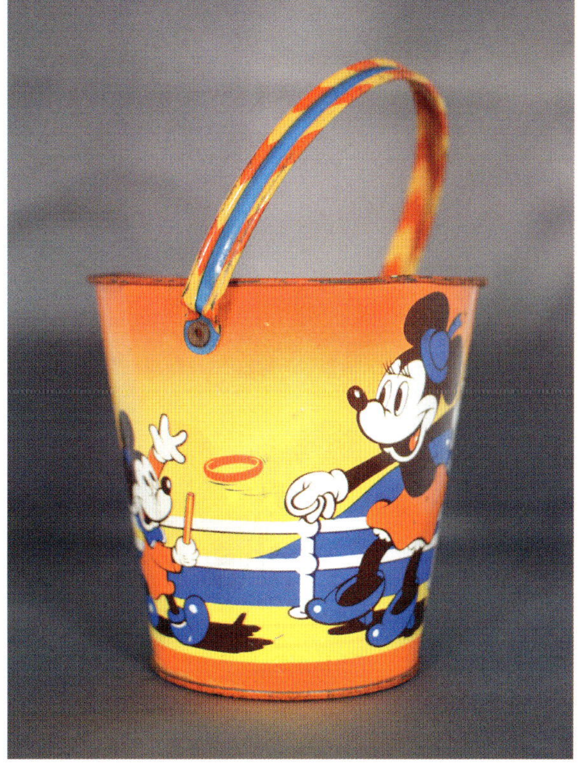

Three views of a 5″ pail with Captain Mickey at the boat controls while Minnie plays with two nephews. Happynak Sand Pail 725 Made in England. Bottom of pail embossed Happynak Series Made in England. With fish logo $200-400

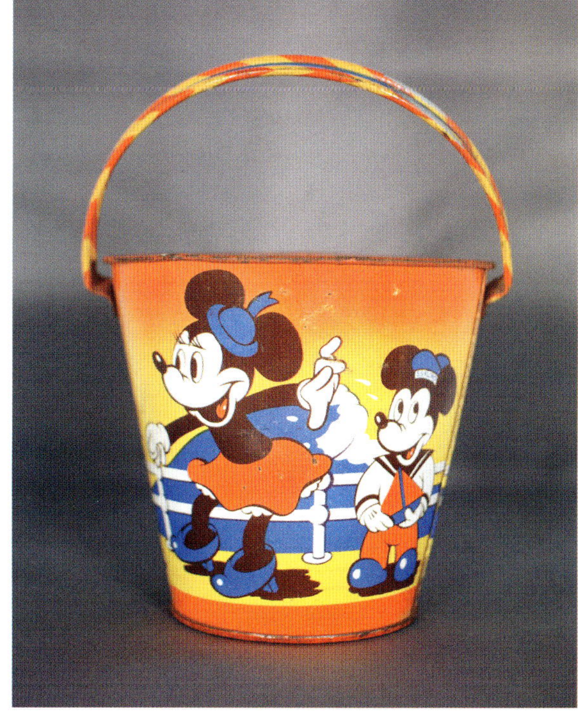

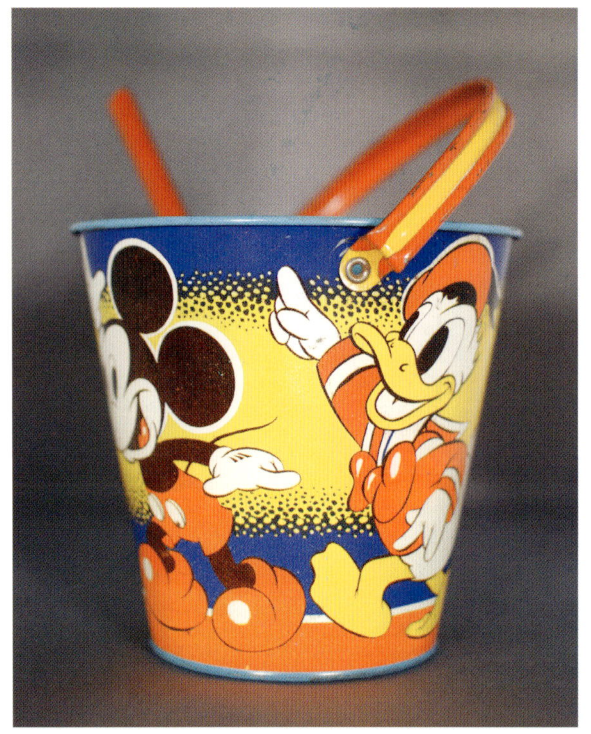

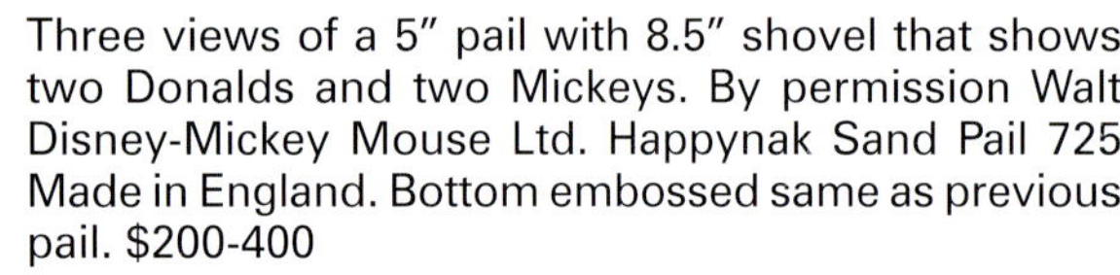

Three views of a 5″ pail with 8.5″ shovel that shows two Donalds and two Mickeys. By permission Walt Disney-Mickey Mouse Ltd. Happynak Sand Pail 725 Made in England. Bottom embossed same as previous pail. $200-400

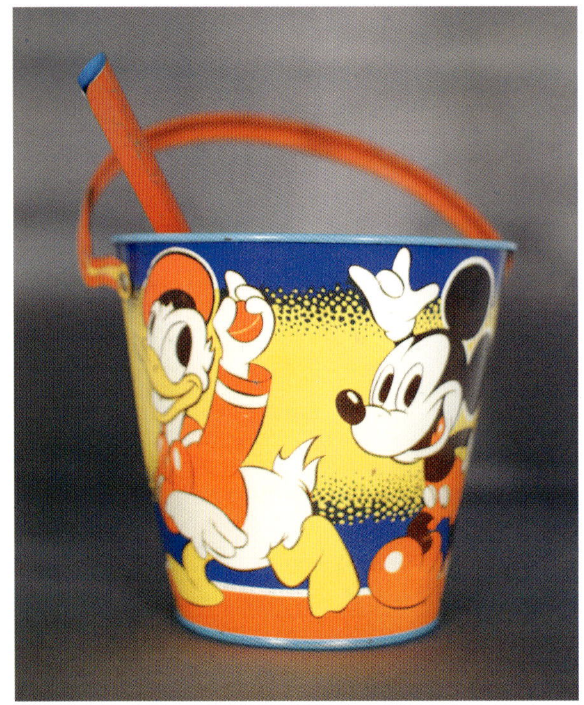

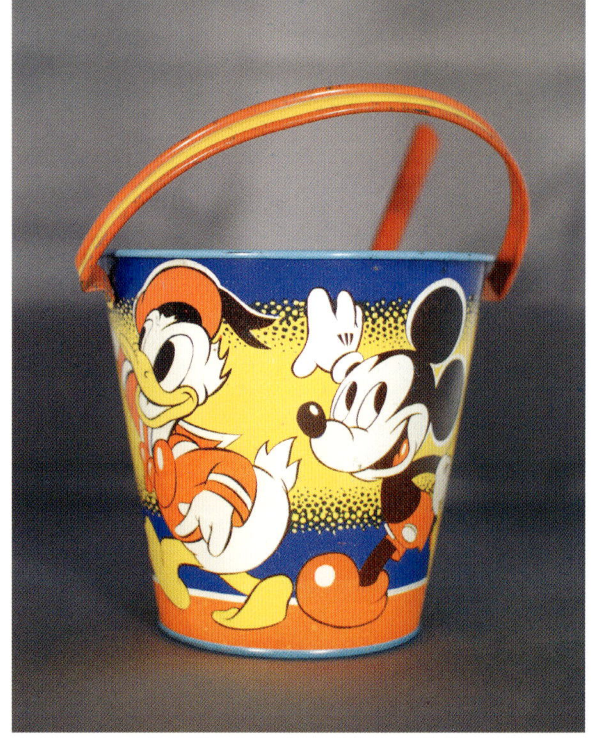

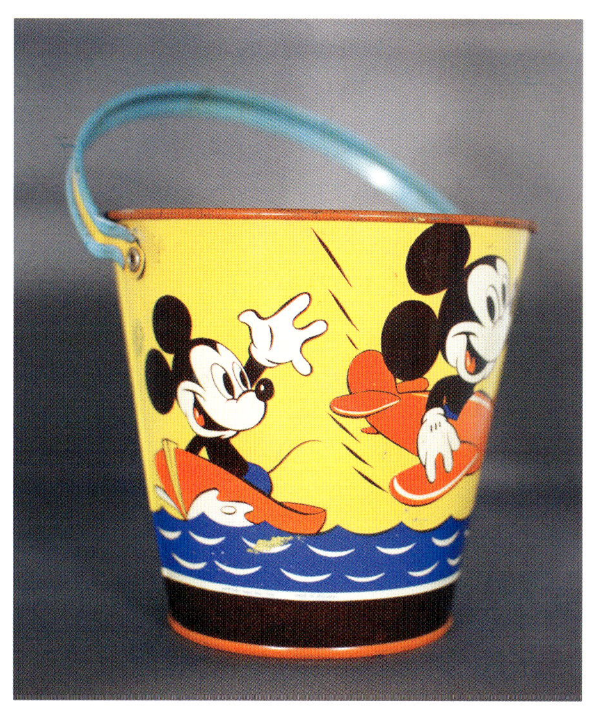

Three views of a 5″ pail with images of Mickey flying and also driving a boat. Same markings as previous pail except No.726 $200-400

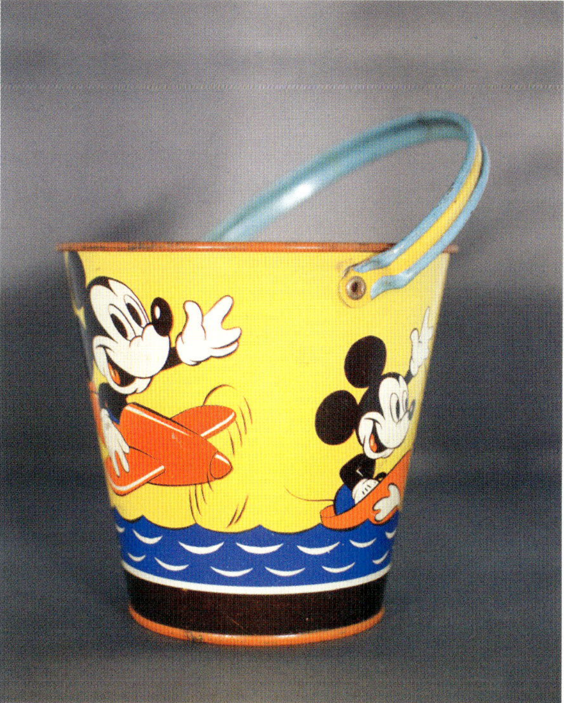

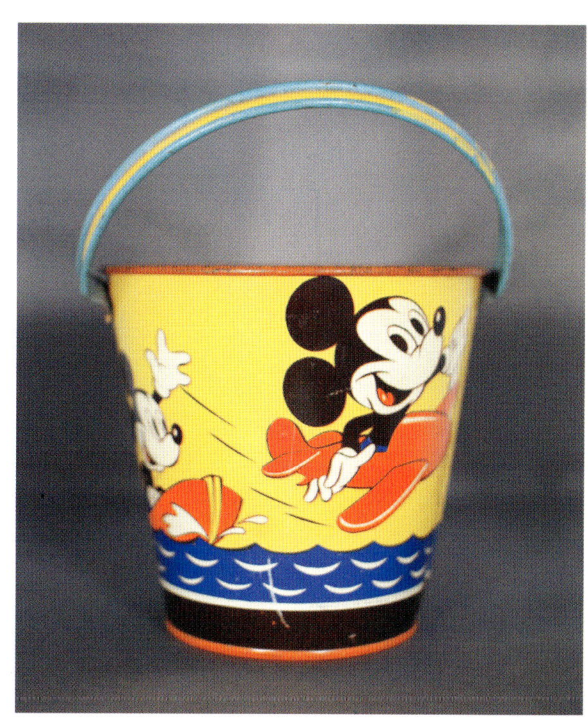

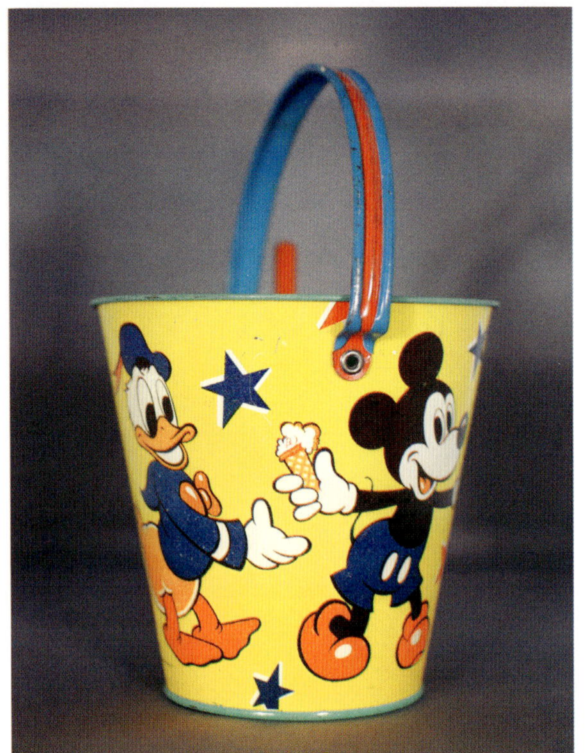

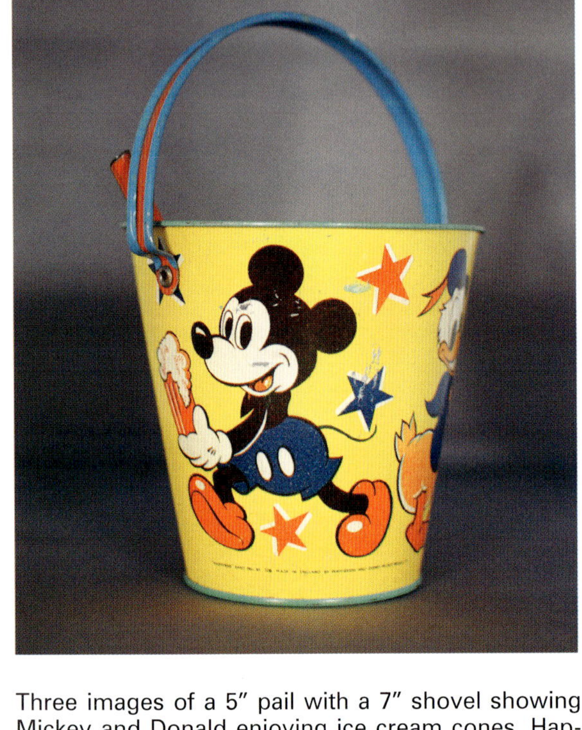

Three images of a 5″ pail with a 7″ shovel showing Mickey and Donald enjoying ice cream cones. Happynak Sea Pail No. 708 Made in England By permission Walt Disney-Mickey Mouse Ltd. Bottom embossed as before $250-450

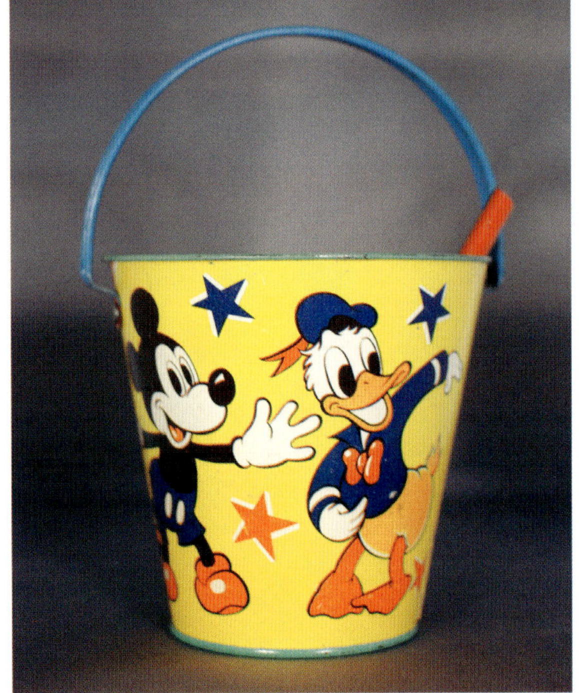

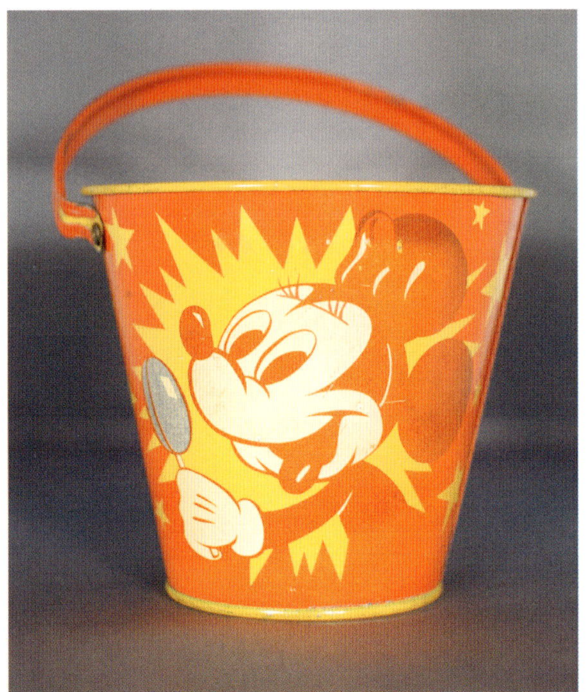

Both sides have the same image on this 5″ sand pail with Mickey enjoying a lollipop! Copyright images probably hidden by seam. Bottom embossed as before. This pail also came in a 3.5″ size with a handle. $100-175 with bail

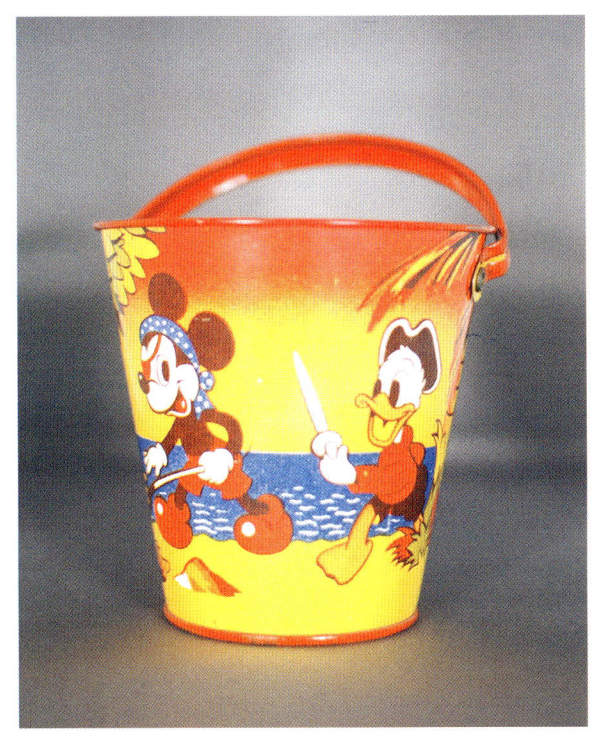

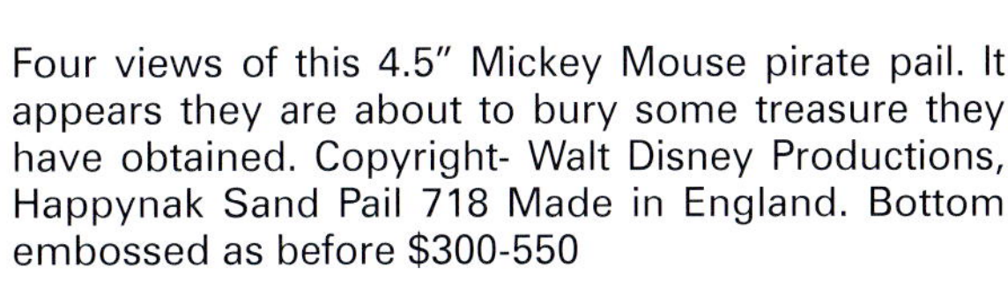

Four views of this 4.5" Mickey Mouse pirate pail. It appears they are about to bury some treasure they have obtained. Copyright- Walt Disney Productions, Happynak Sand Pail 718 Made in England. Bottom embossed as before $300-550

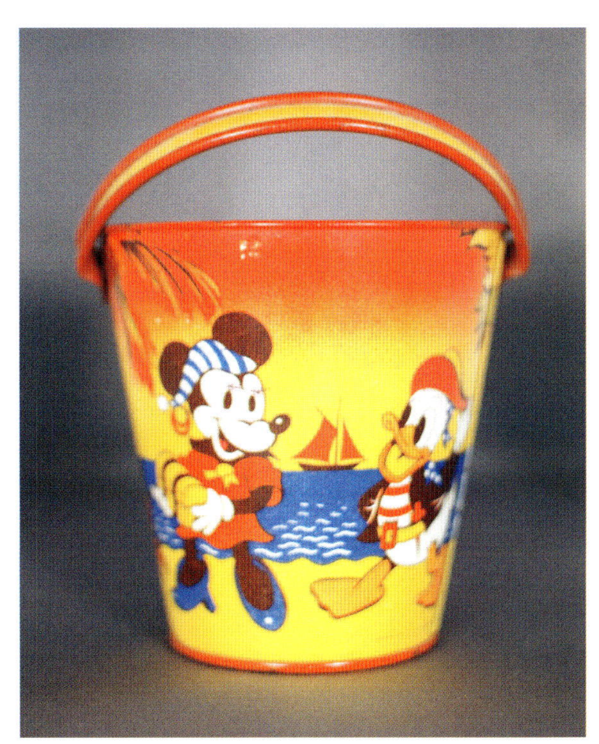

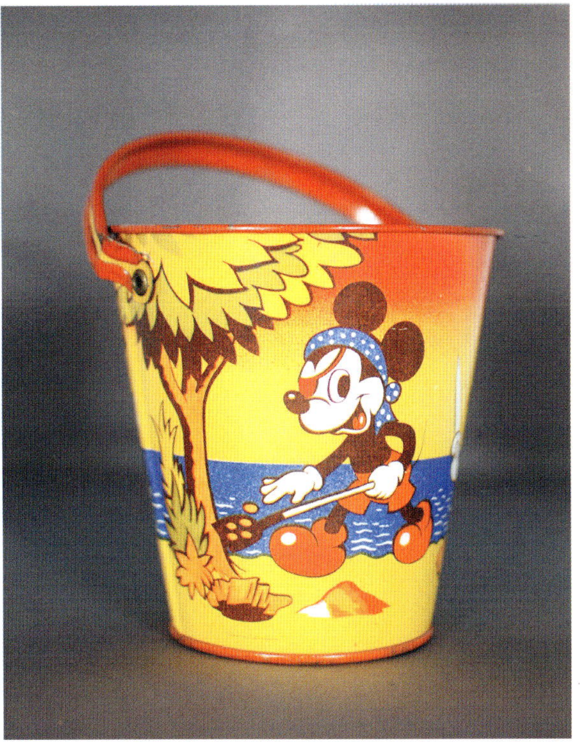

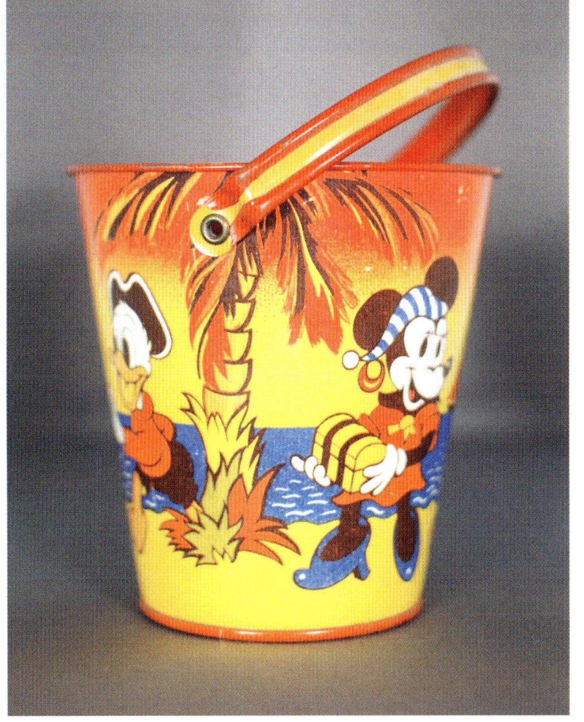

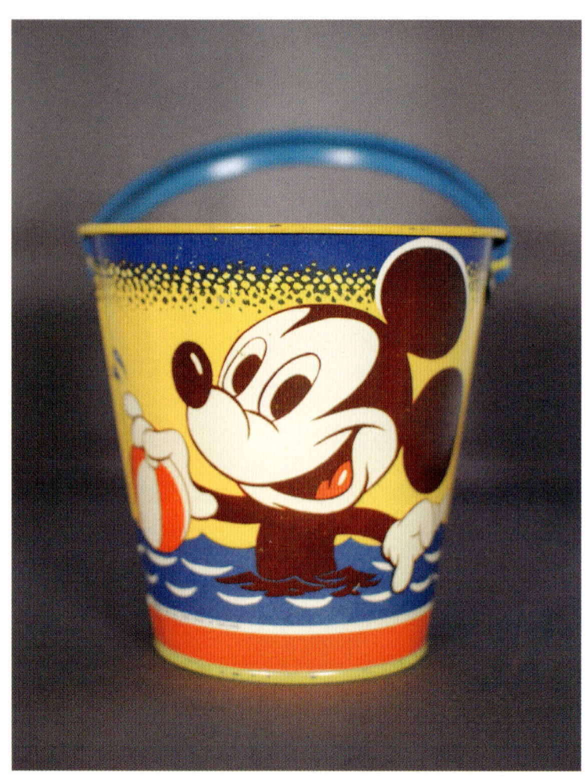

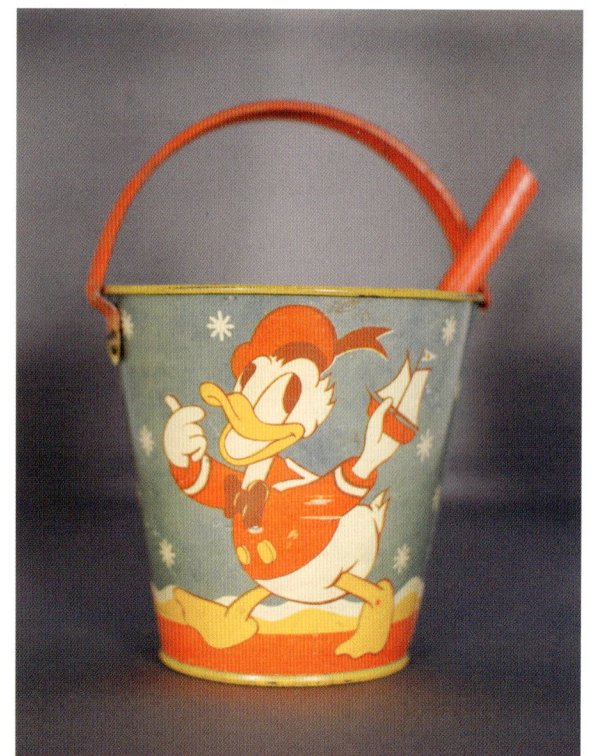

Two views of a 4.5″ pail showing Mickey with a ball and Minnie teasing a fish. By permission Walt Disney-Mickey Mouse Ltd. Happynak Sand Pail 715 Made in England. Same embossing on bottom of pail. *Langer Collection* $200-400

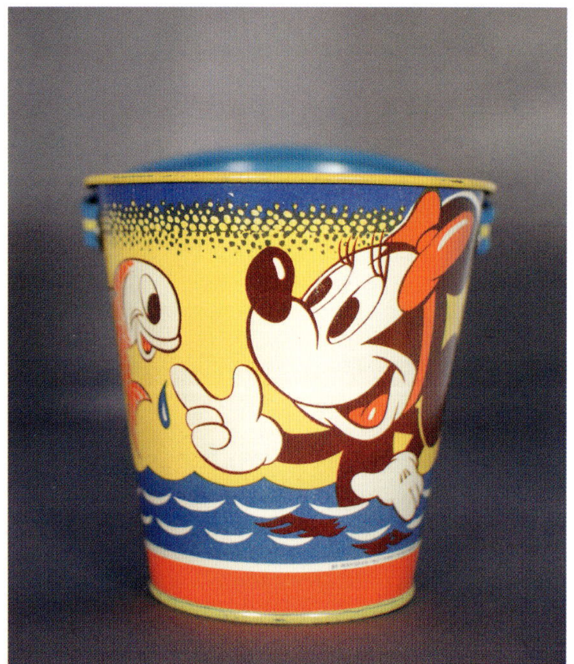

Two scenes from a 4″ pail with 6.25″ shovel illustrating Mickey with a sand pail and Donald with a sail boat. By permission of Walt Disney-Mickey Mouse Ltd. Happynak Sand Pail 714 Made in England. Embossing same on bottom $175-375

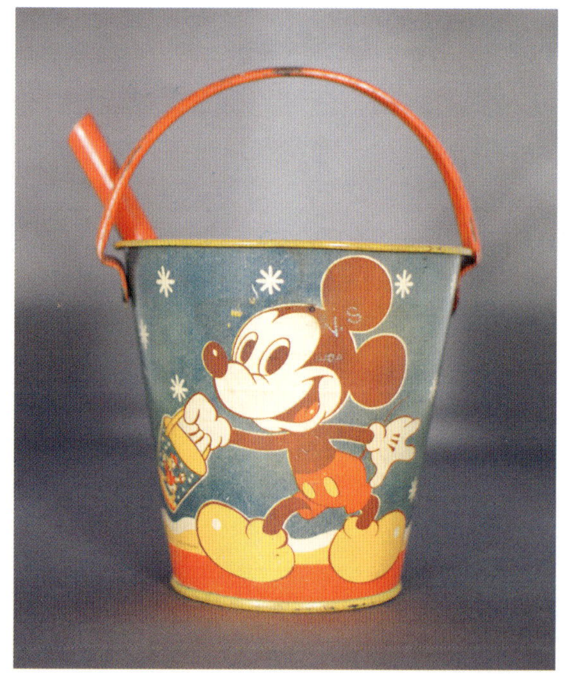

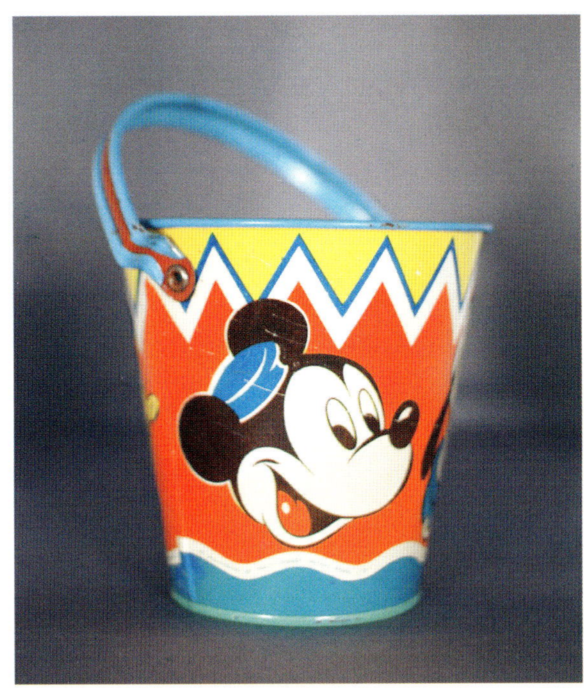

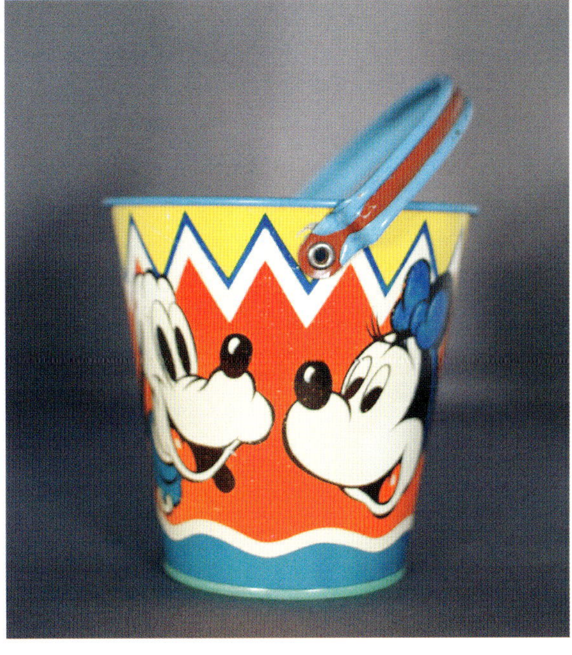

Three views of heads of Mickey, Pluto, Minnie and Donald on this 4" pail. By permission copyright Happynak Pail 706. Embossed bottom $75-125

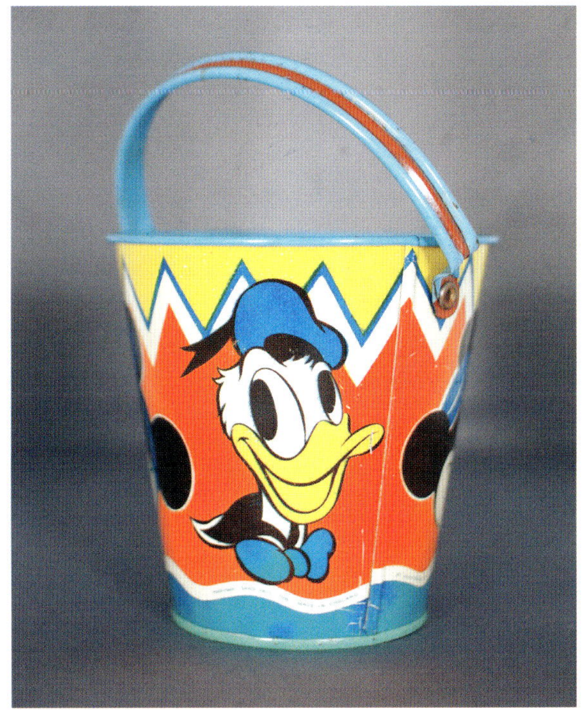

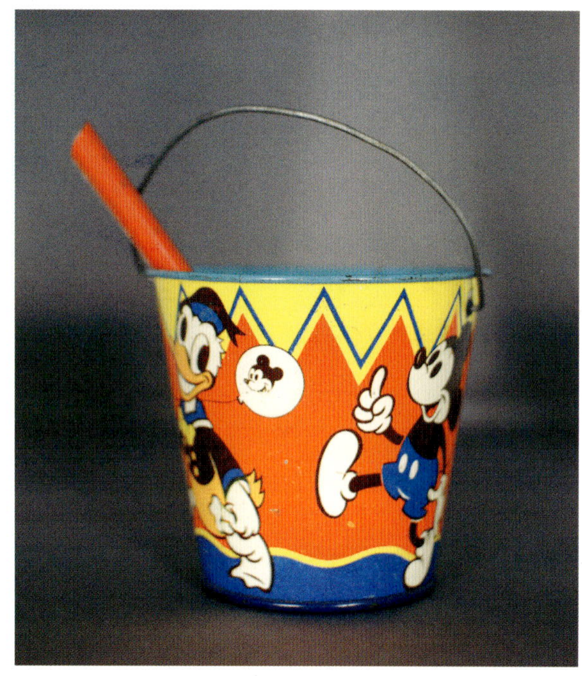

A 4" pail with 6.25" shovel featuring Donald and Mickey, each with a nephew. By permission Copyright Happynak No. 705. Plain bottom $125-150

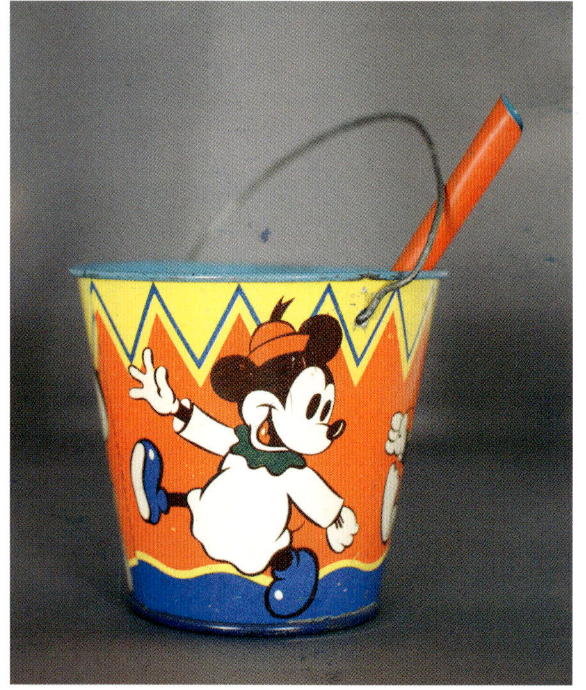

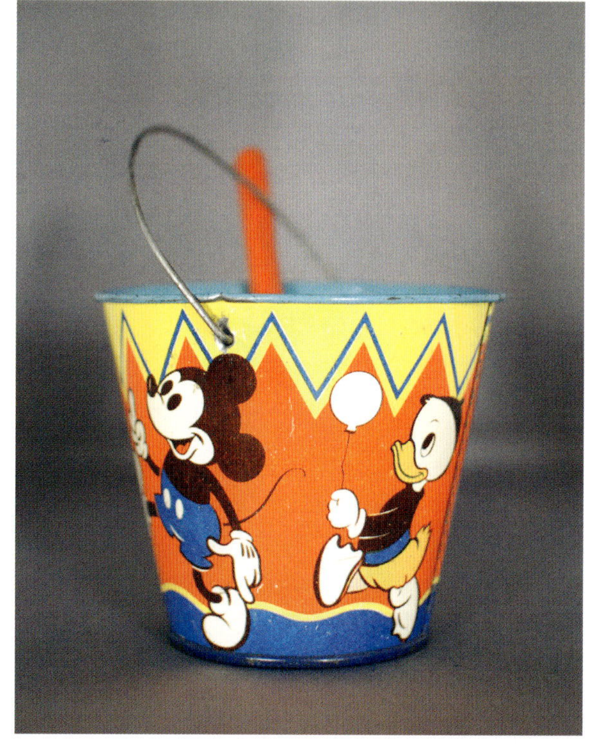

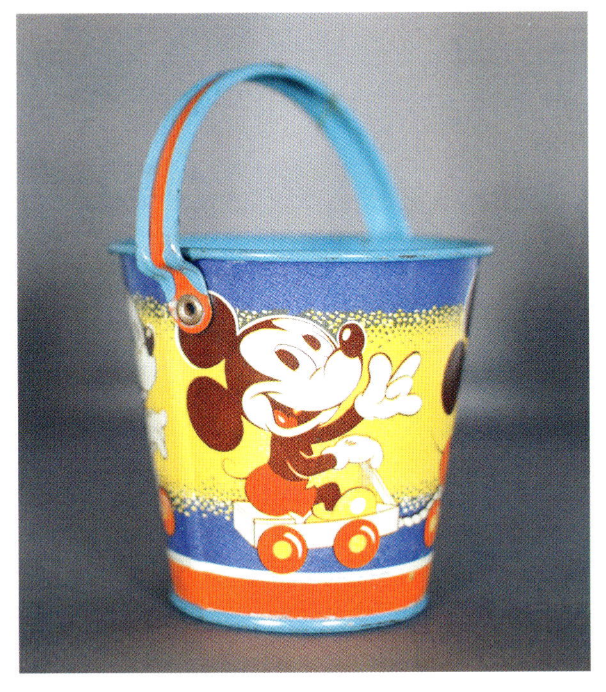

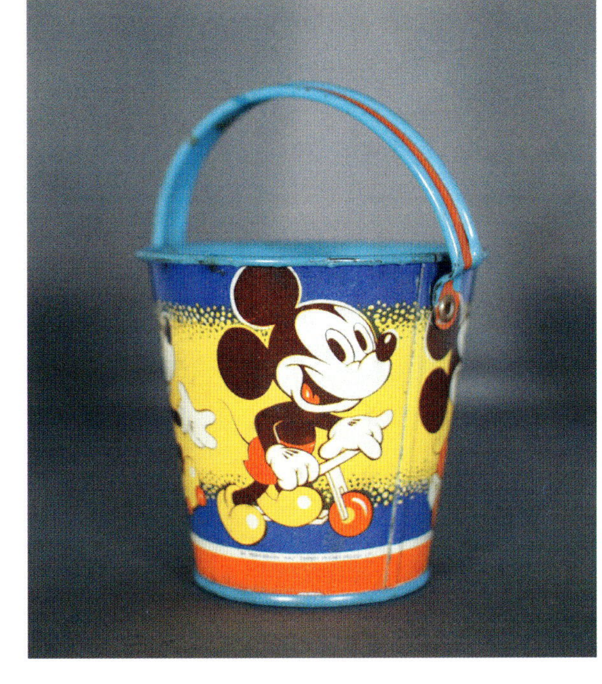

Four scenes of a 3.5" pail featuring Mickey in a wagon, on roller skates, and on a tricycle. By permission Copyright. Happynak pail No. 706 Embossed bottom. *Langer collection* $125-200

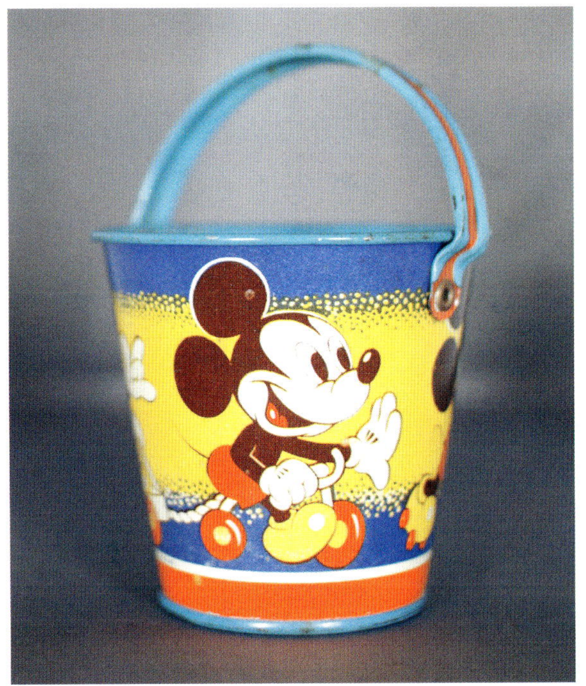

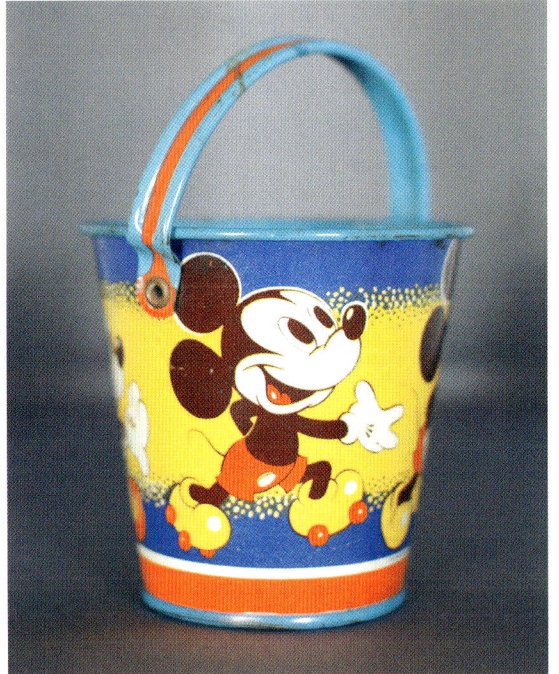

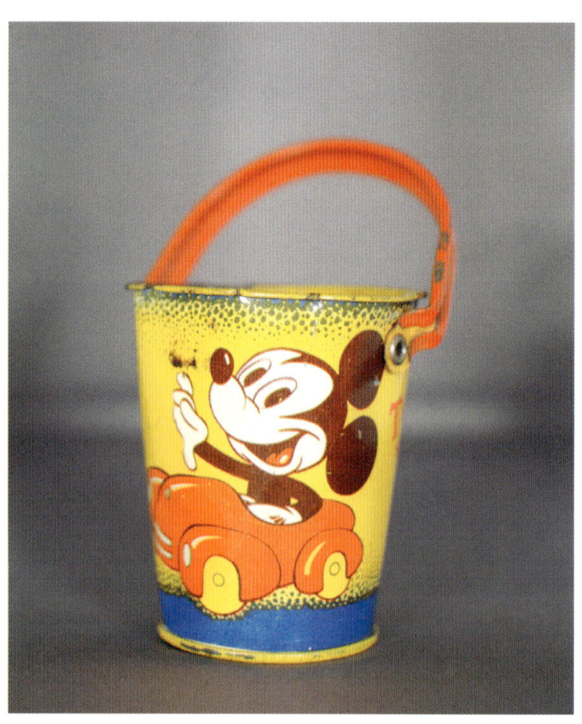

Two views of a 3.25" Tiny Tots Sand Pail. Quite scarce. By permission copyright. Happynak pail No. 701. Embossed bottom. $150-$250

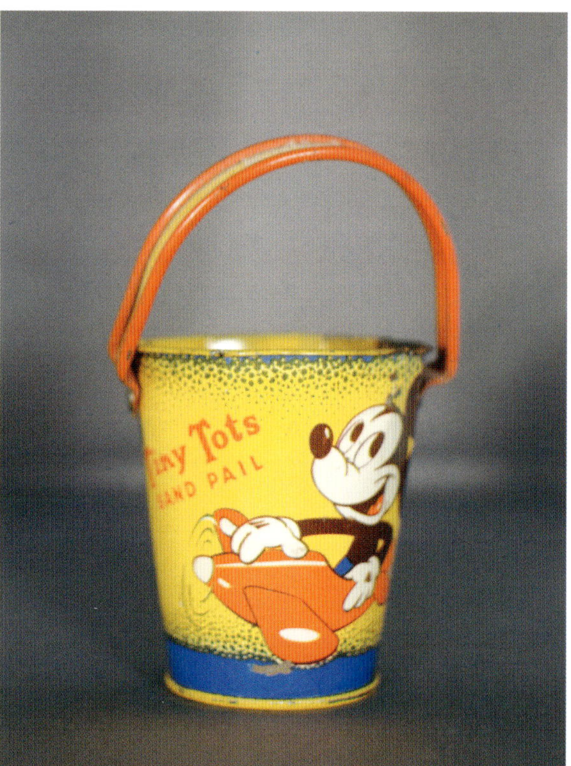

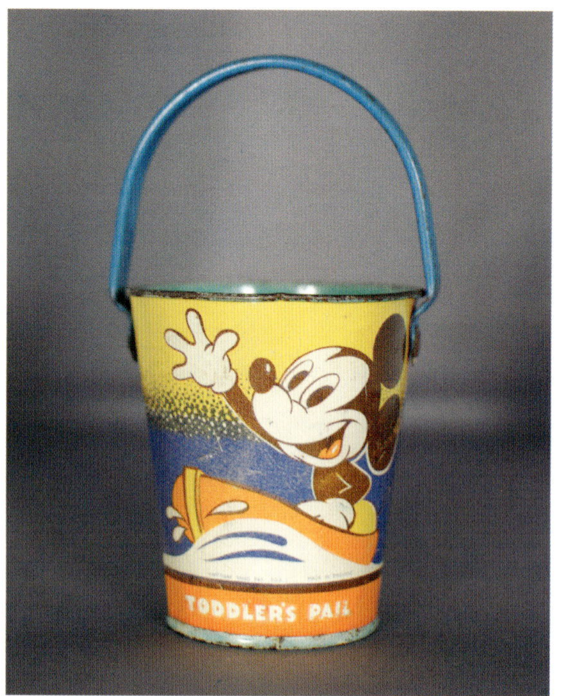

Two views of a 3.25" Toddlers sand pail. Quite scarce. By permission copyright Happynak pail No. 702. embossed bottom $150-250

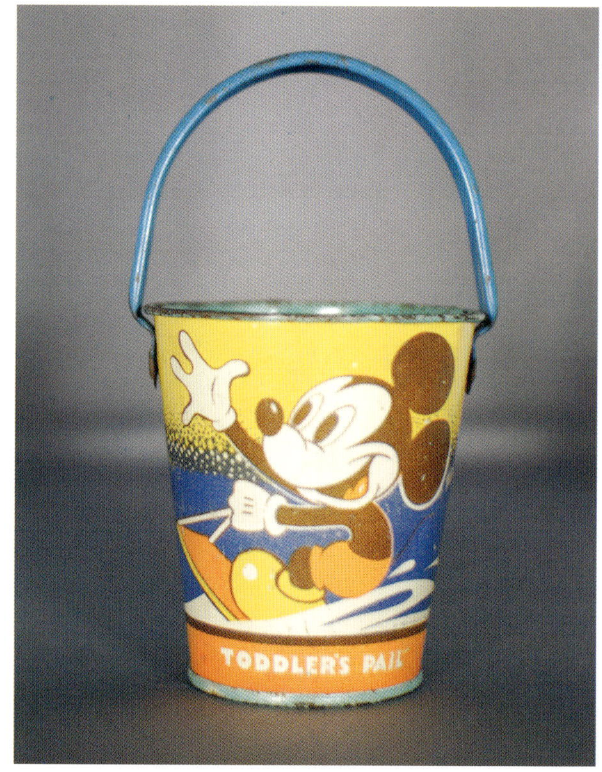

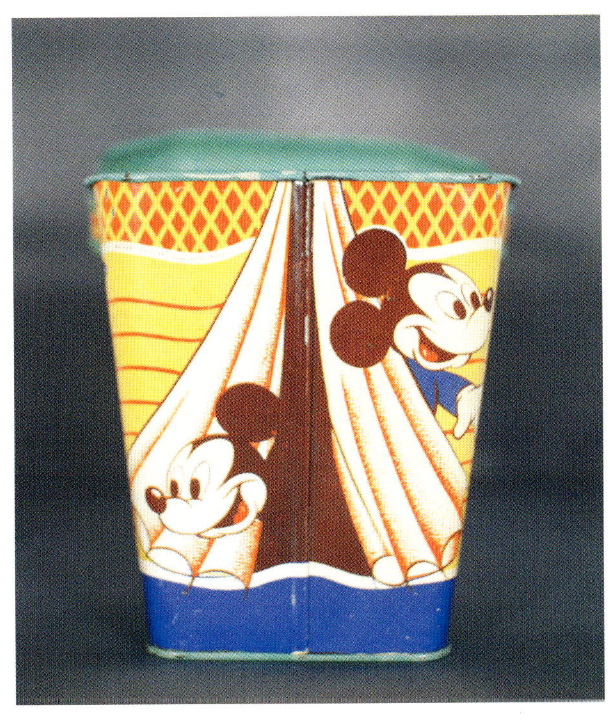

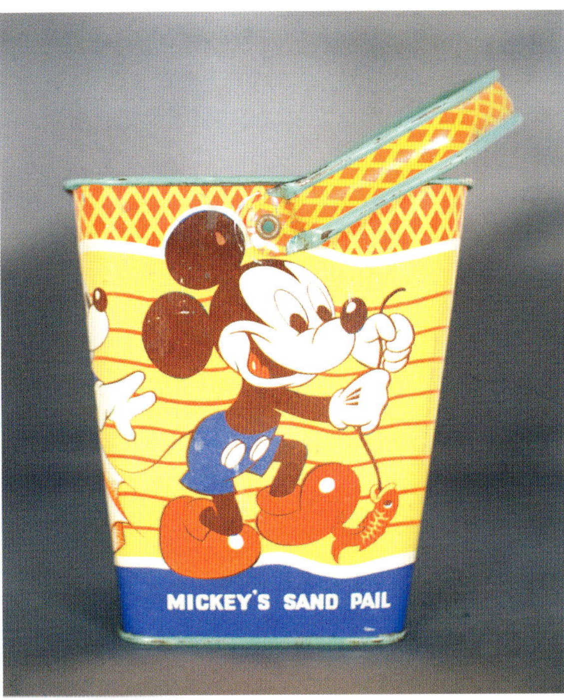

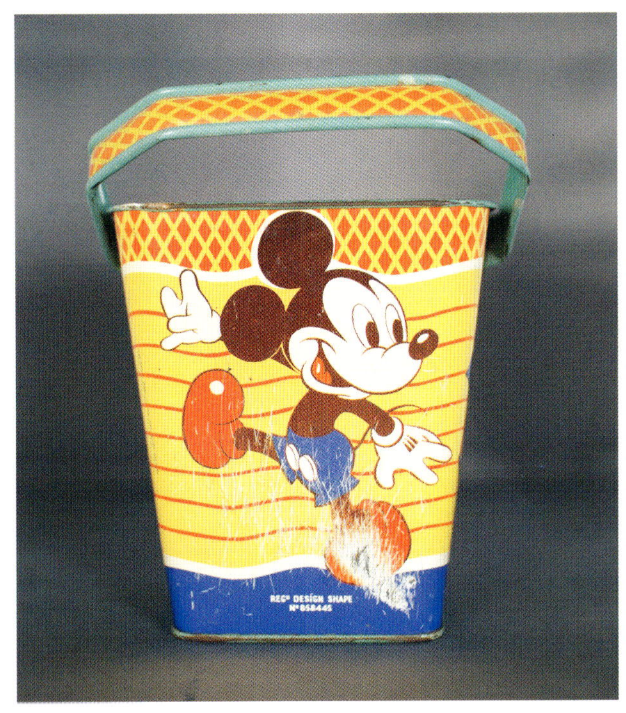

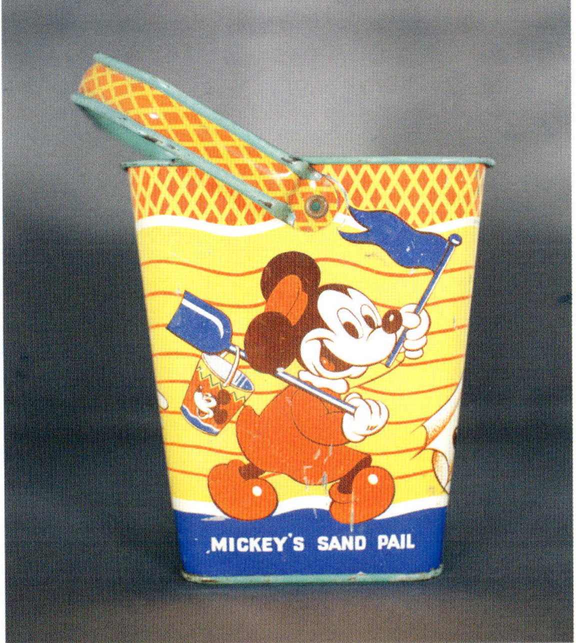

A 5" Mickey Mouse square pail. Unusual as most square pails are by Willow of Australia. Reg'd. Design Shape No.858445. By permission copyright Happynak square sand pail No. 760 Made in England. Embossed bottom as usual. Views of all four sides are shown. $150-250

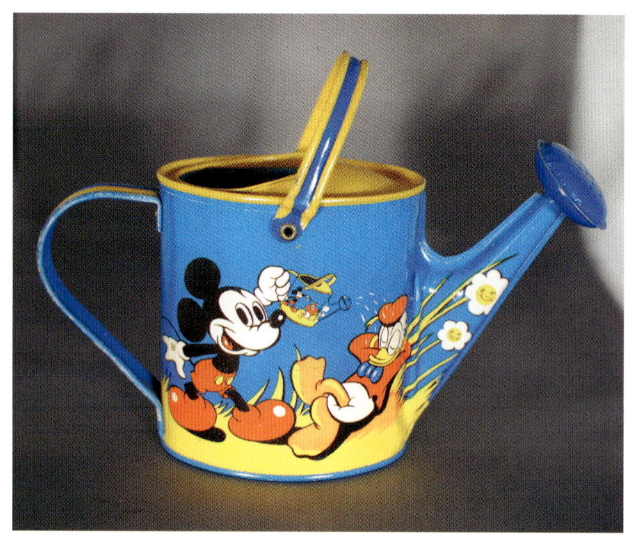

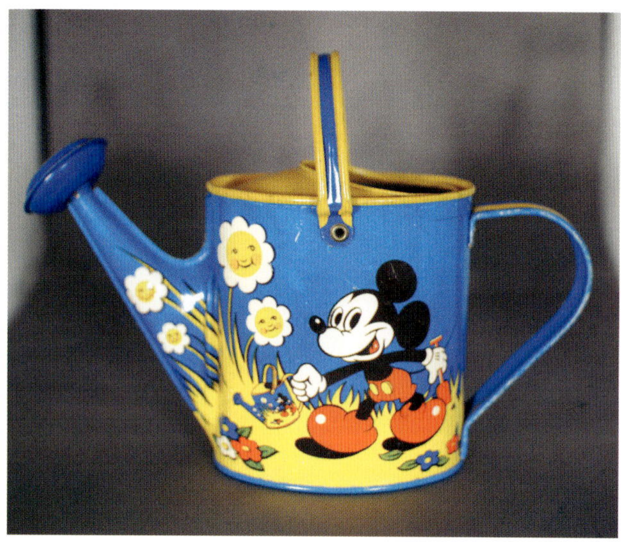

Happynak Mickey Mouse blue watering can. Both sides are pictured. It is interesting to note that these watering cans do not have fixed top handles. By permission copyrights the same on all three watering cans. Bottom says Happynak Toy Patent Applied For, Made in England. The following two cans show the patent #671082 was granted for the watering cans. This one is Happynak No. 772. Quite scarce. $250-450

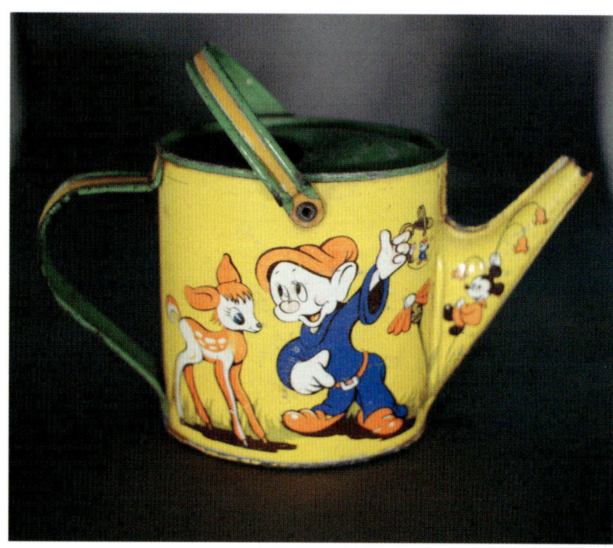

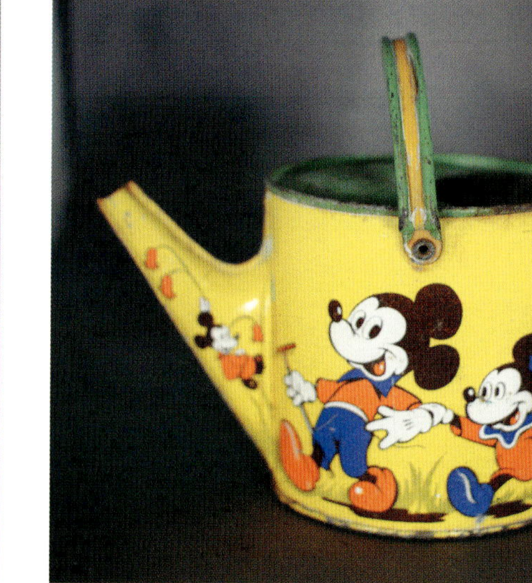

Two views of the yellow Happynak watering can. All cans are 7" tall x 9" from spout to handle. Can # 773. *Langer collection* $125-225

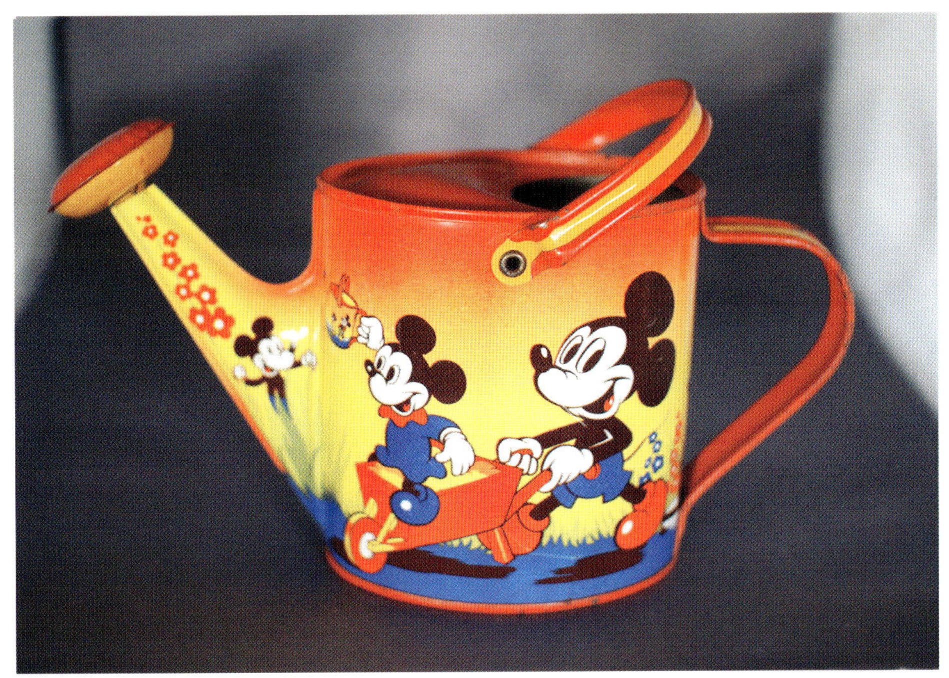

Mickey Mouse Garden Roller. Could be filled with sand or water. It had a 2′ long handle. Roller is 7.5″ x 5″ diameter. Lithographed connection to handle is 8″ x 3.5″. By Permission Walt Disney-Mickey Mouse Happynak Garden Roller 790. Made in England. Seldom seen. $250-350

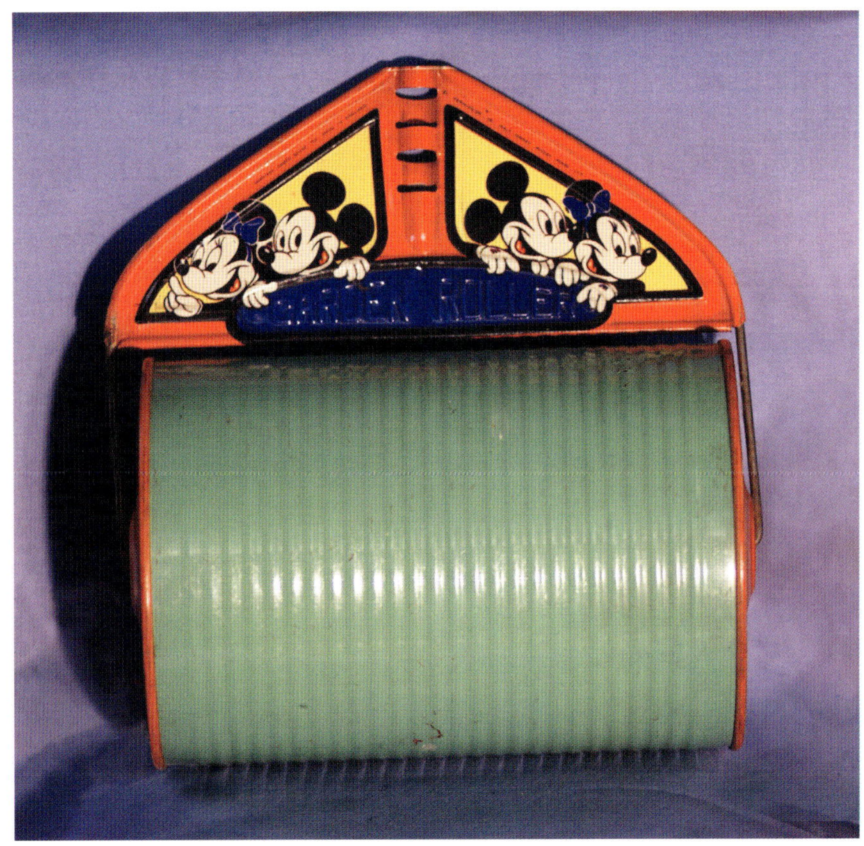

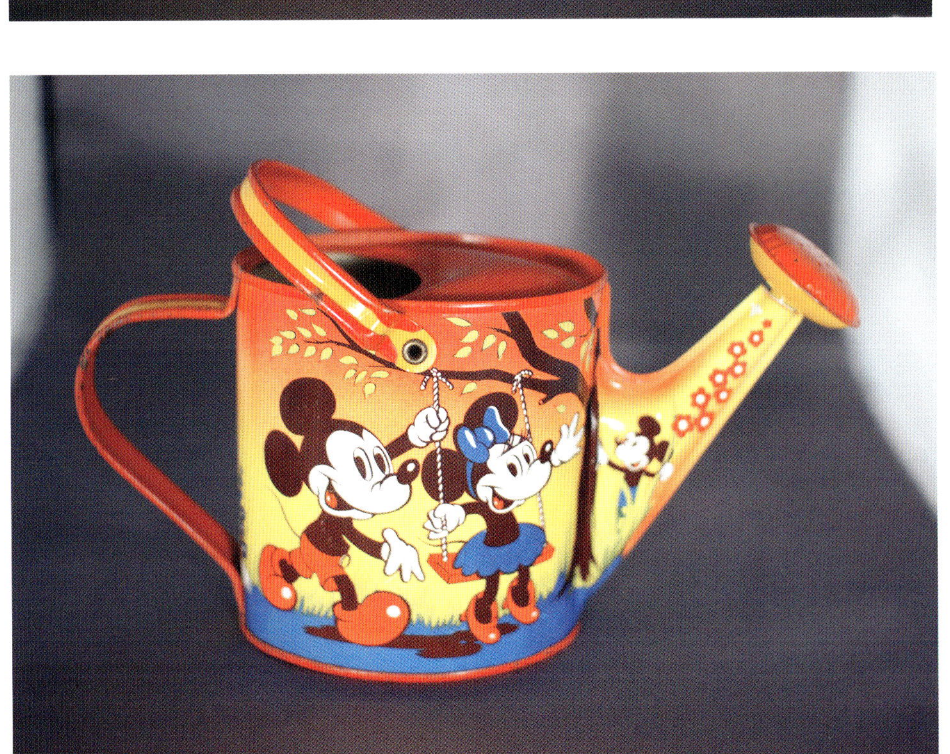

Two views of the red Mickey Mouse watering can. Nice image of Mickey helping Minnie on a swing. Happynak #774. These Happynak watering cans are not seen as often as the sand pails. $250-450

Italy

By 1937 there were 27 licensed vendors of Disney merchandise in Italy. Their Italian offices were in Milan. INGAP was one of Italy's premier toy makers but, at the time they produced this watering can, it did not have a Disney license. Thus they could put Mickey on one side of the sprinkler and Felix on the other. Nevertheless there are wonderful images on the watering can. Unlike Hitler, Mussolini was a great admirer of Mickey

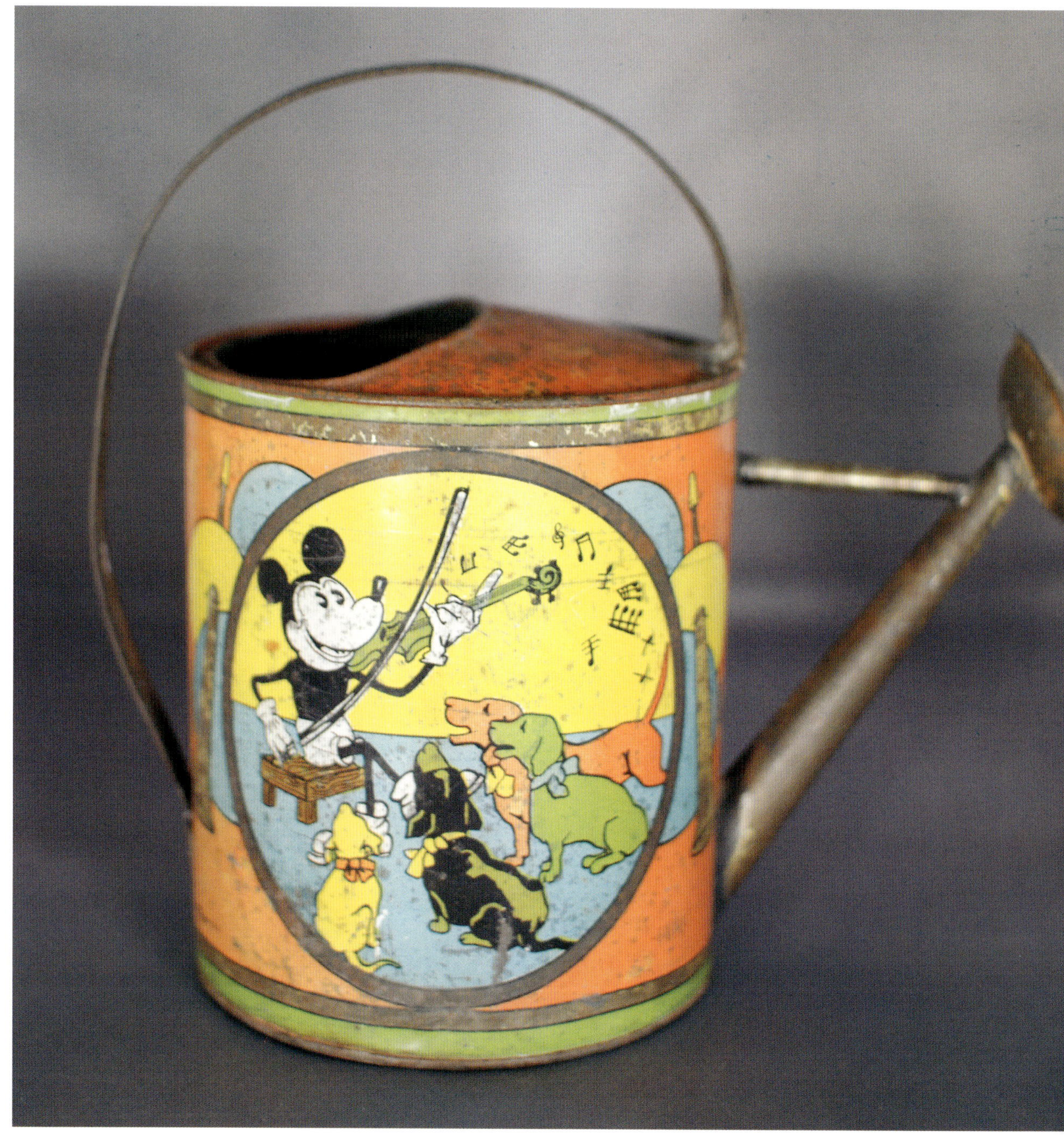

This 8" tall x 9" watering can has a great image of Mickey playing the violin for some admiring dogs. Marked INGAP 853 and Made in Italy. The rod between the spout and the can was added later for strength. Very rare. In this condition $450-750

Japan

Japan produced a great variety of authorized merchandise for licensed vendors around the world including George Borgfeldt of New York. However it appears that sand toys were not among them. The several examples shown here appear to all be unauthorized. These include images of Mickey Mouse, Dumbo and Pinocchio.

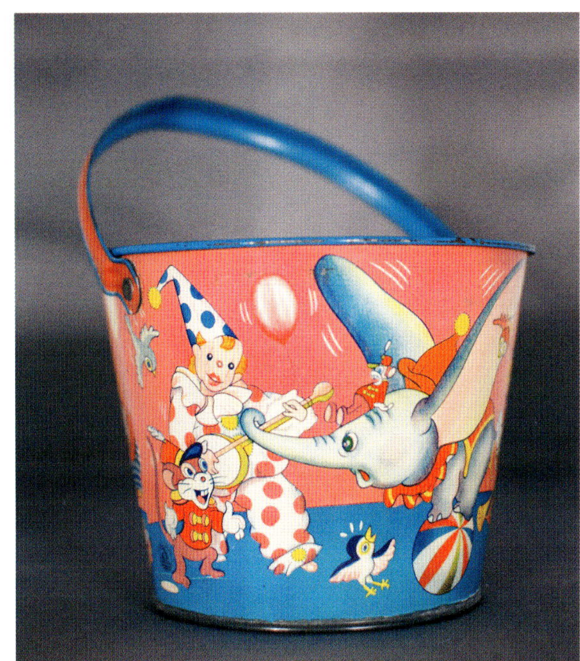

This colorful 4.5" pail features great images of Dumbo and Timothy Mouse. The same image appears on both sides of the pail. A fish mold is on the bottom of the pail. No Disney copyright appears so this is probably unauthorized $200-350

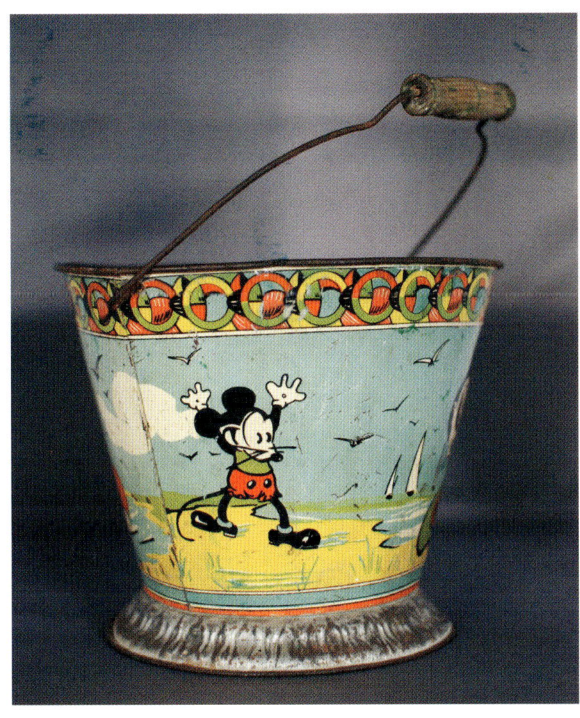

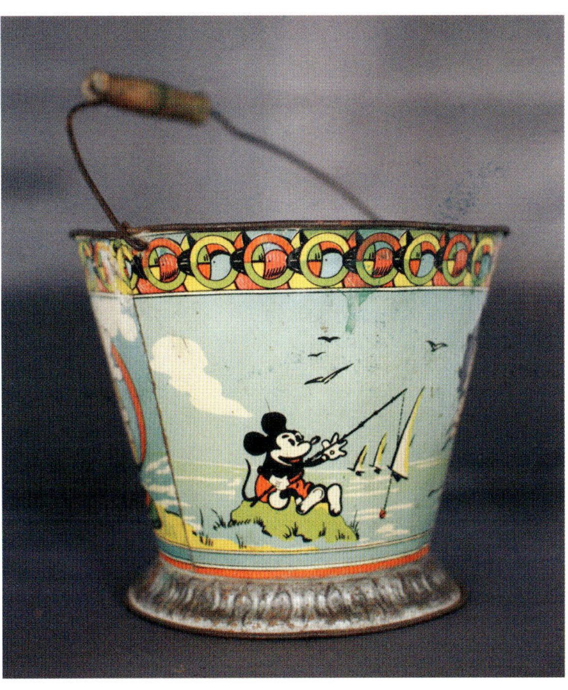

Two views of Mickey from the Betty Boop and Oswald pail. Note the whiskers on Mickey's face. The other shows Mickey fishing. The pail has a raised bottom $1,000-1,500

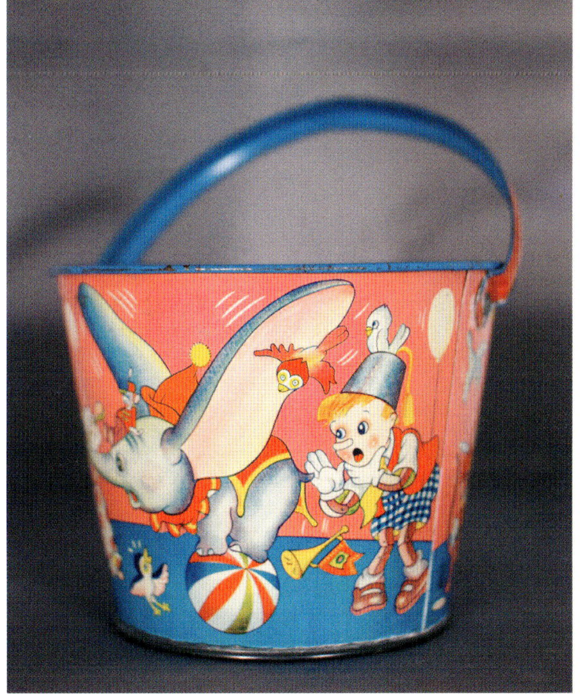

This Mickey Mouse and Betty Boop watering can dates from the mid 1930s. Also shown in Betty Boop chapter. Both sides are pictured. Unmarked. *Birnkrant Collection* $450-850

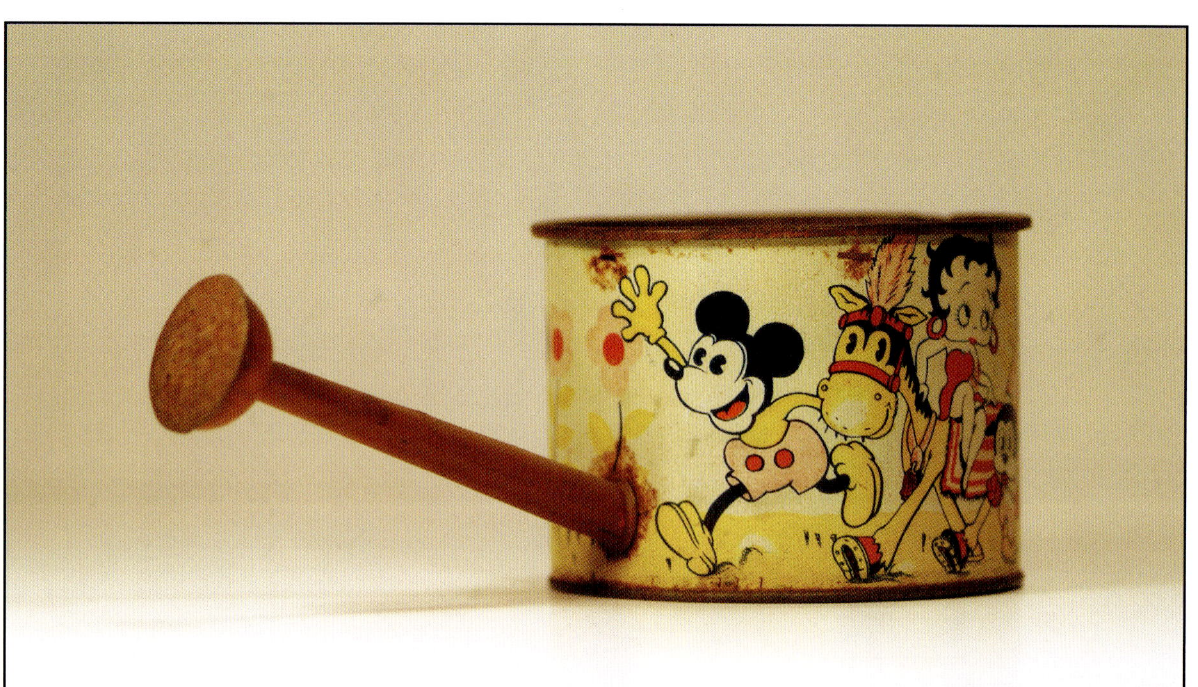

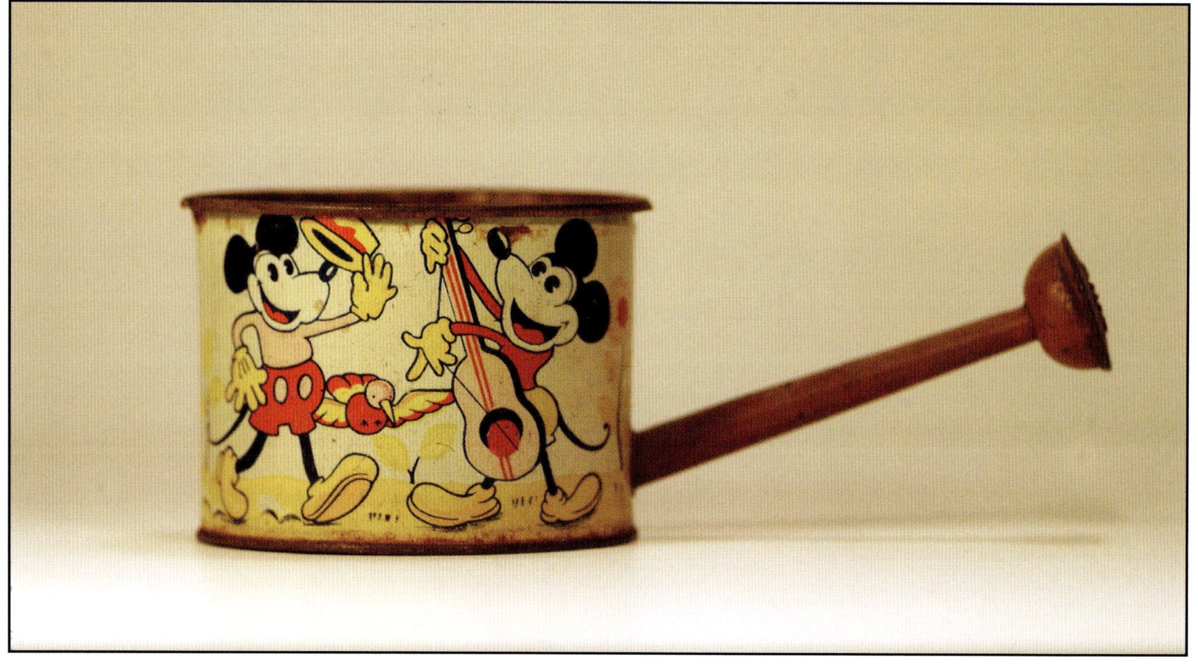

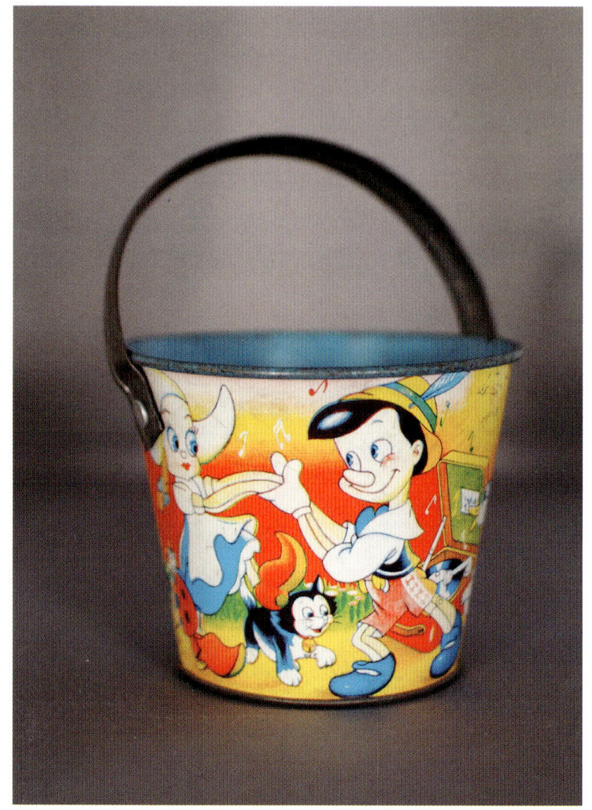

This 3" sand pail has a fine image of Pinocchio and Figaro. The same image appears on both sides of the pail. The bottom has concentric circles. It is probably unauthorized since there are no copyright marks. $200-300.

Mexico

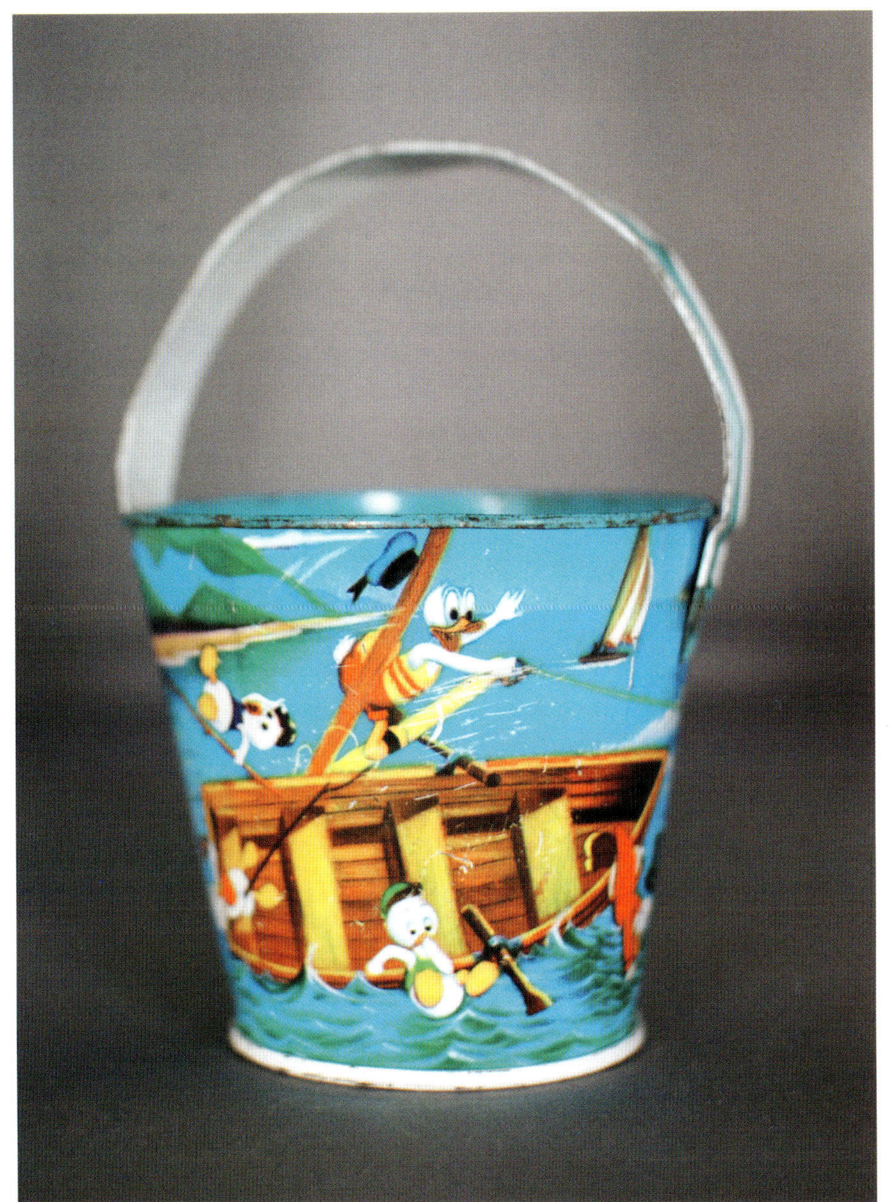

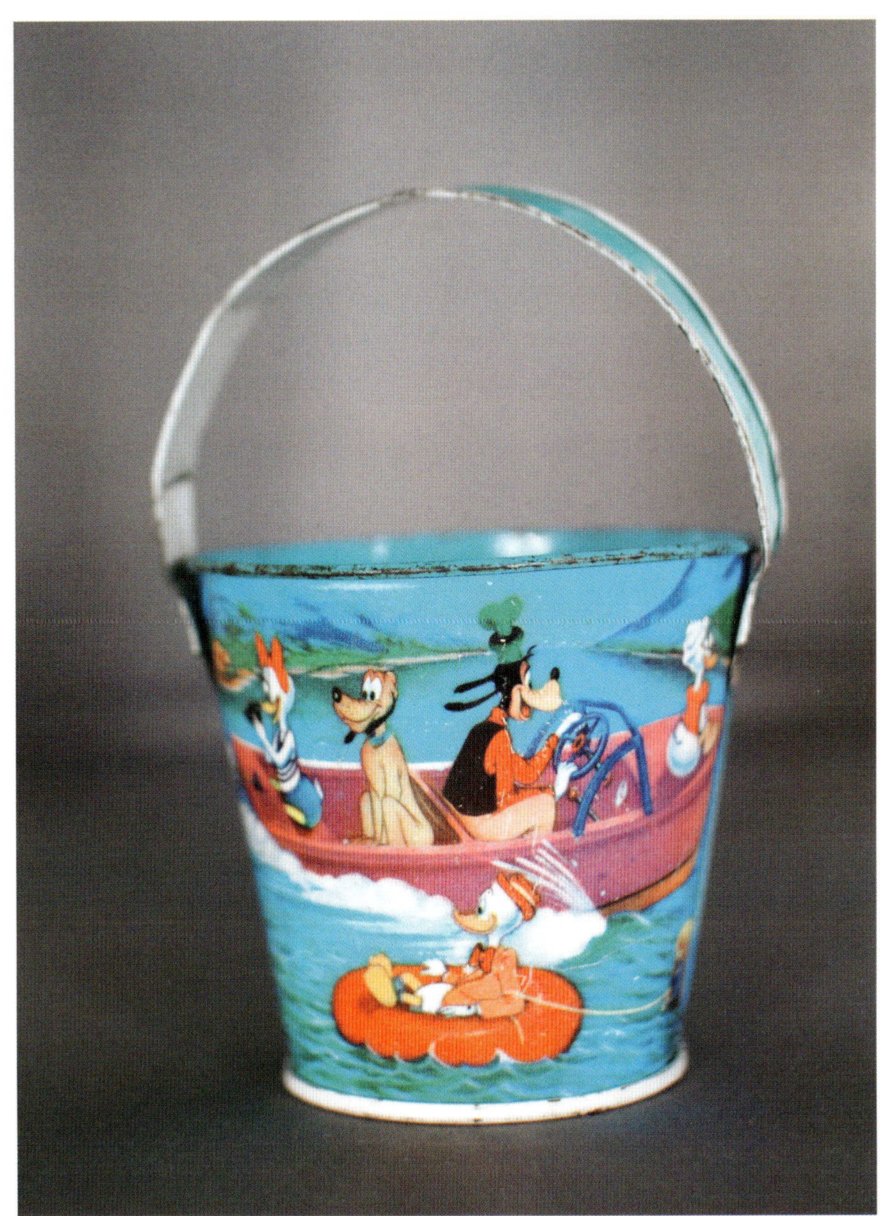

This 3" pail from Mexico shows Donald, Goofy and friends involved in a boating accident. ©Walt Disney Productions (D.R.) Hecho en Mexico $150-200

New Zealand

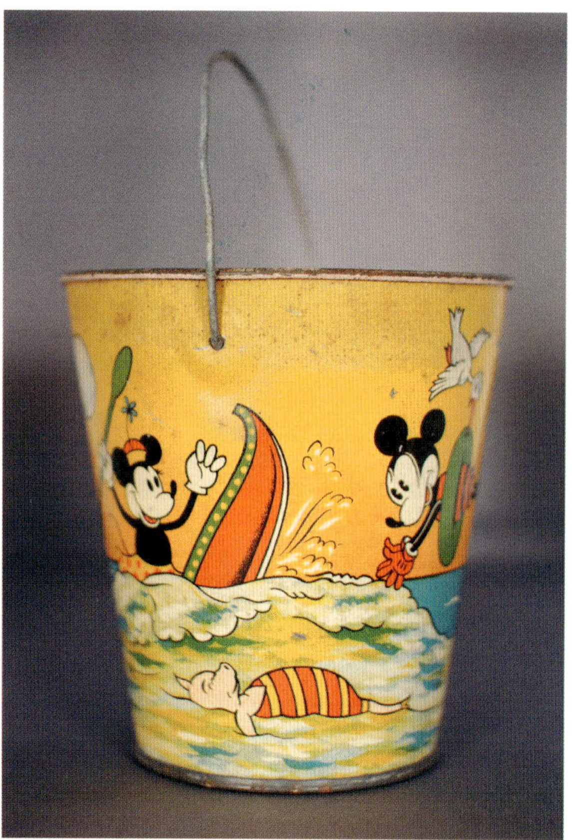

This 4.5" Mickey pail is the only early Disney sand pail produced in New Zealand. The outstanding images speak for themselves. Marked Copyright Walt Disney Ent, Manufactured by Alex Harvey & Sons, Ltd. Auckland. $850-1,250

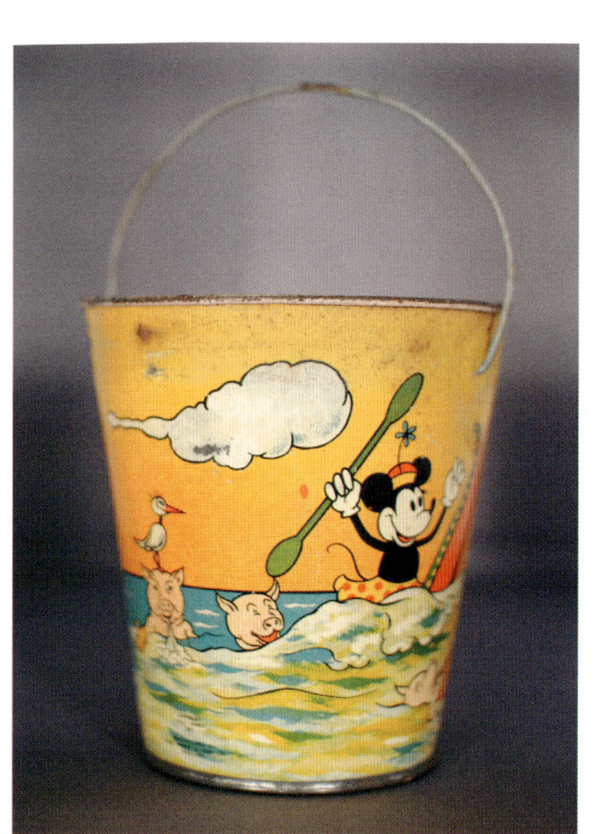

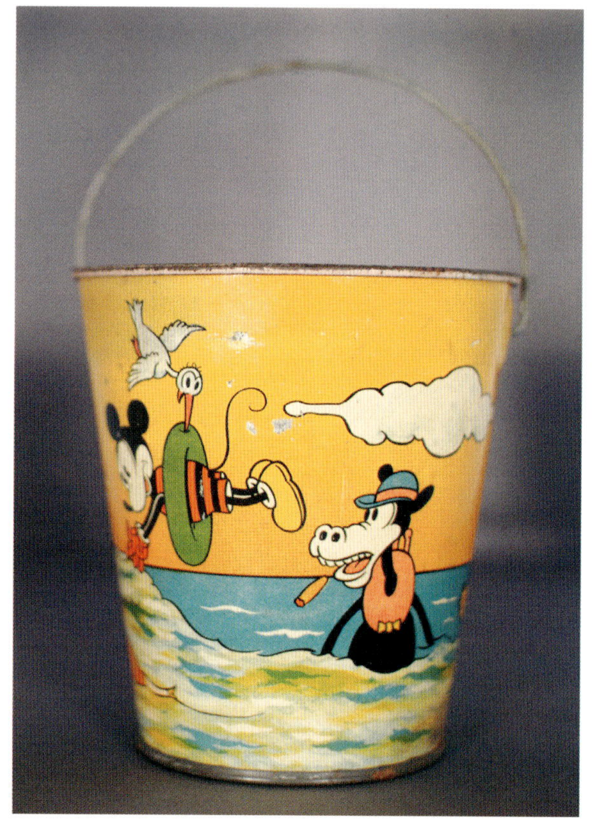

Spain

As far as character toy making in Spain is concerned, Rogelio Sanchis is the beginning and the end. He was a genius at designing and producing toys. His home base was his chateau, "La Isla" where he did his toy manufacturing and also had a fruit packing and shipping business. Among the comic characters he used to design toys were Mickey and Minnie Mouse, Felix the Cat, Laurel and Hardy, Buster Keaton, and Harold Lloyd. Unfortunately, during the height of his toy making career he joined Franco during the Spanish revolution and was killed in 1936. After his death his business was taken over by ASAM (Arrue y San Martin S. Ltd.) Images of invoices of Sanchis and ASAM are shown.

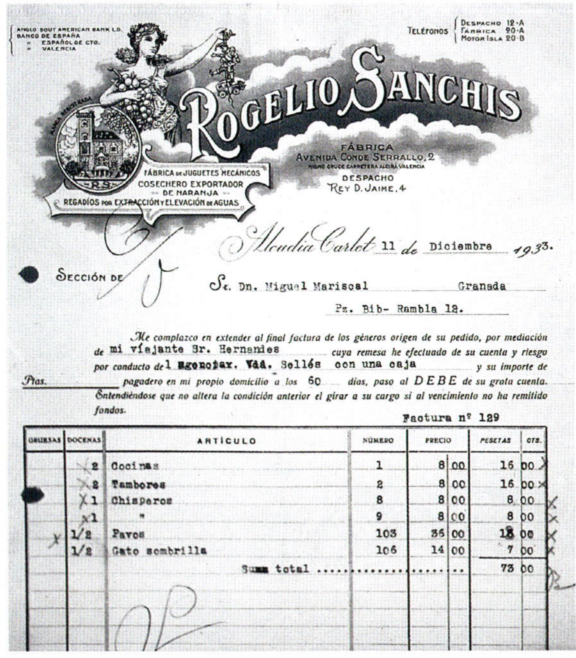

Anglo Sout American Bank Ld.
Banco de España
" Español de Cto.
" Valencia

Teléfonos: Despacho 12-A, Fábrica 20-A, Motor Isla 20-B

ROGELIO SANCHIS

Fábrica de Juguetes Mecánicos
Cosechero Exportador de Naranja
Regadíos por Extracción y Elevación de Aguas

Fábrica: Avenida Conde Serrallo, 2
Despacho: Rey D. Jaime, 4

Alcudia Carlet 11 de Diciembre 1933.

Sección de

Sr. Dn. Miguel Mariscal   Granada
Pz. Bib- Rambla 12.

Me complazco en extender al final factura de los géneros origen de su pedido, por mediación de mi viajante Sr. Hernandes cuya remesa he efectuado de su cuenta y riesgo por conducto del Agenciar. Vdá. Sellés con una caja y su importe de Ptas. pagadero en mi propio domicilio a los 60 días, paso al DEBE de su grata cuenta. Entendiéndose que no altera la condición anterior el girar a su cargo si al vencimiento no ha remitido fondos.

Factura nº 129

Gruesas	Docenas	Artículo	Número	Precio		Pesetas	Cts.
	2	Cocinas	1	8	00	16	00
	2	Tambores	2	8	00	16	00
	1	Chisperos	8	8	00	8	00
	1	"	9	8	00	8	00
	1/2	Pavos	103	36	00	18	00
	1/2	Gato sombrilla	106	14	00	7	00
		Suma total				73	00

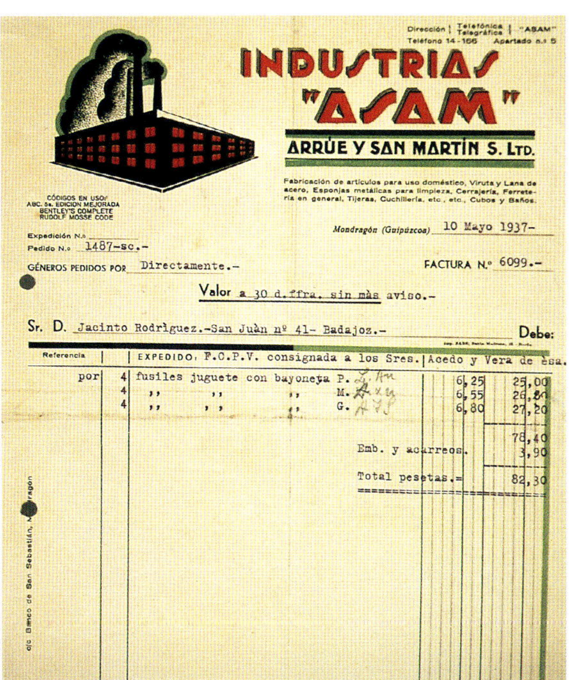

Dirección Telefónica Telegráfica "ASAM"
Teléfono 14-166   Apartado n.º 5

INDUSTRIAS "ASAM"
ARRÚE Y SAN MARTÍN S. LTD.

Fabricación de artículos para uso doméstico, Viruta y Lana de acero, Esponjas metálicas para limpieza, Cerrajería, Ferretería en general, Tijeras, Cuchillería, etc., etc., Cubos y Baños.

Códigos en uso: ABC. 5a. Edicion Mejorada, Bentley's Complete, Rudolf Mosse Code

Mondragón (Guipúzcoa) 10 Mayo 1937-

Expedición N.º
Pedido N.º 1487-sc.-
Géneros pedidos por Directamente.-
Factura N.º 6099.-

Valor a 30 d.ffra. sin màs aviso.-

Sr. D. Jacinto Rodrìguez.-San Juàn nº 41- Badajoz.-   Debe:

Referencia		Expedido: F.C.P.V. consignada a los Sres. Acedo y Vera de èsa.		
por	4	fusiles juguete con bayoneta P.	6,25	25,00
	4	,, ,, ,, M.	6,55	26,20
	4	,, ,, ,, G.	6,80	27,20
				78,40
		Emb. y acarreos.		3,90
		Total pesetas.=		82,30

The Rogelio Sanchis invoice is dated 11 December 1933. The ASAM invoice is dated 10 May 1937. Note the Sanchis invoice incorporates their logo consisting of his chateau "La Isla" and his initials R.S.

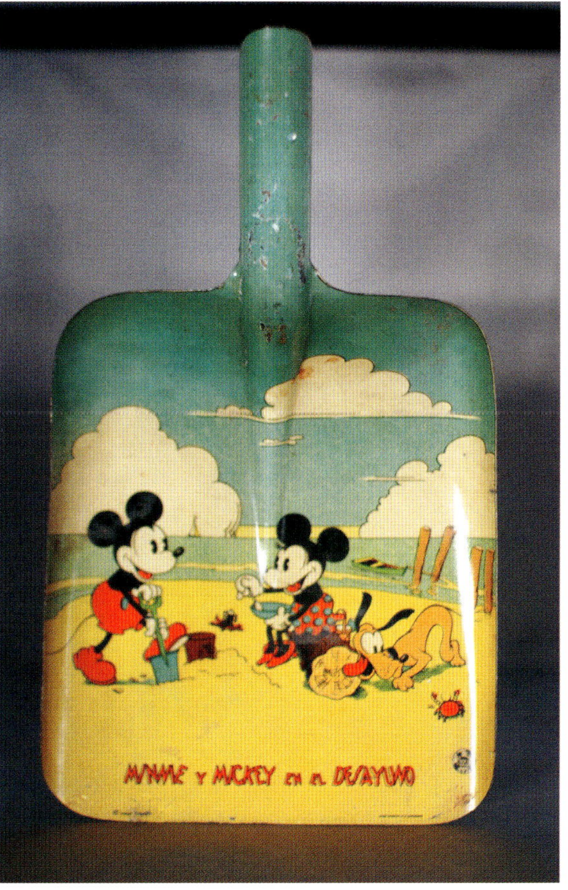

This is the largest character sand shovel made. It measures 12" high x 7" wide. It came with a 2' wood handle. ©Walt Disney. Has R.S. logo. Sanchis was granted the first Spanish Disney license. $850-1,350

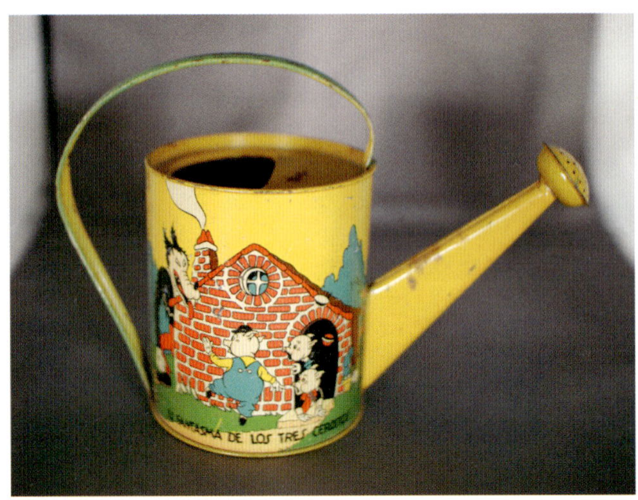

Three Little Pigs and Big Bad Wolf 6" high x 9" watering can. ©Walt Disney. Includes R.S. logo. $350-500

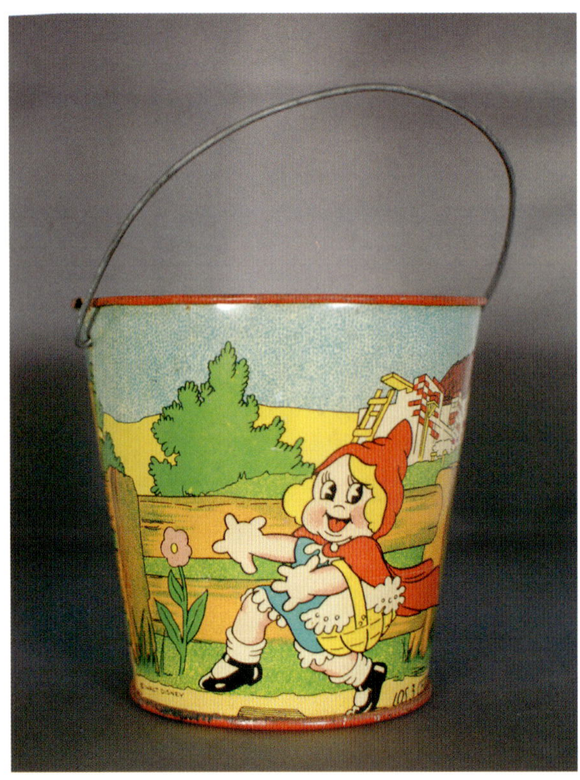

Three Pigs and Red Riding Hood 5" pail by ASAM from 1937. ©Walt Disney. Has ASAM logo. $300-500

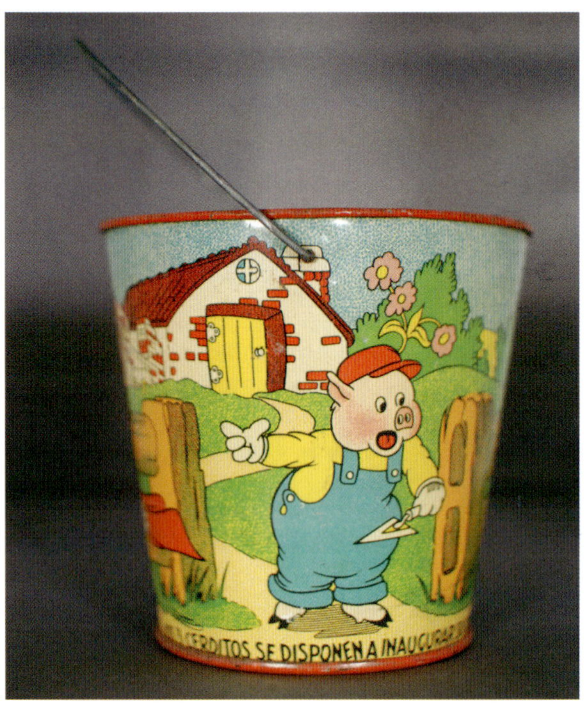

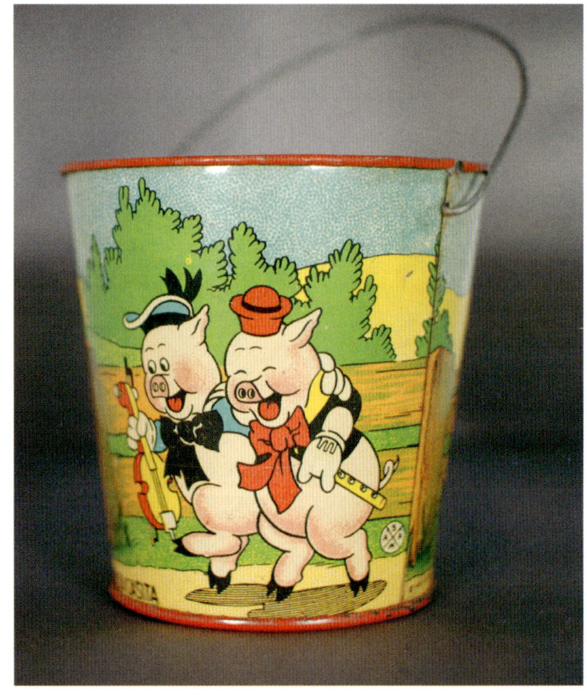

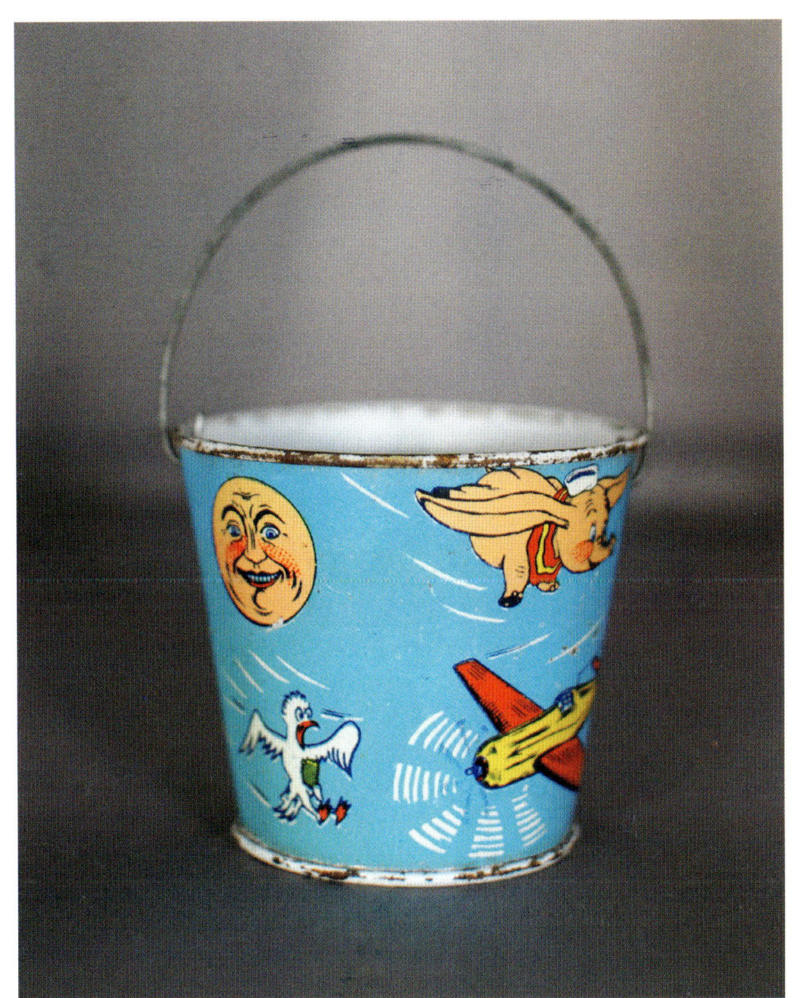

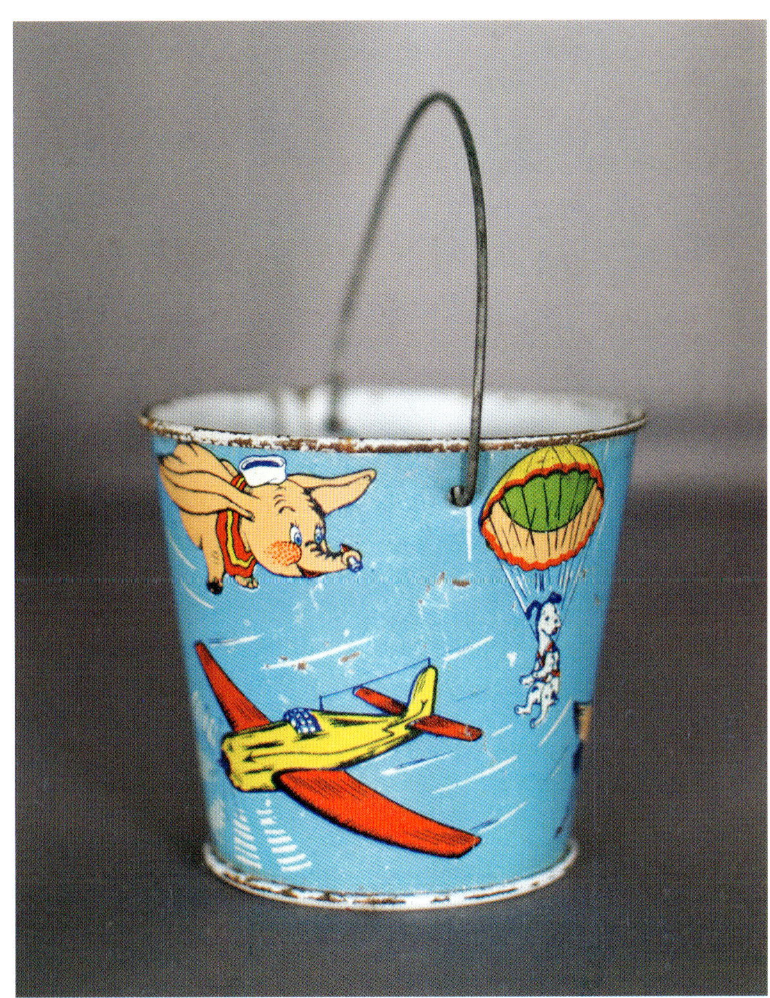

Two views of 2.5″ pail featuring Dumbo. This one is unauthorized. $125-300

Uruguay

Uruguay also produced some licensed merchandise. However, the pictured 2" pail appears to be unauthorized.

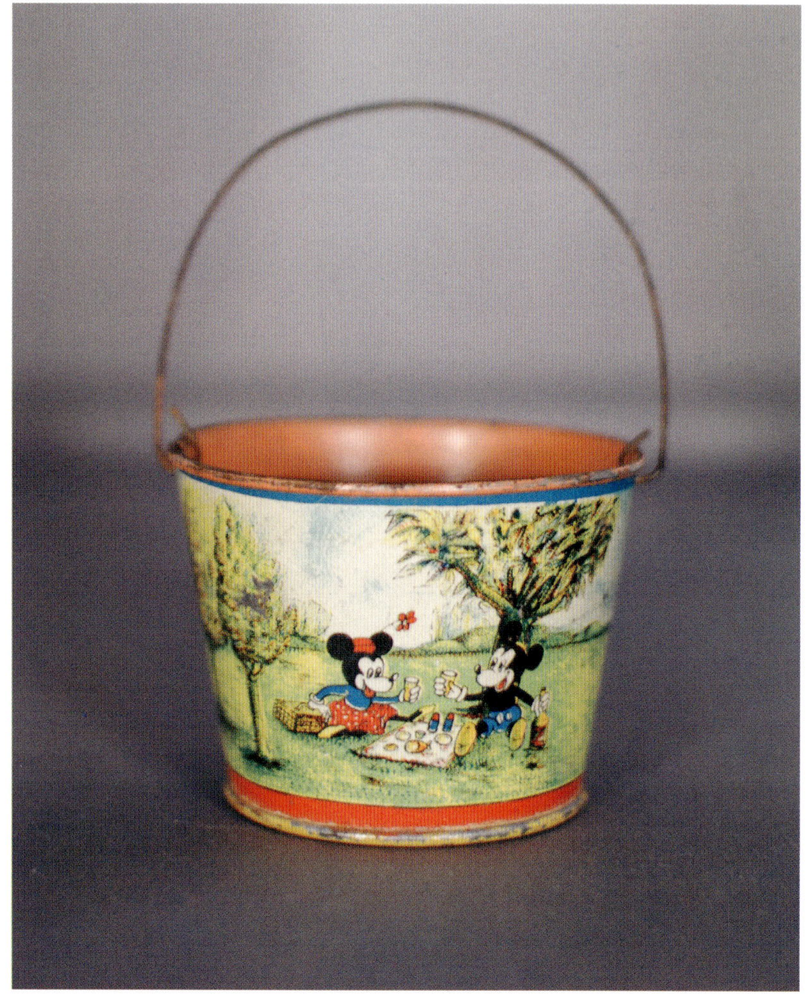

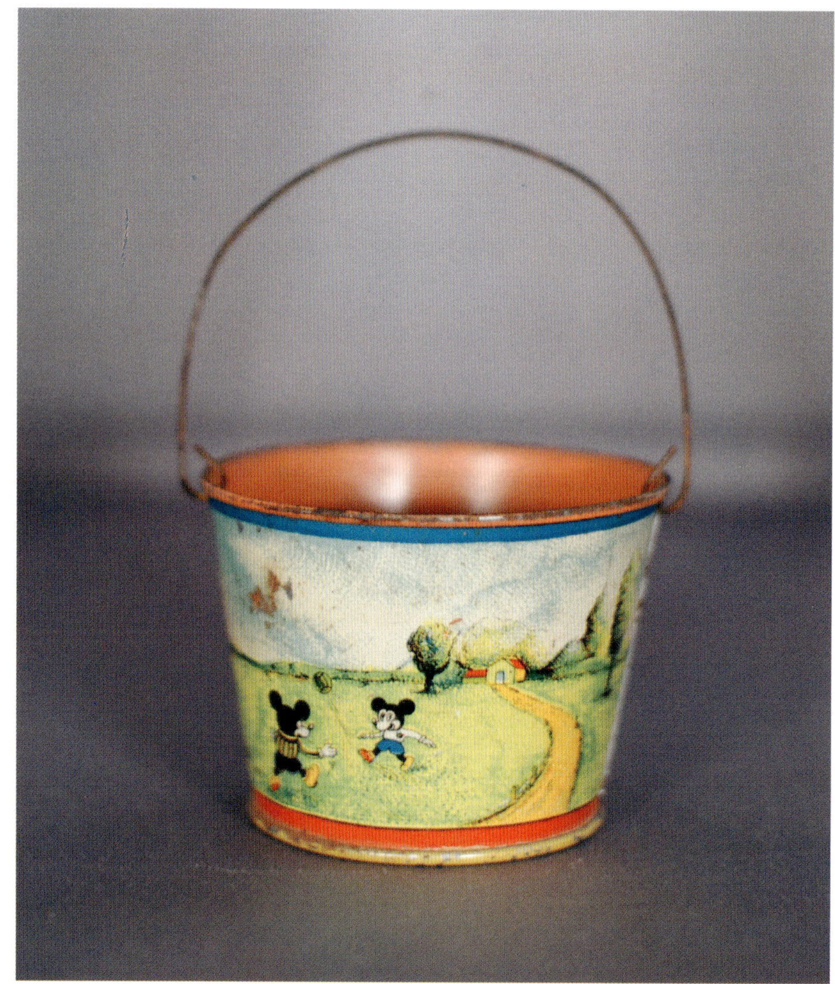

Two views of the small 2" pail from Uruguay. The first image shows Mickey and Minnie enjoying a picnic under a small grove of trees. The reverse side shows Mickey's nephews playing soccer. They are wearing the jerseys of the Uruguayan national team. The pail is unmarked. $200-350

Chapter 9:

Dora the Explorer

A recent character to be featured on sand pails is Dora the Explorer. She is one of the first ones to be taken from a children's TV show. She first appeared in 1999 and became a regular show on the Nickelodeon channel in 2000. Dora was created by Chris Gifford, Valerie Walsh, and Eric Weiner. Several billion dollars worth of associated merchandise have already been sold. Dora's friends include Boots the Monkey, Backpack, Swiper the mischievous fox, Diego, and Baby Jaguar. *Pails courtesy of the Tin Box Co*

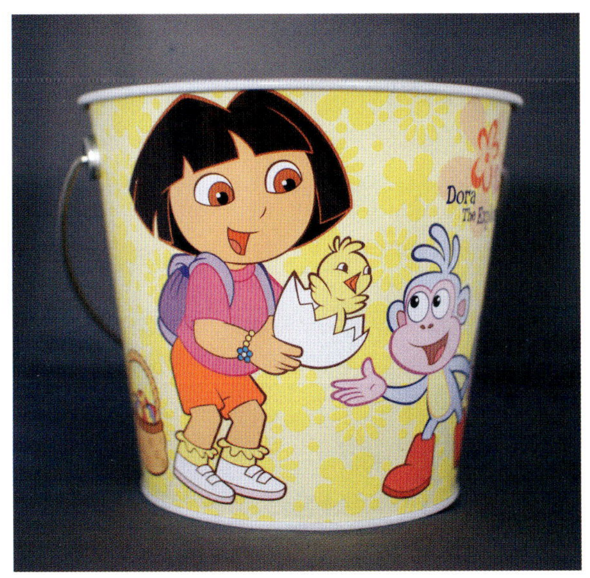

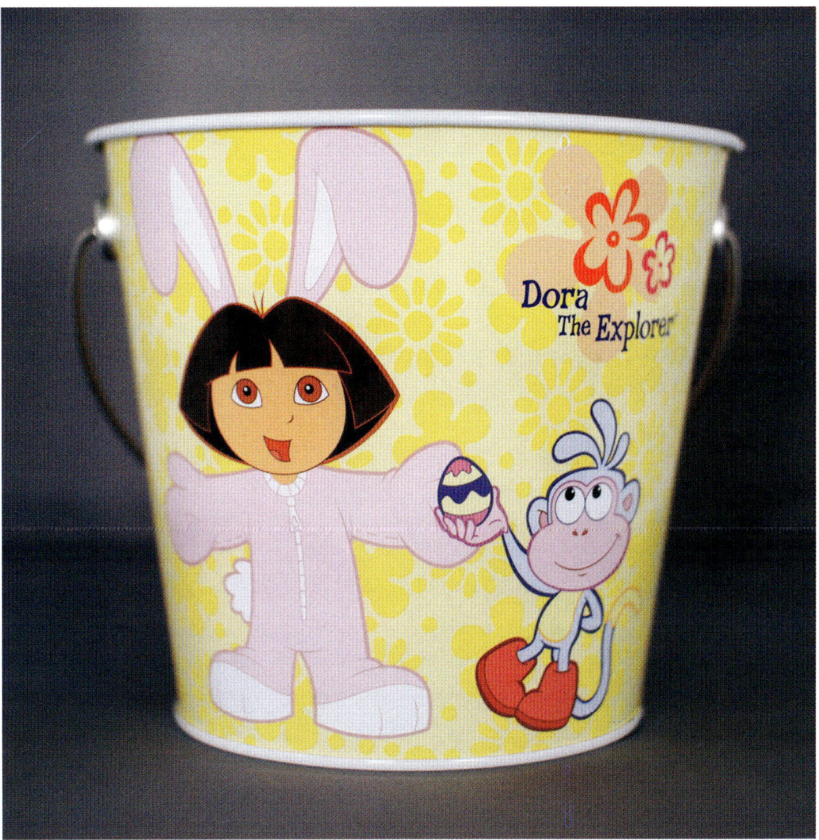

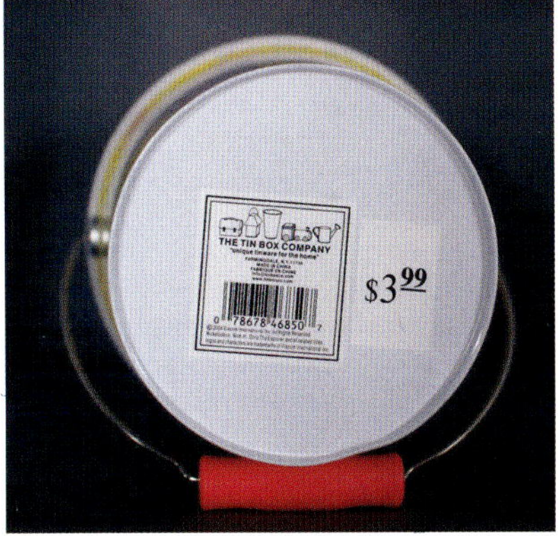

This 5.5" Easter pail features Dora and her friend Boots. The first image features Dora with Backpack and her Easter basket. She is holding a hatched egg in her hand. Next is Dora in her Easter bunny costume with Boots holding an Easter egg. The bottom of the pail is shown with the Tin Box Company label. The pail is marked ©2004 Viacom International Inc. All rights reserved. Nickelodeon, Nick Jr. Dora the Explorer and all related titles, logos and characters are trademarks of Viacom International Inc. $5-15

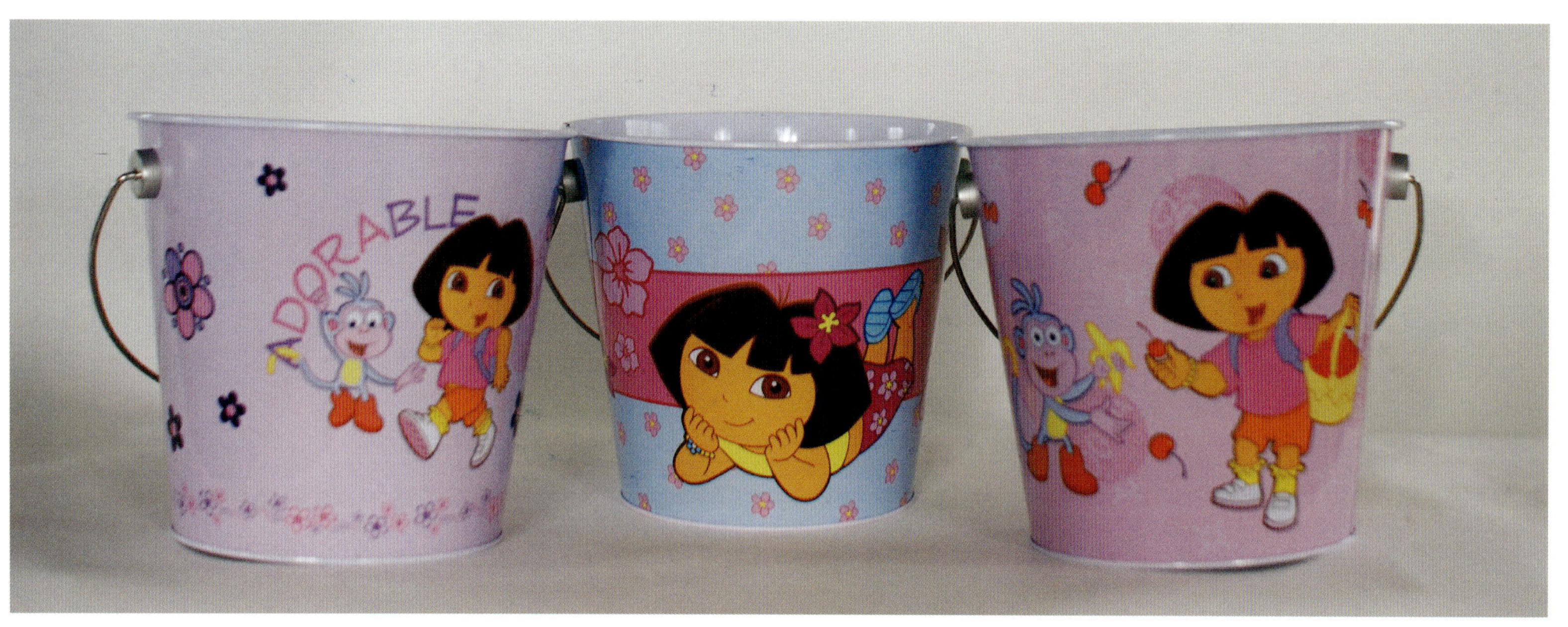

These three 6″ Dora pails were produced in 2006. The pails have images on both sides, hence the two photos. Each is marked ©2006 Viacom International, Inc. All rights reserved. Nickelodeon, Nick Jr., Dora the Explorer and all related titles, logos and characters are trademarks of Viacom International Inc. Tin Box label on bottom $5-15

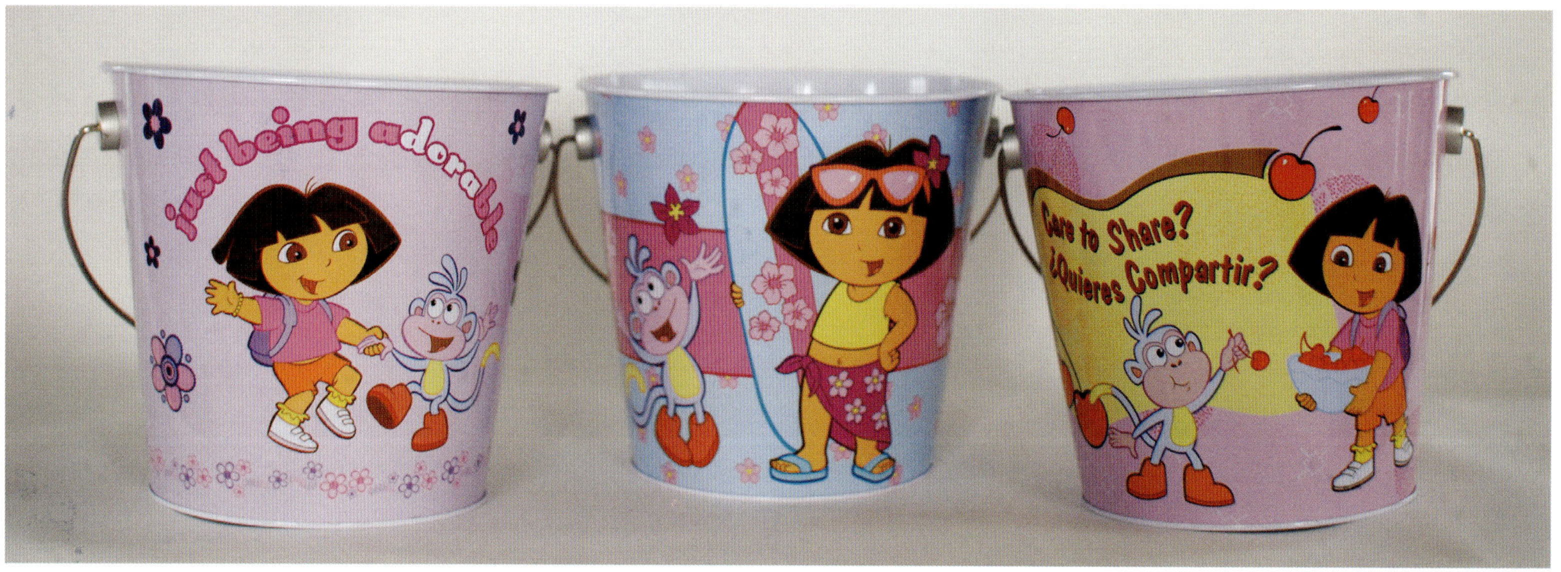

Chapter 10:

Felix the Cat

Felix the Cat is one of the earliest comic characters to remain popular to the present day. Created by Otto Messmer, he first appeared in 1919 in a cartoon short *Feline Follies.* Although created by Messmer, Felix was quickly taken over by Pat Sullivan and his studio. Messmer continued to create story lines and illustrate them but Sullivan received the revenue.

Disney's Mickey Mouse quickly surpassed Felix in popularity because Walt immediately embraced sound for his cartoon shorts, while Sullivan and Felix lagged way behind. When Sullivan passed away in 1933, Felix essentially became dormant until revived for a television series in the 1950s. Fortunately Otto Messmer was still around to help.

Recently produced Felix pails by Schylling demonstrate how Felix has survived.

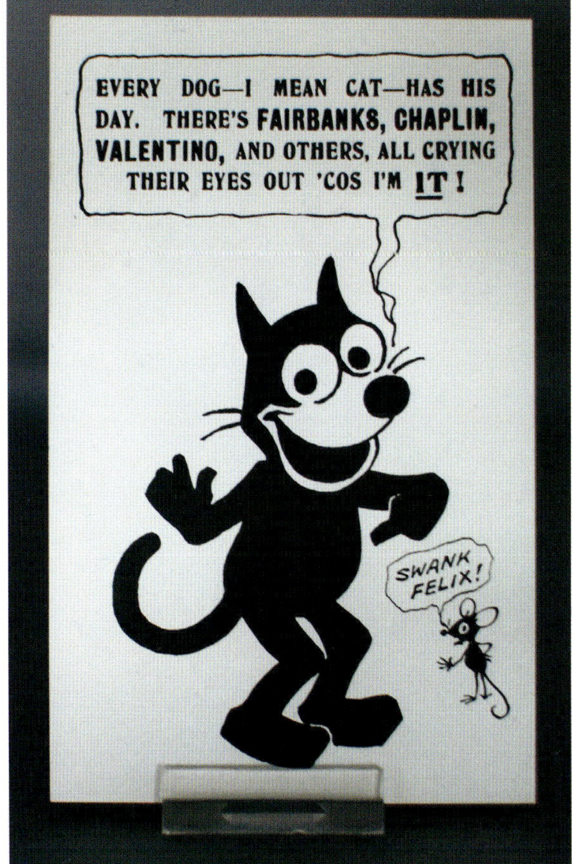

Felix post card featuring Felix bragging that he is "IT" over Fairbanks, Chaplin and Valentino. Published by Bamforth & Co., Ltd.of Holmfirth, England and New York. Printed in England. $15-30

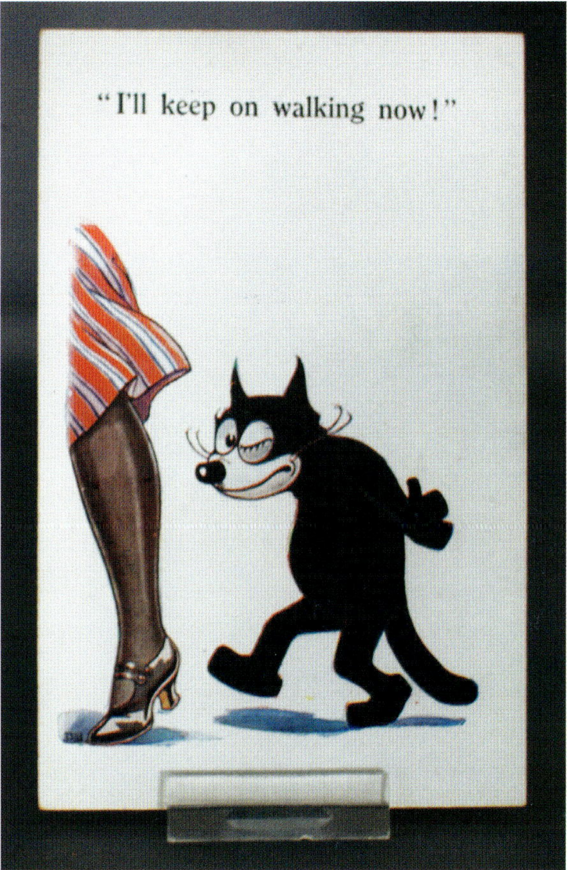

Felix post card "I'll keep on walking!" by Inter Art Co. Code #4830 $15-30

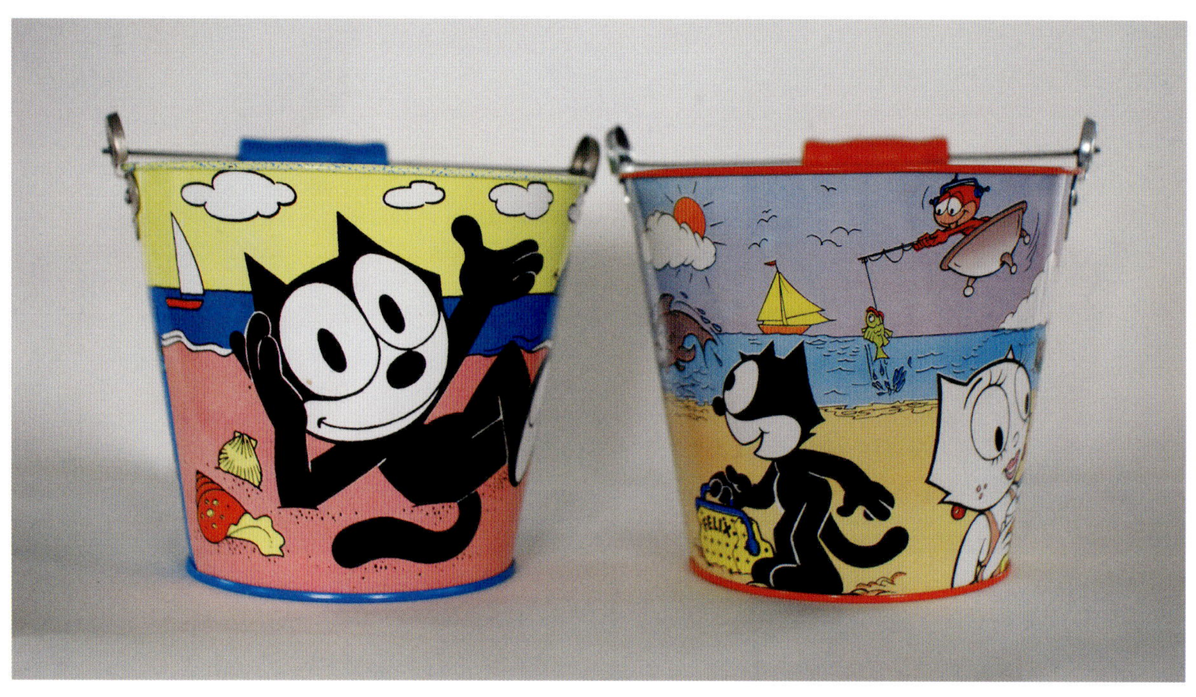

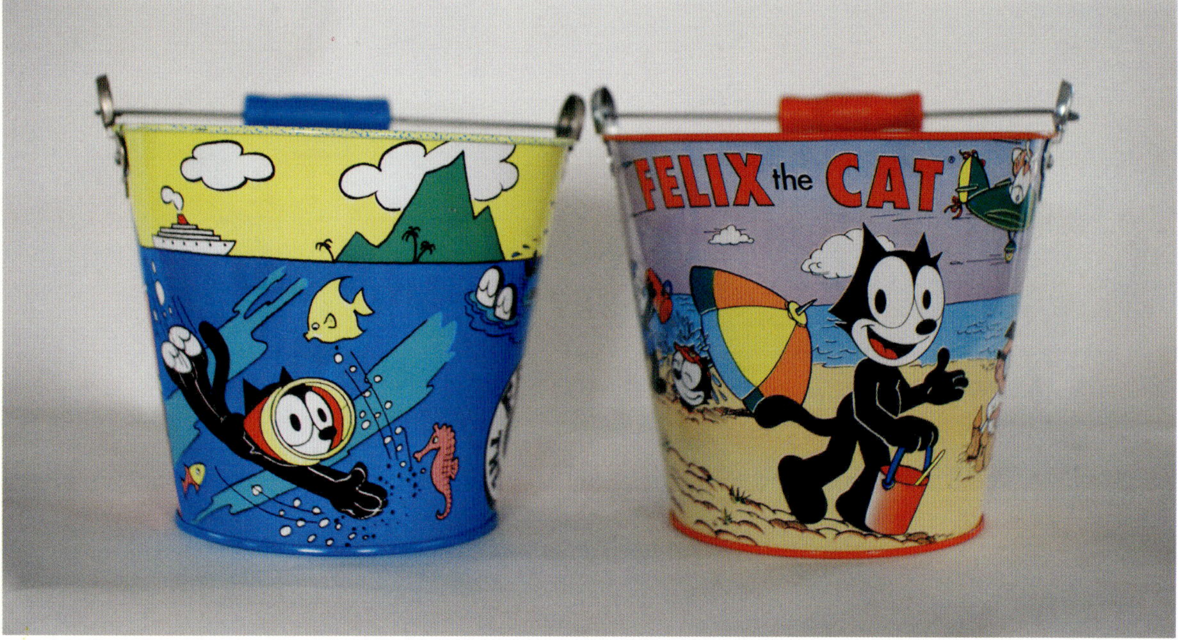

Two views of two contemporary 6" Felix sand pails imported by Schylling. Made in Estonia. Trademark and ©Felix the Cat Productions Licensed by Determined Productions $10-15

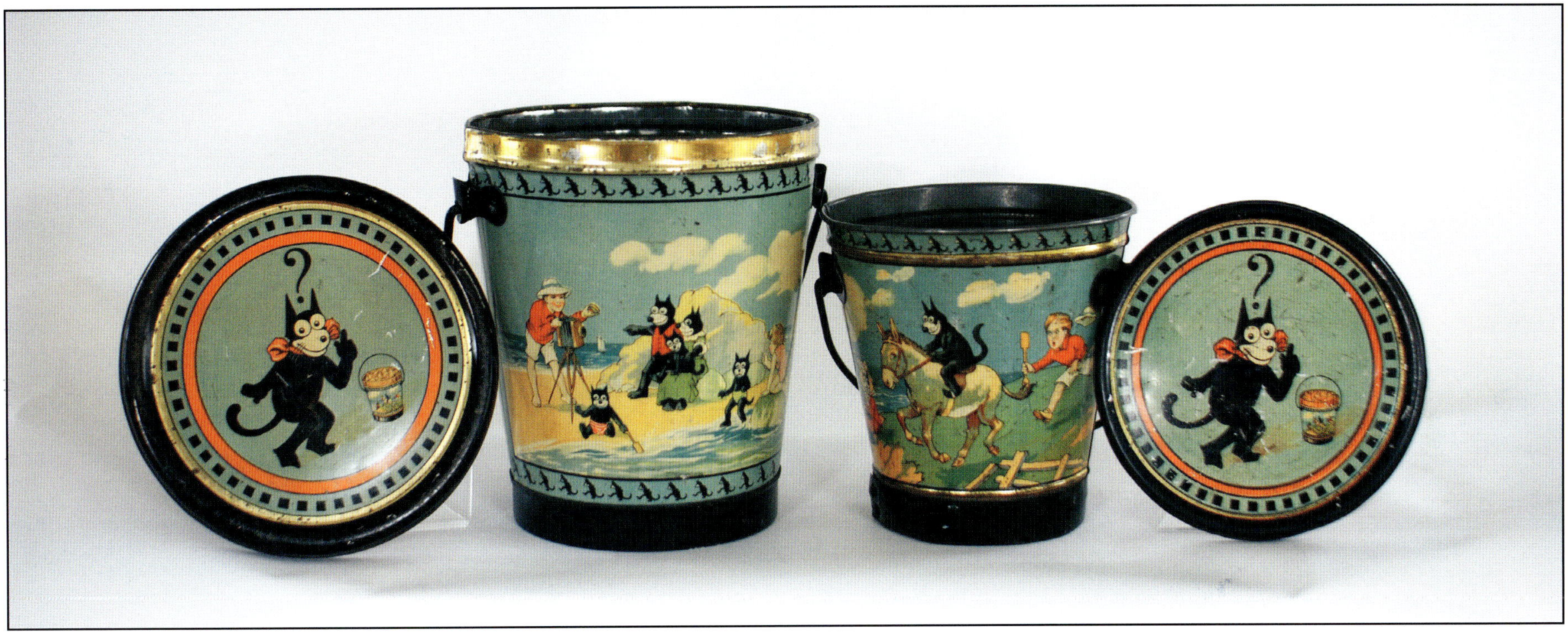

Felix The Cat 6.5" and 8" covered toffee pails. The same images appear on both pails that date from the mid 1920s. Both pails are exceedingly rare, particularly in great condition. The 6.5" example has a built up .5" bottom. The image shown on this pail is that of the Felix family being photographed on the beach. The cover is 6.5" in diameter. Both pails were manufactured in Great Britain by the E.T. Gee & Sons, Ltd. Liverpool. In addition to this mark, it also has No.1038 and Patent No. 178742. A band of walking Felixes appears around the top of the pail. The 8" pail has a second band around the bottom of the pail. Otherwise all images are the same, although larger. The diameter of the cover is 7". The pail is marked: G No. 1034 and Pat. Nos. 178742 & 208369. Because of the difference in G Nos., it is probable there are other pails in different sizes. Among the finest pails ever produced and one of the most desired. In the condition shown $2,500-3,500.

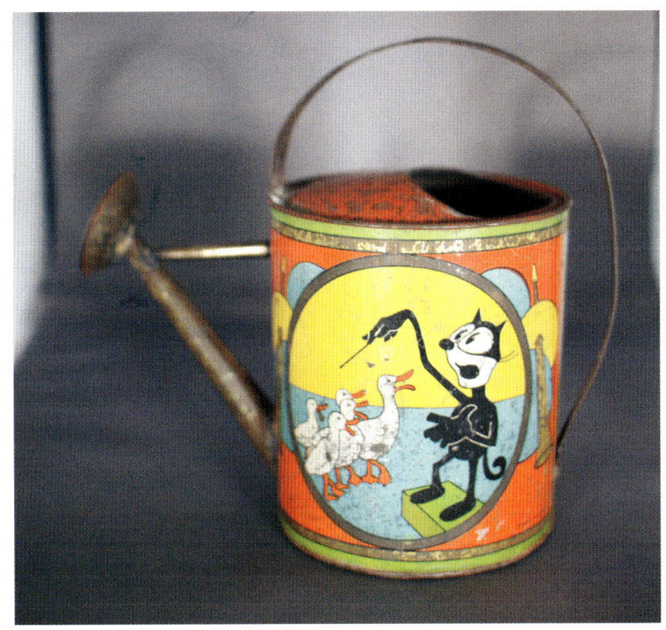

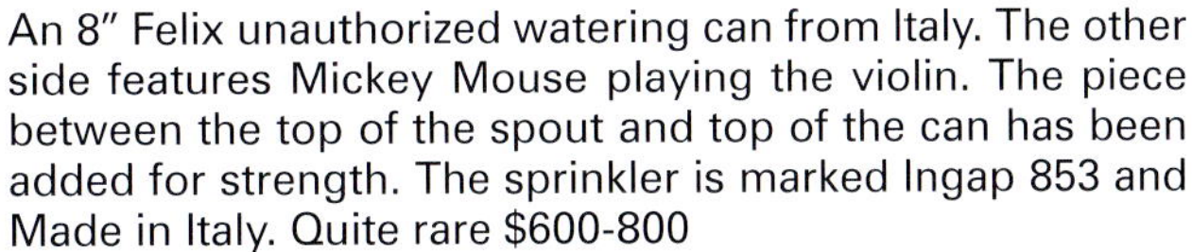

An 8" Felix unauthorized watering can from Italy. The other side features Mickey Mouse playing the violin. The piece between the top of the spout and top of the can has been added for strength. The sprinkler is marked Ingap 853 and Made in Italy. Quite rare $600-800

Chapter 11:

Hanna-Barbera Characters

William Hanna and Joseph Barbera began their six decade collaboration while both were working in the MGM animation studio beginning in 1939. Tom and Jerry were the first well-known animated characters they created, first appearing in 1940. Between 1940 and 1967 they produced 161 shorts for MGM starring Tom and Jerry and winning 7 Academy Awards in the process. When MGM closed their animation studio in 1957, Hanna and Barbara started their own studio and were responsible for creating such famous characters as Huckleberry Hound, Yogi Bear, Quick Draw McGraw, Scooby-Doo, the Flintstones, the Jetsons, and the Smurfs. By far, Hanna-Barbera were responsible for more TV characters than any other studio. William Hanna passed away in 2001 and Joseph Barbera died on December 18, 2006.

The 8″ sand pail pictured here features many of the Hanna-Barbera characters.

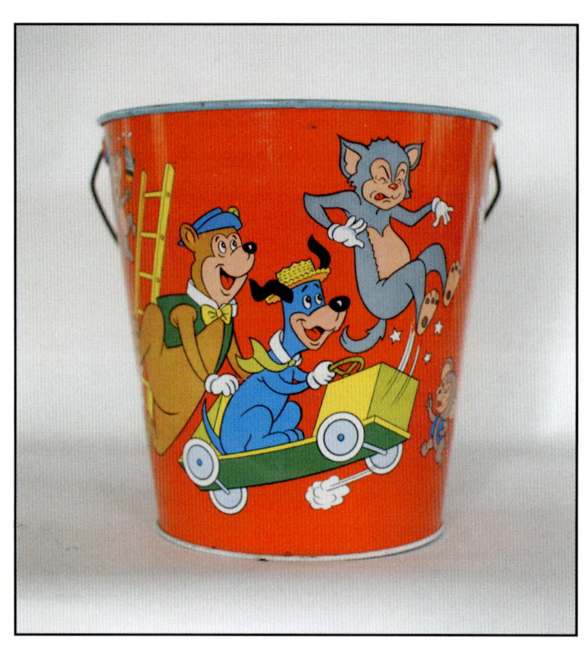

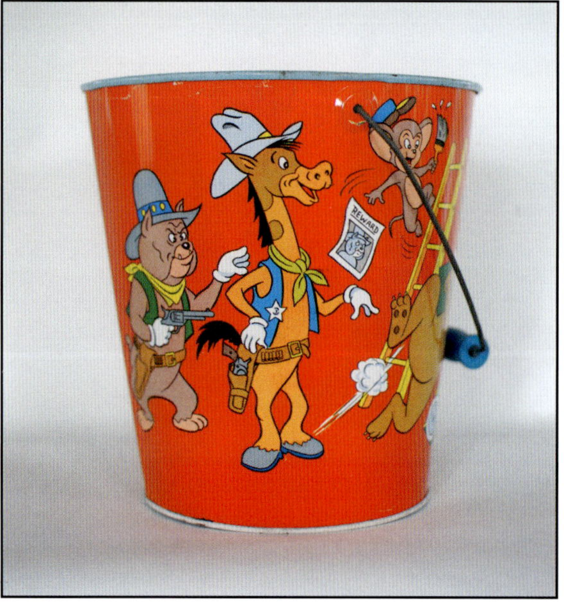

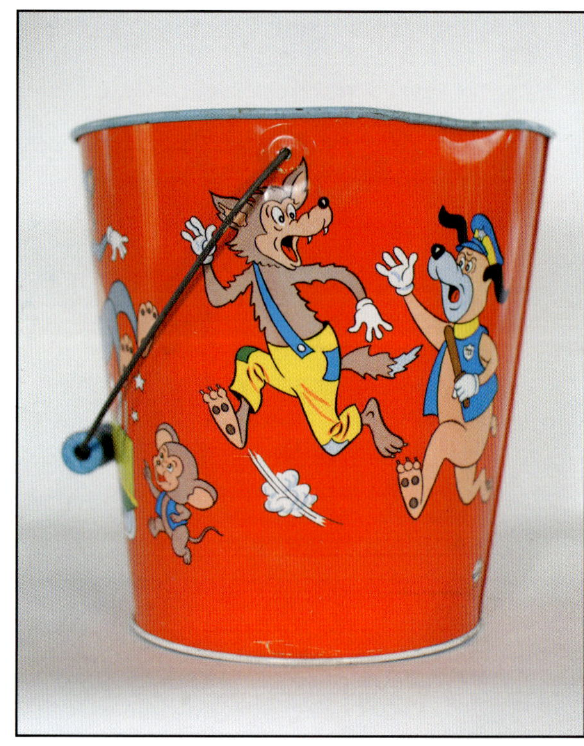

This 8″ sand pail features several Hanna-Barbera characters including Tom and Jerry, Yogi Bear and Quick Draw McGraw. The Ohio Art logo on the pail indicates that it was produced between 1963 and 1971. $75-150

Chapter 12:

Happy Hooligan

Happy Hooligan was one of the earliest comic strip characters, along with the Yellow Kid, the Katzenjammer Kids, and Buster Brown. He was created by Frederick Opper and first appeared in newspaper comic strips in 1900.

The strip was very popular and continued for 32 years until Opper's eyesight failed him.

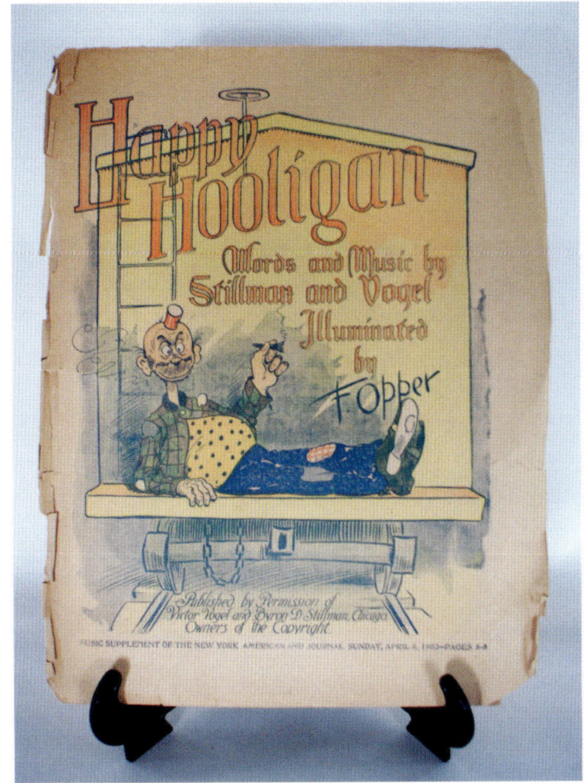

Happy Hooligan's sheet music. Words and music by Stillman and Vogel. Illustrated by F. Opper. Published by permission of Victor Vogel and Bryan D. Stillman, Chicago, Owners of copyright, published April 6, 1902.

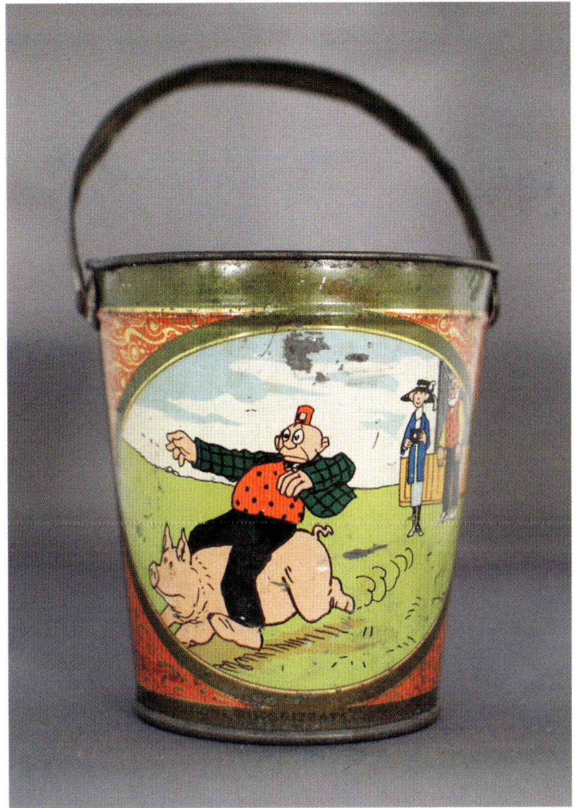

Happy Hooligan sand pail made in Italy. Probably dates from around 1920. The first view is Happy riding a pig. The second shows Happy being knocked off the pig next to a fence. The pail is marked MARCA DEPOSITATA SALIRE SEMPRE and PAL PORRIGIAN SESTO FLORENTINO RIPRODAVIONNE AUTORIZZATA $600-700

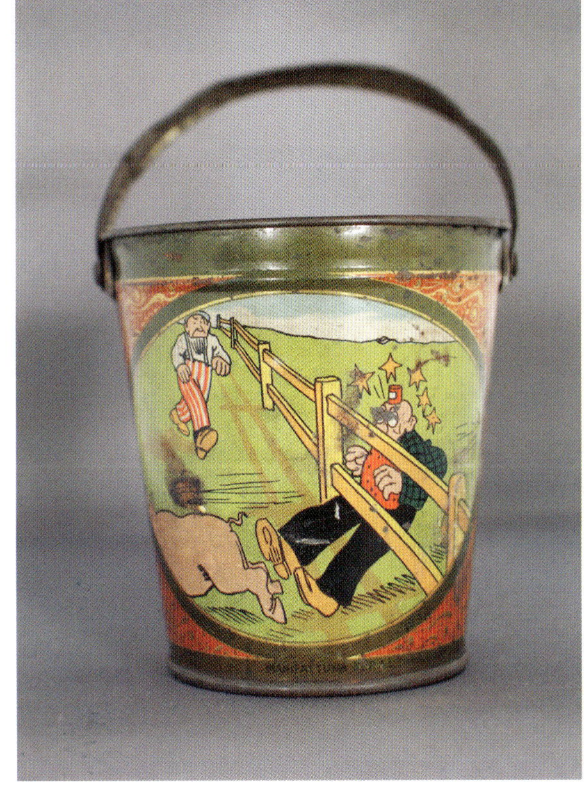

Chapter 13:

Katzenjammer Kids

Katzenjammer Kids is a comic strip created by Rudolph Dirks. It first appeared in a Hearst newspaper *The New York Journal.* This made it the second oldest strip in the world after *The Yellow Kid.* It is the oldest strip continuously published. Between 1912 and 1914 Dirks and Hearst had legal battles, ending with Dirks starting a separate strip, *The Captain and the Kids* that ran continuously for over six decades. The Katzenjammer Kids, now copyright by King Features Syndicate, is still being published and December, 2007 marks 100 years. Incredible!

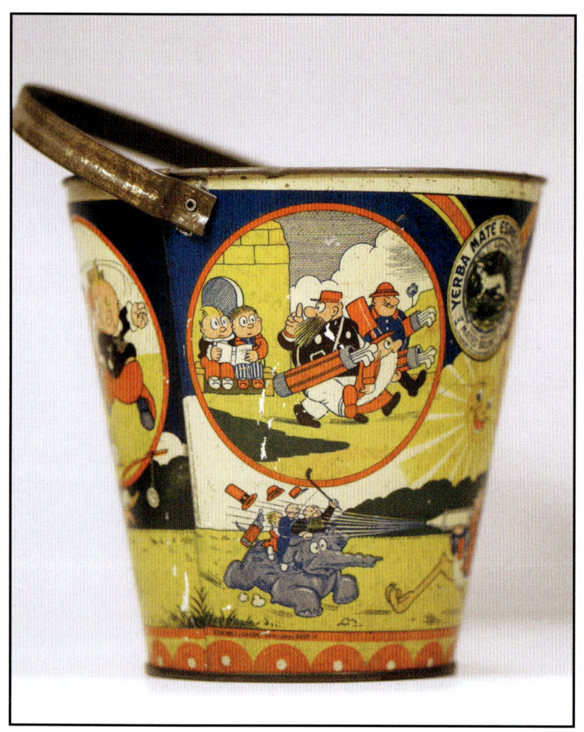

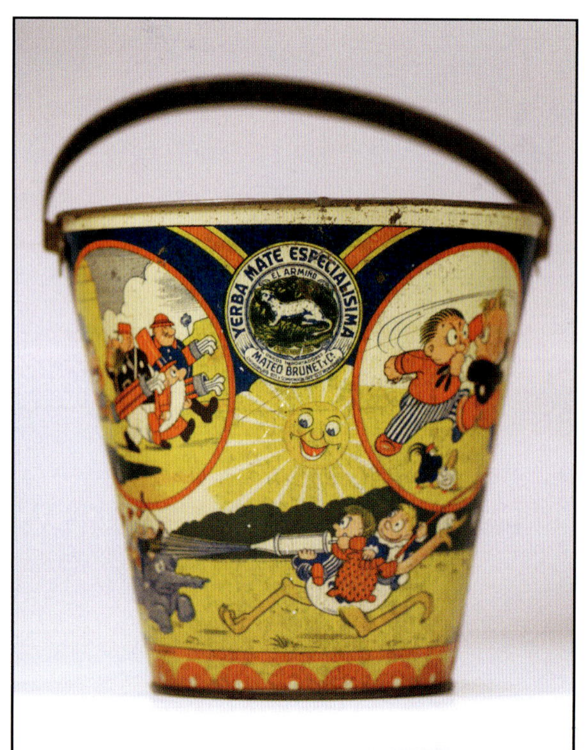

This 6.5" sand pail featuring the Katzenjammer Kids is extremely rare. Three views are shown. Marks are Lostorto y Cici Ltva, CerroLorgo 2000-16 Unicos import-adoo-es 2 w Yeroa Mate Especiellsima, Mateo Brumet y a. *Birnkrant Collection* $750-1,000

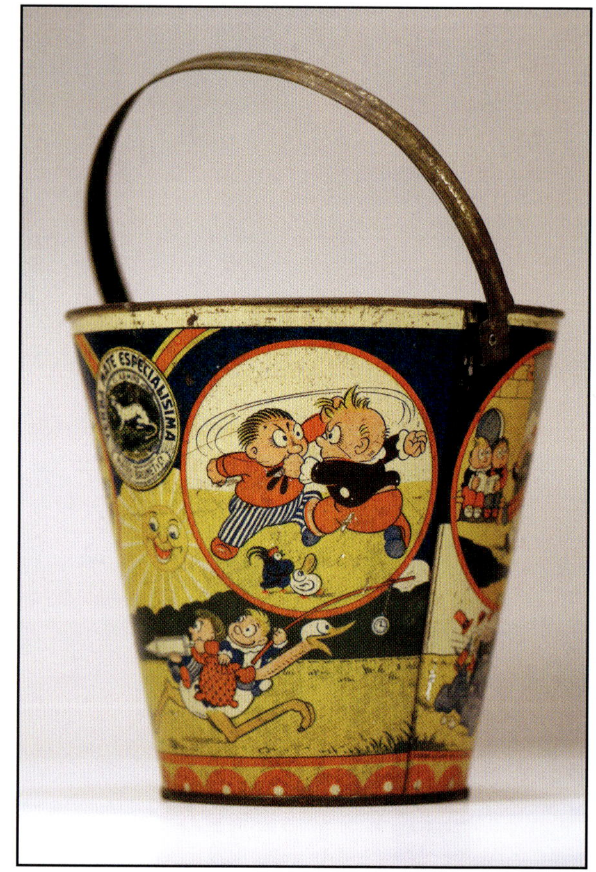

Chapter 14:
Kewpie

Kewpie dolls and toys were derived from illustrations done by Rose O'Neill for *The Ladies Home Journal* in 1909. The dolls and figurines became immensely popular and spawned a number of different items including books and ceramics in addition to the sand pail and shovel illustrated.

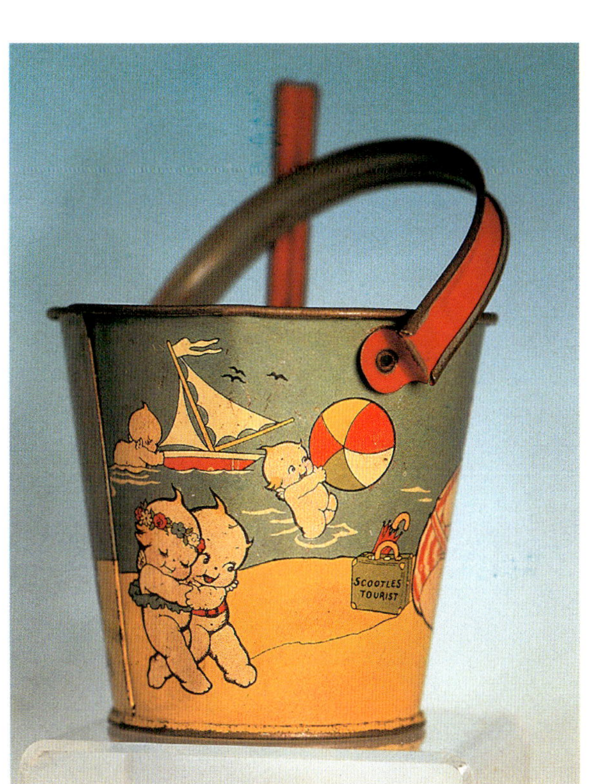

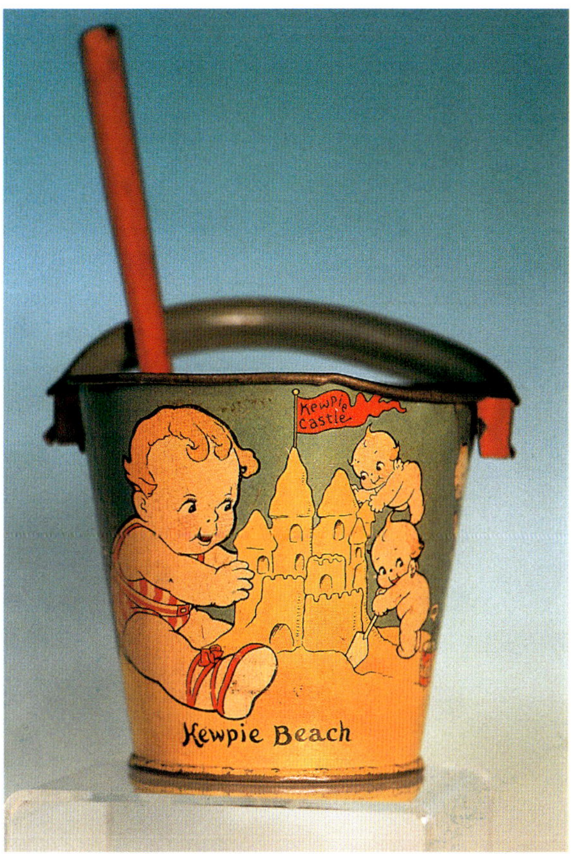

The 3" Kewpie Beach sand pail and shovel dates from 1937. The plain shovel is 6" tall. The three images show the great detail of the sand pail. Note the pennant above the sand castle reads "Kewpie Castle." Signed Rose O'Neill. Copyright 1937 by Rose O'Neill. $250-350

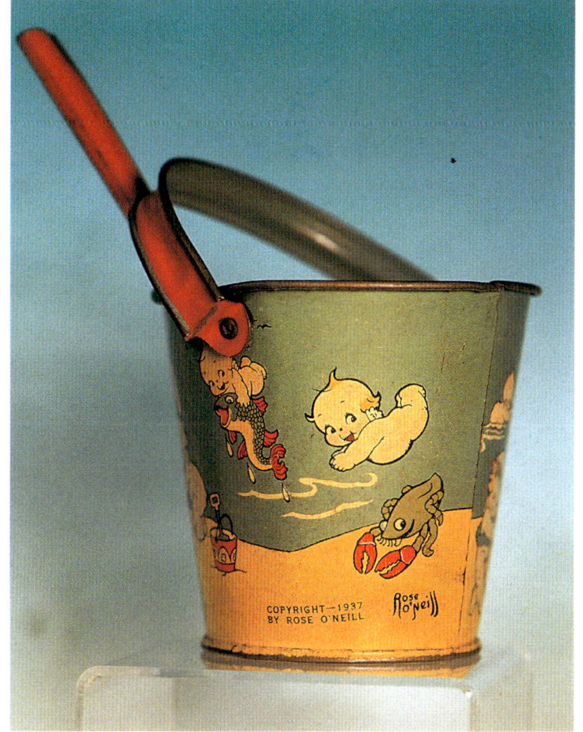

Chapter 15:

Oswald the Lucky Rabbit

Oswald, the Lucky Rabbit, was the creation of Walt Disney in 1926. He signed a contract with Universal to distribute the films he produced. After a successful year, Walt and Roy Disney met with Universal to renew the contract. Much to their dismay, Universal told them that the contract stipulated that Universal owned the rights to Oswald and they would produce films themselves and did not need the Disneys.

This was a tough lesson learned, but it led to the creation of Mickey Mouse in 1928 that proved a lot more successful! This lesson is the principal reason the Disney organization became so adamant about protecting all their characters. The two pails here that feature Oswald are both from Japan. The pails first appeared in the Betty Boop chapter of this book.

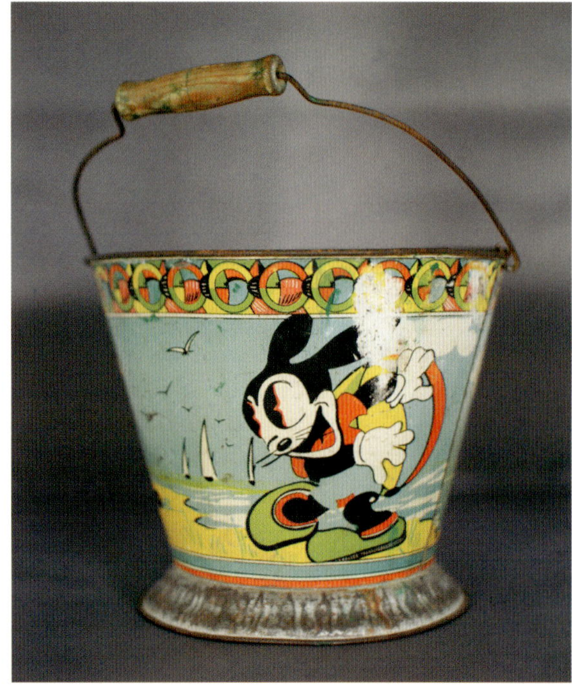

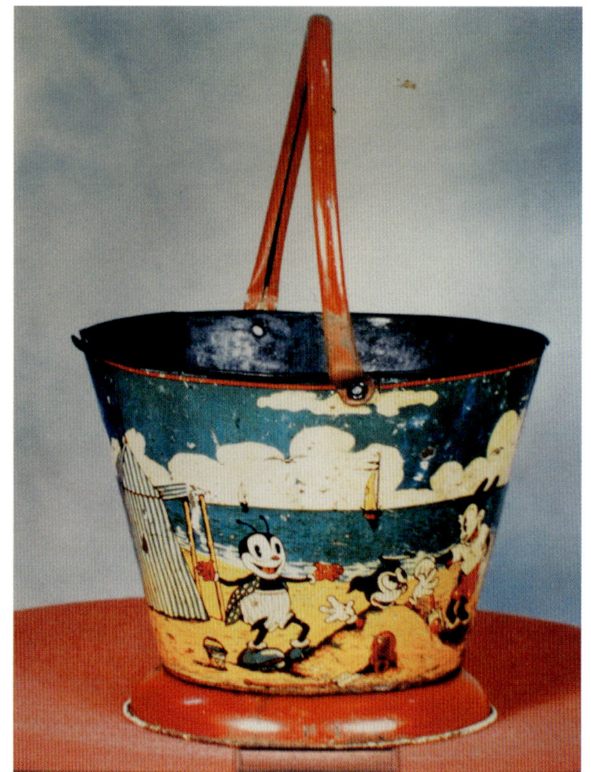

Oswald the Lucky Rabbit sand pails. Both made in Japan and in combination with other comic characters including Betty Boop and Mickey Mouse. The first 5.5" pail has a great image of Oswald. The pail has a raised bottom, two images of Mickey and a large one of Betty Boop. The second pail also has a raised bottom and is about 3.5" tall. In addition to Oswald, to the far right it features images of Felix, Betty Boop, Koko, Bimbo and Mickey and Minnie. 5.5" pail $1,000-1,500; 3.5" pail $500-750

Chapter 16:

Popeye the Sailor

Popeye first appeared in a January, 1929, "Thimble Theatre" comic strip created by Elzie Segar. The "Thimble Theatre" strip featured the daily adventures of the Oyl family which included Olive, her brother Castor, and her father Cole and was started by Segar in 1919. It was another decade before Popeye made his first appearance. Popeye quickly became the star of the strip. Only the Disney characters have had more merchandise produced about them than Popeye. Like Betty Boop, Disney characters, and Felix the Cat, Popeye has continued in popularity to the present day. Besides sand pails, Popeye products include toys, dolls, games, lamps and shades, children's china, books, and post cards.

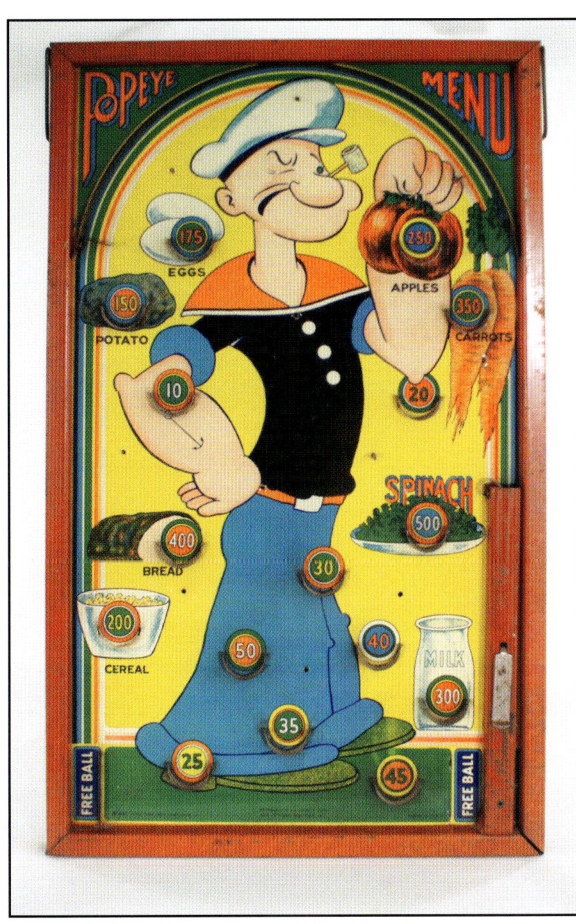

This is a graphic example of another Popeye tin toy that involved shooting marbles. Measuring 22" x 14", it features small pockets with varying values. Naturally spinach, worth 500 points, is the most valuable, going all the way down to 10 points for the pocket carrying the least value. The game is ©1935 Manufactured by the Durable Toy and Novelty Corp., 200 Fifth Ave., New York, NY. And Made in the U.S.A. $200-300

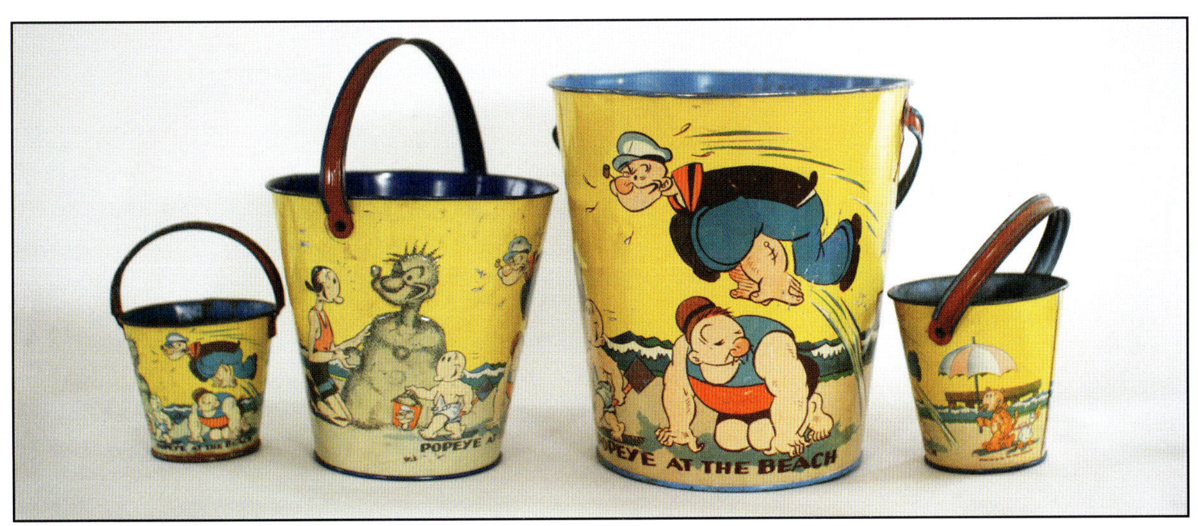

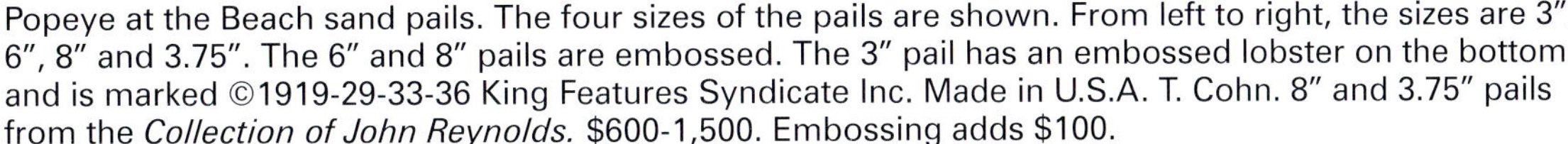

Popeye at the Beach sand pails. The four sizes of the pails are shown. From left to right, the sizes are 3", 6", 8" and 3.75". The 6" and 8" pails are embossed. The 3" pail has an embossed lobster on the bottom and is marked ©1919-29-33-36 King Features Syndicate Inc. Made in U.S.A. T. Cohn. 8" and 3.75" pails from the *Collection of John Reynolds.* $600-1,500. Embossing adds $100.

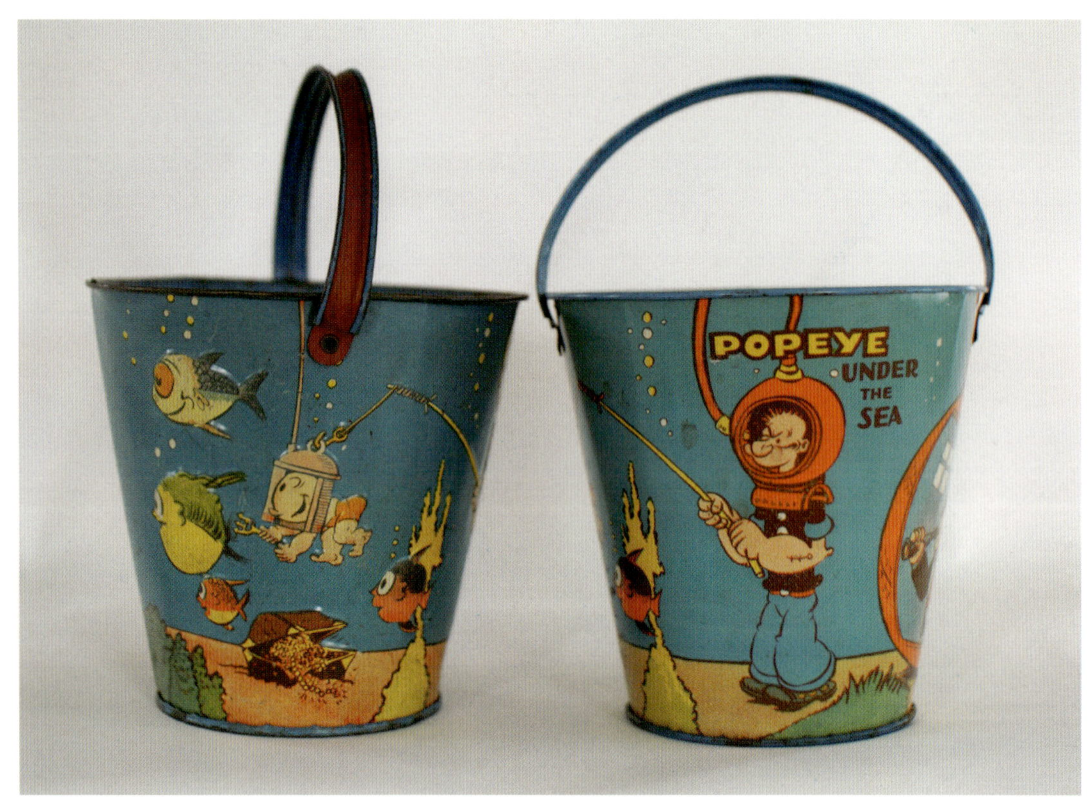

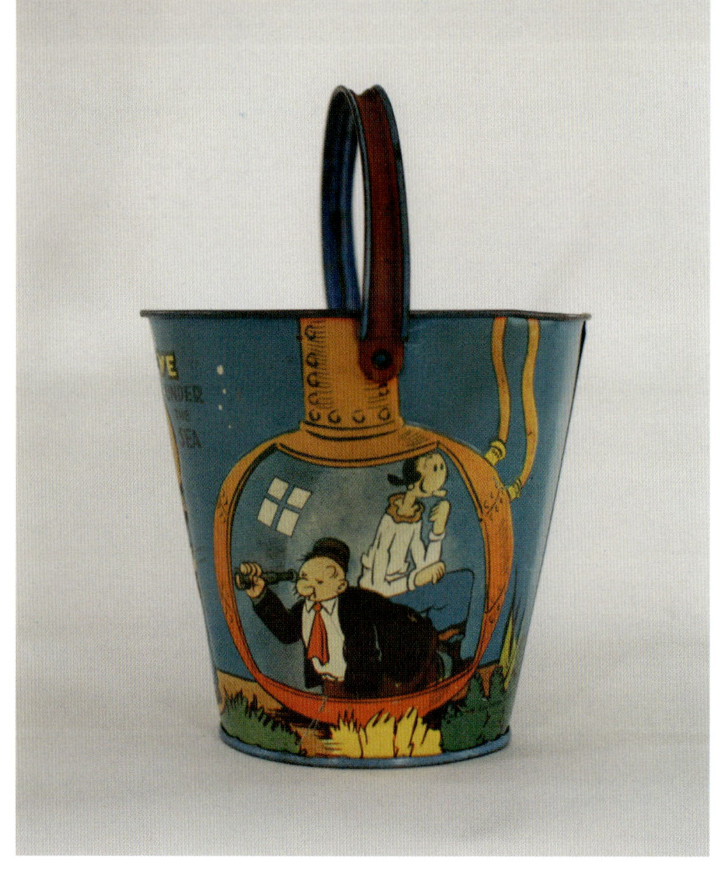

Popeye Under the Sea came in 6″ or 8″ sizes, both embossed and not embossed, like the left of the two pails. The pail on the right is embossed. The single image is of an 8″ pail. Copyrights same as previous pail. Embossed pail is from *Reynolds Collection*. 8″ pail from *Lobel Collection; Keown Photograph.* $750-1,250

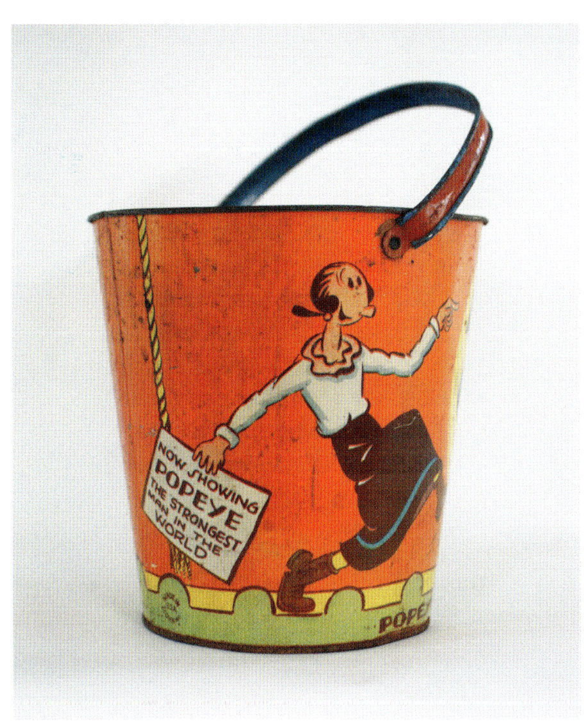

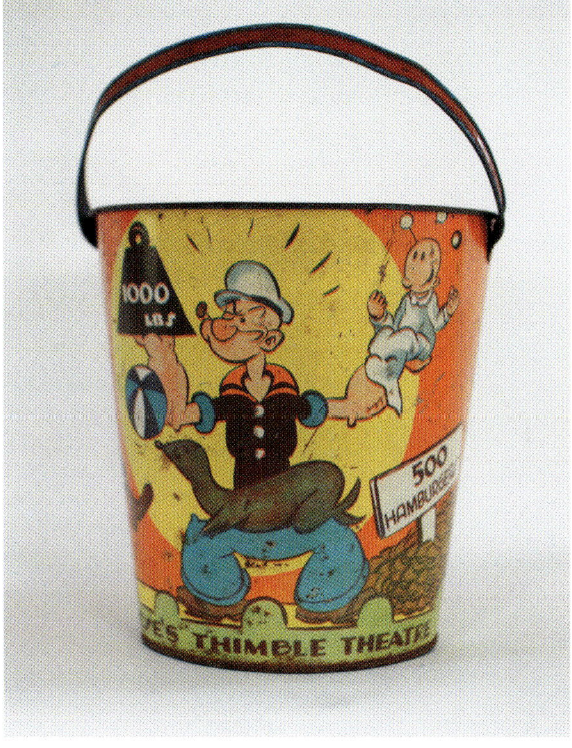

Popeye's Thimble Theatre 8" sand pail. Probably the earliest Popeye sand pail, as it was produced in 1933. Most other Cohn pails were produced after 1936. Copyright same as previous except no 1936. $750-1,250

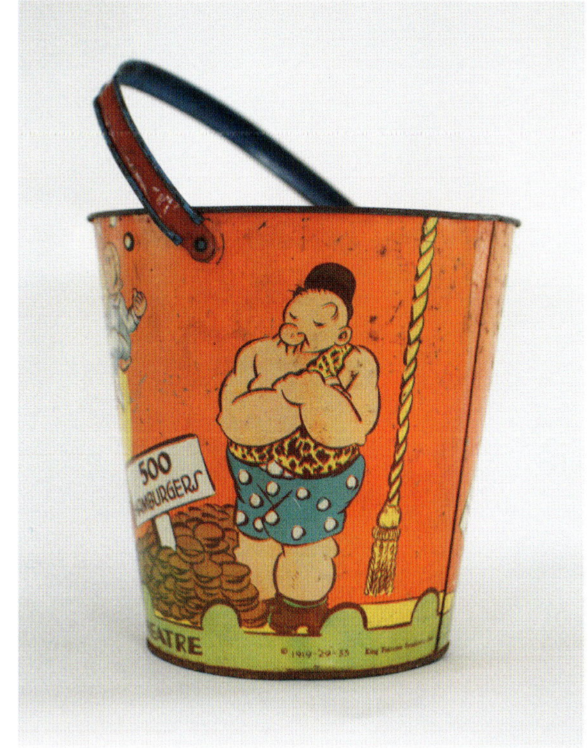

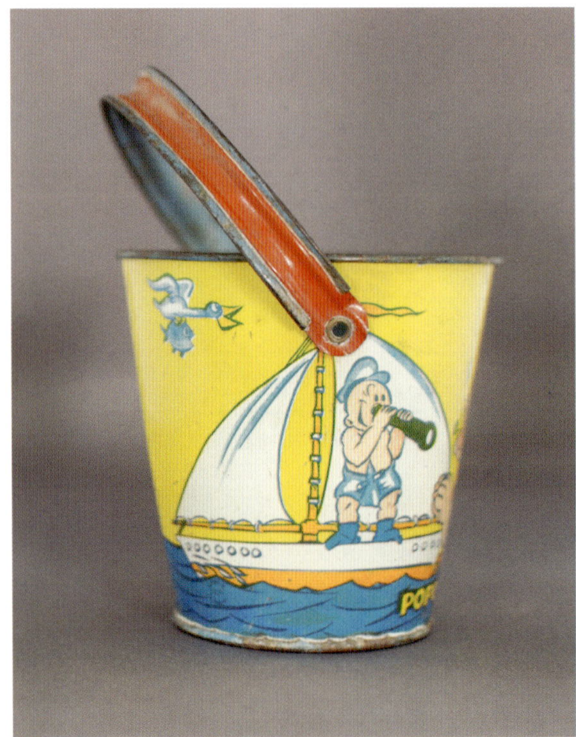

Popeye the Sailor 3.75″ pail. The three views illustrate the creativity of these wonderful toys. King Features copyright and T. Cohn are on the pail. *Reynolds Collection* $500-850

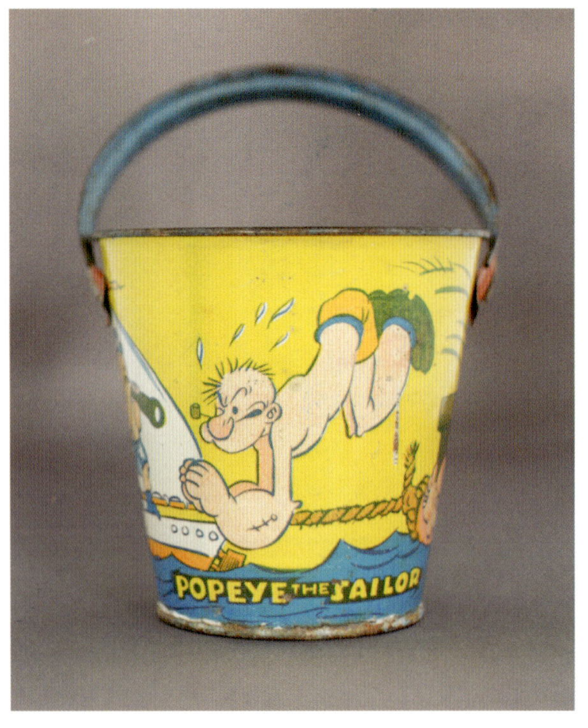

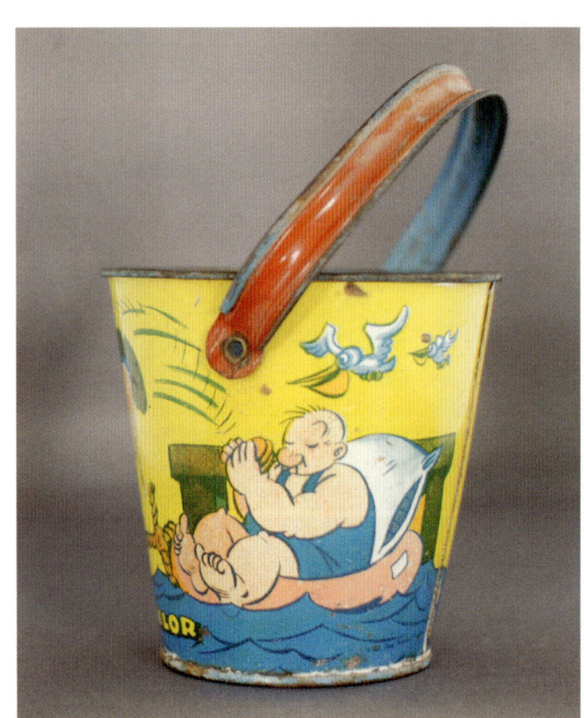

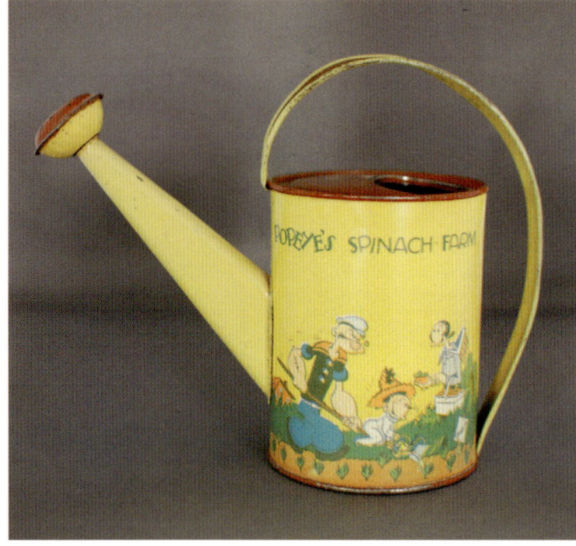

Popeye's Spinach Farm 6″ watering can. Only mark visible is T.Cohn Inc. Bklyn, N.Y. *Reynolds Collection* $300-500

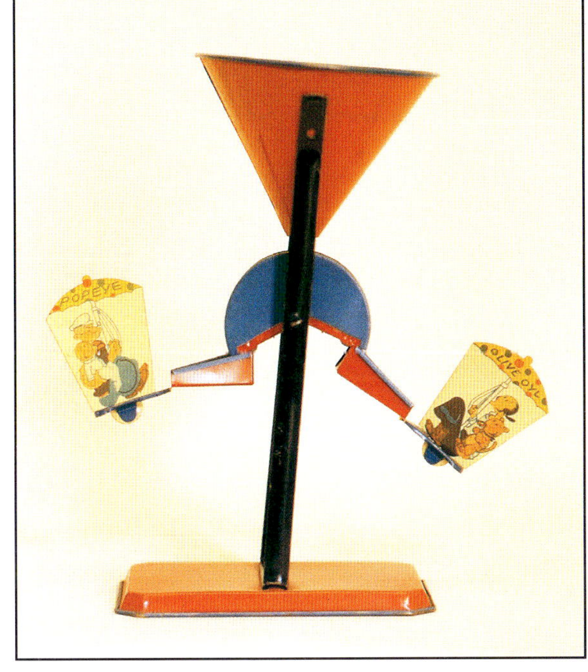

Popeye and Olive Oyl teeter totter sand mill. This unusual toy is 8.25" tall by 7.5" wide. It dates from the late 1940s or early 1950s. Unmarked, but believe to have been made by T. Cohn. *Lobel Collection; Keown Photograph*. $350-600

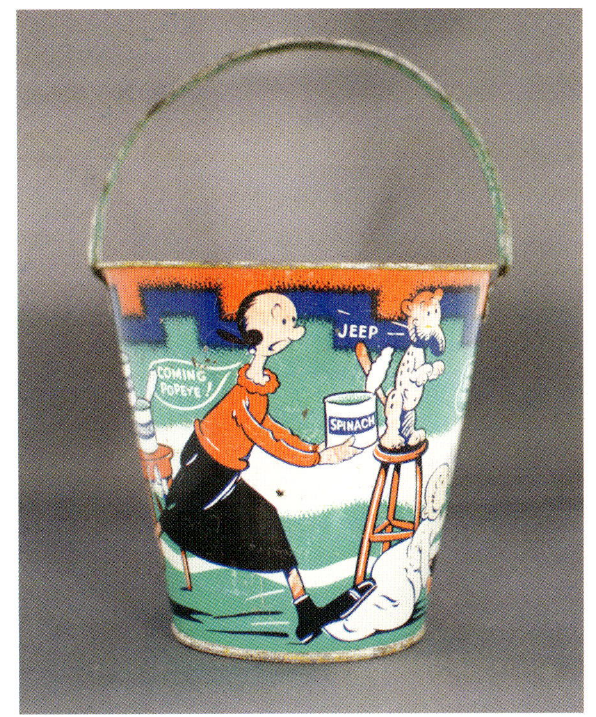

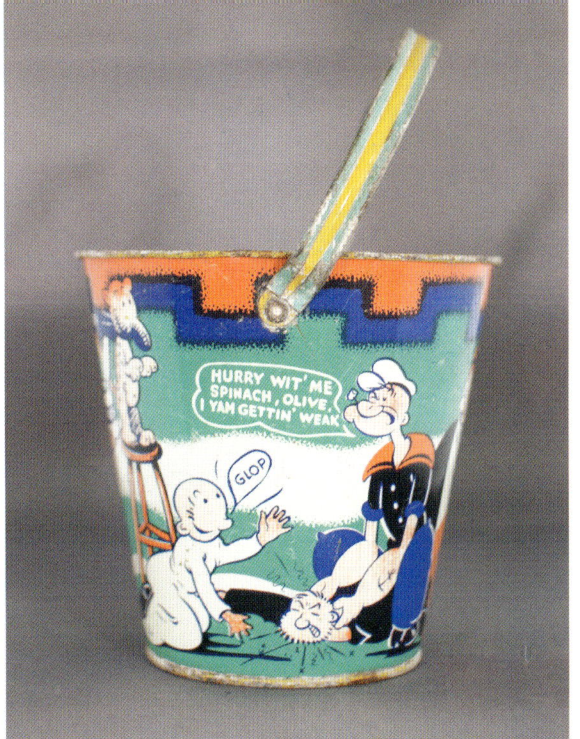

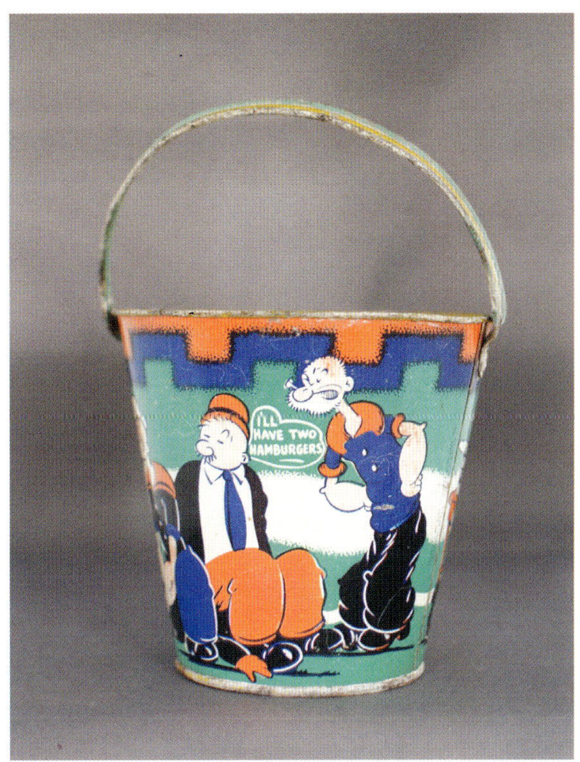

Popeye 5" sand pail from Great Britain. Three views are shown. Marked Copyright by King Features Syndicate, Inc., Happynak Series, Made in Gt. Britain. British Made is embossed on bottom. $700-1,000

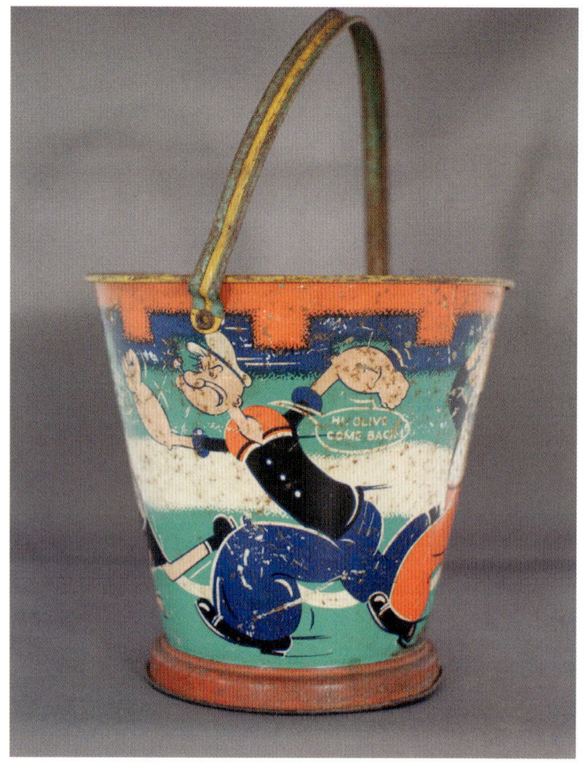

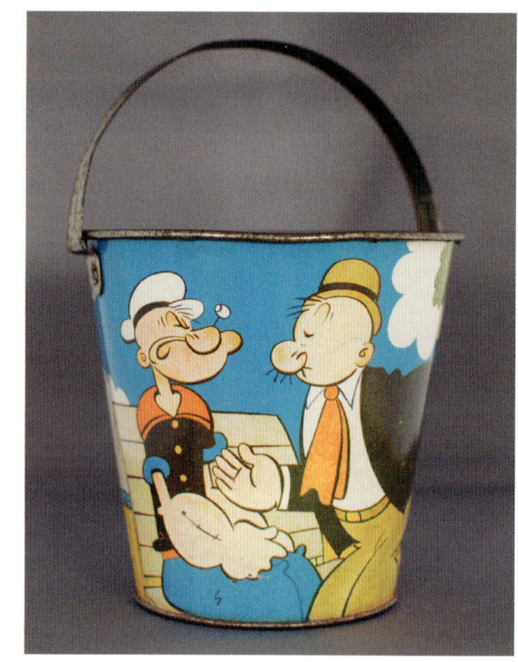

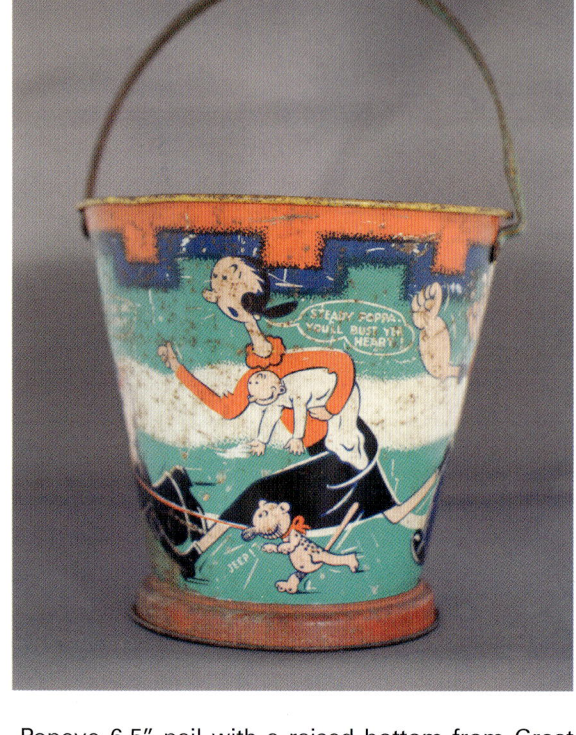

Popeye 6.5" pail with a raised bottom from Great Britain. Three views. Pail has same copyright and embossing on bottom as previous pail Due to condition $250-500

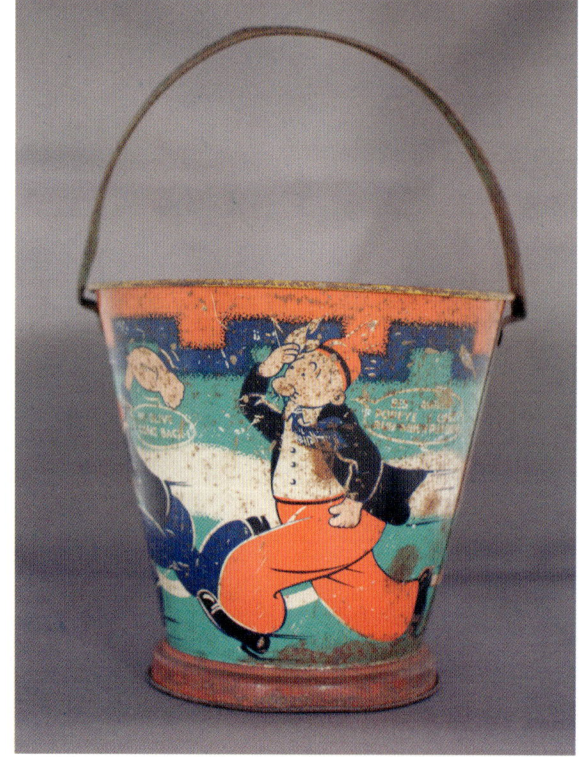

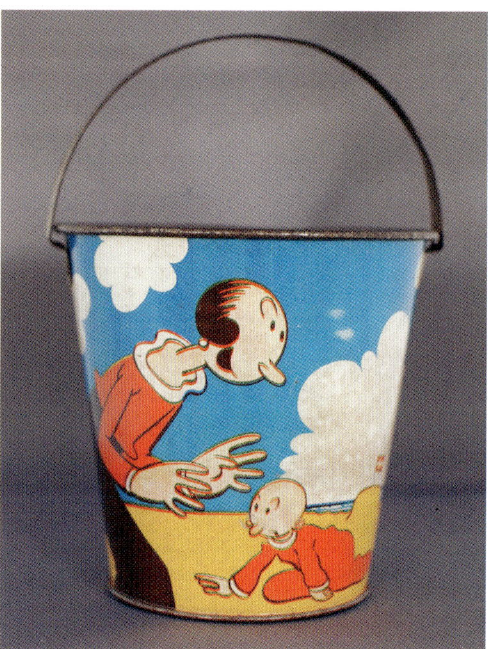

A Popeye 5.5" pail featuring Popeye, Wimpy, Olive Oyl and Sweet Pea. Marked Celludan 2514 $500-700

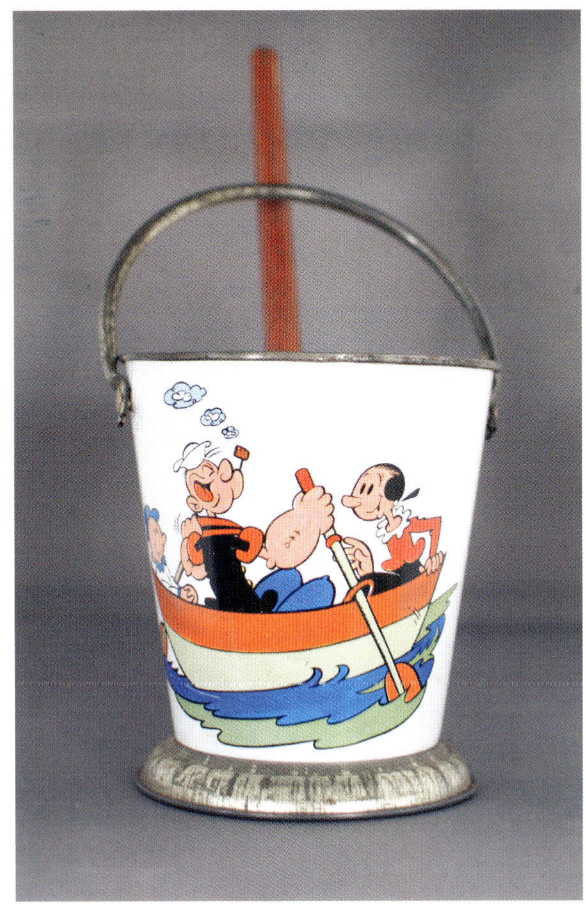

A Popeye 5″ pail from France with a raised bottom and 9.5″ shovel. Marked Virojanglor-Paris. Made in France. Although appearing old, in reality it was produced in the late 60s or early 70s. $200-400

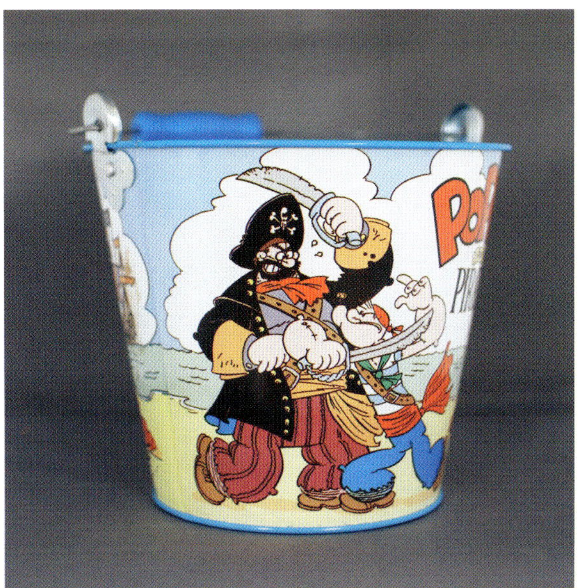

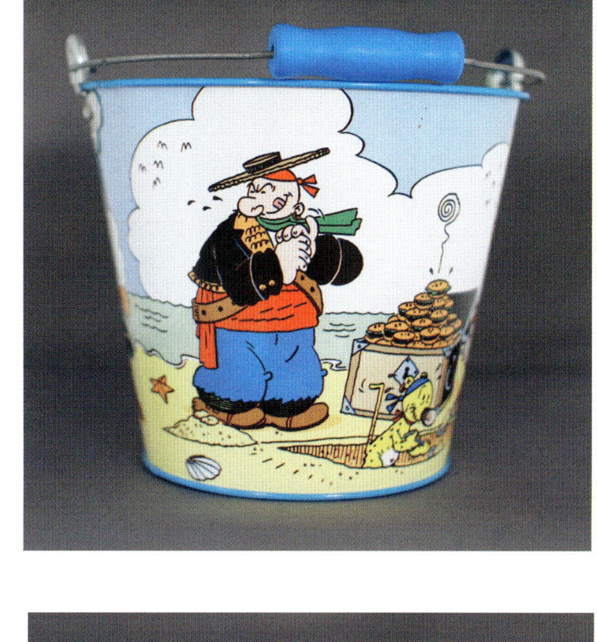

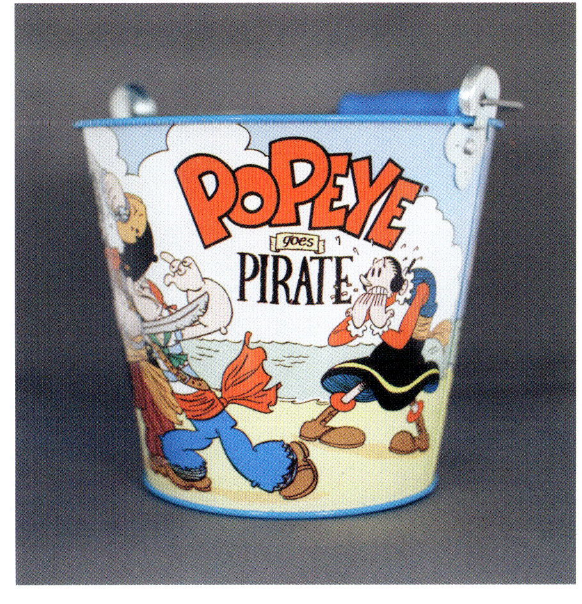

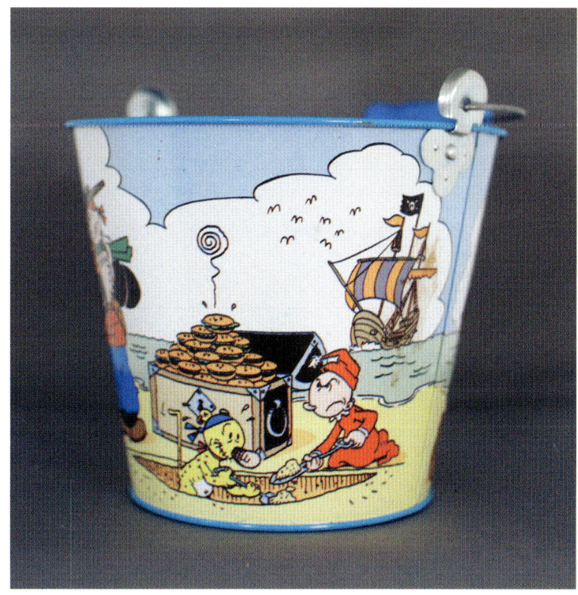

Popeye Goes Pirate. A contemporary 6″ sand pail produced in 1996 by Schylling. Marked on bottom: More Fun from Schylling, Ipswich, MA. 01938. Made in Estonia. Popeye ©1996 King Features Syndicate, Inc.™ The Hearst Corporation $15-25

Chapter 17:
Punch and Judy

The Punch and Judy shows can trace their origin to 16th century Italy. May 9, 1662, is believed to be the first appearance of Punch in the UK. For four centuries puppeteers would operate the marionettes in a puppet theatre. A great variety of merchandise has been created over the years particularly play puppet theaters. This sand pail example features a Punch and Judy theatre on the beach by Chad Valley of England. Interestingly, a couple of young mermaids are in attendance!

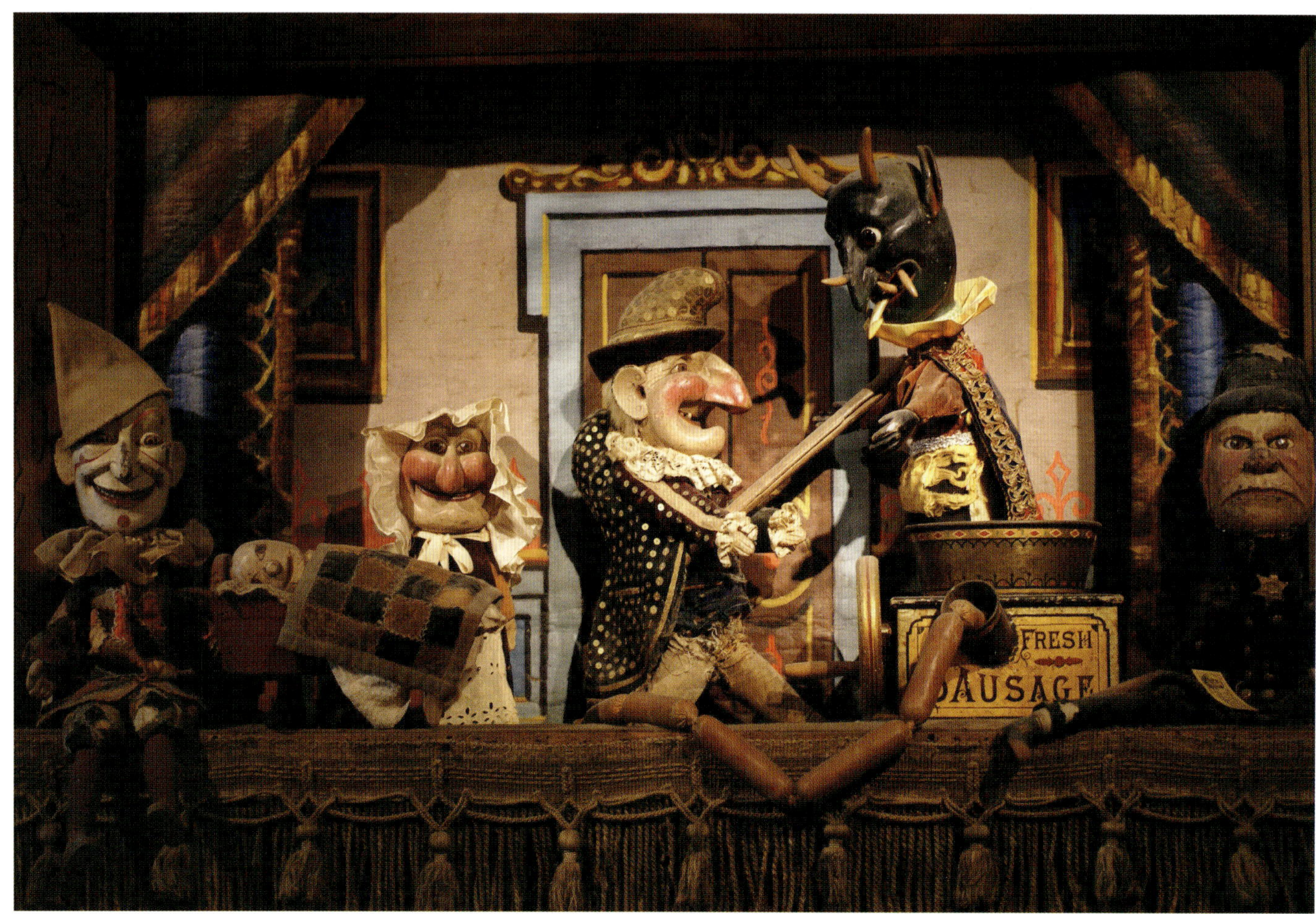

A magnificent Punch and Judy puppet theatre owned and beautifully restored by Mel Birnkrant. Mel even used old material to make some of the costumes.

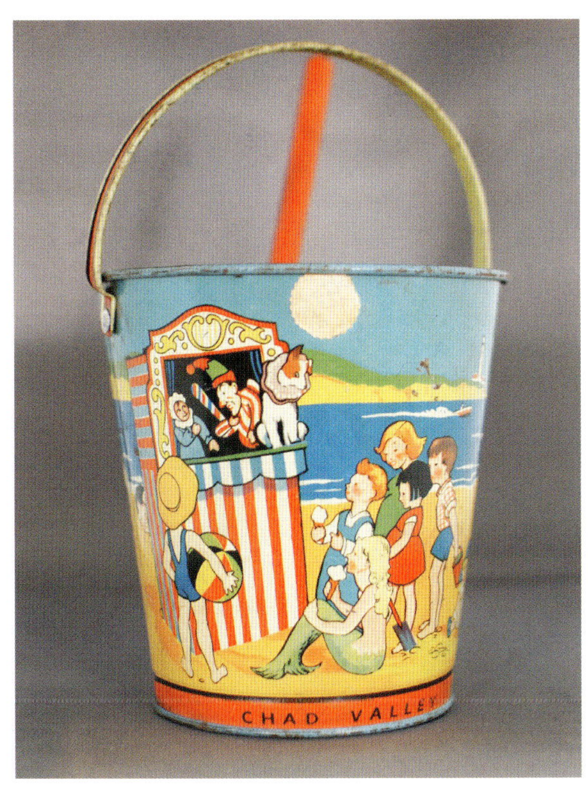

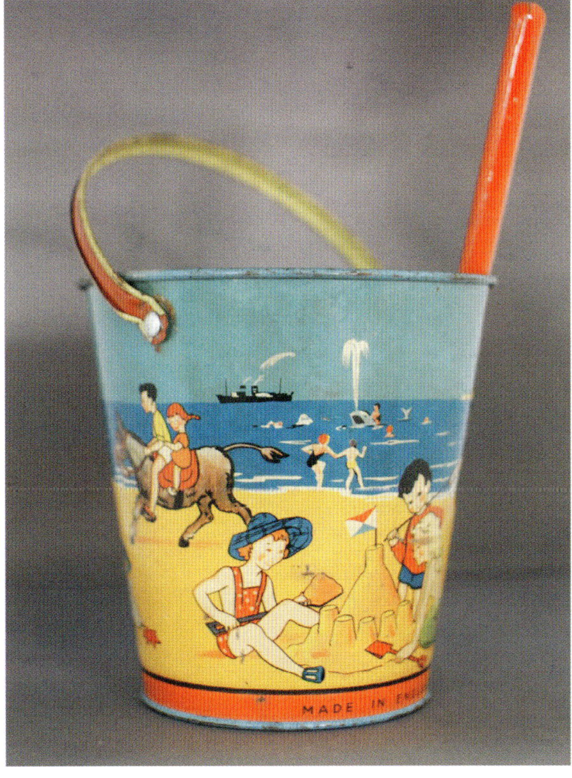

A 6" Punch and Judy sand pail and shovel made by Chad Valley in England. The plain shovel is 9" tall. The first view shows a play being performed by the Punch and Judy players before a rapt audience which includes a mermaid. The second view shows a brother giving his young sister a horseback ride while the third shows a sand castle being built with a mermaid helping and an old salt with his saucy sally boat. $250-400

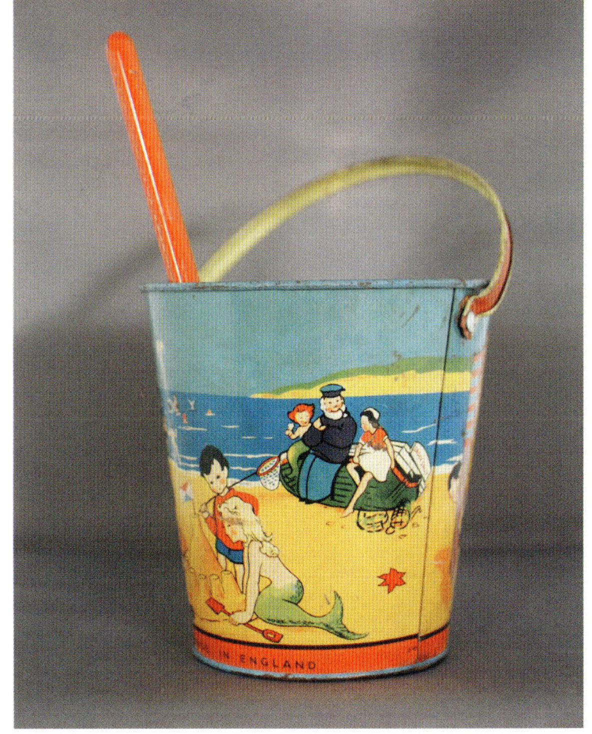

Chapter 18:

Raggedy Ann

Raggedy Ann first appeared as a doll made by Johnny Gruelle for his daughter in 1915. Gruelle wrote and illustrated *Raggedy Ann Stories* in 1918. Because of the great success of Raggedy Ann, Gruelle brought out a sequel to *Raggedy Ann Stories* in 1920 starring Raggedy Andy.

While books represented most of the Raggedy Ann and Raggedy Andy merchandise, items also included dolls, cartoons, feature films and TV productions. Pictured here are one early sand pail and one later example.

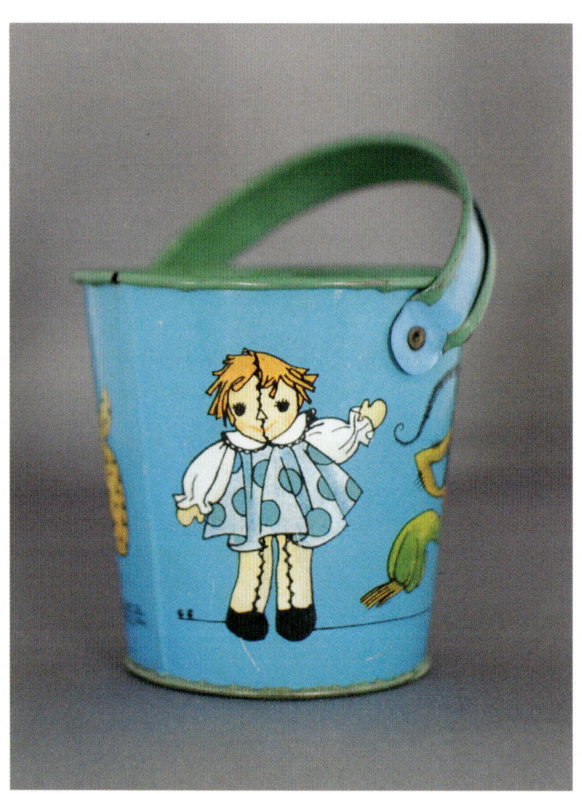

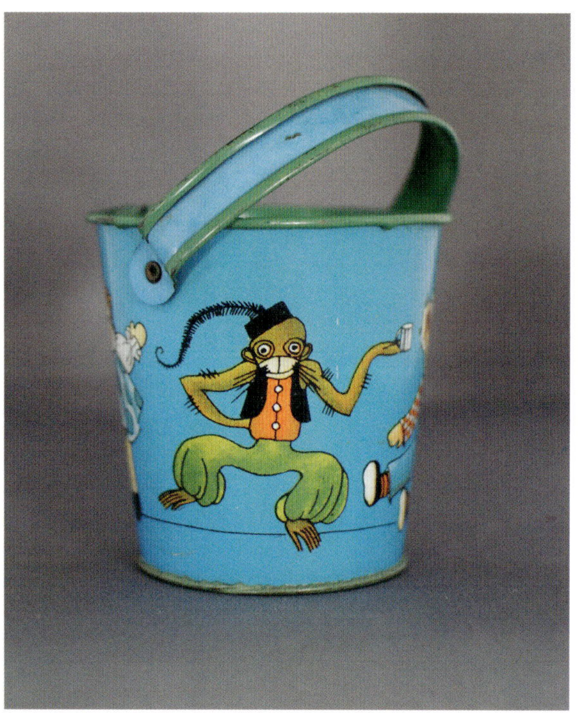

Raggedy Ann 3.5" sand pail by Ohio Art. Four images include Raggedy Ann and Raggedy Andy. From late 1920s or early 1930s. Marked Ohio Art Co. Bryan, O. U.S.A. $200-300

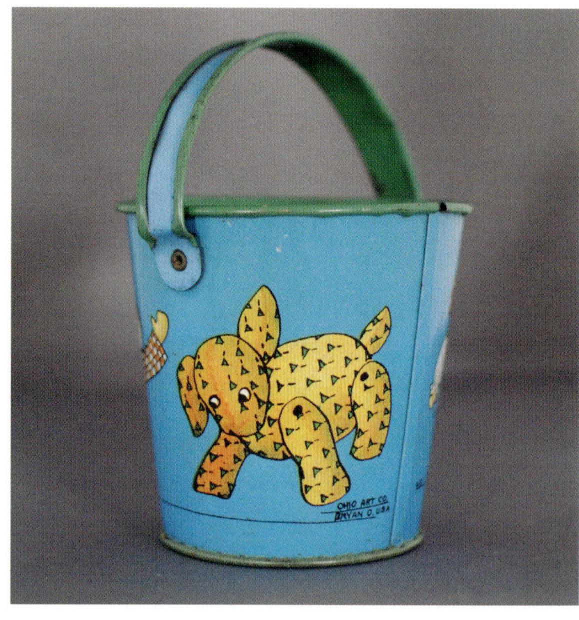

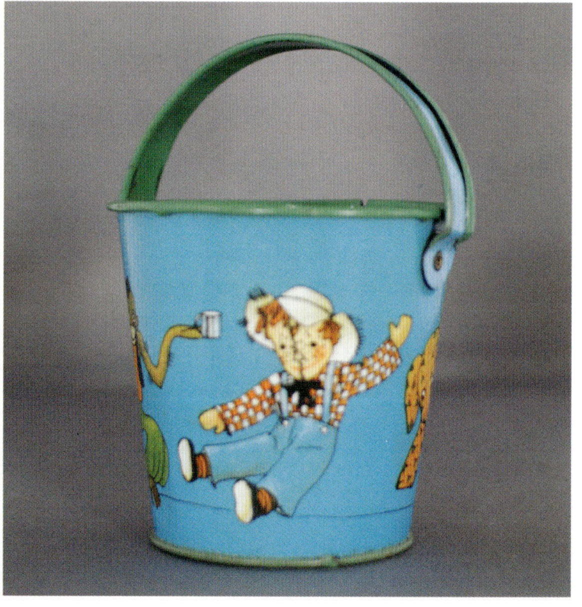

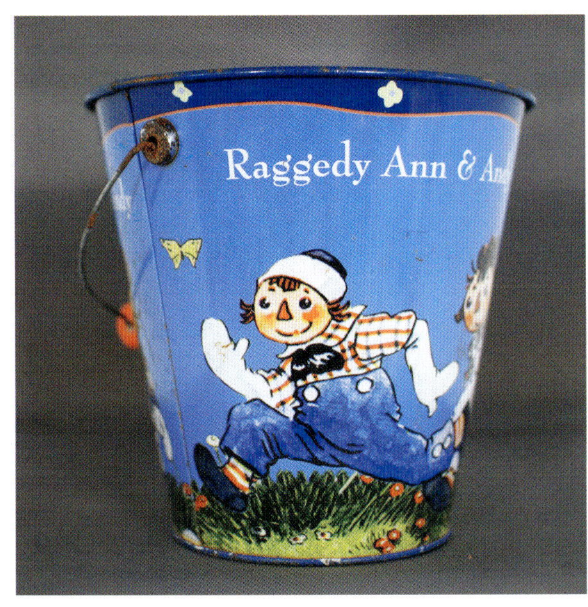

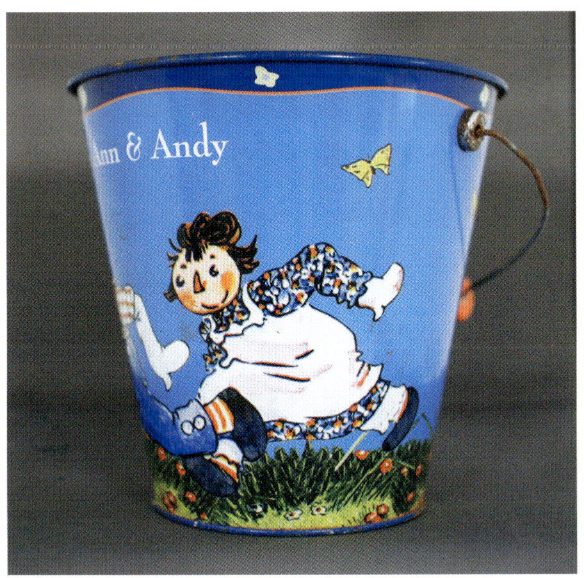

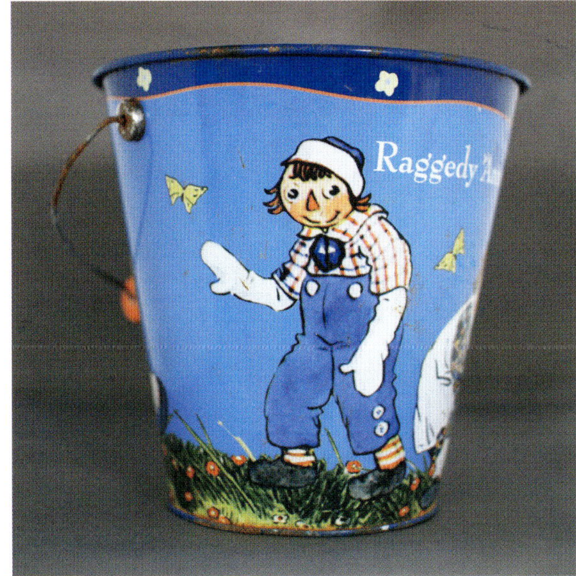

Raggedy Ann and Raggedy Andy 7" contemporary sand pail with shovel. Two images each of Raggedy Ann and Andy. Bottom of pail is marked: © & ™ Simon & Shuster, Inc. Licensed by United Media. Made in China. More Fun from Schylling, Rowley, Ma. 01969. $10-25

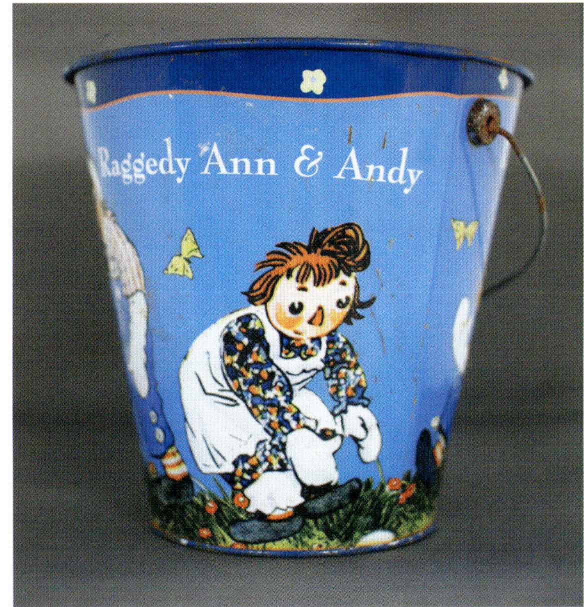

Chapter 19:

Scrappy

The Scrappy character was created in 1931 by Dick Huemer for Charles Mintz's Krazy Kat Studio. Other characters in the series were Scrappy's little brother Oopy, his girlfriend Margy, and a Scotty dog named Yippy.

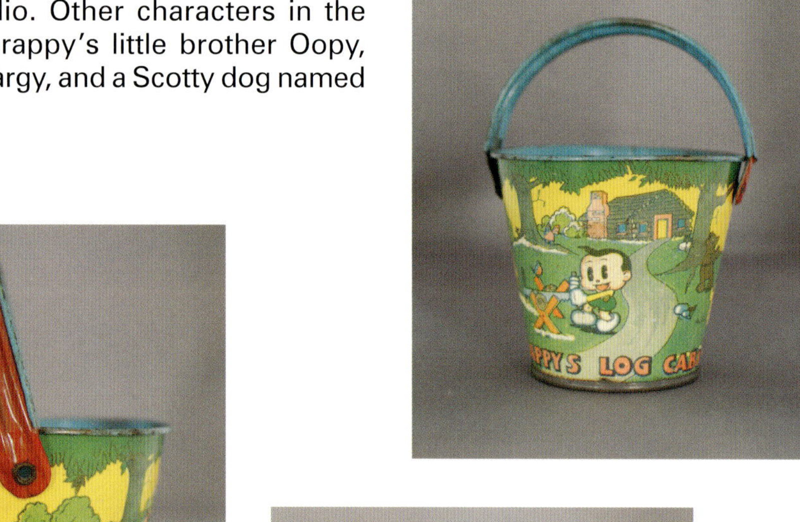

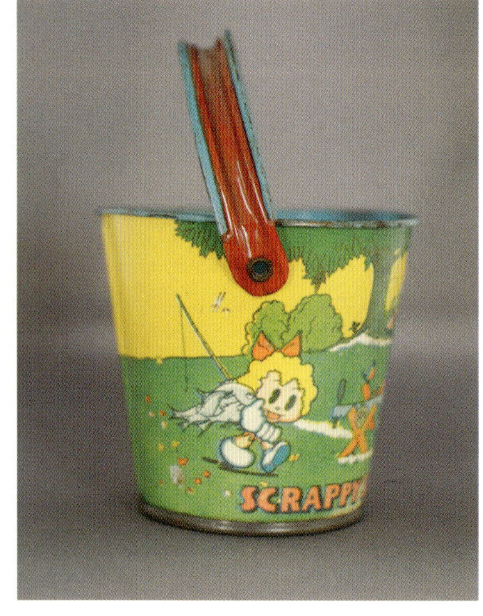

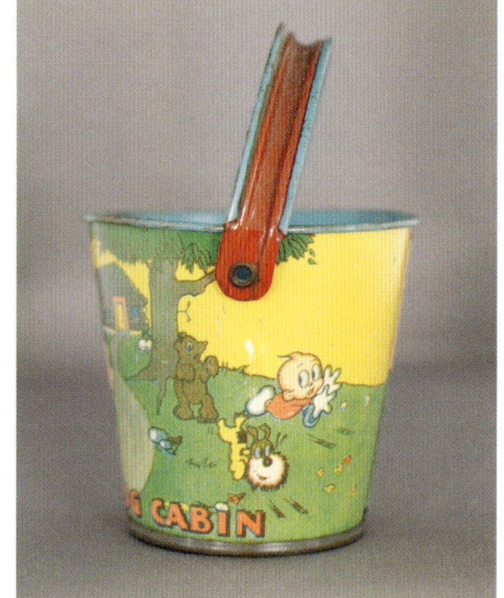

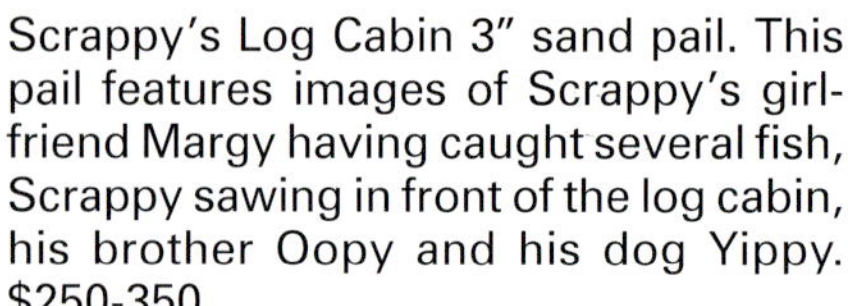

Scrappy's Log Cabin 3" sand pail. This pail features images of Scrappy's girlfriend Margy having caught several fish, Scrappy sawing in front of the log cabin, his brother Oopy and his dog Yippy. $250-350

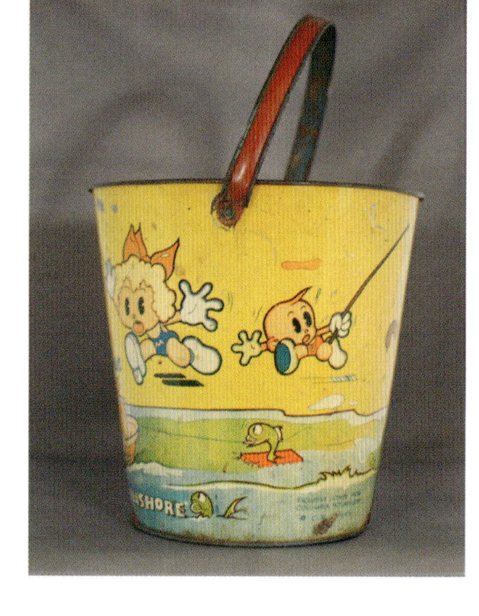

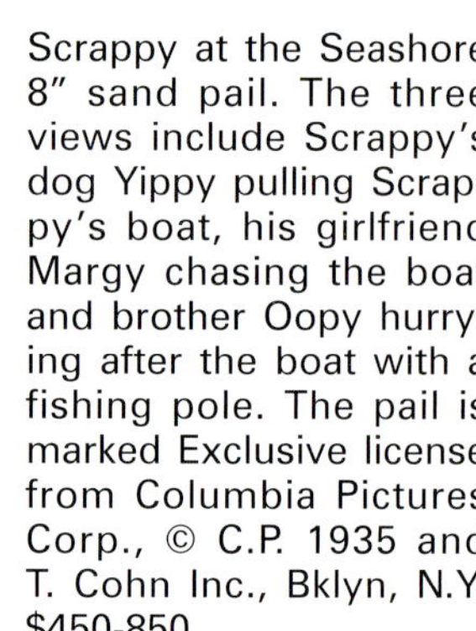

Scrappy at the Seashore 8" sand pail. The three views include Scrappy's dog Yippy pulling Scrappy's boat, his girlfriend Margy chasing the boat and brother Oopy hurrying after the boat with a fishing pole. The pail is marked Exclusive license from Columbia Pictures Corp., © C.P. 1935 and T. Cohn Inc., Bklyn, N.Y. $450-850

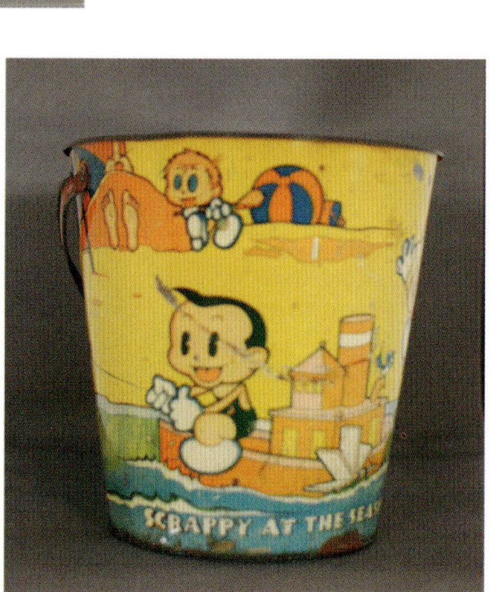

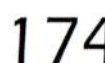

Chapter 20:

SpongeBob SquarePants

SpongeBob is the latest TV cartoon character to decorate sand pails. Created in 1999 by Stephen Hillenburg, SpongeBob appeared first on the Nickelodeon channel. The first pail is an Easter pail and ©2007 by Viacom International. SpongeBob SquarePants and all related titles, logos, and characters are trademarks of Viacom International, Inc.

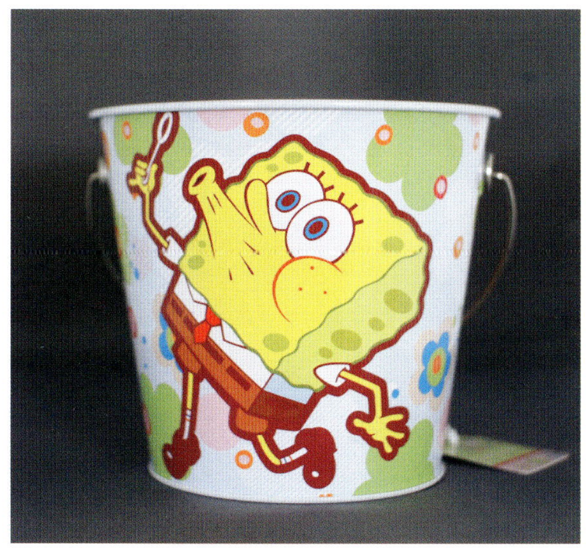

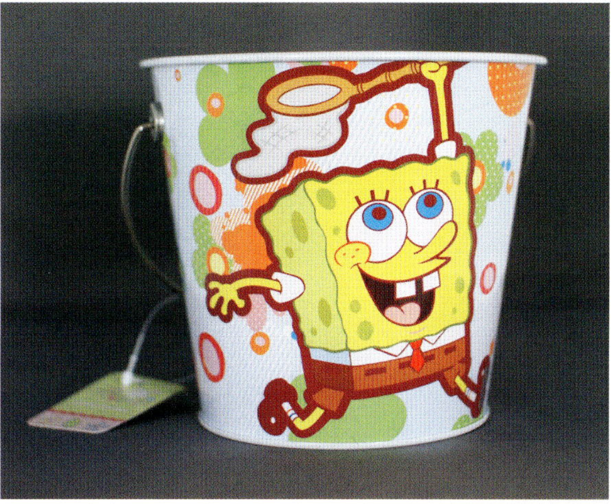

The 5.5" SpongeBob Easter pail has a slightly larger diameter than the other pictured SpongeBob pails. The first view shows SpongeBob blowing bubbles. The other shows him trying to catch the bubbles with a net. Made in China, the pail is imported by the CVS Pharmacy chain. The attached tag indicated the retail price is $3.99 but it was purchased for $2.99. The copyright on the pail reads © 2007 Viacom International Inc. All rights reserved. Nickelodeon, SpongeBob SquarePants and all related titles, logos, and characters are trademarks of Viacom International Inc. Created by Stephen Hillenburg. $5-10

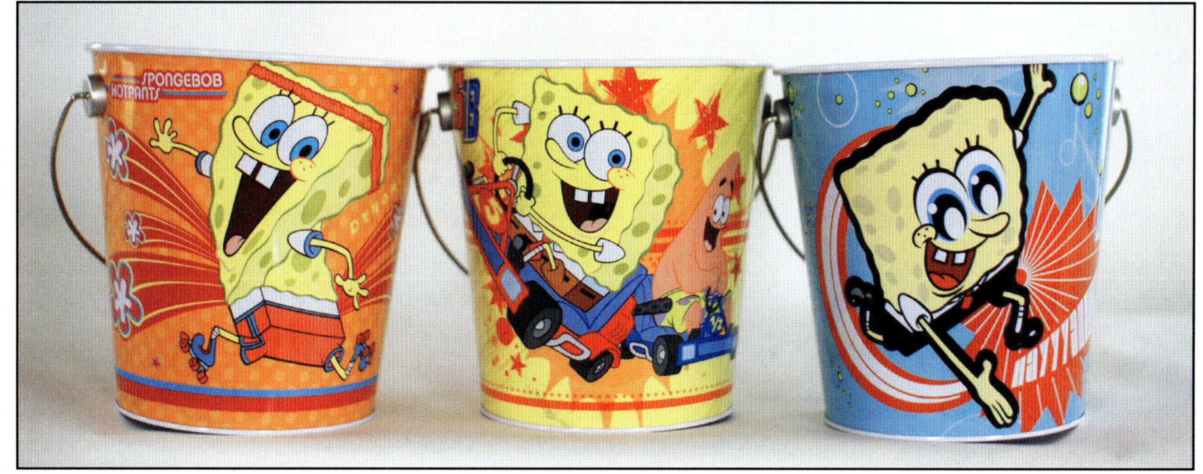

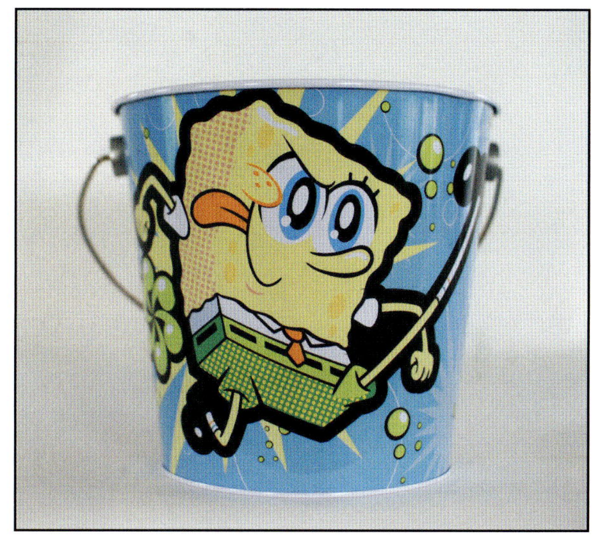

The first image shows the three pails imported by the Tin Box Company in 2007. The pails are 5.5" tall. The second image shows the other side of the third pail of the previous image. The copyright information is identical to that shown on the first SpongeBob pail illustrated. *Pails courtesy of the Tin Box Company* $5-10

Bibliography

Babb, Paul, and Gay Owen. *Bonzo: The Life and Work of George Studdy*. Somerset, England: Richard Dennis, 1988

Grant, John. *Encyclopedia of Walt Disney's Animated Characters*. New York, New York: Harper & Row, 1987

Horman, Karen, and Polly Minick. *Sand Pail Encyclopedia*. Grantsville, Maryland: Hobby House Press, Inc., 2002

Jaffe, Alan, *J. Chein & Co*. *A Collector's Guide to an American Toymaker*. Atglen, Pennsylvania: Schiffer Publishing Ltd., 1997

Kerr, Lisa, with Jim Gilcher. *Ohio Art the World of Toys,* Atglen, Pennsylvania: Schiffer Publishing Ltd., 1997

Lesser, Robert. *A Celebration of Comic Art and Memorabilia*. New York, New York: Hawthorn Books, Inc., 1975

Munsey, Cecil. *Disneyana, Walt Disney Collectibles*. New York, New York: Hawthorne Books, Inc., 1974.

Shine, Bernard C., Principal Consultant. *Walt Disney's Mickey Mouse Memorabilia, The Vintage Years 1928-1938.* New York, New York: Henry N. Abrams Incorporated, 1986.

Sotheby, Parke-Bernet. *Disneyana Auction Catalog of May 14, 1972*. Los Angeles, California: Sotheby, Parke-Bernet, 1972.

Wikipedia, the free encyclopedia. Best source for character information. 2007.